OXFORD GREEK AND LATIN COLLEGE COMMENTARIES

Selected Letters from
Pliny the Younger's *Epistulae*

THE OXFORD GREEK AND LATIN COLLEGE COMMENTARIES series is designed for students in intermediate or advanced Greek or Latin at colleges and universities. Each volume includes, on the same page, the ancient text, a running vocabulary, and succinct notes focusing on grammar and syntax, distinctive features of style, and essential context. The Greek and Latin texts are based on the most recent Oxford Classical Text (OCT) editions whenever available; otherwise, other authoritative editions are used. Each volume features a comprehensive introduction intended to enhance utility in the classroom and student appreciation of the work at hand.

The series focuses on texts and authors frequently taught at the intermediate or advanced undergraduate level, but it also makes available some central works currently lacking an appropriate commentary. The primary purpose of this series is to offer streamlined commentaries that are up-to-date, user-friendly, and affordable. Each volume presents entire works or substantial selections that can form the basis for an entire semester's coursework. Each commentary's close attention to grammar and syntax is intended to address the needs of readers encountering a work or author for the first time.

OXFORD GREEK AND LATIN COLLEGE COMMENTARIES

Selected Letters from Pliny the Younger's *Epistulae*

Commentary by

Jacqueline Carlon

University of Massachusetts Boston

New York   Oxford

OXFORD UNIVERSITY PRESS

Oxford University Press is a department of the University of Oxford.
It furthers the University's objective of excellence in research,
scholarship, and education by publishing worldwide.

Oxford   New York
Auckland   Cape Town   Dar es Salaam   Hong Kong   Karachi
Kuala Lumpur   Madrid   Melbourne   Mexico City   Nairobi
New Delhi   Shanghai   Taipei   Toronto

With offices in
Argentina   Austria   Brazil   Chile   Czech Republic   France   Greece
Guatemala   Hungary   Italy   Japan   Poland   Portugal   Singapore
South Korea   Switzerland   Thailand   Turkey   Ukraine   Vietnam

Published by Oxford University Press
198 Madison Avenue, New York, New York 10016
http://www.oup.com

Library of Congress Cataloging-in-Publication Data
Names: Pliny, the Younger, author. | Carlon, Jacqueline M., 1953- writer of
  added commentary.
Title: Selected letters from Pliny the Younger's Epistulae / Pliny the
  Younger ; commentary by Jacqueline Carlon.
Description: New York ; Oxford : Oxford University Press, [2016] | Series:
  Oxford Greek and Latin college commentaries
Identifiers: LCCN 2015039511 | ISBN 9780199340613
Subjects: LCSH: Pliny, the Younger. Correspondence.
Classification: LCC PA6638 .A4 2016 | DDC 876/.01--dc23 LC record available
  at http://lccn.loc.gov/2015039511

TABLE OF CONTENTS

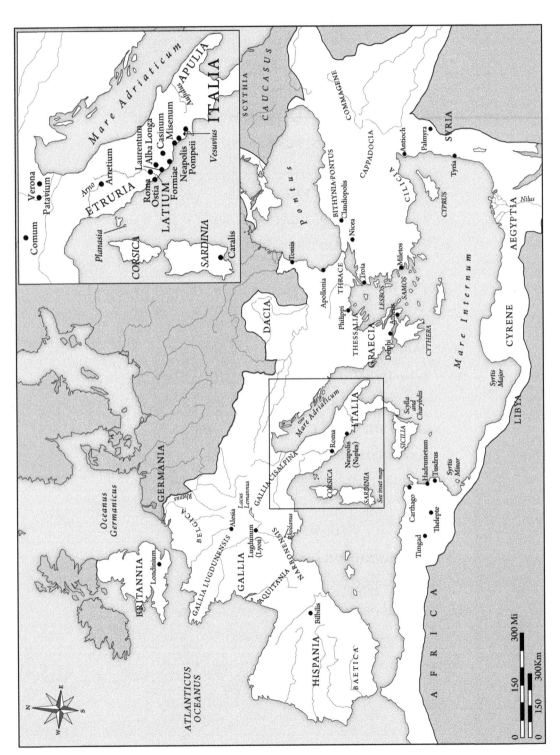

Roman Empire at Its Greatest Extent, ca. 112 AD

ACKNOWLEDGMENTS

I HAD BEEN contemplating putting together a commentary on a selection of Pliny's letters for more than two decades, dating back to when I first began reading them with my students. But it was at the prompting of Stephen Esposito and with the tireless assistance and stalwart support of Barbara Weiden Boyd that this volume came to be; they have my unending gratitude. Many thanks too are owed to Charles Cavaliere at Oxford University Press for his patience and bonhomie; to the anonymous readers of the initial sample text, whose insights were invaluable in shaping its content and approach; to Noelle Zeiner-Carmichael for her sharp eye and careful reading of the manuscript and for her excellent suggestions for revision; and especially to Steven, my husband and best friend, whose support and loving care make all things possible.

INTRODUCTION
PLINY'S LIFE AND TIMES

PLINY THE YOUNGER was born in 61 or 62 CE in the town of Comum, located in Northern Italy in a region that had been the province of Cisalpine Gaul before its incorporation into Italy in 42 BCE. The area had long had the reputation of being rather parochial and conservative, particularly in its adherence to traditional Roman values. The town (modern-day Como) sat on the shore of the southwestern arm of Lacus Larius (Lake Como), which is glacier-fed and the third-largest lake in Italy. In his letters Pliny highlights his ongoing relationships with fellow townsmen and his numerous benefactions for Comum and its people. He reports that he inherited properties from both his mother and father in locations around the lake. Indeed, he apparently was the sole surviving progeny of both parents' equestrian families and thus had substantial resources.

Of Pliny's father we know very little beyond his name: Lucius Caecilius Secundus. That he died before Pliny had reached maturity is clear from the testamentary appointment of Verginius Rufus as the boy's guardian (*Ep.* II.I). Information about his mother (presumably Plinia) is equally elusive. We know her only from brief appearances in his letters, and it is not she but her brother who gives him the name by which we now call him.

Gaius Plinius Secundus, commonly referred to as Pliny the Elder, was a military commander in Germany, an imperial procurator in several provinces, and a prolific author whose staggering literary output is attested by his nephew (*Ep.* III.V). Only his thirty-seven-volume *Natural History* survives, but he also wrote extensive histories, works on oratory and grammar, a biography, and even a manual on throwing the javelin. The elder Pliny was not in Italy during much of the younger Pliny's formative years, but the prominence of his position in his nephew's life is clear from the latter's letters on the eruption of Vesuvius (s. VI.XVI and VI.XX); at the time of the disaster, the three family members—Plinia, her son, and her brother—were living together at Misenum, where the elder Pliny was in command of the Roman fleet. His death in the eruption prompted the testamentary adoption of his nephew, who was subsequently called Gaius Plinius Caecilius Secundus—Pliny the Younger.

There is no doubt that Pliny admired his uncle's accomplishments—his love of literature, his courage, his work ethic, his great deeds. But his own ambitions were focused on the courts and the political arena, not on a military career. He took as models a number of prominent Roman senators and studied rhetoric with the foremost instructors of his time, including Quintilian, and he must have shown a marked talent for the courtroom, as he gave his first speech in the Centumviral Court at the age of eighteen (*Ep.* v.viii).

Political careers in the principate were markedly different from those pursued during the Republic, when magistrates had autonomy and the full power assigned to their office. In Pliny's time the emperor held a collection of powers separated from the offices with which they used to be aligned. But there was still great cachet and status to be gained from serving the emperor and thus the state, and the office of consul retained its prestige, despite the fact that it had become more honorary than functional. Indeed, the emperor frequently served as one of the two ordinary consuls (*consul ordinarius*) by whose names the year was marked; these eponymous consuls were replaced at varying intervals during the year (generally for two, four, or six months) by suffect consuls (*consul suffectus*), a lesser honor than ordinary consul. In Pliny's time the emperor "recommended" candidates, and the Senate elected them. Thus the emperor was able to reward capable and loyal men and to recruit talented administrators; it is clear that he relied on a network of senatorial elite both to serve the needs of the empire and to bring to his attention new talent to expand the upper ranks with capable individuals. Undoubtedly, this is how the younger Pliny's career in public service was launched, with the careful guidance and promotion of men like Corellius Rufus (s. iii.iii) and Julius Frontinus (s. iv.viii and ix.xix), as well as his guardian Verginius Rufus (s. vi.x and ix.xix).

As a young man Pliny served in several minor magistracies and as military tribune, followed by a rather traditional but impressive *cursus:* quaestor, senator, plebeian tribune, praetor, prefect of the military treasury, prefect of the treasury of Saturn, suffect consul in 100, curator of the Tiber, augur, and finally legatus Augusti in the province of Bithynia-Pontus beginning in 109 or 110, where his fiscal acumen was sorely needed (s. section on Book x of the letters). The exact date of his death is unknown, but it is probably no later than 112, while he was still serving as the Emperor Trajan's legate.

The political views that Pliny expresses in his letters are profoundly affected by the emperors under whom he lived. Indeed, it is not extreme to say that the history of Rome under imperial rule runs parallel with the biographies of its emperors. Pliny came of age under Flavian rule, and his first experience in the courtroom might have come to the attention of the emperor Titus, but it was under Domitian that his political career gained momentum. Just how quickly he advanced is a topic of great scholarly debate because, despite the many positive aspects of his reign, in his later years Domitian seemed at war with a number of Pliny's fellow senators, charging them with treason and having them executed. Some senators, like Pliny's archenemy

Regulus (s. II.XX and IV.II), became informers, others either openly or subtly opposed the emperor, and still more stood idly by as his opponents were eliminated. Those who survived and perhaps even prospered under Domitian were left, after his murder, with the need to explain their action or inaction. Pliny would have his reader believe that he was opposed to Domitian's tyrannical treatment of his fellow senators, that he courted danger at every turn, but his political success, seemingly little delayed in those difficult times if at all, suggests his quiet compliance. In any case, with Domitian dead and Rome securely under the control of the "optimus princeps" Trajan, Pliny was free to criticize the villainous Domitian, contrasting his wicked behavior with the excellence of his successor, and to recast and distance himself from his own past (s. particularly C, chap. 1).

While Pliny's letters survive intact, in them he makes clear that he also published a number of his speeches and at least dabbled in poetry, as part of what seems a lively literary circle. Of his speeches, only his *Panegyricus*—a revised and expanded version of his *gratiarum actio*, the speech he gave in thanks to Trajan for the honor of the consulship—survives (s. VI.XXVII for Pliny's approach to the speech). With such a specialized purpose, this sole extant example of his oratory can hardly be considered representative of his rhetoric in general, which was primarily exercised in the courts; it can, however, give us insight into his style. Publication of speeches was a longstanding Roman tradition, beginning well before Cicero's time, but it is Cicero who offers Pliny a compelling model to follow, as Pliny repeatedly in his letters refers to and compares himself with the great Republican statesman and author, albeit often highlighting their differing political circumstances (s. III.XV, III.XXI, and IV.VIII). It may well be that, having read Cicero's letters, Pliny was inspired to assemble his own collection, with the care and precision that Cicero himself was denied by his execution but that he would surely have exercised had he lived long enough to oversee their publication.

We must depend on Pliny's letters for glimpses of his personal life. Married at least twice, perhaps three times, he extols the virtues of his last wife Calpurnia, clearly many years younger than he but a woman who reflects his values and undertakes his interests as her own (s. IV.XIX). Pliny has been credited with being the first Roman to write openly and unabashedly of marital love, as his letters to his wife attest (s. VI.IV and VI.VII). But he remained childless, left to petition the emperor through a friend for the *ius trium liberorum* and the benefits it granted (*Ep.* X.II; s. also II.XIII.8n). With little family through which to shape and define his life, Pliny cultivated relationships with a variety of upstanding men and women, many of whom are known only through his epistolary portrayals of them, which offer the reader a clear lens, albeit colored by Pliny's literary agenda, through which to view elite Roman life in the late first and early second centuries CE.

THE LETTERS

BOOKS I–IX

Pliny's claim in the opening letter of his collection that he has assembled his missives randomly, as they came into his hands, is undoubtedly a literary trope; consideration of the arrangement of his letters makes clear that he is quite intentional in their selection and placement, which together create a comprehensive and idealized image of his life and character. Furthermore, the letters resonate thematically with one another, coming together to form a series of subtly intertwined and highly refined narratives. These are not letters dictated quickly as mere correspondence, but are rather carefully crafted pieces, essays in miniature that generally focus on a single topic, with greetings and closings that align them with epistolary conventions. This is not to say that they are not "genuine" letters; Pliny may certainly have exchanged such literary gems with any number of correspondents; but when he decided to bring them together into what amounts to a portrayal of his life, he most assuredly edited and polished their content. To what extent we can never know.

The addressees of Books I–IX are compelling in their variety. In the 247 letters, there are more than 100 distinct recipients, many of whom are unknown outside of the letters. They appear to represent a true cross section of Pliny's life: men and women, senators and equestrians, friends and young protégés, fellow writers and advocates, family members and casual acquaintances. Many hail from Northern Italy, but others have important connections well south of Rome and even in the provinces. Nearly half, unsurprisingly, are of senatorial rank, but many others in their anonymity leave the reader a vague impression of their ordinariness, thus making letters to them seem like everyday fare, despite their literary refinement.

Pliny does have a number of regular correspondents who receive three or more letters: first and foremost his fellow senator, the historian Tacitus (s. I.VI, VI.XVI, and VI.XX), then a number of people from his hometown and its environs, including his wife's grandfather; the letters to each recipient serve to highlight his various roles—politician, orator, author, benefactor, friend, husband, etc. Topics include: Pliny's own experiences in the courtroom, in literary circles, and in council with the emperor; repeated discussions of how he spends his time, particularly his free time away from his many obligations; letters of advice, recommendation, or condolence; brief historical accounts; and even the latest gossip.

Running through many of the letters is a consistent subtext, through which Pliny offers models of behavior for his readers: ideal men and women at various stages of life and in various social and political settings, with Pliny himself serving as the leading exemplum of a life well and suitably lived. Added to this subtext is the occasional interjection of a villain to serve as a counterpoint to the overwhelmingly positive character of the people who appear in the corpus.

In what form the letters were published is an open question. The term "publication" itself is misleading; "circulation" is more apt. The first two books may have appeared together, dating as they seem to before Pliny's term as consul, or perhaps the nine books appeared in three triads. Letters in later books occasionally assume familiarity with material in earlier books, so it is at least fair to assume that the nine-book collection retains an order intended by Pliny. But each book was also a self-contained unit of a single scroll, with letters meant to be read in sequence that consider a variety of topics yet often share images, language, and points of reference. The nine books together do the same on a grand scale. Thus the corpus subtly invites reading and rereading with a multitude of approaches. It is possible among these to focus on a single book; to trace a particular topic throughout the nine books; to examine letters to a given addressee; to juxtapose the positive and negative exempla Pliny offers; or to consider a selection of letters by their purpose (consolation, recommendation, etc.). Pliny offers no directive, no indication whatsoever to his audience of how the work should be read, and so invites each reader to revisit, rethink, and reimagine the letters of the *Epistulae* and, most important, their ever-present author, with only one clear conclusion: that Pliny plays with reflection, reframing, and resonance so skillfully that his arrangement seems random one moment and deliberate the next, a testament to his artistry in the creation of what is arguably a new genre—"autobiography" in letters.

BOOK X

The differences between the letters of Books I–IX and Book X are startling. The entirety of this last book comprises Pliny's letters to the Emperor Trajan and, for most of them, the emperor's response. The letters are neither casual nor highly literary, as they are focused on the business of the empire. The first fourteen are requests for privileges, expressions of gratitude for the grant of those privileges, or letters of support for the emperor. The remaining 107 letters pertain to Pliny's service as the imperial legate to the province of Bithynia-Pontus, and as such they constitute an invaluable resource for historians of the early empire, not only because they illuminate Trajan's thinking about imperial rule in the provinces but also because they provide a window into how the emperor managed the day-to-day administration of so vast an empire.

Bithynia-Pontus was a Roman province composed of two kingdoms that had briefly been subsumed under Hellenistic rule but had regained self-rule for more than two centuries before the arrival of the Romans; the territory, which bordered the western half of the southern shore of the Black Sea, was fully annexed in 63 BCE as part of Pompey's Eastern Settlements. Pliny was already familiar with the province, having defended two of its former governors against whom the Bithynians had brought charges (*Ep.* IV.IX and V.XX). This insider information, along with his marked talent for finances, must have made Pliny the obvious choice to deal with a province experiencing a series of fiscal crises, as the letters of Book X reveal. Pliny's knowledge of Greek language and culture would also have been critical to his success in a province that had long been populated by Greek colonies and had become thoroughly Hellenized.

Pliny's demeanor in the letters of Book X, as he persistently consults the emperor and defers to his judgment, has suffered a great deal of criticism from modern readers, with accusations that include sycophancy and extreme indecisiveness. Such accusations, however, fail to take into account the uniqueness of Pliny's assignment—as imperial legate to a senatorial province—and the resulting notable lack of precedent for him to follow in dealing with judicial and financial matters there. Trajan does occasionally countermand Pliny's thinking, but more often he reasserts the confidence he had displayed in Pliny's ability when he had first assigned him to the position. These letters reveal a respectful and working relationship between the two men, one that is predicated on Pliny's understanding and acknowledgment of Trajan's supreme position and his display of appropriate deference to that authority. His is a successful relationship with an autocrat, and the letters of Book X offer *exempla* for those who followed him.

Did Pliny decide to append the correspondence with Trajan to his literary collection, as a means of highlighting his relationship with the emperor and his service to the state, or was Book X included by an editor after Pliny's death? While he could not edit what was official communication with the emperor, he could certainly have chosen what to include. Unlike the letters of the first nine books, those in Book X are in strict chronological order, creating a documentary testament of Pliny's association with the emperor. Whether by his own intention or that of an editor, the addition of Book X provides the same benefit to Pliny's epistolary agenda—an imperial stamp of approval and patent evidence of his value to the empire.

STYLE

Despite its deceptively informal context, that is, regular correspondence, Pliny's prose in the first nine books is neither simple nor spontaneous. He was no casual correspondent, but rather a highly trained rhetorician whose writing reflects the attendant care and precision such instruction compelled. Still, the letters have all the elements required of letters: addressees and opening remarks that set forth a reason for writing or that claim to respond to previous requests or to revisit past events; extensive use of the first and second persons in the body of the letter; frequent use of epistolary tenses; and a closing paragraph that is often either self-effacing or aphoristic. In fact, it is this epistolary frame that allows Pliny to expound upon his own actions, opinions, and insights, in seeming response to prompting from his addressee. As personal correspondence, the letters provide motivation for writing as well as the illusion of deep intimacy—a carefully fashioned window into Pliny's inmost thoughts. Thus Pliny can deal with virtually any topic, all the while shaping his own image.

While he frequently nods to Cicero as a model, it is the substance of the great Republican's life, not his Latinity, that Pliny admires. Rarely given to writing in periods, Pliny tends toward parataxis, leading the reader through his thought process to each point of his argument. Of the many rhetorical devices Pliny employs, the most common are asyndeton and anaphora. His prose is marked by the juxtaposition of opposing ideas (antithesis) and the accumulation of single words in descriptive lists (often lacking conjunctions), but it also includes the occasional unexpected grammatical turn (variatio) that seems to mark him as a contemporary of Tacitus, whose writing is rife with syntactical surprise. Pliny also shares with the great historian the frequent ellipsis of forms of the verb *esse* and a fondness for the pithy phrase (sententia) with which he often ends his letters, particularly those that are rather philosophical in nature.

Finally, as Pliny writes and arranges his letter collection, he not only incorporates epistolary conventions but also dabbles in a variety of prose genres. Individual letters can be read as brief excerpts from history or philosophy, or from didactic or encyclopedic prose. Pliny chooses not to write in any of these genres, all the while demonstrating his ability to excel in each of them should he ever choose to do so. The letter collection becomes an ideal canvas for the display of his consummate literary skill.

By contrast, the letters of Book x are clearly not meant to be literary pieces, but neither are they carelessly composed. Pliny's focus is on clarity of expression, as his meticulously constructed narratives attest. With painstaking care, he lays out his concerns, his attention focused not on any rhetorical flourish, but on expediency. These are documents that reveal a competent and diligent imperial administrator, a complement to the literary author of the earlier books.

SCHOLARSHIP

For many years, scholarship on Pliny's *Epistulae* tended to be cursory at best. The letters were mined extensively for social and political insights into the late first and early second centuries of the Roman Empire, without much consideration of the nature of the work as a whole. Much ink was spilled regarding the "authenticity" of the letters, of concern to historians in particular, who wanted to rely on Pliny's authority. There is now general consensus that at the very least the letters are carefully edited versions of what was likely actual correspondence.

In the last twenty years, there has been a marked resurgence of interest in Pliny's work as literature, beginning with extensive consideration of his self-representation in the *Epistulae*. Other scholarship has focused on literary allusion in the letters; various approaches to reading the text (by the whole book, by topic, by addressee, etc.); Pliny's artistic arrangement of the letters and intertextuality within the corpus; and close and careful analysis of his style. Particularly fruitful are comprehensive reading strategies for the letters that highlight the various narrative strains of the collection.

See also the section on Further Reading.

THIS VOLUME

Making a selection of fifty letters for this text was a difficult task, particularly for someone familiar with Pliny's complete corpus. Each letter demands to be read, but there is scarcely room for fifty (an homage to the great A. N. Sherwin-White's *Fifty Letters of Pliny*. Oxford: Oxford University Press, 1967), not to mention the entire collection of 368. Ideally, I would have someone unfamiliar with Pliny begin at the beginning and read to the end. When possible, I would suggest the reading of a minimum of a whole book at a time. But the purpose of this volume is to introduce Pliny to intermediate readers, with the hope of sparking their interest in looking more closely at the whole work. Thus, I have included letters on a variety of topics that will give readers a comprehensive but accessible introduction to the *Epistulae*, as they consider Pliny's style and his political and personal life, as well as the social and historical context in which the letters were composed.

A number of important themes are represented in this selection of letters, and I would encourage readers to juxtapose individual letters within these themes to get a better sense of what Pliny does throughout the whole corpus, as he revisits and recasts topics that are important in his life. Some of the most prominent themes, and the letters in this volume that address them, are:

1. *Otium/Negotium* (Leisure/Business). Pliny and his peers were expected to be engaged in productive activity, either in the *negotium* of serving the state, overseeing their households, and managing their estates, or in the proper use of their *otium*, which was to be spent in activities that led to self-improvement: reading, writing, and exercise (s. I.VI, I.IX, IV.XXIII, IX.XXXVI). Improper use of *otium*, epitomized by obsession with the games, led to dissipation (s. IX.VI).

2. Patronage/Generosity. Roman society had always been held together by the social glue of patronage (*clientela*) and friendship (*amicitia*), the former between those

who were socially unequal, the latter among relative equals. Shared interests, both economic and intellectual, were critical to both horizontal and vertical bonds. Thus Pliny helps not only family members (s. II.IV) and lower-ranking friends (s. II.XIII), but also struggling writers (s. I.XXIV and III.XXI). In addition, as an elite son of Comum, he would have been expected to support the town and its citizens with his financial resources (s. III.VI and VII.XVIII).

3. Freedmen and Slaves. In a steeply stratified society, rank was crucial to self-definition. But Roman rank was also fluid: slaves were regularly manumitted; freedmen could become wealthy; the sons of freedmen might attain political office; and the emperor sometimes chose to elevate the status of worthy individuals. There is no question that Pliny considers the proper treatment of those of lesser rank a mark of good character. He offers contrasting views of how elite men dealt with the treatment of slaves (s. III.XIV and VIII.XVI) and freedmen (s. II.VI and V.XIX), juxtaposing the habits of less-enlightened men with his own practices.

4. Literature. Pliny is part of a thriving literary community, as he makes clear in several letters in which he discusses not only personal exchanges of work (s. III.XV) but also performance venues (s. I.XIII and VIII.XII), as well as how much he values his literary legacy (s. IX.XXIII).

5. Women. Like the men Pliny writes to and about, the women of the letters are overwhelmingly elite and admirable. Among his exemplary characterizations, Pliny offers three portraits of idealized women: bride (s. V.XVI), young wife (s. IV.XIX), and matron (s. VII.XIX). In addition, he offers an obituary for the feisty grandmother of one of his protégés (s. VII.XXIV).

6. Negative Exempla. In contrast to the many positive portraits Pliny presents are a few negative ones that offer his stark criticism of improper behavior: Regulus (s. II.XX and IV.II), Domitian (s. IV.XI), and two unnamed villains—a disrespectful senator (s. IV.XXV) and a neglectful heir (s. VI.X).

In this volume the text of the letters and commentary is preceded by a list of Latin words that appear at least six times; these words will not be glossed in the commentary unless they have an unusual meaning that occurs just once in this anthology. An occasional word, though frequent (like *constare* or *exigere*), has so many idiomatic meanings that listing it just once would not be useful to the reader. Such words will be glossed consistently. The commentary for each of the letters is based on the expectation that the majority of readers will not read this anthology from beginning to end but will instead read selected letters within it. To this end, lexical and grammatical support is repeated for each letter, and no familiarity with earlier letters is assumed. Since the audience for this text may include readers who are unfamiliar with the complexities of Roman social and political structures, explanation is provided where it is needed. This material is *not* repeated from letter to letter, but the reader is referred to earlier remarks by the letter and section number of the topic's first appearance. Rhetorical devices are also noted (in SMALL CAPS), but only those whose use contributes to Pliny's tone or meaning or may interfere with comprehension. For explanation of the abbreviations used in the comments, the reader should consult the list beginning on page xxiii. Rhetorical devices are described in the glossary beginning on page xxvi.

The text of the letters is drawn from the R. A. B. Mynors critical edition (*C. Plini Caecili Secundi Epistularum Libri Decem*. Oxford: Oxford University Press, 1963).

FURTHER READING

GENERAL INTRODUCTION:

Gibson, Roy, and Ruth Morrell. *Reading the Letters of Pliny the Younger: An Introduction.* Cambridge: Cambridge University Press, 2012.

LITERARY ANALYSIS:

Marchesi, Ilaria. *The Art of Pliny's Letters: A Poetics of Allusion in the Private Correspondence.* Cambridge: Cambridge University Press, 2008.

Whitton, Christopher. *Pliny the Younger* Epistles *Book II.* Cambridge: Cambridge University Press, 2013.

SELF-REPRESENTATION:

Carlon, Jacqueline. *Pliny's Women: Constructing Virtue and Creating Identity in the Roman World.* Cambridge: Cambridge University Press, 2009.

Henderson, John G. *Pliny's Statue: The* Letters, *Self-Portraiture, and Classical Art.* Exeter Classical Studies and Ancient History. Liverpool: Liverpool University Press, 2002.

Leach, Eleanor Winsor. "The Politics of Self-Presentation: Pliny's *Letters* and Roman Portrait Sculpture." *Classical Antiquity* 9 (1990): 14–39.

Shelton, Jo-Ann. "Pliny's Letter 3.11: Rhetoric and Autobiography." *Classica et Mediaevalia* 38 (1989): 121–39.

PEOPLE IN THE *EPISTULAE*:

Birley, Anthony R. *Onomasticon to the Younger Pliny: Letters and Panegyric.* Leipzig: K. G. Saur, 2000.

Bradley, Keith R. "The Exemplary Pliny." In *Studies in Latin Literature and Roman History,* edited by Carl Deroux, 15. Brussels: Latomus, 2010, 384–422.

Shelton, Jo-Ann Shelton. *The Women of Pliny's Letters.* New York: Routledge, 2013.

SOCIAL AND POLITICAL COMMENTARY:

Hoffer, Stanley. *The Anxieties of Pliny the Younger.* Atlanta: Scholar's Press, 1999.

Sherwin-White, A. N. *The Letters of Pliny: A Historical and Social Commentary.* Oxford: Oxford University Press, 1966.

STYLE:

Gamberini, Federico. *Stylistic Theory and Practice in the Younger Pliny*. New York: Olms-Weidmann, 1983.

Halla-aho, Hilla. "Epistolary Latin." In *A Companion to the Latin Language*, edited by James Clackson. Malden, Mass.: Wiley Blackwell, 2011, 426–44.

Morello, Ruth, and A. D. Morrison, eds. *Ancient Letters: Classical and Late Antique Epistolography*. Oxford: Oxford University Press, 2007.

TACITUS:

Griffin, Miriam. "Pliny and Tacitus." *Scripta Classica Israelica* 18 (1999): 139–58.

Sinclair, Patrick. *Tacitus the Sententious Historian: A Sociology of Rhetoric in* Annales *1–6*. University Park, Pa.: Pennsylvania State Press, 1995.

Whitton, Christopher. "'Let us tread our path together': Tacitus and the Younger Pliny." In *A Companion to Tacitus*, edited by Victoria Emma Pagán. Malden, Mass.: Wiley Blackwell, 2012, 345–68.

TRAJAN AND BOOK X:

Bennett, Julian. *Trajan: Optimus Princeps*. London: Routledge, 2001.

Coleman, Kathleen M. "Bureaucratic Language in the Correspondence between Pliny and Trajan." *Transactions of the American Philological Association* 142 (2012): 189–238.

Noreña, Carlos F. "The Social Economy of Pliny's Correspondence with Trajan." *American Journal of Philology* 128 (2007): 239–77.

Syme, Ronald. *Tacitus*, 2 vols. Oxford: Oxford University Press, 1958.

Williams, Wynne, ed. *Pliny the Younger: Correspondence with Trajan from Bithynia (Epistles X)*. Warminster: Aris and Phillips, 1990.

COMMENTARY ABBREVIATIONS

Reference Works

AB	Anthony Birley, *Onomasticon to the Younger Pliny: Letters and Panegyric*. Leipzig: K. G. Saur, 2000
AG	*Allen and Greenough's New Latin Grammar*, edited by Anne Mahoney. Newburyport, Mass.: Focus Publishing, 2001
BG	*Gildersleeve's Latin Grammar* by Basil L. Gildersleeve and Gonzalez Lodge. 3rd ed. New York: Boston University Publishing Co., 1894
C	Jacqueline Carlon, *Pliny's Women*. Cambridge: Cambridge University Press, 2009
CIL	*Corpus Inscriptionum Latinarum*. 16 vols. Berlin: Deutsche Akademie der Wissenschaft zu Berlin, 1863–
ILS	*Inscriptiones Latinae Selectae*, edited by Herman Dessau. Berlin, 1892–1916
OCD	*Oxford Classical Dictionary*. 3rd ed., edited by Simon Hornblower and Antony Spawforth. Oxford: Oxford University Press, 1996
OLD	*Oxford Latin Dictionary*, edited by P. G. W. Glare. Oxford: Oxford University Press, 1982
Radice	Betty Radice, ed. and trans. *Pliny Letters and Panegyricus*, 2 vols. Cambridge, Mass.: Harvard University Press, 1969
SW	A.N. Sherwin-White, *The Letters of Pliny: A Historical and Social Commentary*. Oxford: Clarendon, 1966

Symbols in Entries

<	derived from
=	equivalent to, identical with
{>}	derivative

Abbreviations Used in the Grammatical Notes

(1)	first conjugation	advers.	adversative
1st	first	affirm.	affirmative
2nd	second	alt.	alternative
3rd	third	anteced.	antecedent
abl.	ablative	apod.	apodosis
abs.	absolute	appos.	apposition
acc.	accusative	char.	characteristic
accomp.	accompaniment	circumst.	circumstance, circumstantial
act.	active		
adj.	adjective	cl.	clause (cls. = clauses)
adv.	adverb	cogn.	cognate

comm.	command	gerv.	gerundive
compar.	comparative/	Gk.	Greek
	comparison	hist.	historical
compd.	compound	hort.	hortatory
compl.	complementary	idiom.	idiomatic/
conces.	concessive		idiomatically
condit.	condition(al)	i.e.	*id est* = that is (to say),
conj.	conjunction		namely
conjug.	conjugation	impers.	impersonal
constr.	construction	impf.	imperfect
contr.	contracted	impv.	imperative
correl.	correlative	indecl.	indeclinable
C-to-F	contrary-to-fact	indef.	indefinite
dat.	dative	indic.	indicative
dbl.	double	indir.	indirect
decl.	declension	indir. disc.	indirect discourse
defect.	defective	inf.	infinitive
deg.	degree	interrog.	interrogative
delib.	deliberative	intr.	intransitive
demon.	demonstrative	introd.	introducing, intro-
depend.	dependent		duced (by)
depon.	deponent	irreg.	irregular
deriv.	derivative	lit.	literal(ly), in a literary
diff.	different/difference		sense
dim.	diminutive	locat.	locative
dir.	direct	m.	masculine
dur.	duration	mg.	meaning
E.	English	monosyl.	monosyllable/-bic
e.g.	*exempli gratia* =	n.	neuter
	for example	n. (in citations)	note
esp.	especially	n.b.	*nota bene* = note well,
ex.	example (exx. =		take note of
	examples)	negat.	negative
exclam.	exclamation	nom.	nominative
f.	feminine	num.	number
ff.	following	obj.	object
FLV	future less vivid	objv.	objective
FMV	future more vivid	opt.	optative
freq.	frequent(ly)	orig.	originally
frequent.	frequentative	partit.	partitive
fut.	future	pass.	passive
gen.	genitive	pcl.	particle
gen. cond.	general conditional	periphr.	periphrastic
gener.	generally	pers.	person
ger.	gerund	pf.	perfect

pl.	plural	sent.	sentence
plupf.	pluperfect	separ.	separation
pos.	positive	seq.	sequence
poss.	possessive/possession	sg.	singular
postpos.	postpositive	specif.	specification
potent.	potential	stmt.	statement
ppp.	perfect passive participle	subj.	subject(ive)
		subjv.	subjunctive
prep.	preposition	subord.	subordinate
pres.	present	subst.	substantive
pron.	pronoun	superl.	superlative
prot.	protasis	tmp.	temporal
ptc.	participle	usu.	usually
purp.	purpose	vb.	verb
quest.	question	voc.	vocative
ref.	reference	vocab.	vocabulary
reflex.	reflexive	w/	with
relat.	relative	w/out	without
s.	see	wd.	word

GLOSSARY OF RHETORICAL
AND GRAMMATICAL TERMS

ANAPHORA: a rhetorical device in which the same word is repeated at the beginning of successive phrases for emphasis

ASYNDETON: the omission of conjunctions

ELLIPSIS: the omission of a word or words, which must be understood to complete the meaning of the clause

HYPERBATON: the alteration of expected word order or the separation of words that naturally belong together for emphasis or rhetorical effect

IRONY: the use of words in such a way that they convey a meaning that is markedly different from their literal meaning

METONYMY: referring to a thing or concept by using the name of something associated with it

PARENTHESIS: the insertion of explanatory or additional information that is grammatically unconnected with the rest of the sentence; an aside

POLYPTOTON: the repetition of a word root with different inflection

PRAETERITIO: the introduction of a subject made by claiming that it is not under discussion

RHETORICAL QUESTION: a question that is asked for effect or emphasis, rather than in expectation of a response

SENTENTIA: the summation of a point of argument with a witty saying, maxim or quotation

TRANSFERRED EPITHET: the use of an adjective to qualify a noun that does not designate the person or thing actually described

VARIATIO: using two different grammatical structures rather than parallel structures to the same effect

ZEUGMA: the joining of parts of a sentence by a common verb; if the verb changes meaning from one clause to the next, the device is further called *syllepsis*

FREQUENT VOCABULARY

accedo, accedere, accessi, accessus ($<$ ad + cedo, cedere) (1) come to, approach; (2) be added (*OLD* 15a)

accido, accidere, accidi, accisus ($<$ ad + cado, cadere) happen {$>$ accident}

addo, addere, addidi, additus ($<$ ad + do, dare) add, say or write additionally (*OLD* 13)

adhuc (adv.) as yet, thus far, up to that time, to this point

adicio, adicere, adieci, adiectus ($<$ ad + iacio, iacere) add, go on to say

autem (pcl.) moreover; postpos., i.e. not the 1st wd. in its cl. (AG #324j)

certe (adv.) ($<$ certus, -a, -um) certainly, at least

cogito (1) ($<$ con + agito, agitare) consider, have in mind, take into account {$>$ cogitate}

compono, componere, composui, compositus ($<$ con + pono, ponere) (1) compose, write, compile (*OLD* 8a, c); (2) compose one's appearance (*OLD* 13a)

confero, conferre, contuli, collatus ($<$ con + fero, ferre) (1) bring together; (2) reflex.: betake oneself, go; (3) bestow (+ acc.) on (dat.), contribute (*OLD* 9a)

consulo, consulere, consului, consultus (1) intr.: look after, pay attention to (*OLD* 6b); (2) consult on a point of information or law

conuenio, conuenire, conueni, conuentus ($<$ con + uenio, uenire) (1) meet, agree; (2) impers.: be becoming, be suitable, befit (*OLD* 6b/c); (3) be consistent w/ (*OLD* 6 a/b) {$>$ convention}

cot(t)idie (adv.) ($<$ quotus + dies) daily, every day

dein, deinde (adv.) ($<$ de + inde) next, secondly, then

delecto (1) ($<$ de + lacto, lactare) be a source of delight, please {$>$ delectable}

denique (adv.) finally, lastly

desino, desinere, desii ($<$ de + sino, sinere) cease, break off

diligo, diligere, dilexi, dilectus ($<$ dis + lego, legere) love, hold dear

egregius, -a, -um ($<$ ex + grex + -ius) outstanding, splendid {$>$ egregious}

enim (pcl.) for (explaining the reason for the previous stmt.); postpos., i.e. not the 1st wd. in its cl. (AG #324j)

equidem (pcl.) "I for my part" (when used w/ 1st pers.)

ergo (pcl.) in that case, then, therefore

experior, experiri, expertus sum — (< ex + perior) learn by experience, test {> expert}

fio, fieri, factus sum — happen, be done, be made, become

fortasse (adv.) — (< fors) perhaps

honestus, -a, -um — (< honor + -tus) bringing honor, of good repute, honorable

iaceo, iacere, iacui, iacitus — lie, remain {> adjacent}

idem, eadem, idem (adj./pron.) — the same; adj. often used as subst.

ideo (adv.) — for the following reason, for this/that reason

incertus, -a, -um — (< in + certus) (1) uncertain, not predetermined, unsure; (2) undependable (*OLD* 5a)

ingenium, -i (n.) — (< in + gen (from gigno) + -ium) (1) natural ability; (2) literary or poetic talent (*OLD* 5a) {> ingenious}

inquam, inquis, inquit — "I say, you say, he says"; defect. vb. always used PARENTHETICALLY (AG #599c)

inuenio, inuenire, inueni, inuentus — (< in + uenio, uenire) discover, come upon, learn {> invent}

iucundus, -a, -um — (< iuuo + -cundus) pleasant, agreeable, delightful {> jocund}

iudicium, iudici (n.) — (< iudex + -ium) (1) action before a judge, trial; (2) judgment, reasoned decision; (3) favorable opinion, esteem (*OLD* 10) {> judicial}

iuuenis, iuuenis (m.) — young man {> juvenile}; also: *iuuenis, iuuenis* (adj.) young

libellus, -i (m.) — (< liber + -lus) little book, volume, notebook. In the first nine books, Pliny frequently uses the term *libellus* to refer to his poetry.

licet, licere, licuit — it is permitted, granted that {> license}; impers. vb. that often introd. subst. cl. of purp. w/ *ut* freq. omitted (AG #565)

malo, malle — (< magis + uolo, uelle) prefer

metus, -us (m.) — fear, apprehension

mirus, -a, -um — extraordinary, remarkable {> miracle}

modicus, -a, -um — (< modus + -cus) moderate in size or amount {> modicum}

nam (pcl.) — for; introd. explanation of the previous declaration

nescio, nescire, nesciui, nescitus — (< ne + scio, scire) not know, be uncertain; *nescio . . . an*: "I don't know whether" or "I'm inclined to think;" *nescio* often expresses uncertainty about part of a sent.

nouissimus, -a, -um (superl. adj.) — (< nouus -a -um) most recent, latest, final, ultimate

officium, -i (n.)	(ops + facio, facere + -ium) (1) a service, a courtesy; (2) a duty, an obligation; (3) a ceremony (*OLD* 2c)
omnino (adv.)	(< omnis, omne) entirely, altogether
otium, -i (n.)	spare time, freedom from business, leisure (s. Intro.)
opus, operis (n.)	(1) piece of work, effort, activity; (2) building
parum (adv.)	(< paruus) not … enough, too little
patior, pati, passus sum	(1) endure, experience, be subjected to; (2) allow or permit: followed by acc. and inf. (AG #563c)
posco, poscere, poposci	call for, demand
praeterea (adv.)	(< praeter + ea) as well, besides
princeps, principis (adj.)	chief, leading {> principal}; i.e. senatorial rank
princeps, principis (m.)	(1) the leading member; (2) the emperor; the title originally indicated the senator whose name appeared first on the censor's roll and who spoke first in the Senate; it was later revived by the Emperor Augustus to refer to his position in that body (*OCD* s. princeps senatus, 1247). *Optimus Princeps* was a phrase used to describe or refer to the Emperor Trajan early in his reign (largely to contrast his behavior w/ that of Domitian). Later it became an official title (*OCD* s. Trajan, 1544).
primum (adv.)	first of all
proinde (adv.)	(< pro + inde) accordingly
proximus, -a, -um	(< prope + -simus) nearest, next, most recent {> proximity}
quantum, -i (n.) (relat./interrog. pron.)	(< quam + -to + -um) what amount, how(ever) much
quasi (conj.)	as though, as if
quidam, quaedam, quoddam (adj.)	certain; used subst. as pron.: a certain (man, woman, thing) (AG #310); often denotes pers. known to writer but unnamed
quidem (pcl.)	indeed, certainly; emphasizes preceding wd. or phrase; *ne … quidem*: not even
quiesco, quiescere, quieui, quietus	(< quies + -sco) fall asleep, repose in sleep, rest from toil {> quiescent}
ratio, rationis (f.)	(< reor, reri, ratus + -tio) (1) reason, calculation, reckoning, account (*OLD* s. ratio 2d); (2) pattern, plan (*OLD* 13b) {> rational}
rectus, -a, -um	(ppp. of rego, regere) proper, morally upright, straight, direct {> rectify}
reddo, reddere, reddidi, redditus	(< re + do, dare) (1) give back, repay, reflect, restore; (2) reflex.: *se reddere*: return (intr.)

refero, referre, rettuli, relatus	(< res + fero, ferre) (1) bring back, return, redirect; (2) report, recall, mention (*OLD* 18); (3) resemble (*OLD* 19); *gratiam referre*: express thanks; impers. use (*refert*): it makes a difference, it matters
repeto, repetere, repetiui, repetitus	(< re + peto, petere) return to, repeat, recall
requiro, requirere, requisii, requisitus	(< re + quaero, quaerere) look for, seek, ask {> requisition}
rursus (adv.)	again, a second time
sane (adv.)	decidedly, admittedly, to be sure (*OLD* 8a)
secessus, secessus (m.)	(< se + cedo, cedere + -tus) withdrawal from Rome into the country, retreat, privacy {> secession}
sermo, sermonis (m.)	conversation, conversational style, gossip (*OLD* 4)
singuli, -ae, -a	taken separately, individual
solacium, -i (n.)	consolation, comfort, solace
studium, -i (n.)	(< studeo, studere + -ium) zeal, devotion, intellectual pursuits, study (esp. literary study *OLD* 7a)
sufficio, sufficere, suffeci, suffectus	(< sub + facio, facere) be sufficient, adequate {> suffice}
suscipio, suspicere, suscepi, susceptus	(< sub + capio, capere) undertake, support, make a matter of one's concern (*OLD* 7)
tamen (adv.)	yet, however; often postpos., i.e. not the 1st wd. in its cl. (*AG* #324j)
tamquam (conj.)	(< tam + quam) (1) just as if; (2) as though, on the ground that (*OLD* 7)
tantum	(< tantus, -a, -um) adverbial use of acc.) only, just
tantum, -i (n.)	(< tantus, -a, -um) so much; n. adj. used as pron., gener. w/ part. gen., *AG* #346/3
uterque, utraque, utrumque (pron.)	each (of two), both
ualetudo, ualetudinis (f.)	(< ualeo, ualere + -tudo) health, illness
uel (pcl.)	or; (1) implies a choice between two alts., w/out excluding the item not chosen (*AG* #324d); (2) can imply a correction or more precise stmt. of the 1st alt.: "or I should say/or even" (*OLD* 3); *uel . . . uel*: either . . . or
uenia, -ae (f.)	pardon, forgiveness {> venial}
uereor, uereri, ueritus sum	be afraid, regard w/ awe
uerto, uertere, uerti, uersus	turn {> vertex}
uideor, uideri, uisus sum	(1) seem good or right (*OLD* 24); (2) appear after due consideration (legal use) (*OLD* 22)
uoluptas, uoluptatis (f.)	pleasure, delight {> voluptuous}

OXFORD GREEK AND LATIN COLLEGE COMMENTARIES

Selected Letters from
Pliny the Younger's *Epistulae*

BOOK I

I—DEDICATION OF THE *EPISTULAE*

C. PLINIVS SEPTICIO <CLARO> SVO S.

FREQVENTER hortatus es ut epistulas, si quas paulo cura- 1
tius scripsissem, colligerem publicaremque. Collegi non seruato temporis ordine (neque enim historiam componebam),
sed ut quaeque in manus uenerat. Superest ut nec te consilii 2

1.1: Pliny sends his 1st collection of letters to Septicius Clarus. This opening letter serves as a dedication of the work as a whole and is Pliny's opportunity to characterize his own work as an arbitrary collection and arrangement of his correspondence, rather than the careful assembly it clearly is.

Addressee: Gaius Septicius Clarus, equestrian, praetorian prefect 119 CE under Hadrian, dismissed from service to the emperor along with Suetonius Tranquillus, the biographer, in 122 (SW 84, AB 88).

1.1.1

frequenter (adv.) on many occasions, repeatedly (*OLD* 2)

ut . . . colligerem publicaremque subst. cl. of purp. (AG #563) (= indir. comm.) ff. *hortatus es*; the cl. is NOT C-to-F, but rather past gen. condit. (AG #514) w/ subjv. vbs. in depend. cl. (AG #512), apod.: *epistulas . . . colligerem publicaremque* (AG #514), prot.: *si . . . scripsissem*

quas = *aliquas*; some, any; quis, quid: indef. in place of aliquis, aliquid w/ si, nisi, num, ne (AG #310)

paulo somewhat, by a little; abl. of deg. of diff. (AG #414) w/ compar. adv. *curatius* (< ppp. of curo, curare): more carefully

colligo, colligere, collegi, collectus (< con + lego, legere) gather, assemble, bring literary works together (*OLD* 8) {> collect}

publico (1) (< publicus, -a, -um) make public, publish (a book) (*OLD* 3)

seruato temporis ordine abl. abs. (AG #419); seruo (1) watch over, keep, maintain, preserve; ordo, ordinis (f.) order, arrangement (of literary material) (*OLD* 13d) {> ordinal}

ut . . . uenerat tmp. use of *ut* w/ indic. (AG #543); quique, quaeque, quodque (adj.) (< qui, quae, quod + -que) each; *quaeque*: subst. use, i.e. each letter, "as (in the same way as) each had come into my hands"

1.1.2

supersum, superesse (< super + sum, esse) remain, be left over; impers. w/ *ut* and subst. cl. of result (AG #569/2), "the only remaining necessity is (that . . .)" (*OLD* 6b)

nec me paeniteat obsequii. Ita enim fiet, ut eas quae adhuc
neglectae iacent requiram et si quas addidero non supprimam. Vale.

VI—HUNTING AND MORE

C. PLINIVS CORNELIO TACITO SVO S.

1 Ridebis, et licet rideas. Ego, ille quem nosti, apros tres et
quidem pulcherrimos cepi. 'Ipse?' inquis. Ipse; non tamen ut
omnino ab inertia mea et quiete discederem. Ad retia sede-

---

nec ... obsequii paeniteo, paenitere: cause dissatisfaction or regret {> penitent}, impers. vb. of feeling, gener. w/ pers. affected in acc. (*te/me*) and cause in gen. (*consilii/obsequii*) (AG #354b); consilium, -i (n.) advice, counsel; obsequium, -i (n.) (< obsequor, obsequi + -ium) the act of compliance
{> obsequious}; "you do not regret your advice, nor I my compliance [with it]"

ita ... ut correl. (AG #323g), "it will happen thus, that ..."

eas (*epistulas*) implied

neglectus, -a, -um (ppp. of neglego, neglegere < nec + lego, legere) neglected, ignored

si ... supprimam FMV condit. (AG #516c); *quas = aliquas* (s. 1.1.1n.); supprimo, supprimere (< sub +
premo, premere) hold back, suppress

I.VI: Pliny recounts one of his leisure time activities (during his *otium*—s. Freq. Vocab.)—boar hunting, though his participation is not quite what the reader might expect.

Addressee: Publius (?) Cornelius Tacitus, good friend of Pliny, senatorial rank, suffect consul 97 CE;
best known to modern readers as an historian and the author of *Germania, Agricola, Dialogus de
Oratoribus, Annales,* and *Historiae,* he was also a well-regarded orator. He receives more letters than
any other addressee in the 1st nine books, eleven all together, including VI.XVI and VI.XX.

I.VI.1

rideo, ridere laugh {> ridicule}; Pliny's use of POLYPTOTON (*ridebis ... rideas*) highlights the lighthearted nature of the letter

ille quem "that man whom"; Pliny refers to himself in the 3rd pers.

nosco, noscere, noui, notus become acquainted w/, pf.: know; *nosti* = contr. form of *nouisti* (AG #181)

aper, apri (m.) wild boar

ut ... discederem result cl. (AG #537); inertia, -ae (f.) (< iners, inertis + -ia) idleness, disinclination
for activity; quies, quietis (f.) rest, repose, relaxation

rete, retis (n.) net used for hunting or fishing {> retina}. Nets were spread out to snare the boars,
driven into them by hounds. The boars were then killed by men on foot w/ spears. Pliny's task here is
just to watch the nets, since he has no weapons (*OCD* s. hunting, 733).

in proximo close at hand (*OLD* 2a)

uenabulum, -i (n.) (< uenor, uenari + -bulum) hunting spear

lancea, -ae (f.) long light spear, lance

stilus, -i (m.) stylus (for incising letters on wax tablets), pen

pugillares, pugillarium (m.) (< pugnus + -illus + -aris) writing tablets (small enough to be held in
the hand—pugnus, i. (m.) means fist or handful); either wax tablets or *pugillares membranei* (Martial
14.7 and 14.184; SW 100), a folded parchment that was the earliest form of the codex, a book com-
prised of individual pages/sheets, rather than a continuous scroll. Codices were generally bound on
one edge, but could also be folded like a paper fan.

bam; erat in proximo non uenabulum aut lancea, sed stilus
et pugillares; meditabar aliquid enotabamque, ut si manus
uacuas, plenas tamen ceras reportarem. Non est quod con-
temnas hoc studendi genus; mirum est ut animus agitatione
motuque corporis excitetur; iam undique siluae et solitudo
ipsumque illud silentium quod uenationi datur, magna cogitationis incitamenta sunt. Proinde cum uenabere, licebit
auctore me ut panarium et lagunculam sic etiam pugillares
feras: experieris non Dianam magis montibus quam Miner-
uam inerrare. Vale.

2

3

---

meditor, meditari, meditatus sum contemplate, ponder, reflect {> meditate}

enoto (1) (< ex + noto, notare) write down

ut ... reportarem purp. cl. (AG #531/1); *si ... tamen*: correl. (AG #527c), "(even) if ... still"; *(manus) uacuas, plenas ... ceras*: uacuus, -a, -um (< uaco, uacare + -uus) not containing anything, empty {> vacuum}; plenus, -a, -um (< pleo, plere) containing all that it will hold, full {> plenty}; cera, -ae (f.) beeswax, wax; writing-tablet; wax was used as a writing surface, smeared onto wood framed tablets; the writer then used a stylus to scratch words into the wax, which could be heated and smoothed for reuse.

I.VI.2

quod ... genus relat. cl. of char. (AG #535), anteced. *genus*; contemno, contemnere (< con + temno, temnere) scorn, look down on {> contempt}; studeo, studere: devote oneself, study; *studendi* (ger.): gen. of specif. (BG #361) w/ *genus*: genus, generis (n.) a kind or sort of thing (*OLD* 9) {> generic}

mirum est ut ... excitetur subst. use of n. adj. (AG #289) introd. indir. quest. (AG #574); *ut* (interrog. adv.) how; "it is amazing how ..."; animus, -i (m.) mind (as opposed to body); *agitatione motuque*: abl. of means (AG #409); agitatio, agitationis (f.) (< ago, agere + -ito + -tio) movement, exercise; motus, -us (m.) (< moueo, mouere + -tus) movement, motion; excito (1) (< ex + cito, citare) rouse, stir

solitudo, solitudinis (f.) (< solus + -tudo) the state of being alone, solitude

silentium, -i (n.) (< silens + -ium) absence of sound, silence

uenatio, uenationis (f.) (< uenor, uenari + -tio) the hunting of wild animals

cogitatio, cogitationis (f.) (< con + ago, agere + -ito + -tio) the act of thinking, reflection, speculation; *cogitationis*: objv. gen. (AG #347) w/ *incitamenta*; incitamentum, -i (n.) (< in + cito, citare + -mentum) that which urges, incentive, stimulus

I.VI.3

cum uenabere cum tmp. cl. (AG #545); uenor, uenari, uenatus sum: hunt; *uenabere*: alt. 2nd per sg. pass. ending (AG #163)

auctore me abl. abs. (AG #419a); auctor, auctoris (m.) (< augeo, augere + -tor) an authority, one who sets a precedent

ut (adv.) **... sic** (adv.) correl. conj. (AG #323g), "as ... so"

panarium, -i (n.) (< panis + -arium) breadbasket, food basket

laguncula, -ae (f.) (< lagona + -cula) small flask or bottle

non ... inerrare indir. disc. ff. *experieris* (*OLD* 4b and AG #580); *montibus*: dat. of indir. obj. w/ compd vb. *inerrare* (AG #370); inerro (1) (< in 1 erro, errare) wander or roam in {> errant}; Diana, originally a moon goddess, became a goddess of margins and the wilderness (*OCD* 463). Minerva was a goddess of handicrafts, whose domains came to encompass the arts, including writing (*OCD* 984).

ix—CITY LIFE VS. COUNTRY LIFE

C. PLINIVS MINICIO FVNDANO SVO S.

1 Mirum est quam singulis diebus in urbe ratio aut constet
2 aut constare uideatur, pluribus iunctisque non constet. Nam
si quem interroges 'Hodie quid egisti?', respondeat: 'Officio
togae uirilis interfui, sponsalia aut nuptias frequentaui, ille

---

I.IX: Pliny compares a typical day in the city filled with *negotium* to a day in the countryside where he makes the most of his *otium* (s. Freq. Vocab.), and finds the former wanting.

Addressee: Gaius Minicius Fundanus, senatorial rank, suffect consul 107 CE, perhaps also a friend of Plutarch (AB 73)

I.IX.1

mirum est quam *quam* (interrog. adv.) how; subst. use of n. adj. (AG #289) introd. indir. quest. (AG #574), "it is amazing how . . ."

singulis diebus abl. of time when (AG #423)

ratio . . . constet "the account balances" (*OLD* s. ratio 2d); consto (1) (< con + sto, stare) stand still, balance (*OLD* 10b)

plures, plura more, a number of, several (*OLD* 4), too many (*OLD* 5) {> plural}; *pluribus iunctisque (diebus)* parallel to *singulis diebus*; iunctus, -a, -um (< ppp. of iungo, iungere) joined {> junction}

I.IX.2

si . . . interroges . . . respondeat FLV ("should . . . would") condit. (AG #516b); *quem = aliquem* (s. I.I.1n. on quas)

officio . . . interfui *officio*: dat. of indir. obj. w/ compd. vb. *interfui* (AG #370); intersum, interesse, interfui, interfuturus (< inter + sum, esse) attend as a participant, take part in (*OLD* 4); uirilis, uirile (< uir + -ilis) belonging to a man; the *toga uirilis* was assumed by a young man as he became a voting adult, generally between the ages of fourteen and sixteen. The ceremonies that Pliny refers to included a sacrifice, a procession into the forum, registration of the young man's name on the appropriate tribal list, and a celebratory feast (SW 106).

sponsalia, sponsaliorum (n.) (< spondeo, spondere + -alis) betrothal ceremony; in the Republic, betrothal involved the exchange of promises requiring a penalty for any breach. Later the agreement became much more informal, and breach merely required the return of the dowry and any exceptional gifts. The groom-to-be placed an iron ring on the 3rd finger of his espoused, the couple kissed, and a party followed (*OCD* s. betrothal, Roman sponsalia, 240).

nuptiae, nuptiarum (f.) (< nubo, nubere + -ia) marriage ceremony, wedding {> nuptial}; a Roman wedding ritual among the elite included a sacrifice, the signing and witnessing of the marriage contract, a wedding feast and the procession that took the bride from her father's house to her husband's residence (*OCD* s. marriage ceremonies, Roman, 928).

frequento (1) (< frequens + -o) celebrate, observe (a festival, occasion, ceremony) *OLD* 7a)

ille . . . ille . . . ille repeated use of demon. adj. to indicate three different unnamed individuals; here Pliny uses ANAPHORA, ASYNDETON, and ELLIPSIS to emphasize the rapid succession of demands made on a man of his standing when he is in the city. Each cl. depends upon *rogauit*, and the repetition of *ille* pulls the speaker this way and that as each demand is made of him.

ad signandum testamentum gerv. purp. constr. w/ ad (AG #506), best trans. w/ inf. phrase: "to witness a will"; signo (1) (< signum + -o) attest (a will or contract) by affixing a seal (*OLD* 8b); testamentum, -i (n.) (< testor + -mentum) will, testament; a proper will required seven witnesses (SW 107).

me ad signandum testamentum, ille in aduocationem, ille in
consilium rogauit.' Haec quo die feceris, necessaria, eadem, si   3
cotidie fecisse te reputes, inania uidentur, multo magis cum
secesseris. Tunc enim subit recordatio: 'Quot dies quam
frigidis rebus absumpsi!' Quod euenit mihi, postquam in   4
Laurentino meo aut lego aliquid aut scribo aut etiam corpori

Romans were notorious for changing their wills w/ great frequency to reflect their current social
relations, and witnesses to each change were necessary (*OCD* s. inheritance, Roman, 758).

in aduocationem . . . rogauit in aduocationem rogare (idiom.) "to call as an advocate"; aduocatio,
aduocationis (f.) (< ad + uoco, uocare + -tio) a body of legal advisers, the duties of an advocate; in
consilium rogare (idiom.) "to summon as an adviser"; SW (107) suggests that the advocacy to which
Pliny refers is the routine practice of speaking in court on behalf of one of the parties, rather than
anything exceptional. Men of Pliny's rank and experience were often summoned *in consilium* to
advise magistrates or the emperor, primarily on judicial matters. Pliny describes spending several
such days w/ Trajan in *Ep.* VI.XXXI (*OCD* s. consilium principis, 377).

I.IX.3

Haec i.e. the various activities Pliny has just delineated

quo die feceris relat. cl. of char. (AG #535); *quo*: abl. of time when (AG #423); *feceris*: pf. subjv.

necessarius, -a, -um (< necesse + -arius) essential, necessary; supply *uidentur*

si . . . reputes . . . uidentur prot. of FLV condit. but w/ indic. apod. used to emphasize change in point
of view (AG #516/2b n.); reputo (1) (< re + puto, putare) take into consideration, consider; *fecisse
te*: indir. disc. (AG #580) ff. *reputes*; inanis, inane: empty, dead, serving no purpose (*OLD* 13)

multo magis "much more"; *multo*: by much; abl. of deg. of diff. (AG #414)

cum . . . secesseris cum circumst. cl. (AG #546); secedo, secedere, secessi, secessus (< se + cedo,
cedere) detach oneself, withdraw (i.e. from Rome into the country) (*OLD* 3) {> secede}

subeo, subire (< sub + eo, ire) approach, steal in on, come over (a person's mind) (*OLD* 11)

recordatio, recordationis (f.) (< recordor, recordari + -tio) recollection, realization

Quot (interrog. adj.) How many; interrog. used in exclam. (AG #333)

quam frigidis rebus abl. of means (AG #409); *quam* (interrog. adv.): how; emphasizes *frigidis*; frigidus,
-a, -um (< frigus + -idus) cold, lacking warmth or passion, unimportant, tedious (*OLD* 8c); "with
such unimportant matters"

absumo, absumere, absumpsi, absumptus (< ab + sumo, sumere) use up, waste

I.IX.4

Quod (relat. pron.) anteced. previous two sentences; connecting relat., gener. translated "this" (AG
#308f)

euenio, euenire (< ex + uenio, uenire) happen, come about {> event}; w/ dat. of ref. *mihi*

postquam after, when (esp. w/ vbs. in pres. tense: *lego, scribo, uaco*)

Laurentinus, -a, -um Laurentian; referring to one of Pliny's villas; this villa was located near Ostia on
the coastline southwest of Rome; it is described at length in II.XVII. Pliny also owned a villa in Tuscany
at the foot of the Apennines (described in *Ep.* V.VI) and two houses on Lake Como (*Ep.* IX.VII).

corpori uaco uaco (1) have time/leisure for (*OLD* 7a, b) {> vacation}; w/ dat. of ref. *corpori*
(AG #376); "I have time for my body." Pliny means time to devote to exercise; in other letters he
describes interspersing reading and writing w/ long walks around his estates (s. IX.XXXVI).

5   uaco, cuius fulturis animus sustinetur. Nihil audio quod
           audisse, nihil dico quod dixisse paeniteat; nemo apud me
           quemquam sinistris sermonibus carpit, neminem ipse repre-
           hendo, nisi tamen me cum parum commode scribo; nulla spe
           nullo timore sollicitor, nullis rumoribus inquietor: mecum
6   tantum et cum libellis loquor. O rectam sinceramque uitam!

---

cuius fulturis *cuius* (relat. pron.), anteced. *corpori; fulturis*: abl. of means (AG #409); fultura, -ae (f)
    that which supports, a prop; "by whose supports"
sustineo, sustinere (< sub(s) + teneo, tenere) hold up, maintain {> sustain}

I.IX.5

nihil ... nullis In this part of the letter, Pliny uses ANAPHORA and ASYNDETON to the same effect he
    had in his delineation of his many responsibilities in the city earlier in the letter, but in this case the
    absence of distressing elements is emphasized by the repetition of negatives: *nihil, nemo, nulla,* etc.
audisse = contr. form of *audiuisse* (AG #181)
quod ... paeniteat relat. cl. of char. (AG #535); paeniteo, paenitere: cause regret {> penitent}; impers.
    vb. of feeling, gener. w/ pers. affected in acc. and cause in gen. (AG #354b), but here neither is appar-
    ent since inf. cls. represent cause, and pers. is understood to be Pliny; *paeniteat* is used w/ both
    audisse and *dixisse*.
nemo, neminis (m.) (< ne + homo, hominis) no one, nobody
apud me in my presence (*OLD* 8a)
quisquam, quidquam (indef. pron.) anyone, anything
sinistris sermonibus abl. of means (AG #409); sinister, sinistra, sinistrum: on the left side, harmful,
    adverse in influence (*OLD* 4a)
carpo, carpere pick, tear at, criticize (*OLD* 9b) {> carp}
reprehendo, reprehendere (< re + prehendo, prehendere) hold back, rebuke, find fault w/ (*OLD* 5)
nisi tamen me "except, however, myself"; *nisi* (conj.) and *tamen* (adv.) combine to make *me* strong
    advers. to *neminem*
cum ... scribo cum tmp. cl. (AG #545); *commode* (adv.) (< con + modus) properly, suitably, pleas-
    ingly {> commodious}
nulla spe nulla timore abl. of means (AG #490); spes, spei (f.) expectation (often used neutrally, w/out
    either pos. or negat. inference)
sollicito (1) (< sollus + citus (ppp. of cieo, ciere) + -o) disturb, pester {> solicit}
rumor, rumoris (m.) noise, common talk, gossip; *nullis rumoribus*: abl. of means (AG #490)
inquieto (1) (< in + quietus + -o) trouble, disturb the peace and quiet (of someone)

I.IX.6

O ... pulchrius acc. of exclam. (AG #397d); sincerus, -a, -um: sound, whole, simple; dulcis, dulce:
    sweet, delightful {> dulcet}; *paene* (adv.) almost; negotium, -i (n.) (< neg (neque) + otium) busi-
    ness; *negotio*: abl. of compar. (AG #406) w/ *pulchrius* (compar. adj.), which modifies *otium*
O ... μουσεῖον acc. of exclam. (AG #397d); litus, litoris (n.) shore, coast; secretus, -a, -um (ppp. of se +
    cerno, cernere) separate, remote, hidden; *μουσεῖον*: Gr. = museum, -i (n.) a place holy to the Muses,
    a place of inspiration
quam multa interrog. used in exclam. (AG #333), "how many things"; *quam multa ... quam multa*:
    ANAPHORA
dicto (1) (< dico + -to) compose, recite, dictate

O dulce otium honestumque ac paene omni negotio pulchrius!
O mare, o litus, uerum secretumque μουσεῖον, quam multa
inuenitis, quam multa dictatis! Proinde tu quoque strepitum   7
istum inanemque discursum et multum ineptos labores, ut
primum fuerit occasio, relinque teque studiis uel otio trade.
Satius est enim, ut Atilius noster eruditissime simul et face-   8
tissime dixit, otiosum esse quam nihil agere. Vale.

I.IX.7

quoque (adv.) likewise, in the same way too; modifies the cl. *tu . . . relinque*, but by its placement emphasizes *tu* particularly

strepitus, -us (m.) (< strepo, strepere + -tus) noise, din, turmoil; *discursum* and *labores*: dir. objs. of
relinque

iste, ista, istud (demon. adj.) that, those; often used when addressing 2nd pers. (AG #297c), thus: "that
. . . of yours" or "your"

discursus, -us (m.) (< dis + curro, currere + -tus) running about {> discursive}

multum ineptos *multum* (adv.) (< multus) very; modifies *ineptos*; ineptus, -a, -um (< in + aptus) foolish, silly

ut primum as soon as; introd. tmp. cl. w/ indic. (AG #543) (here fut. pf. *fuerit*)

occasio, occasionis (f.) (< ob + cado, cadere + -tio) opportunity

studiis, otio indir. objs. of *trade*; trado, tradere (< trans + do, dare) hand over, surrender {> tradition}

I.IX.8

satius est . . . agere impers. n. subj. introd. acc. + inf. constr. (AG #455/2); *satius* (compar. adj.) prefer-
able, better (*OLD* 7) {> satisfy}; *ut . . . dixit*: "as . . . [Atilius] said," *ut* w/ indic. (AG #527f); *Atilius*:
Atilius Crescens, friend of Pliny, who comments on Atilius' character and his poverty, in *Ep.* VI.VIII
(SW 740, AB 39–40), unknown outside of Pliny's letters; *eruditissime* (superl. adv.) (< eruditus, ppp.
of erudio, erudire) very wisely; *facetissime* (superl. adv.) (< facetus) very wittily {> facetious}; otiosus, -a, -um (< otium + -osus) having ample leisure, not occupied by business; *quam* compar. w/
satius (AG #292); Pliny turns to Atilius for his closing SENTENTIA: "it is more satisfying to be at
leisure than to do nothing."

XIII—PROMISING POETS AND MIDDLING AUDIENCES

C. PLINIVS SOSIO SENECIONI SVO S.

1 Magnum prouentum poetarum annus hic attulit: toto
mense Aprili nullus fere dies, quo non recitaret aliquis.
Iuuat me quod uigent studia, proferunt se ingenia hominum

2 et ostentant, tametsi ad audiendum pigre coitur. Plerique
in stationibus sedent tempusque audiendi fabulis conterunt,

I.XIII: Pliny discusses the state of poetry and its recitation in Rome; while the former flourishes, he is concerned that a substantial and attentive audience is hard to gather. He further emphasizes his own habit of frequenting readings (s. VIII.XII).

Addressee: Quintus Sosius Senecio, senatorial rank, consul ordinarius in 99 CE and again in 107, which indicates an exceptional career, as few men served in this highest of offices even a single time (s. Intro.); also the son-in-law of Julius Frontinus, himself consul three times and the author of works on aqueducts and military strategy (SW 758, AB 90).

I.XIII.1

prouentus, -us (m.) (< pro + uenio, uenire + -tus) harvest, crop

adfero, adferre, attuli, adlatus (< ad + fero, ferre) bring w/ one, yield, produce (*OLD* 18)

Aprilis, Aprile (adj.) months in Latin are expressed as adjs.; *toto mense Aprili*: abl. of time when (AG #423)

nullus . . . dies supply *fuit*; *fere* (adv.) almost, virtually

quo . . . aliquis relat. cl. of char. (AG #535); *quo* (relat. pron.): abl. of time when (AG #423); recito (1) (< re + cito, citare) recite (before an audience); the *recitatio* was a formal occasion for the public reading of a literary work; an author w/ the means (like all of Pliny's literary friends) would hire a hall and issue invitations. Attendance was an expectation, not a mere social nicety (*OCD* 1295–96).

Iuuat me quod vbs. of feeling (*iuuat*) can introduce either a cl. beginning w/ *quod* or *quia* or acc. + inf. constr. (AG #572b); "It pleases me that . . ."

uigeo, uigere flourish, thrive {> vigor}

proferunt . . . ostentant profero, proferre (< pro + fero, ferre) bring forth, make known; *ingenia*: subj. of *proferunt* and *ostentant*; ostento (1) (< ob + tendo, tendere + -to) display, (w/ *se*) exhibit one's qualities (*OLD* 4b) {> ostentatious}

tametsi . . . coitur *tametsi* (conj.) (< tam + etsi) even though; *ad audiendum*: gerv. purp. constr. w/ ad (AG #506), "(in order) to listen"; *pigre* (adv.) (< piger, pigra, pigrum) sluggishly, lazily; Pliny's use of *pigre* signals his disapproval; *coitur*: impers. use of intr. vb. (AG #208d); coeo, coire (< con + eo, ire) come together, gather round; "even though people gather sluggishly to listen"

I.XIII.2

plerusque, -aque, -umque (< plerus + -que) the greater part, most of, m. pl.: "most people"

statio, stationis (f.) (< sto, stare + -tio) place for taking a rest, halting-place, "seats"

audiendi (ger.) gen. of specif. (BG #361) w/ *tempus*

fabula, -ae (f.) talk, gossip {> fabulous}; *fabulis*: abl. of means (AG #409)

contero, conterere (< con + tero, terere) wear away, use up, waste (*OLD* 4)

subinde (adv.) (< sub + inde) promptly, at intervals

sibi . . . librum *iubent* introd. acc. + inf. constr. (AG #563a) w/ *nuntiari*; subjs. of inf.: indir. quests. (AG #574) introd. by *an . . . an . . . an* (ANAPHORA), "they order to be reported to them at intervals whether . . . or . . . or"

ac subinde sibi nuntiari iubent, an iam recitator intrauerit,
an dixerit praefationem, an ex magna parte euoluerit librum;
tum demum ac tunc quoque lente cunctanterque ueniunt,
nec tamen permanent, sed ante finem recedunt, alii dissimulanter et furtim, alii simpliciter et libere. At hercule memoria
parentum Claudium Caesarem ferunt, cum in Palatio spatiaretur audissetque clamorem, causam requisisse, cumque
dictum esset recitare Nonianum, subitum recitanti inopina-

3

---

recitator, recitatoris (m.) (< re + cito, citare + -or) the one reciting; subj. of *intrauerit, dixerit,* and
  euoluerit
intro (1) (< intra + -o) enter
praefatio, praefationis (f.) (< prae + for, fari + -tio) introduction, preface (s. IV.XI.2n.)
ex magna parte to a large extent (*OLD* s. pars 2b)
euoluo, euoluere, euolui, euolutus (< ex + uoluo, uoluere) roll out, unroll (a scroll), read through
  {> evolve}
tum demum not until then, only then (*OLD* s. demum 1b)
tunc quoque even then (*OLD* s. tunc 4d)
lente (adv.) (< lentus, -a, -um) slowly
cunctanter (adv.) (< cunctans, cunctantis) hesitantly
permaneo, permanere (< per + maneo, manere) remain present (*OLD* 3b) {> permanent}
recedo, recedere (< re + cedo, cedere) draw back, move away {> recede}
alii ... libere each instance of *alii* introd. a parallel cl. w/ 2 advs.; *dissimulanter* (adv.) (< dis + pres.
  ptc. of simulo, simulare + -ter) so as to disguise one's purpose {> dissimulate}; *furtim* (adv.)
  (< furtum + -im) secretly {> furtive}; *simpliciter* (adv.) (< simplex, simplicis) openly (*OLD* 4)

I.XIII.3

At hercule *At* (conj.) and yet (expresses contrast); *hercule*: voc., appeal to Hercules, used for emphasis
  or to express strong feelings, *at* w/ *hercule* intensifies imprecation and has expletive force (*OLD*
  s. at 11b)
memoria abl. of time when (AG #423); w/ gen. *parentum*: "in the time of (our parents)" (*OLD* 8b)
Claudius Caesar i.e. Emperor Claudius, who ruled from 41–54 CE and was known for his interest in
  history and literature (*OCD* s. Claudius, 337–38)
Claudium ... uenisse indir. disc. (AG #580) ff. *ferunt* ("they say"), comprising two parallel inf.
  phrases, each w/ a subord. cum tmp. cl. (AG #585b); *cum ... clamorem* should be read w/ *causam
  requisisse,* and *cumque ... dictum esset* w/ *subitum ... uenisse; Claudium Caesarem* is subj. of both infs.
  and implied subj. of *spatiaretur; recitare Nonianum*: indir. disc. (AG #580); "They say that, when
  Caesar was walking ... and had heard ..., he asked ..., and when it was said that ..., he came...."
Palatium, -i (n.) Palatine Hill; where the emperor's palace was located (*OCD* s. Palatine, 1099–1100)
spatior, spatiari, spatiatus sum (< spatium + -o) walk about
audisset = contr. form of *audiuisset* (AG #181)
subitus, -a, -um suddenly appearing; perhaps < ppp. of subeo, subire (*OLD*) but clearly evolved into
  stand-alone adj.
recitanti subst. use (AG #288) of pres. act. ptc.; dat. of agent (AG #375) w/ *inopinatum; inopinatus, -a,
  -um* (< in + ppp. of opinor, opinari) unexpected(ly)

9

4   tumque uenisse. Nunc otiosissimus quisque multo ante roga-
        tus et identidem admonitus aut non uenit aut, si uenit, queritur

5   se diem (quia non perdidit) perdidisse. Sed tanto magis
        laudandi probandique sunt, quos a scribendi recitandique
        studio haec auditorum uel desidia uel superbia non retardat.
        Equidem prope nemini defui. Erant sane plerique amici;
        neque enim est fere quisquam, qui studia, ut non simul et nos

6   amet. His ex causis longius quam destinaueram tempus in
        urbe consumpsi. Possum iam repetere secessum et scribere
        aliquid, quod non recitem, ne uidear, quorum recitationibus

---

I.XIII.4

Nunc sets up contrast w/ *memoria parentum* in preceding sent.

otiosissimus quisque otiosus, -a, -um (< otium + -osus) at leisure; sometimes pejorative, implying that the one it describes is not pursuing any valuable activity (s. otium in Freq. Vocab.); *quisque* w/ superl. (AG #313b); "all the most leisurely men (in turn)"

multo ante *multo*: abl. of deg. of diff. (AG #414), qualifies *ante* (adv.)

rogatus . . . admonitus ppp.; nom. sg. agrees w/ *quisque*, but sense is pl.; *identidem* (< idem + et + idem) again and again, repeatedly; admoneo, admonere, admonui, admonitus (< ad + moneo, monere) remind {> admonish}

si uenit . . . queritur simple condit. (indic.) (AG #514a); queror, queri, questus sum: complain, grumble {> querulous}

se . . . perdidisse indir. disc. (AG #580); perdo, perdere, perdidi, perditus (< per + do, dare) ruin, waste {> perdition}; *perdidit perdidisse*: POLYPTOTON; Pliny uses the device to highlight the questionable judgment and values of the *otiosissimi*, and to heighten the IRONY of their dismay at "wasting" their excessive leisure time by actually doing something.

I.XIII.5

tanto magis so much more; *tanto*: abl. of deg. of diff. (AG #414)

laudandi probandique sunt 2nd (pass.) periphr. conjug. (AG #196 and 500/2); probo (1) (< probus + -o) commend {> probation}

quos (relat. pron.) anteced. implied subj. of *sunt*; "those men . . . whom," dir. obj. of *non retardat*

scribendi recitandique ger., objv. gen. (AG #347) w/ *studio*

haec . . . superbia *auditorum*: gen. pl. noun to be read w/ *desidia* and *superbia* and retaining verbal force over dir. obj. *haec*; desidia, -ae (f.) (< desideo, desidere + -ia) idleness; superbia, -ae (f.) (< super + -bus + -ia) pride, disdain, arrogance; "either the idleness or arrogance of the ones listening to these things"

retardo (1) (< re + tardo, tardare) inhibit, discourage

prope (adv.) almost, nearly

desum, deesse, defui, defuturus (< de + sum, esse) fail, neglect to support; w/ dat. of ref. *nemini* (AG #376); nemo, neminis (m.) (< ne + homo, hominis) no one, nobody

neque . . . amet *qui . . . amet*: relat. cl. of char. (AG #535) that contains a result cl. (AG #537), w/ *amet* as the vb. of each cl. (ZEUGMA); *et* = *etiam*; quisquam, quidquam (indef. pron.) anyone, anything; "For there is scarcely anyone who takes pleasure in literary pursuits who does not also at the same time have regard for me." *His ex causis*: modifier of obj. of monosyl. prep. often precedes prep. (AG #599d)

adfui, non auditor fuisse sed creditor. Nam ut in ceteris
rebus ita in audiendi officio perit gratia si reposcatur. Vale.

xviii—INTERPRETING OMINOUS DREAMS

C. PLINIVS SVETONIO TRANQVILLO SVO S.

Scribis te perterritum somnio uereri ne quid aduersi in   1
actione patiaris; rogas ut dilationem petam, et pauculos dies,

---

I.XIII.6

longius (compar. adj.) modifies *tempus*

destino (1) intend, designate {> destination}

consumo, consumere, consumpsi, consumptus (< con + sumo, sumere) use up, spend

quod . . . recitem relat. cl. of char. (AG #535)

ne uidear, quorum . . . negat. purp. cl. (AG #531/1); *quorum* (relat. pron.): anteced. implied dat. of ref.
  after *uidear*; "lest I should seem to those [at] whose . . ."

recitationibus dat. of indir. obj. w/ compd vb. *adesse* (AG #370)

creditor, creditoris (m.) (< credo + -tor) someone to whom something is owed

ut . . . ita correl. (AG #323g), "as . . . so"

audiendi (ger.) objv. gen. (AG #347) w/ *officio*

perit . . . reposcatur Pliny closes w/ a SENTENTIA; pereo, perire (< per + eo, ire) be lost, perish;
  gratia, -ae (f.) gratitude, favor; *si reposcatur*: mixed condit., prot. of FLV but w/ indic. apod. used to
  emphasize change in point of view (AG #516/2b); reposco, reposcere (< re + posco, poscere)
  demand back; Roman elite social relations were maintained through a system of granting and
  receiving favors for which the benefactor received *gratia* and at the same time obliged the recipient
  to respond appropriately in the future. There is no single word in E. by which to capture the sense of
  obligation that *gratia* implies.

I.XVIII: Pliny writes to calm Suetonius' fears about a dream he has had by relating his own reaction to a
  disturbing dream.

Addressee: Gaius Suetonius Tranquillus, an equestrian whose career consisted of a series of secretarial
  positions including work in the imperial library and with the emperor Hadrian's correspondence.
  Suetonius was the author of a number of biographies, including his *Lives of the Caesars*, which he
  dedicated to Septicius Clarus (s. I.I). Elsewhere in his letters, Pliny assists Suetonius in purchasing a
  farm (s. I.XXIV) and in gaining the *ius trium liberorum* (SW 759, AB 90–1).

I.XVIII.1

te . . . uereri indir. disc. (AG #580); *perterritum*: ppp. of perterreo, perterrere, perterrui, perterritus
  (< per + terreo, terrere); somnium, -i (n.) (< somnus + -ium) dream; *somnio*: abl. of means (AG #409)

ne . . . patiaris subst. cl. ff. vb. of fearing (AG #564); *quid aduersi: quid = aliquid* (s. I.I.1n. on quas),
  aduersi: partit. gen. ff. n. pron. (AG #346/3), aduersus, -a, -um (< ppp. of ad + uerto, uertere) unfavorable, harmful (*OLD* 8), "something harmful"; actio, actionis (f.) (< ago, agere + -tio) action,
  legal process, lawsuit (*OLD* 6a)

ut . . . petam . . . excusem subst. cl. of purp. (AG #563) (= indir. comm.) ff. *rogas* (AG #563); dilatio,
  dilationis (f.) (< differo, differre + -tio) postponement, delay {> dilatory}; peto, petere: reach out
  for, seek {> petition}; pauculus, -a, -um (< paucus, -a, -um + -ulus) pl.: a few; *pauculos dies*: acc. of
  dur. of time (AG #423/2); *proximum: diem* implied; excuso (1) (<. ex + causa + o) excuse, exempt
  from a task, *te* implied

2   certe proximum, excusem. Difficile est, sed experiar, καὶ γάρ
    τ' ὄναρ ἐκ Διός ἐστιν. Refert tamen, euentura soleas an con-
    traria somniare. Mihi reputanti somnium meum istud, quod

3   times tu, egregiam actionem portendere uidetur. Suscepe-
    ram causam Iuni Pastoris, cum mihi quiescenti uisa est socrus
    mea aduoluta genibus ne agerem obsecrare; et eram acturus
    adulescentulus adhuc, eram in quadruplici iudicio, eram
    contra potentissimos ciuitatis atque etiam Caesaris amicos,

---

καὶ γάρ τ' ὄναρ ἐκ Διός ἐστιν   Gr.: "for a dream comes from Zeus"; Homer *Iliad* 1.63

I.XVIII.2

euentura . . . somniare   indir. quest. (AG #574) w/ 2 alts. ff. *refert, utrum* omitted; euenturus, -a, -um:
    fut. act. ptc. of euenio, euenire, eueni, euenturus (< ex + uenio, uenire) come out, happen; *euentura*:
    n. pl. acc. subst. (AG #288), "things about to occur"; *somniare*: compl. inf. w/ *soleas* (AG #456); *an*
    (interrog. pcl.) or; contrarius, -a, -um: opposite, adverse, harmful; *contraria*: n. pl. acc. subst. (AG
    #288), "adverse things"; somnio (1) (< somnus + ium + -o) dream, see in a dream

reputanti . . . meum   reputo (1) (< re + puto, putare) think over, reflect on; *reputanti*: pres. act. ptc.
    modifying *mihi*, dat. of ref. (AG #376) after *uidetur*; somnium meum: dir. obj. of *reputanti*

istud quod   iste, ista, istud (demon. adj.) that, those (of yours); *istud* (supply somnium): subj. of *uide-
    tur*; *quod* (relat. pron.), anteced. *istud*

portendo, portendere   (< por + tendo, tendere) indicate

I.XVIII.3

causa, -ae (f.)   legal case

Iunius Pastor   Pliny's client in the earlier case, unknown apart from this letter

cum . . . obsecrare   cum tmp. cl. (AG #545); socrus, -us (f.) mother-in-law; aduoluo, aduoluere (< ad +
    uoluo, uoluere) roll toward; *aduoluta*: ppp. modifying *socrus*; genu, genus (n.) knee {> genuflect};
    genibus aduolui (idiom.): grovel (+ dat.), fall on one's knees (*OLD* s. aduoluo 2); *ne . . . agerem*:
    negat. subst. cl. of purp. (AG #563) (= indir. comm.); (causam) agere (idiom.) plead a case (*OLD* 42)
    (agere alone can mean give a speech); obsecro (1) (< ob + sacro, sacrare) implore, beg; read *obse-
    crare* w/ *uisa est*

eram acturus   1st periphr. conjug. (act. periphr.) (AG #195 and 498a), "I was about to give my speech";
    eram . . . eram . . . eram: ANAPHORA heightens the drama of Pliny's impending appearance in court.

adulescentulus, -i (m.)   (< adulescens + -ulus) a young man; used in appos. to 1st pers. subj.

quadruplici iudicio   quadruplex, quadruplicis (< quadri + -plex) four-part, fourfold {> quadrupli-
    cate}; a *quadruplex iudicium* was a court that had four separate panels, each of which heard a differ-
    ent portion of a complex case (SW 128, 302–3, 399).

potentissimus, -a, -um   superl. of potens, potentis {> potent}; *potentissimos*: subst. use (AG #288)

quae (relat. pron.)   n. pl. nom., anteced. three preceding stmts. that begin w/ *eram*, subj. of *excutere*;
    quae singula: "which things, taken separately"

excutio, excutere   (< ex + quatio, quatere) shake; *mihi*: dat. of ref. (AG #376) w/ *excutere*, compl. inf.
    (AG #456) w/ *poterant*

tristis, triste   gloomy, grim

quae singula excutere mentem mihi post tam triste somnium
poterant. Egi tamen λογισάμενος illud εἷς οἰωνὸς ἄριστος   4
ἀμύνεσθαι περὶ πάτρης. Nam mihi patria, et si quid carius
patria, fides uidebatur. Prospere cessit, atque adeo illa actio
mihi aures hominum, illa ianuam famae patefecit. Proinde   5
dispice an tu quoque sub hoc exemplo somnium istud in
bonum uertas; aut si tutius putas illud cautissimi cuiusque
praeceptum 'Quod dubites, ne feceris', id ipsum rescribe. Ego   6

I.XVIII.4

Egi . . . illud illud: dir. obj. of *egi*. "that (thing)," referring to the description of the speech he was intending to give in the special court

λογισάμενος . . . εἷς οἰωνὸς ἄριστος ἀμύνεσθαι περὶ πάτρης Gr.; n.b. λογισάμενος is not part of the quote; "[believing that] the one best dream is to fight for one's country" (Homer *Iliad* 12.243)

mihi dat. of ref. (AG #376)

si . . . patria ELLIPSIS of *est*; simple condit. (AG #514a); *quid = aliquid* (s. 1.1.1n. on quas); *carius*: compar. adj. modifying *quid* and followed by *patria*, abl. of compar. (AG #406)

fides, fidei (f.) trust, promise {> fidelity}; *Nam . . . uidebatur* is a highly compressed sent. (SENTENTIA), in which Pliny eloquently presents the depth of his loyalty. Its comprehension requires considerable expansion; "For a promise seems like my country to me, even something dearer than my country, if there is anything."

Prospere (adv.) (< prosperus, -a, -um) successfully

cedo, cedere, cessi, cessus turn out (w/ advs. *OLD* 7) {> cede}

adeo (adv.) to the extent that

illa actio . . ., illa . . . patefecit patefacio, patefacere, patefeci, patefactus (< pateo, patere + facio, facere) open (+ acc.) to (dat.); both cls. w/ subjs. *illa actio* and *illa* (*actio* implied) use vb. *patefecit*; w/ a combination of ANAPHORA and ZEUGMA, Pliny explains how the speech opened the way for his career.

I.XVIII.5

dispicio, dispicere (< dis + specio, specere) consider

an . . . uertas indir. quest. (AG #574) ff. *dispice*; 2nd alt. implied by use of *an*, "whether (or not)"; *quoque* (adv.) modifies the cl., but by its placement emphasizes *tu* particularly.

si . . . rescribe simple condit. (indic.) (AG #514a)

tutius . . . illud . . . praeceptum indir. disc. (AG #580), ELLIPSIS of *fore*; *tutius* (compar. adj.) modifies *praeceptum*; praeceptum, -i (n.) (< ppp. of prae + capio, capere) piece of advice, rule {> precept}; *cautissimi cuiusque*: quisque w/ superl. (AG #313b), "of all the most cautious men" (lit. "of each and every very cautious man"); cautus, -a, -um (< ppp. of caueo, cauere) cautious, wary

Quod . . . feceris *Quod dubites*: relat. cl. of char. (AG #535), dir. obj. of *feceris*; *ne feceris*: negat. jussive subjv. (= hort. subjv.) uses pres. subjv. except in prohibitions, where pf. subjv. may be used (AG #439 n. 1). Pliny quotes an old saying: "You should not do anything about which you are in doubt."

id ipsum "that very thing," i.e. that you (Suetonius) do not wish to proceed

rescribo, rescribere (< re + scribo, scribere) reply, write back

aliquam stropham inueniam agamque causam tuam, ut istam
agere tu cum uoles possis. Est enim sane alia ratio tua, alia mea
fuit. Nam iudicium centumuirale differri nullo modo, istuc
aegre quidem sed tamen potest. Vale.

xxiv—A FARM FOR SUETONIUS

C. PLINIVS BAEBIO HISPANO SVO S.

1 Tranquillus contubernalis meus uult emere agellum, quem
2 uenditare amicus tuus dicitur. Rogo cures, quanti aequum

---

i.xviii.6

stropha, -ae (f.) (< Gr. στροφή) trick, device

ut . . . possis purp. cl. (AG #531/1); *istam*: i.e. *causam*; *cum uoles*: cum tmp. cl. (AG #545); *uoles*: an epistolary fut., indicating that Suetonius had not made a decision about how to proceed at the time the letter was written

alia ratio tua . . . alia mea fuit "yours (is) one line of thought . . . mine has been another"

Nam . . . differri *iudicium centumuirale*: Centumviral Court, subj. of understood *potest* w/ compl. inf. *differri*; differo, differre (< dis + fero, ferre) postpone, defer; the court originally had 105 judges— three from each of the 35 tribes—and in the imperial period 180 (*OCD* s. centumviri, 309–10); it heard civil cases, particularly those concerning inheritance.

nullo . . . potest *nullo modo*: in no way, not at all (*OLD* s. modus 11a); *istuc* (adv.) to the place that you have reached, "in your situation"; *aegre* (adv.) w/ difficulty; Pliny seems to contradict himself as he qualifies what he can do regarding a court delay: "For in no way can a centumviral trial be postponed, in your situation with difficulty indeed, but nevertheless it is possible." The effect Pliny creates w/ this complex stmt. is twofold: to push Suetonius toward proceeding w/ the case and to emphasize should he choose to delay how difficult it will be for Pliny to comply.

i.xxiv: Pliny writes to secure for Suetonius a good price on a small farm that he is interested in purchasing and describes the amenities of the property in question as suited to a scholar rather than to someone needing property for income.

Addressee: Baebius Hispanus, about whom little is known except from Pliny's letters. He may have been from Saguntum (AB 41).

i.xxiv.1

Tranquillus Gaius Suetonius Tranquillus (s. i.xviii)

contubernalis, -is (m.) (< con + taberna + -alis) comrade in arms, intimate friend

emo, emere, emi, emptus buy; *emere*: compl. inf. (AG #456) w/ *uult*

agellus, -i (m.) (< ager + -lus) small plot of land, small farm

uendito (1) (< uendo + -ito) seek to sell, offer for sale {> vend}; *uenditare*: inf. in indir. disc. ff. *dicitur*, w/ pass. vb. of saying, subj. of inf. is nom. (AG #582, BG #528)

i.xxiv.2

cures subst. cl. of purp. (AG #563) (= indir. comm.) ff. *rogo*, omitting *ut* (AG #565a); curo (1) (< cura + -o) look after, see to it (that) (*OLD* 6); *cures* functions as impv. form (AG #449/2c)

est emat; ita enim delectabit emisse. Nam mala emptio
semper ingrata, eo maxime quod exprobrare stultitiam domino
uidetur. In hoc autem agello, si modo adriserit pretium, Tran-   3
quilli mei stomachum multa sollicitant, uicinitas urbis, opportunitas uiae, mediocritas uillae, modus ruris, qui auocet magis
quam distringat. Scholasticis porro dominis, ut hic est, suffi-   4

---

quanti at what value (*OLD* 6b); gen. of quality (price) (AG #345), used instead of abl. of price w/ indef.
value (AG #417)

aequus, -a, -um level, even, fair, reasonable (*OLD* 6a) {> equal}

emat subjv. ff. *cures*; *ut* omitted, as often w/ fac or dic (AG #565); *rogo … emat*: "I ask you to see to it
that he buys it at what value is fair."

emisse pf. act. inf., subj. of *delectabit* w/ implied dir. obj. *eum*

emptio, emptionis (f.) (< emo, emere + -tio) a purchase

ingratus, -a, -um displeasing, disagreeable {> ingratitude}; ELLIPSIS of *est*

eo maxime quod particularly/especially because

exprobo (1) (< ex + probrum + -o) bring (+ acc. *stultitiam*) as a reproach against (+ dat. *domino*);
stultitia, -ae (f.) (< stultus + -ia) stupidity, folly {> stultify}

I.XXIV.3

si … pretium prot. of FMV condit. (AG #516c); *modo* (adv.) only; adrideo, adridere, adrisi, adrisus
(< ad + rideo, ridere) smile at, be pleasing, satisfactory; *adriserit*: fut. pf. indic.; pretium, -i (n.)
price, value

stomachum multa sollicitant stomachus, stomachi (m.) (< Gr. στόμαχος) gullet, stomach; sollicito
(1) (< sollus + ppp. of cieo, ciere + -o) stir, stimulate; stomachum sollicitare (idiom.) tempt the
appetite; *multa*: subj. of *sollictant*, followed by four noun cls. in appos., beginning w/ *uicinitas, oppor-*
tunitas, mediocritas, and *modus*

uicinitas, uicinitatis (f.) (< uicinus + -tas) proximity, nearness {> vicinity}

opportunitas, opportunitatis (f.) (< ob + portus + unus + -tas) convenience

mediocritas, mediocritatis (f.) (< medius + ocris + -tas) moderate size

modus, -i (m.) quantity, size

rus, ruris (n.) countryside, land, country estate {> rural}

qui … auocet … distringat relat. cl. of char. (AG #535); auoco (1) (< ab + uoco, uocare) call away,
distract {> avocation}; distringo, distringere (< dis + stringo, stringere) detain, pull in different
directions; *auocare* implies a pleasant diversion, while *distringere* indicates an unwelcome and un-
comfortable force between conflicting demands.

I.XXIV.4

scholasticis … dominis dat. of ref. (AG #376) w/ *sufficit*; scholasticus, -a, -um (< Gr. σχολαστικός)
concerning a scholar, one who studies

porro (adv.) further, besides

ut hic est *ut* w/ indic. "as" (AG #527f); *hic*: Suetonius

cit abunde tantum soli, ut releuare caput, reficere oculos,
reptare per limitem unamque semitam terere omnesque
uiteculas suas nosse et numerare arbusculas possint. Haec
tibi exposui, quo magis scires, quantum esset ille mihi ego
tibi debiturus, si praediolum istud, quod commendatur his
dotibus, tam salubriter emerit ut paenitentiae locum non
relinquat. Vale.

---

abunde (adv.) (< abundus, -a, -um) quite, fully, enough and to spare {> abundant}

tantum ... ut introd. series of results (AG #537/2 n. 2) expressed by *possint* and compl. infs. (*releuare, reficere, reptare, terere, nosse, numerare*) (AG #465); *soli*: partit. gen. (AG #346/3); solum, soli (n.) soil, ground

releuo (1) (< re + leuo, leuare) reduce the load, lighten, ease {> relieve}

reficio, reficere (< re + facio, facere) restore, refresh

repto (1) (< repo, repere + -to) move slowly, stroll about {> reptile}

limes, limitis (m.) boundary {> limit}

semita, -ae (f.) side path

tero, terere wear away, form by treading

uitecula, -ae (f.) (< uitis + -cula) little vine {> viticulture}

nosco, noscere, noui, notus become acquainted w/, pf.: know; *nosse* = contr. form of *nouisse* (AG #181)

numero (1) (< numerus + -o) count

arbuscula, -ae (f.) (< arbor +-cula) small or young trees

expono, exponere, exposui, expositus (< ex + pono, ponere) put out, explain (*OLD* 6) {> expository}

quo ... scires relat. cl. of purp., introd. by *quo* because of compar. *magis* (AG #531/2a)

quantum ... debiturus indir. quest. (AG #574) ff. *scires* and apod. of a FMV condit. (AG #516d); *esset . . . debiturus*: 1st periphr. conjug. (act. periphr.) (AG #195 and 498a); *ille*: subj. closest to the vb., thus vb. is 3rd pers. rather than 1st (BG #287 Remark a); "how much he is going to owe to me and I to you . . ."

si ... emerit prot. of FMV condit. (AG #516c); praediolum, -i (n.) (< praedium + -olum) small estate; commendo (1) (< con + mando, mandare) entrust, make attractive (*OLD* 6); dos, dotis (f.) quality, attribute; *his dotibus*: abl. of means (AG #409); *salubriter* (adv.) (< saluber, salubris) profitably, at a favorable price {> salubrious}; *emerit*: fut. pf. indic.

ut ... relinquat result cl. (AG #537), implied subj.: *praediolum*; paenitentia, -ae (f.) (< paeniteo + -ia) regret {> penitent}

BOOK II

IV—HELPING A FEMALE RELATIVE

C. PLINIVS CALVINAE SVAE S.

Si pluribus pater tuus uel uni cuilibet alii quam mihi   1
debuisset, fuisset fortasse dubitandum, an adires hereditatem
etiam uiro grauem. Cum uero ego ductus adfinitatis officio,   2
dimissis omnibus qui non dico molestiores sed diligentiores
erant, creditor solus exstiterim, cumque uiuente eo nubenti

II.IV: Pliny writes to a young woman concerning the troubled estate her father has left her and his own plans to provide financial assistance, as he has done for her benefit in the past.

Addressee: Calvina, a young woman who has an undefined family connection (through marriage, i.e. *adfinitas*) to Pliny's family (AB 46).

II.IV.1

Si ... fuisset ... dubitandum past C-to-F condit. (AG #517); plures, plura (compar. adj.) more, subst. use: "more people"; *pluribus*: dat. of ref. (AG #376); quilibet, quaelibet, quidlibet (indef. pron.) anyone whosoever (AG #151c, 312); *uni cuilibet alii quam mihi*; *alii*: dat. sg. agreeing w/ *cuilibet*: "to any individual besides me"; *dubitandum fuisset*: impers. use of 2nd (pass.) periphr. conjug. (AG #500/3) w/ *tibi* implied, "you would have had to hesitate"

an ... grauem indir. quest. (AG #574) introd. by *dubitandum*; *an*: "whether" ("or not" implied); adeo, adire (< ad + eo, ire) approach, accept the responsibilities of (OLD 10c) {> adit}; hereditas, hereditatis (f.) (< heres + -tas) inheritance {> heredity}; *etiam* (pcl.) qualifies *uiro*, dat. of ref. (AG #376); grauis, graue: burdensome {> gravity}; as her father's heir Calvina inherited all of his debts. She might have decided to refuse the estate, provided that she could have found a sympathetic praetor (OCD s. inheritance, Roman, 758).

II.IV.2

cum ... exstiterim cum causal cl. (AG #549); *uero* (pcl.) (< uerus + -o) truly, yet (OLD 7b) {> verify}; adfinitas, adfinitatis (f.) (< ad + finis + -tas) relation by marriage; *dimissis omnibus*: abl. abs. (AG #419); dimitto, dimittere, dimisi, dimissus (< dis + mitto, mittere) discharge, pay off (a creditor); *non dico*: trans. w/ *molestiores* as an aside; molestus, -a, -um: troublesome, annoying, "I'm not saying rather annoying"; diligens, diligentis (< pres. ptc. of diligo, diligere) attentive, scrupulous {> diligent}; *creditor*: appos. to 1st pers. subj. of *exstiterim*, "as sole creditor"; exsisto, exsistere, exstiti (< ex + sisto) appear, emerge; in calling the creditors "*diligentiores*," Pliny makes them justified in seeking repayment and himself more heroic in covering the debts.

cum ... contulerim 2nd cum causal cl., parallel w/ *cum ... exstiterim*

uiuente eo abl. abs. (AG #419a), *eo*: Calvina's father

nubo, nubere get married {> nubile}; used only for women and may orig. have referred to the act of the bride veiling herself before the ceremony; *nubenti*: pres. act. ptc., modifies *tibi*, dat. of ref. (AG #376)

tibi in dotem centum milia contulerim, praeter eam summam quam pater tuus quasi de meo dixit (erat enim soluenda
de meo), magnum habes facilitatis meae pignus, cuius fiducia
debes famam defuncti pudoremque suscipere. Ad quod te ne
uerbis magis quam rebus horter, quidquid mihi pater tuus
3   debuit, acceptum tibi fieri iubebo. Nec est quod uerearis ne
sit mihi onerosa ista donatio. Sunt quidem omnino nobis

---

dos, dotis (f.) (cognate w/ do, dare) dowry; it was not unusual to borrow funds for a dowry, whose value
    was crucial in arranging an advantageous marriage for one's daughter. The dowry was part of the mar-
    riage contract, which was legally binding, as would have been any loans taken to secure its payment.

milia, milium (n.) thousands; *centum milia* = 100,000 (*sesterces* implied); Calvina's father was likely a
    member of the equestrian order—an eques Romanus), which would have required the ownership of
    at least 400,000 sesterces' worth of property; the minimum for senators was 1,000,000 sesterces
    (*OCD* s. senate, 1385–87).

summa, -ae (f.) amount of money {> sum}

pater dixit dicere here: "declare one's intention of giving" (*OLD* 11)

erat . . . meo referring to the *summam* paid by Calvina's father; *erat . . . soluenda*: 2nd (pass.) periphr.
    conjug. (AG #196 and 500/2); soluo, soluere (< se + luo, luere) loosen, pay (a debt) (*OLD* 18 and
    19) {> solvent}; *de meo*: partit. use of abl. w/ de (AG #346c), "from my (resources)." Pliny is declar-
    ing that the moneys for repayment were taken from a larger pool of funds.

facilitas, facilitatis (f.) (< facio, facere + -ilis + -tas) ease, readiness, ability; *facilitatis*: objv. gen.
    (AG #347) w/ *pignus*; pignus, pignoris (n.) pledge, guarantee

fiducia, -ae (f.) (< fido, fidere) assurance, confident expectation of (+ gen.) {> fiduciary}; *fiducia*: abl.
    of means (AG #409)

fama, -ae (f.) news, rumor, reputation; like all elite Romans, Pliny is concerned w/ securing a long-lasting
    and excellent reputation. So while he advises Calvina to look after her father's *fama*, his actions on her
    behalf also increase his own standing.

defunctus, -a, -um (< ppp. of de + fungor, fungi) dead; *patris* implied

pudor, pudoris (m.) (< pudeo, pudere + -or) feeling of shame, honor

Ad . . . horter negat. purp. cl. (AG #531/1) w/ postponement of *ne*; *quod* (relat. pron.) refers to Pliny's
    previous stmt., i.e. the care of Calvina's father's reputation; *te*: dir. obj. of *horter*; *ne horter* (*ad quod*):
    "lest I encourage you (to do this, i.e. to accept your father's estate)"; *uerbis . . . rebus*: abl. of means
    (AG #409); res, rei (f.) material goods, things tangible

quisquis, quidquid (indef. pron.) (< quis, quid) anyone, anything (AG #151b)

acceptum fieri (idiom.) be set down to the credit of (+ dat. *tibi*) (*OLD* s. acceptus 2b)

II.IV.3

Nec est quod "And there is no reason that"

quod uerearis relat. cl. of char. (AG #535)

ne . . . donatio subst. cl. ff. vb. of fearing (AG #564); *mihi*: dat. of ref. (AG #376) w/ *onerosa*; onerosus,
    -a, -um (< onus + -osus) burdensome {> onerous}; donatio, donationis (f.) (< dono + -tio) gift

quidem (pcl.) admittedly (*OLD* 4)

nobis dat. of poss. (AG #373)

modicae facultates, dignitas sumptuosa, reditus propter con-
dicionem agellorum nescio minor an incertior; sed quod
cessat ex reditu, frugalitate suppletur, ex qua uelut fonte
liberalitas nostra decurrit. Quae tamen ita temperanda est, 4
ne nimia profusione inarescat; sed temperanda in aliis, in te
uero facile ei ratio constabit, etiamsi modum excesserit.
Vale.

---

facultas, facultatis (f.) ability, power, pl.: resources, means (*OLD* 5b) {> faculty}

dignitas, dignitatis (f.) (< dignus + -tas) rank, status (*OLD* 3a)

sumptuosus, -a, -um (< sumo, sumere + -tus + -osus) costly, expensive; Pliny here refers to the need
  for him as a senator to maintain a particular lifestyle.

reditus, -us (m.) (< redeo, redire + -tus) return, revenue; men of senatorial rank were expected to earn
  their income from activities associated w/ their land: farming, husbandry, mining, wine production, etc.

condicio, condicionis (f.) (< con + dico, dicere + -io) situation, state of health (*OLD* 6a and d)

agellus, -i (m.) (< ager + -lus) small plot of land, small farm

minor an incertior both compar. adjs. modify *reditus*; "(revenue) that is (I'm inclined to think) too
  small or too undependable"

quod (relat. pron.) subst. use: "that which"

cesso (1) (< cedo, cedere + -to) hold back, fail {> cessation}

frugalitas, frugalitatis (f.) (< frux + -alis + -tas) temperance, self-restraint; *frugalitate*: abl. of means
  (AG #409); *frugalitas* is an imperial virtue, one that Pliny assigns to Trajan in his *Panegyricus* (3, 41,
  49, 51, 88) and that appears repeatedly throughout the letters to define proper behavior and Pliny's
  character (C 124, 159–60).

suppleo, supplere (< sub + pleo, plere) make up, complete {> supplement}

uelut (adv.) (< uel + ut) just as

fons, fontis (m.) a spring {> font}; *fonte*: abl. w. implied *ex*

liberalitas, liberalitatis (f.) (< liber + -alis + -tas) generosity, munificence

decurro, decurrere (< de + curro, currere) run down, flow

II.IV.4

Quae (relat. pron.) anteced. *liberalitas*, connecting relat. gener. translated "this" (AG #308f)

temperanda est 2nd (pass.) periphr. conjug. (AG #196 and 500/2); tempero (1) (< tempus) restrain
  {> temperance}

ne . . . inarescat *ita* in main cl. would ordinarily signal result cl. beginning w/ *ut*, but *ne* (rather than the
  usual *ut non*) can introduce a result cl., as it does here, when it "implies an effect intended" (AG #537
  n. 2a); *nimia profusione*: abl. of means (AG #409); nimius, -a, -um: excessive, immoderate; profusio,
  profusionis (f.) (< pro + fundo, fundere + -tio) pouring out, lavish spending, extravagance; inaresco, inarescere (< in + areo, arere + -sco) become dry, dry up

in aliis "with respect to others"

in te . . . excesserit FMV condit. (AG #516a); *in te*: "in your case"; *ei* (is, ea, id): dat. of ref. (AG #376),
  "for it (Pliny's *liberalitas*)"; *ratio constabit*: "the account will balance" (*OLD* s. ratio 2d); consto
  (1) (< con + sto, stare) stand still, balance (*OLD* 10b); etiamsi (conj.) even if; modus, -i (m.) measure, correct amount, limit; excedo, excedere, excessi, excessus (< ex + cedo, cedere) exceed, go
  beyond; *excesserit*: fut. pf.

vi—HOW TO TREAT DINNER GUESTS

C. PLINIVS AVITO SVO S.

1 Longum est altius repetere nec refert, quemadmodum
acciderit, ut homo minime familiaris cenarem apud quendam,
ut sibi uidebatur, lautum et diligentem, ut mihi, sordidum

2 simul et sumptuosum. Nam sibi et paucis opima quaedam,
ceteris uilia et minuta ponebat. Vinum etiam paruolis lagunculis in tria genera discripserat, non ut potestas eligendi, sed

---

II.vi: Pliny criticizes the varied treatment of guests at a recent dinner party, whose host presented different qualities of food and drink to his guests based on their status, and thus offers a sharp contrast
to his own generosity outlined in II.iv and his concern for his freedman as expressed in v.xix.
Addressee: Iunius Avitus, a young senator, who was a protégé of Pliny's. In *Ep*. VIII.xxiii, Pliny offers an
obituary for Avitus in which he is an exemplum of the ideal young man, dying tragically on the eve of
a brilliant career (SW 750, AB 63).

II.vi.1

Longum est w/ inf. (*OLD* 12), "It is too long a business [to] ..."

altius (compar. adv.) (< altus) more deeply, thoroughly {> altitude}

quemadmodum acciderit indir. quest. (AG #574); *quemadmodum* (interrog. adv.) (< quem + ad +
modum) how; *acciderit*, impers. use w/ *ut*, introd. subst. cl. of result (AG #569/2): happen, come
about (that)

homo minime familiaris appos. to subj. of *cenarem* ("I"); *minime* (adv.) not at all, by no means; familiaris, familiare (< familia + -aris) closely associated by friendship, well known (as if part of a household, familia); "as a man by no means well known"

ceno (1) (< cena + -o) dine

apud (prep. + acc.) at the home of

ut ... ut ... sumptuosum *ut* w/ indic. "as" (AG #527f), ELLIPSIS of *uidebatur* after 2nd *ut*; *lautum, diligentem, sordidum, sumptuosum*: all modify *quendam* (the host of the dinner party), 1st pair = the
host's opinion of himself, 2nd pair = Pliny's assessment of him; lautus, -a, -um (< ppp. of lauo,
lauare) clean, splendid, luxurious; diligens, diligentis (< pres. ptc. of diligo, diligere) attentive,
scrupulous; sordidus, -a, -um (< sordeo, sordere + -idus) unwashed, lacking refinement, vulgar
{> sordid}; sumptuosus, -a, -um (< sumo, sumere + -tus + -osus) expensive, extravagant

II.vi.2

sibi et paucis dat. of ref. (AG #376); *paucis*: subst. use

opimus, -a, -um choice, rich; n. acc. pl. subst.

ceterus, -a, -um the rest, the other; used in pl. as pron., "the others"; *ceteris*: dat. of ref. (AG #376)

uilia, minuta n. acc. pl. subst.; uilis, uile: cheap, ordinary; minutus, -a, -um: small, meager

pono, ponere place, set before one, serve {> position}

paruolis lagunculis abl. of means (AG #409); paruolus, -a, -um (< paruus, -a, -um + -ulus) tiny; laguncula, -ae (f.) (< lagona + -cula) small flask or bottle

genus, generis (n.) type, class, variety

discribo, discribere, discripsi, discriptus (< dis + scribo, scribere) distribute, allot, assign

ut ... ne ... esset purp. cls. (AG #531/1), introd. by parallel *non ... sed*; *eligendi*: ger., objv. gen. (AG
#347) w/ *potestas*; potestas, potestatis (f.) (< potis + -tas) ability, power; eligo, eligere (< ex + lego,

ne ius esset recusandi, aliud sibi et nobis, aliud minoribus
amicis (nam gradatim amicos habet), aliud suis nostrisque
libertis. Animaduertit qui mihi proximus recumbebat, et an   3
probarem interrogauit. Negaui. 'Tu ergo' inquit 'quam consuetudinem sequeris?' 'Eadem omnibus pono; ad cenam enim,
non ad notam inuito cunctisque rebus exaequo, quos mensa

---

legere) choose, select {> eligible}; *recusandi*: ger., objv. gen. (AG #347) w/ *ius*; ius, iuris (n.) the right
{> jury}; recuso (1) (< re + causa + -o) protest, object, decline {> recuse}

aliud … aliud … aliud explains *tria genera*: "one … another … another," each w/ dat. of ref. (AG
#376): *sibi et nobis, minoribus amicis, suis nostrisque libertis*; using ANAPHORA, Pliny recreates the
rather abrupt presentation of the various qualities of wine. Lesser friends (*minoribus amicis*) would
have been freeborn Romans (as opposed to freedmen) who were of lower rank than the host.

gradatim (adv.) (< gradus + -atus + -im) by degrees, in order of precedence

habeo, habere have, treat (*OLD* 22), regard (*OLD* 24)

libertus, -i (m.) (< liber + -tus) freedman; the freeing of slaves was so common an occurrence in
Rome that laws set a minimum age (for both slave and master) and a limit to the number of slaves
who could be manumitted. Once formally freed, the freed person became a Roman citizen. But
freedmen still had legal and social obligations to their former masters and often remained part of the
household; they were expected to show continued deference and loyalty. Informal manumission
made the freed person a Junian Latin w/ limited rights and kept the freedman financially bound to
his master (*OCD* s. freedmen, freedwomen, 609, and Latini Iuniani, 821).

II.VI.3

animaduerto, animaduertere, animaduerti, animaduersus (< animum + ad + uerto, uertere) pay
attention, notice; subj. of *animaduertit*: relat. cl.; *qui* (relat. pron.), subst. use (AG #307c): "(the man)
who"

mihi dat. w/ adj. *proximus* (AG #384)

recumbo, recumbere (< re + cumbo, cumbere) recline {> recumbent}. Roman dining customs
placed couches on three sides of the table, leaving the fourth open for the food to be set and re-
moved. On each couch reclined three diners. So Pliny must be on one of the outside edges, speaking
w/ the fellow in the middle position (*OCD* s. dining-rooms, 469–70).

an … probarem indir. quest. (AG #574) ff. *interrogauit*; *an*: "whether" ("or not" implied); probo
(1) (< probus + -o) regard as right, approve

quam (interrog. adj.) modifies *consuetudinem*; consuetudo, consuetudinis (f.) (< con + suesco +
-tudo) habit, convention

cena, -ae (f.) dinner; such dinner parties were often elaborate affairs and were critical to the cultivation
and maintenance of Roman social relations; seating was regularly determined by the host based on
rank and the closeness of his relationship w/ the guest.

nota, -ae (f.) mark, brand, mark of quality; can be used to mean a mark of disgrace or disapproval

inuito (1) invite; implied dir. obj. *eos*

cunctis rebus abl. of specif. (AG #418); cunctus, -a, -um: the whole, pl.: all

exaequo (1) (< ex + aequo, aequare) make level or equal

quos … aequaui *quos* (relat. pron.), subst. use (AG #307c): "those whom," dir. obj. of both *exaequo* and
aequaui; POLYPTOTON emphasizes Pliny's commitment to fair treatment of his guests; *mensa et toro*:
abl. of specif. (AG #418); torus, tori (m.) cushion (used on a dining couch); aequo (1) (< aequus + -o)
make equal, put on equal terms, regard as equal; *ad cenam … aequaui*: "For I invite them to dinner,
not to a branding (i.e. an exercise in ranking them), and those whom I have put on equal terms at
table and couch (in the dining room), I make equal in all things."

4   et toro aequaui.' 'Etiamne libertos?' 'Etiam; conuictores
enim tunc, non libertos puto.' Et ille: 'Magno tibi constat.'
'Minime.' 'Qui fieri potest?' 'Quia scilicet liberti mei non
5   idem quod ego bibunt, sed idem ego quod liberti.' Et hercule si gulae temperes, non est onerosum quo utaris ipse

---

II.VI.4

Etiamne . . . Etiam Repetition of a key part of a quest. in its answer was one way to answer the quest. affirmatively; Latin has no simple word for "yes."

conuictor, conuictoris (m.) (< con + uiuo, uiuere + -tor) friend, companion, dinner guest

tunc (adv.) (< tum + -ce) at that moment

puto (1) (< putus + -o) consider; implied dir. obj. *eos*

Magno tibi constat *magno*: abl. of price (AG #416); *tibi*: dat. of ref. (AG #376); consto (1) (< con + sto, stare) stand together, cost (*OLD* 11a); "It costs you a lot"

Minime (adv.) not at all, by no means; used as single wd. response, the most common way of responding negatively to a quest. Latin has no simple word for "no."

Qui (interrog. adv.) how (AG #150b) (*OLD* s. qui^2) = *quo*

scilicet (pcl.) (< prob. scire + licet) it is clear (that), you may be sure (that)

bibo, bibere drink {> bibulous}; ELLIPSIS of vb. requires *bibunt* (or another form of bibere) to be used at least 2x, w/ *liberti* and w/ *ego*; 3rd pers. pl. vb. agrees w/ subj. *liberti* in 1st cl. (BG #287 Remark a); i.e. Pliny serves the kind of wine that freedmen drink to everyone, including himself, when freedmen are his guests

II.VI.5

hercule voc., an appeal to Hercules, used for emphasis or to express strong feelings

si . . . temperes prot. of FLV condit. w/ apod. in indic., indicating a change in point of view (AG #516b n.); gula, -ae (f.) throat, gullet; *gulae*: dat. w/ intr. vb. *temperes* (AG #367); tempero (1) (< tempus) restrain oneself, exercise moderation (in respect to)

onerosus, -a, -um (< onus + -osus) burdensome

quo utaris ipse relat. cl. of char. (AG #535) serves as dir. obj. of *communicare*; *quo*: subst. use of relat. pron. (AG #307c): "that which," abl. w/ *uti*, depon. vb. that takes abl. of means, not acc. dir. obj. (AG #410); utor, uti, usus sum: make use of, consume {> utility}; communico (1) (< con + munis + -ico) share {> commune}

plures, plura (compar. adj.) more, a number of, several (*OLD* 4)

illa i.e. *gula*; *illa . . . illa*: ANAPHORA and ASYNDETON make this a strong stmt. against greed.

reprimenda . . . redigenda est 2nd (pass.) periphr. conjug. (AG #196 and 500/2); reprimo, reprimere (< re + premo, premere) hold in check, repress; *quasi* (adv.) "as it were" (*OLD* 9a); in ordinem redigere: bring into line, reduce to the common level (*OLD* s. redigo 10d); ordo, ordinis (f.) a line, order {> ordinal}

si . . . parcas prot. of FLV condit. w/ apod. in indic., indicating a change in point of view (AG #516b n.); sumptus, -us (m.) (< sumo, sumere + -tus) expenditure; *sumptibus*: dat. of indir. obj. w/ *parcas*, vb. that functions as if it were intr. (AG #367); parco, parcere: act sparingly w/ respect to, be economical w/

quibus . . . consulas relat. cl. of char. (AG #535), anteced. *sumptibus*; *quibus*: dat. of indir. obj. w/ *consulas* as intr. vb. (AG #367c); *aliquanto* (adv.) (< alius + quantus) to some extent, somewhat: modifies *rectius* (compar. adv.) (< rectus, -a, -um) more correctly, properly; *continentia* and *contumelia*: abl. of means (AG #409); continentia, -ae (f.) (< pres. ptc. of con + tineo, tinere + -ia) self-restraint {> continence}; contumelia, -ae (f.) insulting language, rough treatment {> contumely}; alienus, -a, -um (< alius + -enus) belonging to another, inflicted on others

communicare cum pluribus. Illa ergo reprimenda, illa quasi
in ordinem redigenda est, si sumptibus parcas, quibus aliquanto rectius tua continentia quam aliena contumelia consulas.

Quorsus haec? ne tibi, optimae indolis iuueni, quorundam   6
in mensa luxuria specie frugalitatis imponat. Conuenit autem
amori in te meo, quotiens tale aliquid inciderit, sub exemplo
praemonere, quid debeas fugere. Igitur memento nihil magis   7
esse uitandum quam istam luxuriae et sordium nouam societatem; quae cum sint turpissima discreta ac separata, turpius
iunguntur. Vale.

II.VI.6

Quorsus (interrog. adv.) to what end, w/ what in view; *Quorsus haec?* (vb. like *dico* or *expono* implied):
"Why do I tell you all this?"

ne . . . imponat purp. cl. (AG #531/1); *tibi*: dat. of indir. obj. w/ compd. vb. *imponat* (AG #370); *optimae
indolis iuueni*: appos. to *tibi*; indoles, indolis (f.) (< indu + -alies) innate character; *quorundam in
mensa*: "at the table of certain men" (like the host Pliny has described); luxuria, -ae (f.) (< luxus)
extravagance; *specie*: abl. of quality (also called descriptive abl.) (AG #415); species, speciei (f.)
(< specio, specere + -ies) appearance, semblance; frugalitas, frugalitatis (f.) (< frux + -alis + -tas)
temperance, self-restraint (s. II.IV.3n.); impono, imponere: lay on, deceive, trick (intr. use *OLD* 16)
{> impose}

amori . . . meo dat. of indir. obj. w/ compd. vb. *conuenit* (AG #370); *amor in*: "love for" (AG #221/12)
+ acc. *te*; wd. order has Avitus (*te*) surrounded by Pliny's love.

quotiens . . . inciderit relat. cl. of char. (AG #535); *quotiens* (relat. adv.) (< quot + -iens) whenever;
tale aliquid: "any such thing"; incido, incidere, incidi (< in + cado, cadere) fall, occur (*OLD* 10a)
{> incident}

sub exemplo "in the form of an example" (*OLD* s. sub 5a)

praemoneo, praemonere (< prae + moneo, monere) warn in advance {> premonition}; *praemonere*:
subj. of *conuenit*, introd. *quid . . . fugere*, indir. quest. (AG #574)

II.VI.7

Igitur (conj.) therefore

memento . . . societatem *memento*: fut. impv. sg., regularly used instead of pres. impv. (AG #449a);
memini, meminisse: remember; *nihil . . . societatem*; indir. disc. (AG #580); *esse uitandum*:
2nd (pass.) periphr. conjug. (AG #196 and 500/2); uito (1) avoid; sordes, sordis (f.) filth, stinginess,
greed, moral turpitude {> sordid}; societas, societatis (f.) (< socius + -tas) partnership, alliance

quae . . . iunguntur *quae* (relat. pron.), n. pl. subj. of *sunt*, anteced. *luxuriae et sordium*; *cum . . . separata*:
cum conces. cl. (AG #549); turpis, turpe: offensive, repulsive {> turpitude}; *discreta ac separata*: n.
pl. adj., modifying *quae*; discretus, -a, -um (< ppp. dis + cerno, cernere) placed apart, separate; sep-
aratus, -a, -um (< ppp. se + paro, parare) unconnected; iungo, iungere: yoke, join, bring close together; Pliny ends his assessment w/ this closing SENTENTIA, which serves to add point to his
disgust.

xiii—RECOMMENDING AN OLD FRIEND

C. PLINIVS PRISCO SVO S.

1 Et tu occasiones obligandi me auidissime amplecteris, et
2 ego nemini libentius debeo. Duabus ergo de causis a te
potissimum petere constitui, quod impetratum maxime
cupio. Regis exercitum amplissimum: hinc tibi beneficiorum
larga materia, longum praeterea tempus, quo amicos tuos
exornare potuisti. Conuertere ad nostros nec hos multos.

II.XIII: Pliny writes on behalf of his childhood friend Voconius Romanus to secure for him a military
post, most likely as a tribune; he highlights Romanus' outstanding qualities and emphasizes the past
assistance Pliny has provided. Romanus is a prominent figure in Pliny's writing, the recipient of
eight letters, a testament to their close relationship.
Addressee: Identified only by cognomen, Priscus may be Lucius Neratius Priscus, suffect consul in
97 CE (AB 74, 83) or Lucius Javolenus Priscus (Octavius Tidius Tossianus), suffect consul in 86 CE
(SW 174–5, 749). Both were jurisconsults.

II.XIII.1
occasiones . . . me *obligandi*: ger., objv. gen. (AG #347) w/ *occasiones*, w/ dir. obj. *me*; occasio, occasionis
(f.) (< ppp. of ob + cado, cadere + -tio) opportunity; obligo (1) (< ob + ligo, ligare) tie, place under
a moral obligation {> obligate}
auidissime (superl. adv.) (< auidus, -a, -um < aueo + -idus) most eagerly {> avid}
amplector, amplecti, amplexus sum (< ambi + plecto, plectare) embrace, seize eagerly upon
nemo, neminis (m.) (< ne + homo, hominis) no one, nobody; *nemini*: dat. of ref. (AG #376)
libentius (compar. adv.) (< libens, libentis) more willingly, gladly

II.XIII.2
duabus de causis modifier of obj. of monosyl. prep. often precedes prep. (AG #599d)
potissimum (adv.) especially, above all
peto, petere ask; petere takes *a/ab* + abl. of pers. asked rather than acc. dir. obj. (AG #396a); *petere*:
objv. inf. (AG #563d) ff. *constitui*
quod (relat. pron.) subst. use: "that which"
impetro (1) (< in + patro, patrare) obtain by request, gain; *impetratum*: supine expressing purp.
(AG #509), supine gener. appears after vb. of motion; here, movement is delivery of the letter.
Regis (vb.) 2nd pers. sg. pres.
amplus, -a, -um large, impressive in size {> ample}
hinc (adv.) from this (i.e. the army)
tibi dat. of poss. (AG #373), ELLIPSIS of *est*
beneficium, -i (n.) (< bene + facio, facere + -ium) service, kindness, benefit {> beneficiary}
largus, -a, -um generous, bountiful
materia, -ae (f.) (< mater + -ia) material, means, potential (*OLD* 8)
quo (relat. pron.) abl. of time within which (AG #424a)
exorno (1) (< ex + orno, ornare) equip, add distinction to, glorify
conuerto, conuertere (< con + uerto, uertere) turn to, direct one's attention to; pass. form w/ middle
sense: actively and deliberately turn oneself; *Conuertere*: pres. pass. sg. impv.
nostros . . . multos i.e. *amicos*

Malles tu quidem multos; sed meae uerecundiae sufficit unus   3
aut alter, ac potius unus. Is erit Voconius Romanus. Pater ei   4
in equestri gradu clarus, clarior uitricus, immo pater alius
(nam huic quoque nomini pietate successit), mater e primis.
Ipse citerioris Hispaniae (scis quod iudicium prouinciae illius,
quanta sit grauitas) flamen proxime fuit. Hunc ego, cum simul   5
studeremus, arte familiariterque dilexi; ille meus in urbe ille

---

II.XIII.3

malles   apod. of implied pres. C-to-F condit. (AG #517), prot. omitted (AG #522): "[if you were able to choose] you would prefer"

uerecundiae   dat. of indir. obj. w/ compd. vb. *sufficit* (AG #370); uerecundia, -ae (f.) (< uereor + -cundus + -ia) modesty, restraint

ac (conj.)   and; draws particular attention to what follows (AG #524b)

potius (adv.)   rather, more exactly

II.XIII.4

Voconius Romanus   life-long friend and protégé of Pliny. Pliny takes a strong personal interest in his advancement.

ei (**is, ea, id**)   dat. of poss. (AG #373), ELLIPSIS of *sunt/erant*; using ELLIPSIS and ASYNDETON, Pliny gives a quick sketch of his friend's lineage.

equester, equestris, equestre   (< equus + -es + -estris) equestrian (on equestrian rank s. II.IV.2n. on milia)

gradus, -us (m.)   step, stage, order

clarus, -a, -um   bright, well-known, famous {> clarity}

uitricus, -i (m.)   stepfather; qualified by *immo pater alius* in appos.; *immo* (pcl.): rather, more precisely; "more precisely a second father"

huic nomini   dat. of indir. obj. w/ compd. vb. *successit* (AG #370); succedo, succedere, successi, successus (< sub + cedo, cedere) move up in position to, become successor to

pietas, pietatis (f.)   (< pius + -tas) dutiful respect; *pietate*: abl. of means (AG #409); the possession of *pietas* was an integral part of Roman identity. A proper Roman man saw to his duty to serve the gods, the state, and his family. The value of this virtue is clearly expressed in the characterization of Aeneas in Virgil's *Aeneid* (*OCD* s. pietas, 1182).

e primis   "from the first [ranks]," i.e. senatorial rank (s. II.IV.2n. on milia)

Hispania, -ae (f.)   citerior, citerius (< citer) nearer; Citerior Hispania: Nearer Spain, a province that encompassed most of the eastern coast of Spain; under Augustus it became part of Hispania Tarraconensis. Pliny uses the old designation to emphasize the long-standing traditions about the area, which he highlights in his aside about its excellent reputation.

quod ... quanta ... sit   indir. quest. (AG #574) ff. *scis*; quantus, -a, -um (interrog. adj.) (< quam + -to + -us) how great; grauitas, grauitatis (f.) (< grauis + -tas) weight, seriousness of conduct, influence

flamen, flaminis (m.)   a priest for a particular god; in the provinces, the *flamen* oversaw the imperial cult and provided funding for the games (SW 177). Radice calls it "the highest dignity available" (122).

proxime (adv.)   most recently

II.XIII.5

Hunc   i.e. Voconius

cum ... studeremus   cum circumst. cl. (AG #546); studeo, studere: devote oneself, study

arte (adv.)   (< artus, -a, -um) firmly, intimately

familiariter (adv.)   (< familia + -aris) as a close friend, thoroughly

      in secessu contubernalis, cum hoc seria cum hoc iocos miscui.

6   Quid enim illo aut fidelius amico aut sodale iucundius? Mira

7   in sermone, mira etiam in ore ipso uultuque suauitas. Ad hoc

      ingenium excelsum subtile dulce facile eruditum in causis

      agendis; epistulas quidem scribit, ut Musas ipsas Latine loqui

8   credas. Amatur a me plurimum nec tamen uincitur. Equidem

---

ille ... contubernalis ELLIPSIS of *erat*; *ille ... ille*: ANAPHORA and ASYNDETON; while *meus* clearly
modifies *contubernalis,* its placement immediately ff. *ille* emphasizes the intimacy Pliny and
Voconius shared

contubernalis, contubernalis (m.) (< con + taberna + -alis) comrade in arms, intimate friend

cum ... cum ANAPHORA and ASYNDETON stress Pliny's closeness w/ Voconius; *cum hoc*: abl. of
accomp. (AG #413)

serius, -a, -um important, serious; n. pl. acc. subst.: "serious matters"

iocus, -i (m.) joke

misceo, miscere, miscui, mixtus mix, share (*OLD* 6)

II.XIII.6

Quid ... iucundius? RHETORICAL QUESTION, ELLIPSIS of *est; illo*: abl. of compar. (AG #406); *amico/
sodale*: appos. to *illo*—read w/ compar. adj. *fidelius/iucundius* respectively; fidelis, fidele (< fides +
-elis) faithful, loyal; sodalis, sodalis (m.) comrade, companion

mira ... suauitas *mira ... mira*: ANAPHORA and ASYNDETON; both modify *suauitas,* ELLIPSIS of *est*; os,
oris (n.) mouth, voice, eloquence {> oral}; uultus, -us (m.) countenance, facial expression; suauitas,
suauitatis (f.) (< suauis + -tas) pleasantness, charm

II.XIII.7

Ad hoc ... agendis Pliny leaves unstated a vb. like *additur; excelsum ... eruditum*: Pliny's use of ASYN-
DETON creates a piling on of adjs. to emphasize Voconius' innate talent; all of the adjs. are terms
used to describe oratorical ability; excelsus, -a, -um: lofty, elevated; subtilis, subtile (< sub + tela +
-is) fine, precise {> subtle}; dulcis, dulce: delightful, sweet-sounding; facilis, facile: easy, natural,
unforced; eruditus, -a, -um (< ppp. of ex + rudis + -io) learned {> erudition}; causam agere: plead
a case; *in causis agendis*: gerv. constr. (AG #503)

ut ... credas result cl. (AG #537); *Musas ... loqui*: indir. disc. (AG #580) ff. *credas*; Musa, Musae (f.)
Muse; *Latine* (adv.) (< Latinus, -a, -um) derived from adj. that denotes a population, used to specify
the language that those people spoke; thus, *Latine loqui* means "to speak Latin"; the nine Muses were
goddesses, traditionally daughters of Zeus and Mnemosyne, who inspired creativity in artists, phi-
losophers, and thinkers in general (*OCD* s. Muses, 1002). Their home was Mount Olympus, and thus
Pliny assumes that they speak Greek rather than Latin.

plurimum (adv.) most of all, to the greatest extent

uinco, uincere overcome, outdo, exceed {> invincible}; i.e. Voconius loves Pliny equally in return

II.XIII.8

iuuenis ... iuueni ... contuli *iuuenis*: appos. to subj. "I"; *iuueni*: dat. of indir. obj. w/ compd. vb. *contuli*
(AG #370); "I, as a young man, bestowed on [him] as a young man"

per aetatem "in accordance with my age"

nuper (adv.) recently

ius, iuris (n.) the right; *trium liberorum ius*: the right of three children; part of the Augustan marriage
laws, this right gave precedence for public offices to married men w/ children. In addition, those men
were exempt from serving as guardians (*OCD* s. ius liberorum, 791). By Pliny's time, the right was
sometimes awarded at the discretion of the emperor to those who were neither married nor parents.

iuuenis statim iuueni, quantum potui per aetatem, auidissime contuli, et nuper ab optimo principe trium liberorum
ius impetraui; quod quamquam parce et cum delectu daret,
mihi tamen tamquam eligeret indulsit. Haec beneficia mea   9
tueri nullo modo melius quam ut augeam possum, praesertim cum ipse illa tam grate interpretetur, ut dum priora
accipit posteriora mereatur. Habes qualis quam probatus   10
carusque sit nobis, quem rogo pro ingenio pro fortuna tua
exornes. In primis ama hominem; nam licet tribuas ei quantum amplissimum potes, nihil tamen amplius potes amicitia

---

impetro (1) (< in + patro, patrare) obtain by request

quod (relat. pron.) anteced. *ius*

quamquam ... daret conces. cl. w/ subjv. (usu. indic. w/ *quamquam*) (AG #527e); *parce et cum delectu*: VARIATIO; *parce* (adv.) (< parcus, -a, -um) sparingly, in a restricted manner; delectus, -us (m.) (< ppp. of diligo, diligere) discrimination; *cum delectu*: abl. of manner (AG #412)

tamquam ... eligeret condit. cl. of compar. (AG #524); eligo, eligere (< ex + lego, legere) select, choose

indulgeo, indulgere, indulsi, indultus look favorably upon, accede (to a request) {> indulge}, intr. vb. w/ dat. *mihi* (AG #367)

II.XIII.9

tueor, tueri, tutus sum look on, watch over, preserve, safeguard

nullo modo in no way

quam ut augeam result cl. introd. by *quam ut* (AG #535c); augeo, augere: increase in number, extend {> augment}; "(I can safeguard these services of mine in no way better) than to add to [them]."

praesertim (adv.) (< prae + sero + -im) especially

cum ... interpretetur cum causal cl. (AG #549); *illa*: i.e. *beneficia*; *grate* (adv.) (< gratus, -a, -um) w/ gratitude; interpretor, interpretari, interpretatus sum (< interpres + -o) regard, comprehend

ut ... mereatur result cl. (AG #537); *dum* (conj.) while, in or by (doing something) (*OLD* 4a); prior, prius (compar. adj.) (< primus) previous, earlier; posterior, posterius (compar. adj.) (< posterus) later; *priora ... posteriora*: *beneficia* implied; mereor, mereri, meritus sum: earn, deserve {> merit}

II.XIII.10

qualis quam ... nobis indir. quest. (AG #574); *qualis quam*: ASYNDETON; qualis, quale (interrog. adv.) what kind of (character), what (he is) like; *quam* (interrog. adv.) how, modifies *probatus*; probatus, -a, -um (< ppp. of probo, probare) esteemed, pleasing; *nobis*: dat. w/ adj. (AG #384)

quem ... rogo ... exornes relat. cl., anteced. Voconius, implied subj. of *sit*; followed by subst. cl. of purp. after *rogo* (AG #563) (= indir. comm.); omission of *ut* (AG #565a); *pro ingenio pro fortuna tua*; *tua* agrees w/ closest noun (AG #287) but should be read w/ both abls., *ingenio* and *fortuna*; ANAPHORA and ASYNDETON: here as elsewhere in the letter, the combination of these two devices draws attention and adds point to these characteristics; exorno (1) (< ex + orno) equip, ennoble

In primis above all else, first and foremost

tribuo, tribuere grant, bestow on {> attribute}; *ei* (is, ea, id): dat. sg., indir. obj. of *tribuas*; *quantum amplissimum potest*: relat. cl., dir. obj. of *tribuas*: "the greatest amount you are able"

amicitia, -ae (f.) (< amicus + -ia) friendly association; *amicitia*: abl. of compar. (AG #406) w/ *amplius*; while *amicitia* could certainly involve true affection, it often denoted a relationship among relative equals that was mutually beneficial, politically and socially (*OCD* s. amicitia, 72).

11   tua; cuius esse eum usque ad intimam familiaritatem capacem
quo magis scires, breuiter tibi studia mores omnem denique
uitam eius expressi. Extenderem preces nisi et tu rogari diu
nolles et ego tota hoc epistula fecissem; rogat enim et quidem
efficacissime, qui reddit causas rogandi. Vale.

---

cuius ... scires *cuius ... capacem*: indir. disc. (AG #580) ff. *scires*; *cuius* (relat. pron.), anteced. *amicitia*, gen. w/ *capax* (AG #349c); *usque* (adv.) all the way (to), persistently; intimus, -a, -um (< in + -timus) deepest, most intimate; familiaritas, familiaritatis (f.) (< familia + -aris + -tas) close friendship, close relationship; capax, capacis (< capio + -ax) capable of, fit for {> capacity}; *quo ... scires*: relat. cl. of purp., introd. by *quo* because of compar. *magis* (AG #531/2a)

studia mores omnem ... uitam ASYNDETON; mos, moris (m.) custom, practice, pl.: character {> moral}

exprimo, exprimere, expressi, expressus (< ex + premo, premere) portray, describe; *cuius ... expressi*: "I have described in a few words for you his studies, character and finally his whole life so that you might know more fully that he is fit for your friendship all the way to the deepest of relationships."

II.XIII.11

extenderem ... nisi et ... nolles et ... fecissem apod. of pres. C-to-F condit. (AG #517) w/ two prot. introd. by *et ... et*, one pres. C-to-F, one past C-to-F: "I would ... both if you were not ... and if I had not ..."; extendo, extendere (< ex + tendo, tendere) continue, prolong; prex, precis (f.) prayer, entreaty; *diu* (adv.) w/ negat.: any further, any longer (*OLD* 2); *tota epistula*: abl. of means (AG #409); *hoc*: n. acc. sg., refers to *extenderem preces*

rogat ... rogandi a typical Plinian SENTENTIA, beginning and ending nicely w/ forms of the same vb., i.e. POLYPTOTON; subj.: "(The man) who ..."; *efficacissime* (superl. adv.) (< ex + facio, facere + -ax) most effectively {> efficacious}; causam reddere: give an explanation or reason (*OLD* s. reddo 13c); *rogandi*: ger., objv. gen. (AG #347) w/ *causas*

II.XVII: In this detailed description of his villa at Laurentum, Pliny leads the reader through its many rooms, gardens, and surrounding structures. Various scholars have attempted reconstructions of the villa, relying only on Pliny's description, as its site has not yet been discovered. Yet Pliny's goal is not to reconstruct a model, but rather to convey the ambience and refinement of this country estate, to reveal it as a most suitable place for him to enjoy the kind of *otium* (s. Freq. Vocab.) he mentions in I.IX and discusses at length in IX.XXXVI, as well as the kind of retirement he outlines in IV.XXIII. Addressee: Gallus, identified by cognomen only, likely the Gallus who receives another letter *Ep.* VIII. XX that is also an exegesis, offering a detailed description of Lake Vadimon (S-W 180).

II.XVII.1

miror, mirari, miratus sum (< mirus + -o) wonder, be amazed

cur ... delectet indir. quest. (AG #574); Laurentinus, -a, -um: belonging to Laurentum (a town on the coast of Latium); *Laurentinum*: n. subst., the estate at this location; *si ita mauis*: PARENTHESIS; Laurens, Laurentis (adj.) belonging to Laurentum; like *Laurentinum*, n. subst. referring to the estate; Pliny offers two names for his villa; *Laurens* is the more poetic word, used by two of Pliny's contemporaries, the poets Silius Italicus (1.110, 669; 3.83, 8.598) and Statius (*Silu.* 1.2.163) to mean Roman (*OLD* 2); Pliny describes Italicus's suicide in *Ep.* III.VII. Since this villa was the closest of his estates to Rome, *Laurens* might be read as "my Roman villa"; *tanto opere* (also tantopere) (adv.) to such a great degree, so much

cum ... spatium cum tmp. cl. (AG #545); cognosco, cognoscere, cognoui, cognitus (< con + nosco, noscere) get to know, become aware; *cognoueris*: fut. pf.; opportunitas, opportunitatis (f.) (< ob + portus + unus + -tas) convenience; litus, litoris (n.) shore, coast

XVII—PLINY'S LAURENTIAN VILLA

C. PLINIVS GALLO SVO S.

Miraris cur me Laurentinum uel (si ita mauis), Laurens   1
meum tanto opere delectet; desines mirari, cum cognoueris
gratiam uillae, opportunitatem loci, litoris spatium. Decem   2
septem milibus passuum ab urbe secessit, ut peractis quae
agenda fuerint saluo iam et composito die possis ibi manere.
Aditur non una uia; nam et Laurentina et Ostiensis eodem
ferunt, sed Laurentina a quarto decimo lapide, Ostiensis ab
undecimo relinquenda est. Vtrimque excipit iter aliqua ex
parte harenosum, iunctis paulo grauius et longius, equo
breue et molle. Varia hinc atque inde facies; nam modo   3

II.XVII.2

milia, milium (n.) thousands; milia passuum: miles; *milibus*: abl. of deg. of diff. indicating distance (AG #425b)

secedo, secedere, secessi, secessus (< se + cedo, cedere) detach oneself, withdraw (i.e. from Rome into the country) (*OLD* 3) {> secede}

ut...manere result cl. (AG #537); *peractis...fuerint*: abl. abs. w/ relat. cl. of char. (AG #535) used subst. (AG #419b), "when the things that have to be done are completed"; saluus, -a, -um: unimpaired, intact, not lost; compositus, -a, -um (< ppp. of compono, componere) well-arranged, well-ordered; *saluo...die*: abl. abs. (AG #419); i.e. the villa is close enough that it can be reached after a day's business is concluded in Rome

adeo, adire (< ad + eo, ire) approach {> adit}; *aditur*: subj. *uilla* understood

Laurentina, Ostiensis *uiae* understood; Ostiensis, Ostiense: of or belonging to Ostia; the city of Ostia, located at the mouth of the Tiber River, expanded around an early fort placed there to control both military and economic access to the river that led to and served the city of Rome. Ostia's remains are extensive and make it one of the most studied ancient Roman cities (*OCD* 1081–82).

eodem (adv.) (< idem, eadem, idem) to the same place

lapis, lapidis (m.) stone, milestone; roads in the countryside (i.e. not leading to Rome or a provincial capital) were measured and marked by distance from the principal city/town in the area. In Pliny's time, milestones appeared every 1500 paces or *leuga* (a Gallic measure that becomes league in E.) (*OCD* 979–80).

relinquenda est 2nd (pass.) periphr. conjug. (AG #196 and 500/2); subj. *uia* understood

Vtrimque (< uterque + im) on/from both sides

aliqua ex parte modifier of obj. of monosyl. prep. often precedes prep. (AG #599d)

harenosus, -a, -um sandy, unpaved; Pliny here is referring to the unpaved side roads leading to his villa from either the Via Laurentina or the Via Ostiensis, both of which would have been paved, as part of the extensive system of Roman roads that linked cities and towns throughout the empire.

iunctis...equo dat. of ref. (AG #376); iunctus, -a, -um (< ppp. iungo, iungere) joined; *iunctis*: a yoked pair of horses, i.e. a carriage

paulo somewhat, by a little; abl. of deg. of diff. (AG #414) w/ compar. *grauius* and *longius*

mollis, molle soft, tolerable, gentle

II.XVII.3

facies, faciei (f.) sight, scene; ELLIPSIS of *est*

modo...modo (adv.) first...then, now...now

occurrentibus siluis uia coartatur, modo latissimis pratis dif-
funditur et patescit; multi greges ouium, multa ibi equorum
boum armenta, quae montibus hieme depulsa herbis et
tepore uerno nitescunt. Villa usibus capax, non sumptuosa

4   tutela. Cuius in prima parte atrium frugi, nec tamen sordidum; deinde porticus in D litterae similitudinem circumactae, quibus paruola sed festiua area includitur. Egregium
hae aduersus tempestates receptaculum; nam specularibus

5   ac multo magis imminentibus tectis muniuntur. Est contra
medias cauaedium hilare, mox triclinium satis pulchrum,

---

occurro, occurrere (< ob + curro, currere) hurry to meet, present itself

coarto (1) (< con + arto, artare) crowd, confine

pratum, -i (n.) meadow

diffundo, diffundere (< dis + fundo, fundere) spread out

patesco, patescere (< pateo, patere + -sco) made open

ouis, ouis (m./f.) sheep

bos, bouis (m./f.) bull or cow, pl.: cattle {> bovine}; *boum*: gen. pl.

armentum, -i (n.) herd; ELLIPSIS of *sunt*; using ASYNDETON, Pliny amplifies the number of herds.

montibus abl. of separ. (AG #401) w/ *depulsa* (modifying *quae*); depello, depellere, depuli, depulsus (< de + pello, pellere) drive off, drive down

herbis ... tepore uerno abl. of means (AG #409); tepor, teporis (< tepeo, tepere + -or) mild heat, warmth; uernus, -a, -um (< uer + -nus) occurring in spring, springtime {> vernal}

nitesco, nitescere (< niteo + -sco) take on a healthy shine, become sleek

capax, capacis (< capio + -ax) roomy {> capacity}; w/ *usibus*: abl. of specif. (AG #418)

sumptuosus, -a, -um (< sumo, sumere + -tus + -osus) expensive, extragavant; w/ *tutela*: abl. of specif. (AG #418); tutela, -ae (f.) maintenance

II.XVII.4

frugi (indecl. adj.) moderate, frugal; ELLIPSIS of *est*

sordidus, -a, -um (< sordeo, sordere + -idus) lacking refinement, vulgar {> sordid}

porticus, -us (m./f.) covered walkway, colonnade

in ... similitudinem similitudo, similitudinis (f.) (< similis, simile + -tudo) resemblance, similarity; *D litterae*, dat. of ref. (AG #376): "to the letter D"

circumago, circumagere, circumegi, circumactus (< circum + ago, agere) lead around, bend, or form round; *circumactae*: nom. pl. w/ *porticus*, ELLIPSIS of *sunt*

quibus (relat. pron.) anteced. *porticus*

paruolus, -a, -um dim. of paruus, -a, -um

festiuus, -a, -um (< festus + -iuus) excellent, fine

aduersus (prep.) against (+ acc.)

tempestas, tempestatis (f.) (< tempus + -tas) weather, storm

receptaculum, -i (n.) (< recipio, recipere + -to + -culum) refuge, shelter; ELLIPSIS of *sunt*

specularis, speculare (< speculum + -aris) of mirrors; n. pl. subst.: windows made of transparent stone (gener. forms of mica or gypsum—*OLD* 2b)

immineo, imminere overhang {> imminent}

tectum, -i (n.) (< ppp. of tego, tegere) roof, building, house

munio, munire protect w/ a structure

quod in litus excurrit ac si quando Africo mare impulsum est,
fractis iam et nouissimis fluctibus leuiter adluitur. Vndique
ualuas aut fenestras non minores ualuis habet atque ita a
lateribus a fronte quasi tria maria prospectat; a tergo
cauaedium porticum aream porticum rursus, mox atrium
siluas et longinquos respicit montes. Huius a laeua retractius   6
paulo cubiculum est amplum, deinde aliud minus quod altera
fenestra admittit orientem, occidentem altera retinet; hac
et subiacens mare longius quidem sed securius intuetur. Huius   7
cubiculi et triclinii illius obiectu includitur angulus, qui

II.XVII.5

cauaedium, -i (n.) inner court

hilaris, hilare cheerful, lighthearted

triclinium, -i (n.) (< Gr. τρικλίνιον) dining room; so called because of the three couches placed in the room on which diners reclined (s. II.VI.3n. on Roman dining)

excurro, excurrere (< ex + curro, currere) run out, extend

si quando if ever, whenever

Africus, -a, -um African; m. sg. subst.: southwest wind

impello, impellere, impuli, impulsus (< in + pello, pellere) push forward, drive in

fractus, -a, -um (< ppp. of frango, frangere) broken {> fracture}

fluctus, -us (m.) (< fluo, fluere + -tus) wave {> fluctuate}

adluo, adluere touch w/ water, lap

ualuae, -arum (f. pl.) folding doors; *ualuis*: abl. of compar. (AG #406)

latus, lateris (n.) side {> lateral}; *a lateribus a fronte*: w/ ASYNDETON, Pliny makes the three sided view a single vista.

prospecto (1) (< prospicio, prospicere + -to) gaze out at, look out on; subj. *triclinium* understood

a tergo . . . montes Pliny's use of ASYNDETON in describing the view back through the house from the dining room, connects all of the places he has just described and sets the villa immediately next to the forest. The continuity is broken w/ the conj. *et*, which nicely locates the mountains in the distance; longinquus, -a, -um: far off, remote; respicio, respicere (< re + specio, specere) look round, look back

II.XVII.6

huius i.e. the *triclinium*

laeua, -ae (f.) left hand side; *a laeua*: on the left

retractus, -a, -um (< ppp. of re + traho, trahere) lying far back

paulo somewhat, by a little; abl. of deg. of diff. (AG #414)

admitto, admittere (< ad + mitto, mittere) grant access, let in

oriens, orientis (m.) (< pres. ptc. of orior, oriri, *sol* understood) rising sun

occidens, occidentis (m.) (< pres. ptc. of occido, occidere, *sol* understood) setting sun

hac i.e. the west-facing window; abl. of means (AG #409); *et = etiam*

subiaceo, subiacere (< sub + iaceo, iacere) lie underneath, lie at the foot

securus, -a, -um (< se + cura + -us) free from care/anxiety

intueor, intueri, intuitus sum (< in + tueor, tueri) look at, look upon, regard (as); subj. *cubiculum* understood

II.XVII.7

Obiectus, -us (m.) (< obicio, obicere + -tus) interposition, opposing position

angulus, -i (m.) corner

purissimum solem continet et accendit. Hoc hibernaculum,
hoc etiam gymnasium meorum est; ibi omnes silent uenti,
exceptis qui nubilum inducunt, et serenum ante quam usum

8 loci eripiunt. Adnectitur angulo cubiculum in hapsida
curuatum, quod ambitum solis fenestris omnibus sequitur.
Parieti eius in bibliothecae speciem armarium insertum est,

9 quod non legendos libros sed lectitandos capit. Adhaeret

---

contineo, continere (< con + teneo, tenere) retain, embrace

accendo, accendere heighten, intensify (*OLD* 3)

hibernaculum, -i (n.) (< hiberno, hibernare + -culum) winter quarters; *meorum*: i.e. the members of the household

exceptis … eripiunt abl. abs. w/ relat. cl. (AG #535) used subst. (AG #419b); nubilus, -a, -um (< nubes + -ilus) cloudy; n. sg. subst.: cloud; serenum, -i (n.) clear sky; usus, -us (m.) (< utor, uti + -tus) enjoyment, use, function; eripio, eripere (< ex + rapio, rapere) snatch away, take away; "with the exception of those (winds) that bring in clouds and take away clear sky before they take away the function of the location,"—i.e. the area is usable except during an actual storm

II.XVII.8

adnecto, adnectere (< ad + necto, nectare) connect, attach to; compd. vb + dat. *angulo* (AG #370)

(h)apsis, (h)apsidis (f.) (< Gr. ἀψίς) segment of a circle {> apse}; *hapsida*: Gr. acc. sg.

curuatus, -a, -um (< ppp. of curuo, curuare) curved, bent

ambitus, -us (m.) (< ambio, ambire + -tus) circuit, cycle

parieti … insertum est paries, parietis (m.) wall of a building; bibliotheca, -ae (f.) (< Gr. βιβλιοθήκη) library; species, speciei (f.) (< specio, specere + -ies) appearance; armarium, -i (n.) (< arma + -arium) cabinet, bookcase; insero, inserere, inserui, insertus (< in + sero, serere) put in, thrust in, joined; compd. vb + dat. *parieti* (AG #370)

legendos … lectitandos gerv.; lectito (1) (< leo, legere + -ito) read repeatedly

II.XVII.9

adhaereo (< ad + haereo, haerere) be near, adjoin {> adhere}

dormitorium membrum bedroom; dormitorius, -a, -um: pertaining to sleep; membrum, -i (n.) apartment, room (*OLD* 3b)

transitu interiacente abl. abs. (AG #419); transitus, -us (m.) passage

qui … ministrat suspendo, suspendere, suspendi, suspensus (< sub + pendo, pendere) placed in a raised position (*OLD* 4); tubulatus, -a, -um (< tubus + -ulus + -atus) fitted w/ pipes; concipio, concipere, concepi, conceptus (< con + capio, capere) draw in, take in; uapor, uaporis (m.) heat, warmth; *salubri temperamento*: abl. of quality (AG #415a) saluber, salubris; healthy, beneficial {> salubrious}; temperamentum, -i (n.) (< tempero, temperare + -mentum) a mean between hot and cold; digero, digerere (< dis + gero, gerere) distribute; ministro (1) (< minister + -o) provide, control, regulate (*OLD* 4); Pliny describes an underfloor heating system (hypocaust) that was common in elite Roman housing and public baths.

libertus, -i (m.) (< liber + -tus) freedman (s. II.VI.2 n.)

detineo, detinere (< de + tineo, tinere) retain, reserve; *usibus*: dat. of purp. (AG #382)

plerisque … mundis abl. abs. (AG #419); plerusque, -aque, -umque (< plerus + -que) the greater part, most of, pl.: most; mundus, -a, -um: elegant, refined

ut … possint result cl. (AG #537); hospes, hospitis (m./f.) guest, visitor

dormitorium membrum transitu interiacente, qui suspensus
et tubulatus conceptum uaporem salubri temperamento huc
illuc digerit et ministrat. Reliqua pars lateris huius seruorum
libertorumque usibus detinetur, plerisque tam mundis, ut
accipere hospites possint. Ex alio latere cubiculum est poli-   10
tissimum; deinde uel cubiculum grande uel modica cenatio,
quae plurimo sole, plurimo mari lucet; post hanc cubiculum
cum procoetone, altitudine aestiuum, munimentis hibernum;
est enim subductum omnibus uentis. Huic cubiculo aliud et
procoeton communi pariete iunguntur. Inde balinei cella   11
frigidaria spatiosa et effusa, cuius in contrariis parietibus duo
baptisteria uelut eiecta sinuantur, abunde capacia si mare in
proximo cogites. Adiacet unctorium, hypocauston, adiacet

II.XVII.10

politus, -a, -um (< ppp. of polio, polire) refined, elegant

grandis, grande large

cenatio, cenationis (f.) (< ceno, cenare + -tio) dining room (likely smaller and less elegant than a
   triclinium); ELLIPSIS of *est*

luceo, lucere shine w/ reflected light, sparkle (*OLD* 2)

procoeton, procoetonis (m.) (< Gr. προκοιτών) antechamber; ELLIPSIS of *est*

altitudine, munimentis abl. of specif. (AG #418) w/ *aestiuum* and *hibernum* respectively; aestiuus, -a,
   -um (< aestus + iuus) designed for the summer; munimentum, -i (n.) (< munio, munire +
   mentum) defense, safeguard; hibernus, -a, -um: designed for the winter

subduco, subducere, subduxi, subductus (< sub + duco, ducere) remove, rescue (*OLD* 5)

iungo, iungere yoke, join, bring close together

II.XVII.11

balineum, -i (n.) (< Gr. βαλανεῖον) baths; many Roman villa complexes incorporated private baths for
   the use of the household and visitors. Rooms within the baths varied by the preferences of the owner
   but might include many of the same spaces as public baths: a changing room; cold, hot, and warm
   rooms, using both dry and moist heat; pools, baths, and basins of various temperatures; and even
   swimming pools (*OCD* 236).

cella frigidaria cooling room (in a bath) (*OLD* frigidarius); cella, -ae (f.) chamber

spatiosus, -a, -um (< spatium + -osus) expansive {> spacious}

effusus, -a, -um (< ppp. of ex + fundo, fundere) poured out, spacious{> effusive}

contrarius, -a, -um opposite

baptisterium, -i (n.) (Gr.) plunge bath

eicio, eicere, eieci, eiectus (< ex + iacio, iacere) extend, thrust forth {> eject}

sinuo (1) (< sinus + -o) bend in a curve, present a curved form {> sinuous}

abunde (adv.) (< abundus, -a, -um) quite, enough and to spare {> abundant}

si . . . cogites prot. of FLV condit. (AG #516b), apod. omitted; *in proximo*: close at hand (*OLD* 2a)

adiaceo, adiacere (< ad + iaceo, iacere) lie beside, be contiguous {> adjacent}; ASYNDETON here
   unifies the rooms into bathing complex, rather than unrelated areas.

unctorium, -i (n.) (< unguo, unguere + -torium) room used for oiling the body

hypocauston, -i (n.) (< Gr. ὑπόκαυστον) heating system

12

propnigeon balinei, mox duae cellae magis elegantes quam
sumptuosae; cohaeret calida piscina mirifica, ex qua natantes
mare adspiciunt, nec procul sphaeristerium quod calidissimo
soli inclinato iam die occurrit. Hic turris erigitur, sub qua
diaetae duae, totidem in ipsa, praeterea cenatio quae latissimum mare longissimum litus uillas amoenissimas possidet.

13

Est et alia turris; in hac cubiculum, in quo sol nascitur
conditurque; lata post apotheca et horreum, sub hoc triclinium, quod turbati maris non nisi fragorem et sonum
patitur, eumque iam languidum ac desinentem; hortum et

14

gestationem uidet, qua hortus includitur. Gestatio buxo aut

---

propnigeon, -i (n.) (< Gr. προπνιγεῖον) hot room, sweating room

cohaereo, cohaerere (< co + haereo, haerere) be connected {> coherent}

calidus, -a, -um (< caleo, calere + -idus) hot

piscina, -ae (f.) (< piscis + -ina) swimming pool

mirificus, -a, -um (< mirus + -ficus) causing wonder, amazing

nato (1) swim; *natantes*: subst. use, i.e. swimmers

adspicio, adspicere (< ad + specio, specere) catch sight of, gaze upon

procul (adv.) some way off, far away

sphaeristerium, -i (n.) (< Gr. σφαιριςτήριον) court for ball games; ELLIPSIS of *est*

calidissimo soli dat. of indir. obj. w/ compd. vb. *occurrit* (AG #370)

inclinato die abl. abs. (AG #419); inclino (1) lean to one side, bend downwards; "in the afternoon"

II.XVII.12

turris, turris (f.) (< Gr. τύρρις) tower, upper storey {> turret}

erigo, erigere (< ex + rego, regere) raise, set up, lift {> erect}

diaeta, -ae (f.) (< Gr. δίαιτα) annex, room, apartment; ELLIPSIS of *sunt*

totidem (indecl. adj.) (< tot + idem) the same number, as many; i.e. *diaetae*; *ipsa*: i.e. *turris*

amoenus, -a, -um pleasing, charming

possideo, possidere (< potis + sedeo, sedere) have (land) in one's control, take in; Pliny's repeated use of superlatives combines w/ ASYNDETON to stress the exceptional view from this 2nd-storey dining room.

II.XVII.13

nascor, nasci, natus sum be born {> natal}

condo, condere put away, lay to rest (*OLD* 4a); this is the 3rd time that Pliny has referred to sunrise and sunset, differently each time (s. II.XVII.6 and 8), a wonderful ex. of VARIATIO.

apotheca, -ae (f.) (< Gr. ἀποθήκη) storeroom (particularly for wine)

post (adv.) behind

horreum, -i (n.) storeroom (particularly for grain); ELLIPSIS of *sunt*

turbatus, -a, -um (< ppp. of turbo, turbare) turbulent, stirred up

non nisi only

fragor, fragoris (m.) crash, roar

sonus, -i (m.) sound, noise

languidus, -a, -um (< langueo, languere + -idus) faint, weak

gestatio, gestationis (f.) (< gestio, gestire + -tio) an area for driving or walking, a drive

rore marino, ubi deficit buxus, ambitur; nam buxus, qua
parte defenditur tectis, abunde uiret; aperto caelo apertoque
uento et quamquam longinqua aspergine maris inarescit.
Adiacet gestationi interiore circumitu uinea tenera et um-   15
brosa, nudisque etiam pedibus mollis et cedens. Hortum
morus et ficus frequens uestit, quarum arborum illa uel
maxime ferax terra est, malignior ceteris. Hac non deteriore
quam maris facie cenatio remota a mari fruitur, cingitur
diaetis duabus a tergo, quarum fenestris subiacet uestibulum
uillae et hortus alius pinguis et rusticus. Hinc cryptoporticus   16

II.XVII.14

buxus, -i (f.) box-tree, boxwood

ros marinus rosemary; ros, roris (m.) dew

deficio, deficere (< de + facio, facere) be lacking, come to an end {> deficient}

ambio, ambire (< ambi + eo, ire) surround, encircle {> ambient}

qua parte "on the side which"

uireo, uirere be vigorous, thrive

aperto . . . maris *aperto caelo apertoque uento*: abl. abs. (AG #419); *longinqua aspergine*: abl. of means
    (AG #409); aspergo, asperginis (f.) (< ad + spargo, spargere) sprinkling, spray; all three are agents/
    causes in this ex. of VARIATIO.

inaresco, inarescere (< in + areo, arere + -sco) become dry, dry up

II.XVII.15

gestationi dat. of indir. obj. w/ compd. vb. *adiacet* (AG #370)

interiore circumitu abl. of place where w/o prep. (AG #429); circumitus, -us (m.) (< circum + eo, ire
    + -tus) surrounding area

uinea, -ae (f.) vines

tener, -a, -um delicate, of tender age

umbrosus, -a, -um (< umbra + -osus) shady

cedo, cedere submit, yield (OLD 10) {> cede}; *nudis . . . pedibus*: dat. of ref. (AG #376)

morus, -i (f.) black mulberry tree

ficus, -i (f.) fig tree

frequens, frequentis crowded

uestio, uestire (< uestis + -io) clothe, cover

ferax, feracis (< fero, ferre + -ax) productive, fertile

malignus, -a, -um spiteful, harmful {> malign}

hac . . . facie abl. of means w/ depon. vb. *fruitur* (AG #410); deterior, deterius (compar. adj.) less desir-
    able, less valuable; remotus, -a, -um (< ppp. remoueo, remouere) distant, out of the way; fruor, frui,
    fructus sum: enjoy

cingo, cingere encircle, lie round

quarum . . . subiacet *fenestris*: dat. of indir. obj. w/ compd. vb. *subiacet* (AG #370); "under whose win-
    dows lies"; sg. vb. makes the items that follow part of a whole view (AG #317b)

uestibulum, -i (n.) forecourt, entrance {> vestibule}

pinguis, pingue rich, fertile

rusticus, -a, -um (< rus) of the country; w/ *hortus*: likely a kitchen garden

II.XVII.16

cryptoporticus, -us (f.) (< Gr. κρυπτός + porticus) covered gallery, cloister

prope publici operis extenditur. Vtrimque fenestrae, a mari
plures, ab horto singulae sed alternis pauciores. Hae cum
serenus dies et immotus, omnes, cum hinc vel inde uentis
17   inquietus, qua uenti quiescunt sine iniuria patent. Ante
cryptoporticum xystus uiolis odoratus. Teporem solis in-
fusi repercussu cryptoporticus auget, quae ut tenet solem sic
aquilonem inhibet summouetque, quantumque caloris ante
tantum retro frigoris; similiter africum sistit, atque ita
diuersissimos uentos alium alio latere frangit et finit. Haec
18   iucunditas eius hieme, maior aestate. Nam ante meridiem
xystum, post meridiem gestationis hortique proximam partem

---

extendo, extendere (< ex + tendo, tendere) stretch, continue

prope (adv.) almost, nearly

publici operis gen. of quality (AG #345); i.e. to the length of one in an urban building

Vtrimque fenestrae ELLIPSIS of *sunt*

singulae sed alternis *alternis* (adv.) in alternate positions; perhaps (ff. Radice 139) "individual windows in every other arch"

Hae i.e. *fenestrae*

cum ... patent pair of cum tmp. cl. (AG #545) each w/ ELLIPSIS of *est*; immotus, -a, -um
(< ppp. of in + moueo, mouere) tranquil; *omnes* (supply *patent*); *inquietus* (supply *dies*); inquietus, -a, -um (< in + ppp. of quiesco, quiescere) unsettled; *qua* (relat. adv.) in which direction;
pateo, patere: be open; i.e. the windows on either side may be opened or closed as needed to
block the wind

II.XVII.17

xystus, -i (m.) (< Gr. ξυστός) garden walkway, terrace; ELLIPSIS of *est*

uiola, -ae (f.) violet

odoratus, -a, -um (< odor + -atus) smelling of, fragrant

infundo, infundere, infudi, infusus (< in + fundo, fundere) pour on

repercussus, -us (m.) (< re + per + quatio, quatere + -tus) reflection {> repercussion}

quae (relat. pron.) anteced. *cryptoporticus*

ut ... sic correl. conj. (AG #323g), "as ... so"

aquilo, aquilonis (m.) the north wind

inhibeo, inhibere (< in + habeo, habere) restrain, hold back {> inhibit}

summoueo, summouere (< sub + moueo, mouere) drive off, banish

quantum, -i (n.) ... **tantum, -i** (n.) correl., "as much (w/ partit. gen. *caloris*) ... as (w/ partit. gen.
frigoris), ELLIPSIS of *est*; calor, caloris (m.) heat; *retro* (adv.) backwards, back; frigor, frigoris (m.)
cold

sisto, sistere bring to a standstill, stop (*OLD* 6a)

diuersus, -a, -um (< ppp. of diuerto, diuertere) different

alium alio consecutive forms of alius = dbl. stmt. (AG #315c): "one wind on one side, the other wind
on the other side"

frango, frangere break, shatter, soften (*OLD* 10)

iucunditas, iucunditatis (f.) (< iuuo, iuuare + -cundus + -tas) pleasantness, charm; ELLIPSIS of *est*

umbra sua temperat, quae, ut dies creuit decreuitue, modo
breuior modo longior hac uel illa cadit. Ipsa uero crypto-   19
porticus tum maxime caret sole, cum ardentissimus culmini
eius insistit. Ad hoc patentibus fenestris fauonios accipit
transmittitque nec umquam aere pigro et manente ingrauescit. In capite xysti, deinceps cryptoporticus horti,   20
diaeta est amores mei, re uera amores: ipse posui. In hac
heliocaminus quidem alia xystum, alia mare, utraque solem,
cubiculum autem ualuis cryptoporticum, fenestra prospicit
mare. Contra parietem medium zotheca perquam eleganter   21
recedit, quae specularibus et uelis obductis reductisue modo

II.XVII.18

umbra sua still referring to the cryptoporticus

tempero (1) (< tempus) regulate (in terms of temperature) (*OLD* 5b) {> temperance}

ut ... decreuitue *ut* w/ indic. "as" (AG #527f); cresco, crescere, creui, cretus: increase, lengthen
   {> crescent}; decresco, decrescere, decreui, decretus (< de + cresco, crescere) dwindle, fade

hac (adv.) **uel illa** (adv.) on this side or that, on one side or the other

II.XVII.19

careo, carere lack, be w/out, be deprived; w/ abl. of separ. *sole* (AG #401)

ardentissimus, -a, -um (superl. adj.) (< ardens, ardentis) most fiery, brilliant; i.e. *sol*

culmen, culminis (n.) peak, highest point in the sky; *culmini*: dat. of indir. obj. w/ compd. vb. *insistit*
   (AG #370); insisto, insistere (< in + sisto, sistere) stand on {> insist}

ad hoc moreover, in addition (*OLD* ad 23b)

patentibus fenestris abl. abs. (AG #419)

fauonius, -i (m.) west wind

aer, aeris (m.) (< Gr. ἀήρ) air

piger, pigra, pigrum sluggish, lazy

ingrauesco, ingrauescere (< in + grauis + -esco) become stuffy

II.XVII.20

deinceps (adv.) then, next

cryptoporticus gen. sg.

amores mei my beloved, my favorite

heliocaminus, -i (m.) (< Gr. ἡλιοκάμινος) sun room

alia ... alia (adv.) in one direction ... in the other direction

prospicio, prospicere (< pro + specio, specere) give a view of; read *prospicit* w/ both *heliocaminus* and
   cubiculum; *ualuis, fenestra*: abl. of means (AG #409)

II.XVII.21

zotheca, -ae (f.) (< Gr. ζωθήκη) recess, bay

perquam (adv.) extremely, exceedingly

recedo, recedere (< re + cedo, cedere) draw back, move away {> recede}

quae aufertur *specularibus ... reductis*: abl. abs. (AG #419); uelum, -i (n.) curtain; obduco, obducere
   (< ob + duco, ducere) draw over as a cover; aufero, auferre (< ab + fero, ferre) take away, remove;
   i.e. moveable glass doors and curtains make it possible to include or exclude this alcove from the
   bedroom

adicitur cubiculo modo aufertur. Lectum et duas cathedras
capit; a pedibus mare, a tergo uillae, a capite siluae: tot
facies locorum totidem fenestris et distinguit et miscet.

22   Iunctum est cubiculum noctis et somni. Non illud uoces
seruolorum, non maris murmur, non tempestatum motus
non fulgurum lumen, ac ne diem quidem sentit, nisi fenestris
apertis. Tam alti abditique secreti illa ratio, quod interiacens
andron parietem cubiculi hortique distinguit atque ita

23   omnem sonum media inanitate consumit. Adplicitum est
cubiculo hypocauston perexiguum, quod angusta fenestra
suppositum calorem, ut ratio exigit, aut effundit aut retinet.
Procoeton inde et cubiculum porrigitur in solem, quem

---

lectus, -i (m.) bed, couch

cathedra, -ae (f.) (< Gr. καθέδρα) arm chair

a pedibus...siluae ELLIPSIS of *sunt*

distinguet, miscet subj. *diaeta* understood; distinguo, distinguere: pick out, keep separate; misceo, miscere: mix, share (*OLD* 6)

II.XVII.22

somnus, -i (m.) sleep {> somnolent}

motus, -us (m.) (< moueo, mouere + -tus) movement, motion

fulgur, fulguris (n.) flash of lightning

lumen, luminis (n.) light, brightness {> luminous}

fenestris apertis abl. abs. (AG #419)

abditus, -a, -um (< ppp. of abdo, abdere) hidden

secretum, -i (n.) (< ppp. of se + cerno, cernere) seclusion

(est) quod subst. cl. introd. by *quod* (AG #572), "that"

interiaceo, interiacere (< inter + iaceo, iacere) lie between

andron, andronis (m.) (< Gr. ἀνδρών) passage, corridor

sonus, -i (m.) sound

inanitas, inanitatis (f.) (< inanis + -tas) empty space

consumo, consumere (< con + sumo, sumere) use up, swallow up

II.XVII.23

adplico (1) (< ad + plico, plicare) place near; compd. vb + dat. *cubiculo* (AG #370)

perexiguus, -a, -um (< per + exiguus) very small

angustus, -a, -um narrow, congested; *angusta fenestra*: "through a narrow opening"

ut ratio exigit *ut* w/ indic. "as" (AG #527f); exigo, exigere (< ex + ago, agere) demand, require (*OLD* 9a); i.e. Pliny could open the vent when he wanted heat

effundo, effundere (< ex + fundo, fundere) send forth, discharge

porrigo, porrigere (< por + rego, regere) extend; *porrigitur*: sg. because the two areas comprise a single unit

oblicus, -a, -um at an angle

II.XVII.24

cum...recepi cum tmp. cl. (AG #545); se recipere: retire, withdraw (*OLD* 12)

praecipue (adv.) (< prae + capio, capere + -uus) especially

orientem statim exceptum ultra meridiem oblicum quidem
sed tamen seruat. In hanc ego diaetam cum me recepi, abesse   24
mihi etiam a uilla mea uideor, magnamque eius uoluptatem
praecipue Saturnalibus capio, cum reliqua pars tecti licentia
dierum festisque clamoribus personat; nam nec ipse meorum
lusibus nec illi studiis meis obstrepunt. Haec utilitas haec   25
amoenitas deficitur aqua salienti, sed puteos ac potius fontes
habet; sunt enim in summo. Et omnino litoris illius mira
natura: quocumque loco moueris humum, obuius et paratus
umor occurrit, isque sincerus ac ne leuiter quidem tanta

Saturnalia, -ium (n. pl.) festival of Saturn; *Saturnalibus*: abl. of time when (AG #423); the celebration
  began on December 17 and continued for as many as seven days (duration was lengthened or short-
  ened under various emperors). It included the exchange of gifts and the inversion of roles within the
  household, w/ slaves taking various liberties (albeit temporary), including dining before their masters, and masters dressing casually. The time was set aside for feasts and amusements—thus the
  noise that Pliny mentions (*OCD* 1360–61).
cum . . . personat cum tmp. cl. (AG #545); licentia, -ae (f.) (< licens + -ia) lack of restraint, immoderate behavior {> license}; festus, -a, -um: festal, celebrating a festival; persono (1) (< per + sono,
  sonare) resound
lusus, -us (m.) (< ludo, ludere + -tus) game
obstrepo, obstrepere (< ob + strepo, strepere) overpower w/ sound, counteract; compd. vb + dat.
  lusibus, studiis (AG #370); *obstrepunt*: read w/ both *ipse* (i.e. Pliny) and *illi*; the latter is subj. closest
  to the vb., thus vb. is 3rd pers. rather than 1st (BG #287 Remark a); Pliny, of course, could hardly
  have disturbed the merriment w/ his studies, but perhaps he might have had to shout at the revelers
  to quiet them down.

II.XVII.25
utilitas, utilitatis (f.) (< utilis + -tas) advantage, usefulness, convenience
amoenitas, amoenitatis (f.) (< amoenus + -tas) pleasantness
aqua saliente abl. of separ. w/ *deficitur* (AG #401); salio, salire: jump, spurt, gush; Pliny is likely referring to an absence of water features, e.g. fountains.
puteus, -i (m.) well
potius (adv.) rather, more exactly
fons, fontis (m.) spring {> font}
in summo on the surface (of the ground)
et . . . natura ELLIPSIS of *est*
quocumque . . . humum gen. condit. using 2nd pers. sg. in prod. and indic. in apod. (AG #518a),
  introd. by an indef. relat. (AG #519); *quacumque* (relat. adv.) wherever; *loco*: abl. of place where w/o
  prep. (AG #429); humus, -i (f.) soil
obuius, -a, -um (< ob + uia + -us) presenting itself, lying exposed
umor, umoris (m.) (< umeo, umere + -or) moisture
sincerus, -a, -um sound, clear; ELLIPSIS of *est*

26   maris uicinitate corruptus. Suggerunt adfatim ligna proximae
     siluae; ceteras copias Ostiensis colonia ministrat. Frugi
     quidem homini sufficit etiam uicus, quem una uilla discernit.
     In hoc balinea meritoria tria, magna commoditas, si forte
     balineum domi uel subitus aduentus uel breuior mora cal-

27   facere dissuadeat. Litus ornant uarietate gratissima nunc
     continua nunc intermissa tecta uillarum, quae praestant
     multarum urbium faciem, siue mari siue ipso litore utare;
     quod non numquam longa tranquillitas mollit, saepius fre-

---

uicinitas, uicinitatis (f.) (< uicinus + -tas) proximity, nearness {> vicinity}
corruptus, -a, -um (< ppp. of con + rumpo, rumpere) impure, adulterated

II.XVII.26

suggero, suggerere (< sub + gero, gerere) supply
adfatim (adv.) sufficiently, amply
lignum, -i (n.) wood
uicus, -i (m.) village
discerno, discernere (< dis + cerno, cernere) separate, divide off; i.e. there is a village nearby, separated from Pliny's estate by just a single property
meritorius, -a, -um (< mereo + -torius) let out for hire; ELLIPSIS of *sunt*
commoditas, commoditatis (f.) (< commodus + -tas) convenience
si ... dissuadeat prot. of FlV condit. (AG #516b); *forte* (adv.) (< fors) by chance, as luck would have it;
subitus, -a, -um: suddenly appearing (perhaps < ppp. of subeo, subire (*OLD*) but clearly evolved
into stand-alone adj.); aduentus, -us (m.) (< ad + uenio, uenire + -tus) arrival; calfacio, calfacere
(< caleo, calere + facio, facere) make hot, heat; *aduentus/mora*: subj. of *dissuadeat*; *balineum*: dir.
obj. of *calfacere*; presumably it would have taken some time to get the baths in the villa ready for use.

II.XVII.27

orno (1) (< ordo + -o) decorate, adorn {> ornate}
uarietate gratissima abl. of manner omitting *cum* (AG #412b)
continuus, -a, -um (< con + teneo, tenere + -uus) uninterrupted, w/out pause
intermitto, intermittere, intermisi, intermissus (< inter + mitto, mittere) discontinue, interrupt
praesto (1) (< prae + sto, stare) make available, furnish (*OLD* 9a)
siue ... utare prot. of FLV condit. but w/ indic. apod. (relat. cl. *quae ... faciem*) used to emphasize
change in point of view (AG #516/2b n.); *siue ... siue*: alt. condit. (AG #525c); utor, uti, usus sum:
make use of {> utility}; *utare*: depon. vb. that takes abl. of means (not acc. dir. obj. AG #410)
quod (relat. pron.) anteced. *litore*
tranquillitas, tranquillitatis (f.) quiet state of affairs, tranquillity
mollio, mollire (< mollis + -io) make soft, soften

quens et contrarius fluctus indurat. Mare non sane pretiosis
piscibus abundat, soleas tamen et squillas optimas egerit.
Villa uero nostra etiam mediterraneas copias praestat, lac in
primis; nam illuc e pascuis pecora conueniunt, si quando
aquam umbramue sectantur.

Iustisne de causis iam tibi uideor incolere inhabitare diligere secessum? quem tu nimis urbanus es nisi concupiscis.
Atque utinam concupiscas! ut tot tantisque dotibus uillulae
nostrae maxima commendatio ex tuo contubernio accedat.
Vale.

28

29

---

induro (1) (< in + duro, durare + -o) make hard, harden

II.XVII.28
pretiosus, -a, -um (< pretium + -osus) valuable
abundo (1) (< ab + undo, undare) overflow, abound {> abundant}
solea, -ae (f.) sole (flat fish)
squilla, -ae (f.) shrimp
egero, egerere (< ex + gero, gerere) bring forth, yield
lac, lactis (n.) milk {> lactate}
in primis above all else, first and foremost
pascuum, -i (n.) (< pasco + -uus) pasture
pecus, pecoris (n.) herd, flock
sector, sectari, sectatus sum (< ppp. of sequor, sequi) pursue

II.XVII.29
Iustis . . . secessum using ASYNDETON, Pliny stresses how much he treasures this retreat
quem . . . concupiscis simple condit. (indic.) (AG #514a); *quem* (relat. pron.), anteced. *secessum*; urba-
    nus, -a, -um (< urbs + -anus) pertaining to the city, witty, urbane; concupisco, concupiscere (< con
    + cupio, cupere + -sco) desire ardently, covet
concupiscas opt. subjv. w/*utinam* (AG #442)
ut . . . accedat purp. cl. (AG #531/1); *dotibus*: dat. of indir. obj. w/ compd. vb. *accedat* (AG #370); dos,
    dotis (f.) quality, attribute; commendatio, commendationis (f.) (< commendo, commendere + -tio)
    recommendation, esteem; contubernium, -i (n.) (< con + taberna + -ium) cohabitation,
    association

xx—REGULUS THE LEGACY HUNTER

C. PLINIVS CALVISIO SVO S.

1   Assem para et accipe auream fabulam, fabulas immo; nam
me priorum noua admonuit, nec refert a qua potissimum

2   incipiam. Verania Pisonis grauiter iacebat, huius dico Pisonis,
quem Galba adoptauit. Ad hanc Regulus uenit. Primum
impudentiam hominis, qui uenerit ad aegram, cuius marito
inimicissimus, ipsi inuisissimus fuerat! Esto, si uenit tantum;

3   at ille etiam proximus toro sedit, quo die qua hora nata esset

---

II.xx: Pliny recounts a series of episodes that demonstrate the despicable behavior of his archenemy
Regulus (also the subject of IV.II), whom he casts here in the role of the *captator*, a legacy hunter,
i.e. someone who cultivates the vulnerable in order to receive otherwise undeserved legacies.

Addressee: Calvisius Rufus, a close friend and fellow townsman of Pliny, who receives six letters from
Pliny that focus on proper behavior, both in business matters and in leisure (SW 202, AB 46–7).

II.xx.1

as, assis (m.) a bronze coin, penny; the value of Roman coinage varied drastically in different time
periods and under individual emperors, both in the weight of each denomination and in its metal
content; an 'as' was a small bronze or copper coin, w/ four being equal in value to a sestertius, and
eight a denarius (devalued from the original ten that gave the denarius its name); there were also
various fractions of all three coins, as well as a gold coin, the aureus (*OCD* s. Roman coinage,
358–61), which was the equivalent of 25 denarii.

aureus, -a, -um (< aurum + -eus) golden

fabula, -ae (f.) tale, gossip {> fabulous}

immo (pcl.) rather, more precisely

prior, prius (compar. adj.) (< primus) previous, earlier; *priorum, fabulorum* understood: gen. ff. vb.
of reminding *admonuit* (AG #351); admoneo, admonere, admonui, admonitus (< ad + moneo,
monere) remind {> admonish}

a qua . . . incipiam indir. quest. (AG #574); *potissimum* (adv.) especially; incipio, incipere (< in +
capio, capere) begin {> incipient}

II.xx.2

Verania Pisonis Verania's husband L. Calpurnius Piso Frugi Licinianus held no political office in
Rome until his adoption by the emperor Galba, when he became heir apparent to the principate.
She receives exceptional praise in Tacitus' account of her husband's assassination, because she
demanded and received the right to bury him (*Hist.* 1.47). It was standard Roman practice to refer
to a married woman by her gentilicium followed by her husband's name in poss. gen.

grauiter (adv.) (< grauis) seriously; i.e. seriously ill

Pisonis Pliny's repetition of Piso's name emphasizes Verania's status.

adopto (1) (< ad + opto, optare) adopt legally; adoption of adult men was not unusual in Rome, as it
offered Roman men who were childless a means to pass on their names and their fortunes. Although
Piso's adoption led to his death, the adoption of competent successors by a series of childless emperors (Nerva, Trajan, Hadrian, and Antoninus Pius) provided the principate w/ almost 100 years of
unprecedented stability (*OCD* s. adoption, 13).

Regulus M. Aquil(l)ius Regulus made his reputation in the courts as an advocate, particularly in his
prosecutions of three men of consular rank under Nero for which he was handsomely rewarded both
financially and w/ a priesthood and the office of quaestor. His career stalled under the Flavians until

interrogauit. Vbi audiit, componit uultum intendit oculos
movet labra, agitat digitos computat. Nihil. Vt diu miseram exspectatione suspendit, 'Habes' inquit 'climactericum
tempus sed euades. Quod ut tibi magis liqueat, haruspicem   4
consulam, quem sum frequenter expertus.' Nec mora, sacri-   5

Domitian, under whom his prosecutorial career was revived (SW 93–4, AB 37–8, *OCD* 133–4). Regulus serves in the *Epistulae* as a type of anti-Pliny, behaving in all the ways a Roman man should not.

impudentia, -ae (f.) (< in + pudens + -ia) shamelessness, impudence; *impudentiam*: acc. of exclam.
(AG #397d)

qui uenerit relat. cl. of char. (AG #535), anteced. *hominis*

aeger, aegra, aegrum ill, ailing; *aegram*: subst. use (AG #288)

maritus, -i (m.) husband {> marital}; *marito*: dat. w/ adj. *inimicissimus* (AG #384)

ipsi i.e. Verania; dat. w/ adj. *inuisissimus* (AG #384); inuisissimus, -a, -um (superl. adj.) (< inuisus, -a,
-um < ppp. of in + uideo, uidere) extemely odious; i.e. she could not stand the sight of him

II.XX.3

Esto fut. impv. of sum, esse; "So be it" (*OLD* 8b)

si . . . tantum simple condit. (indic.) (AG #514a)

at (conj.) but (introd. a new point in the argument AG #324d)

torus, -i (m.) conjugal bed; *toro*: dat. w/ adj. *proximus* (AG #384)

quo . . . esset indir. quest. (AG #574); *quo die qua hora*: Pliny's use of ASYNDETON suggests the speed at
which Regulus verbally assails Verania. Regulus is about to make a display of his astrological knowledge for which he needs Verania's date and time of birth. Astrology, which had its origins in the Hellenistic world, became quite popular in Rome, w/ a number of adherents, including the emperor
Tiberius and many of his successors (*OCD* s. astrology, 195).

audiit = contr. form of *audiuit* (AG #181)

componit . . . computat uultus, -us (m.) countenance, facial expression; intendo, intendere
(< in + tendo, tendere) stretch, direct (one's eyes) (*OLD* 6c); labrum, -i (n.) lip; agito
(1) (< ago, agere + -ito) set in motion, busy oneself in (*OLD* 11a) {> agitate}; digitus, -i (m.) finger
{> digital}; computo (1) (< con + puto, putare) calculate, reckon; again Pliny's use of ASYNDETON
emphasizes the rapid-fire nature of Regulus' impudent actions that easily overwhelmed his victim.
The shift to the hist. use of pres. tense further enlivens his fabula (AG #469).

Vt . . . suspendit tmp. use of *ut* w/ indic. (AG #543), "while"; *miseram*: *eam* understood; exspectatio,
ionis (f.) (< ex + specto, spectare + -tio) expectancy, the state of waiting in suspense; suspendo,
suspendere (sub + pendo, pendere) hang, keep a person in a state of uncertainty (*OLD* 7a)

climactericus, -a, -um (< Gr. κλιμακτηρικός) critical; a κλιμακτήρ (a 'rung') was an astrological term
that indicated a critical point in a human life; it occurred every seven years (*OLD*).

euado, euadere (< ex + uado, uadere) come through to the other side (*OLD* 3a), escape

II.XX.4

quod (relat. pron.) anteced. *tempus*

ut . . . liqueat purp. cl. (AG #531/1); liqueo, liquere: appear clear, be free from doubt

haruspex, haruspicis (m.) a type of diviner; to reinforce his astrological calculations, Regulus now brings
in external support in the form of a *haruspex*. The Romans used three types of divination: augury, the
consulation of the Sybilline books, and haruspicy. *Haruspices* were Etruscan aristocrats who were called
on to interpret prodigies and portents and to read the entrails of sacrificed animals, particularly the liver,
in order to obtain divine insight into the future (*OCD* s. divination, 488, and haruspices, 667–8).

consulo, consulere consult (in divination)

frequenter (adv.) on many occasions, repeatedly (*OLD* 2)

ficium facit, adfirmat exta cum siderum significatione congruere. Illa ut in periculo credula poscit codicillos, legatum
Regulo scribit. Mox ingrauescit, clamat moriens hominem
nequam perfidum ac plus etiam quam periurum, qui sibi per

6   salutem filii peierasset. Facit hoc Regulus non minus scelerate
quam frequenter, quod iram deorum, quos ipse cotidie fallit,
in caput infelicis pueri detestatur.

7   Velleius Blaesus ille locuples consularis nouissima uale-
tudine conflictabatur: cupiebat mutare testamentum. Regulus qui speraret aliquid ex nouis tabulis, quia nuper captare
eum coeperat, medicos hortari rogare, quoquo modo spiri-

II.xx.5

adfirmo (1) (< ad + firmo, firmare) confirm, corroborate; *exta … congruere*: indir. disc. (AG #580);
exta, extorum (n.) internal organs of an animal; sidus, sideris (n.) heavenly body, constellation; sig-
nificatio, significationis (f.) (< signum + facio, facere + io) outward sign, indication; congruo, congruere: agree, coincide {> congruent}

ut … credula *ut* w/ indic. "as" (AG #527f), *est* understood; credulus, -a, -um (< credo, credere +ulus)
prone to believe or trust {> credulous}

codicillus, -i (m.) a supplement to a will, pl.: writing tablets {> codicil}; Roman wills among the elite
were often complex documents that not only named heirs but also left legacies of varying amounts to
friends and associates based on closeness of relationships and the esteem in which the named individuals were held. Thus a will might need to be revised or amended frequently as circumstances warranted.

legatum, -i (n.) (< ppp. of lego, legare) legacy, bequest

ingrauesco, ingrauescere (< in + grauis + -esco) grow worse

hominem … periurum indir. disc. (AG #580), ELLIPSIS of *esse*; nequam (indecl. adj.) morally worth-
less, depraved; perfidus, -a, -um (< per + fidus + -us) treacherous, deceitful; periurus, -a, -um: one
who has deliberately broken an oath {> perjury}

qui … peierasset relat. cl. in indir. disc., subjv. vb. when opinion is of someone other than the author
(AG #591); salus, salutis (f.) (< saluus) safety, well-being; peiero (1) (< per + iuro, iurare) swear
falsely; *peierasset* = contr. form of *peierauisset* (AG #181); Pliny uses POLYPTOTON (*periurum …
perierasset*) to drive home Aurelia's assessment of Regulus' character.

II.xx.6

scelerate (adv.) (< sceleratus < scelus + -atus) atrociously, w/ incredible wickedness

quod (conj.) inasmuch as, because

fallo, fallere escape the clutches of, elude (*OLD* 7a)

infelix, infelicis (< in + felix) unfortunate, ill-fated

detestor, detestari, detestatus sum (< de + testis + -or) call down

II.xx.7

Velleius Blaesus Nothing certain is known about this former consul, though he may be referred to by
the poets Statius (*Silv.* II.1.191, 3.77) and Martial (VIII.38) (SW 203).

locuples, locupletis (< locus + *pleo*) rich (in lands)

consularis, consulare (< consul + -aris) of consular rank, having been a consul

conflicto (1) (< con + fligo, fligere + -to) harass, distress

tum homini prorogarent. Postquam signatum est testa-   8
mentum, mutat personam, uertit adlocutionem isdemque
medicis: 'Quousque miserum cruciatis? quid inuidetis bona
morte, cui dare uitam non potestis?' Moritur Blaesus et,
tamquam omnia audisset, Regulo ne tantulum quidem.
Sufficiunt duae fabulae, an scholastica lege tertiam poscis?   9
est unde fiat. Aurelia ornata femina signatura testamentum   10
sumpserat pulcherrimas tunicas. Regulus cum uenisset ad

---

testamentum, -i (n.) (< testor + -mentum) will, testament (s. I.ix.2n. on ad signandum testamentum)
qui speraret relat. cl. of char. (AG #535); "as the sort of man who expected..."
tabula, -ae (f.) writing tablet
nuper (adv.) recently
capto (1) (< capio, capere + -to) court the favor of in order to receive a legacy (*OLD* 9b)
coepi, coepisse (pf. stem only) begin
medicus, -i (m.) (< medeor, mederi + -cus) doctor {> medicine}
hortari rogare hist. infs. (AG #463), w/ whose use Pliny creates the sense of factual narrative
quoquo ... prorogarent indir. quest. (AG #574); quisquis, quidquid (indef. pron.) (< quis, quid)
    anyone, anything—except in abl. when it is used as an adj. (AG #151b n.2); *quoquo*: some; spiritus, -us
    (m.) (< spiro, spirare + -tus) breath, life (by METONYMY); prorogo (1) (< pro + rogo, rogare) prolong

II.XX.8
signo (1) (< signum + -o) attest (a will or contract) by affixing a seal (*OLD* 8b)
persona, -ae (f.) mask (used in a play), character
adlocutio, -ionis (f.) (< ad + loquor, loqui + -tio) manner of addressing
Quousque (interrog. adv.) how far, how long
crucio (1) (< crux + -o) torture {> excruciate}
quid (interrog. adv.) why (*OLD* quis, quid 16a)
inuideo, inuidere (< in + uideo, uidere) begrudge (dat. of pers.) of (abl. of thing) (*OLD* 2c)
    {> invidious}
tamquam ... audisset condit. cl. of compar. (AG #524); *audisset* = contr. form of *audiuisset* (AG #181)
tantulus, -a, -um (< tantus + -ulus) so small, such a little; subst.: so small an amount; *est* understood;
    i.e. in Blaesus' will

II.XX.9
scholasticus, -a, -um (< Gr. σχολαστικός) concerning a school of rhetoric, of a scholar; traditionally a
    rhetorical argument contained no more than three major points (Quintilian IV.5.3 and *Rhetorica ad
    Herennium* 1.17).
tertius, -a, -um third {> tertiary}
est unde fiat lit. "there is (a place) whence it may be done"; i.e. "it can be done"

II.XX.10
Aurelia Pliny gives insufficient detail to identify this woman, although his use of the adj. *ornata* makes
    it clear that she was of senatorial rank; ornatus, -a, -um: rich, distinguished {> ornate}
sumo, sumere, sumpsi, sumptus put on
cum uenisset cum circumst. cl. (AG #546)

11   signandum, 'Rogo' inquit 'has mihi leges.' Aurelia ludere
      hominem putabat, ille serio instabat; ne multa, coegit
      mulierem aperire tabulas ac sibi tunicas quas erat induta
      legare; obseruauit scribentem, inspexit an scripsisset. Et
      Aurelia quidem uiuit, ille tamen istud tamquam morituram
      coegit. Et hic hereditates, hic legata quasi mereatur accipit.
12   Ἀλλὰ τί διατείνομαι in ea ciuitate, in qua iam pridem
      non minora praemia, immo maiora nequitia et improbitas

---

has . . . leges subst. cl. of purp. (AG #563) (= indir. comm.) ff. *Rogo, ut* omitted; *has*: i.e. *tunicas*; lego
      (1) (< lex + o) bequeath, leave as a legacy

II.xx.11
ludere hominem indir. disc. (AG #580) ff. *putabat*; ludo, ludere: play, joke
serio (adv.) not playfully, seriously
insto (1) (< in + sto, stare) press on
ne multa in brief, to cut a long story short (*OLD* multus, -a, -um 3b)
cogo, cogere, coegi, coactus (< con + ago, agere) compel; w/ obj. inf. *aperire* (AG #563d); aperio,
      aperire: open {> aperture}
induo, induere, indui, indutus put on
obseruo (1) (< ob + seruo, seruare) keep an eye on
inspicio, inspicere, inspexi, inspectus (< in + specio, specere) inspect, examine
an scripsisset indir. quest. (AG #574) introd. by *inspexit; an*: "whether" ("or not" implied)
iste, ista, istud (demon. adj.) that, those
tamquam morituram condit. cl. of compar. (AG #524), *eam* understood, ELLIPSIS of *esset*
hereditas, hereditatis (f.) (< heres + -tas) inheritance {> heredity}
quasi mereatur condit. cl. of compar. (AG #524); mereor, mereri, meritus sum: earn, deserve
      {> merit}

II.xx.12
Ἀλλὰ τί διατείνομαι Gr.: "But why do I stir myself up"; Pliny refers here to Demosthenes
      (s. IX.XXIII.5n.) *De Corona* 142.
ciuitas, ciuitatis (f.) (< ciuis + -tas) state
iam pridem for a long time, well before now; w/ pres. tense: action begun in past but continuing in
      pres. (AG #466)
nequitia, -ae (f.) (< nequam + -ia) depravity, villainy
improbitas, improbitatis (f.) (< in + probus + -tas) dishonesty, shamelessness

quam pudor et uirtus habent? Adspice Regulum, qui ex   13
paupere et tenui ad tantas opes per flagitia processit, ut ipse
mihi dixerit, cum consuleret quam cito sestertium sescentiens
impleturus esset, inuenisse se exta duplicia, quibus portendi miliens et ducentiens habiturum. Et habebit, si modo   14
ut coepit, aliena testamenta, quod est improbissimum genus
falsi, ipsis quorum sunt illa dictauerit. Vale.

---

pudor, pudoris (m.) (< pudeo, pudere + -or) honor

II.xx.13

adspicio, adspicere (< ad + specio, specere) behold, look at {> aspect}

ex paupere et tenui *uita* understood; pauper, pauperis: poor; tenuis, tenue: thin, meager, modest

ops, opis (f.) power, pl.: financial resources

flagitium, -i (n.) disgrace, shameful act

procedo, procedere, processi, processus (< pro + cedo, cedere) move forward, advance

ut . . . dixerit *ut* w/ indic. "as" (AG #527f)

cum consuleret cum circumst. cl. (AG #546)

quam . . . esset indir. quest. (AG #574); *quam* (interrog. adv.) how; *cito* (adv.) quickly; sestertium, -i
  (n.) 100,000 sesterces (s. II.xx.1n. on as); *sescentiens* (adv.) 600 times, w/ *sestertium* = 60,000,000
  sesterces; impleo, implere: fill up, amount to, attain to the full

inuenisse . . . habiturum series of indir. disc. (AG #580) ff. *dixerit*; (1) *inuenisse . . . duplicia*; duplex,
  duplicis: double; (2) *quibus portendi*; *quibus* (relat. pron.): abl. of means (AG #409), anteced. *exta*;
  portendo, portendere: indicate; *portendi*: pres. pass. inf.; relat. cl. in indir. disc. uses inf. form when
  relat. pron. functions as demon. (AG #583b); (3) *(se) habiturum (esse)* ff. *portendi*; *miliens* (adv.): a
  thousand times; *ducentiens* (adv.): two hundred times; *sestertium* understood, thus twice 60,000,000
  or 120,000,000 sesterces

II.xx.14

habebit, si . . . dictauerit FMV condit. (AG #516c); *modo* (adv.) only; *ut coepit*: ut w/ indic. "as" (AG
  #527f); alienus, -a, -um (< alius + -enus) belonging to another; improbissimus, -a, -um (superl. adj.)
  (< improbus, -a, -um) most shameless, greedy; genus, generis (n.) a kind or sort of thing (*OLD* 9)
  {> generic}; falsum, -i (n.) fraud; *ipsis quorum sunt illa*: "to those very people whose (wills) they are";
  dicto (1) (< dico + -to) compose, recite, dictate

BOOK III

iii—RECOMMENDING A TUTOR

C. PLINIVS CORELLIAE HISPVLLAE SVAE S.

Cum patrem tuum grauissimum et sanctissimum uirum   1
suspexerim magis an amauerim dubitem, teque et in memoriam eius et in honorem tuum unice diligam, cupiam necesse
est atque etiam quantum in me fuerit enitar, ut filius tuus
auo similis exsistat; equidem malo materno, quamquam illi
paternus etiam clarus spectatusque contigerit, pater quoque

III.III: Pliny writes to recommend a tutor for the grandson of one of his mentors and in doing so gives
details of just what qualities should be sought for a young man from so distinguished a family.

Addressee: Corellia Hispulla was the daughter of Corellius Rufus, whom Pliny praises as his guide and
guardian (*Ep.* I.XII). She was likely married to the well-known jurisconsult Lucius Neratius Priscus
(AB 51–52, C 73–75).

III.III.1

Cum ... dubitem 1st half of compd. cum causal cl. (AG #549) containing indir. quest. (AG #574)
suspexerim ... an amauerim, ff. *dubitem*; *an* (pcl.) or ("whether" implied); grauissimus, -a, -um
(superl. adj.) (< grauis, graue) venerable (*OLD* 13a) {> gravity}; sanctissimus, -a, -um (superl. adj.)
(< sanctus, -a, -um) most upright, virtuous (*OLD* 4); suspicio, suspicere, suspexi, suspectus
(< sub + specio, specere) look up to, admire

teque ... diligam 2nd half of cum causal cl.; *unice* (adv.) (< unicus, -a, -um) particularly, especially
{> unique}; in this uncharacteristically convoluted series of cls., Pliny lays out the reasons he is
compelled to make what is likely an unsolicited recommendation.

cupiam ... enitar subst. cl. of result w/ *ut* omitted (AG #569 n. 2) ff. *necesse est*; *quantum ... fuerit*:
relat. cl. of char. (AG #535); enitor, eniti, enixus sum (< ex + nitor, niti) strive, take pains

ut ... exsistat purp. cl. (AG #531/1); auus, -i (m.) grandfather; *auo*: dat. w/ adj. (AG #384); exsisto,
exsistere (< ex + sisto) emerge, prove to be

maternus, -a, -um (< mater + -nus) maternal; *auo* understood

quamquam ... contigerit conces. cl. w/ subjv. (usu. indic. w/ *quamquam*) (AG #527e); paternus, -a,
-um (<pater + nus) paternal; *auus* understood; clarus, -a, -um: bright, well-known, famous
{> clarity}; spectatus, -a, -um (<ppp. of specto, spectare) distinguished, of observed merit; contingo, contingere, contigi, contactus (< con + tango, tangere) fall to one's lot, be granted to (dat.)
(*OLD* 8a)

2   et patruus inlustri laude conspicui. Quibus omnibus ita de-
           mum similis adolescet, si imbutus honestis artibus fuerit,

3   quas plurimum refert a quo potissimum accipiat. Adhuc
           illum pueritiae ratio intra contubernium tuum tenuit, prae-
           ceptores domi habuit, ubi est erroribus modica uel etiam
           nulla materia. Iam studia eius extra limen proferenda sunt,
           iam circumspiciendus rhetor Latinus, cuius scholae seueritas

---

patruus, -i (m.) (< pater + -uus) father's brother, uncle

inlustri laude abl. of specif. (AG #418); inlustris, inlustre: brilliant, distinguished {> illustrious}

conspicuus, -a, -um (< con + specio, specere + -uus) notable, famous; *conspicui* modifying both *pater* and *patruus*, ELLIPSIS of *sunt*

III.III.2

Quibus ... adolescet, si ... fuerit FMV condit. (AG #516c); *quibus* (relat. pron.), anteced. all the male relatives mentioned above; *ita demum* (adv.) only (if) (*OLD* demum 2b); adolesco, adolescere: grow up, reach manhood {> adolescent}; imbuo, imbuere, imbui, imbutus: drench, give (acc. of pers.) initial instruction in (*OLD* 4a); *honestis artibus*: abl. of means (AG #409)

quas (relat. pron.) anteced. *artibus*; dir. obj. of *accipiat*

plurimum (adv.) most of all, to the greatest extent

a quo ... accipiat relat. cl. of char. (AG #535); *potissimum* (adv.) especially, above all; w/ use of superls. *plurimum* and *potissimum*, Pliny insists fervently that his teacher will be critical in the shaping of the boy's character.

III.III.3

pueritia, -ae (f.) (< puer + -itia) boyhood

contubernium, -i (n.) (< con + taberna + -ium) cohabitation, living together

praeceptor, praeceptoris (m.) (<prae + capio, capere + -tor) teacher, tutor; it was not unusual for elite Roman children to receive formal instruction within their homes from private tutors beginning at about seven years of age. In early adolescence, generally at age thirteen or fourteen, boys contin-ued their education w/ a teacher of rhetoric and left the careful vigilance of their household. Thus it was imperative to find a well-respected instructor, who would carefully guard his student's reputa-tion in addition to providing proper instruction (*OCD* s. Roman education, 509–10).

erroribus dat. of purp. (AG #382)

materia, -ae (f.) (< mater + -ia) means, potential (*OLD* 8)

limen, liminis (n.) threshold; i.e. the household (METONYMY) {> liminal}

proferenda sunt ... circumspiciendus 2nd (pass.) periphr. conjug. (AG #196 and 500/2); profero, proferre (< pro + fero, ferre) bring forth; circumspicio, circumspicere (< circum + specio, specere) look around for, search for

rhetor, rhetoris (m.) (< Gr. ῥήτωρ) one who teaches public speaking or the art of persuasion {> rhetoric}

cuius ... constet relat. cl. of char. (AG #535); seueritas, seueritatis (f.) (< seuerus + -tas) strictness, sternness; pudor, pudoris (m.) (< pudeo, pudere + -or) feeling of shame, honor; *in primis*: above all else, first and foremost; castitas, castitatis (f.) (< castus + -tas) moral purity, integrity {> chastity}; consto (1) (< con + sto, stare) be fixed or established (*OLD* 8a); Pliny's use of ASYNDETON to list the requirements of the school to which Corellia's son must go stresses the seriousness of the quali-ties he sets forth. The sg. vb. *constet* makes these three virtues inseparable.

pudor in primis castitas constet. Adest enim adulescenti   4
nostro cum ceteris naturae fortunaeque dotibus eximia corporis pulchritudo, cui in hoc lubrico aetatis non praeceptor
modo sed custos etiam rectorque quaerendus est. Videor ergo   5
demonstrare tibi posse Iulium Genitorem. Amatur a me;
iudicio tamen meo non obstat caritas hominis, quae ex
iudicio nata est. Vir est emendatus et grauis, paulo etiam
horridior et durior, ut in hac licentia temporum. Quantum   6
eloquentia ualeat, pluribus credere potes, nam dicendi facultas aperta et exposita statim cernitur; uita hominum altos

---

III.III.4

adulescens, adulescentis (m.) (< pres. ptc. adolesco, adolescere) young person; *adulescenti*: dat. of poss. (AG #373)

dos, dotis (f.) quality, attribute

eximius, -a, -um (< ex + emo, emere + -ius) exceptional, remarkable

pulchritudo, pulchritudinis (f.) (< pulcher + -tudo) handsomeness, beauty

cui (relat. pron.) anteced. *adulescenti*

lubricus, -a, -um slippery; n. subst.: a dangerous period or situation (*OLD* 4b)

custos, custodis (m.) guardian, protector {> custody}

rector, rectoris (m.) (< rego, regere + -tor) guide, tutor

quaerendus est 2nd (pass.) periphr. conjug. (AG #196 and 500/2); quaero, quaerere: search for, seek

III.III.5

demonstro (1) (< de + monstro, monstrare) recommend

Iulius Genitor Julius Genitor is unknown outside of Pliny's letters, but he was clearly well known to Pliny, who addresses three letters to him (*Ep.* III.XI, *Ep.* VII.XXX, and IX.XVII).

iudicio meo dat. of indir. obj. w/ compd. vb. *obstat* (AG #370); obsto (1): (< ob + sto, stare) stand in the way

caritas, caritatis (f.) (< carus + -tas) affection, esteem; *hominis*: objv. gen. (AG #347)

emendatus, -a, -um (< ppp. of emendo, emendare) faultless

grauis, graue serious {> gravity}

paulo somewhat, by a little; abl. of deg. of diff. (AG #414)

horridus, -a, -um (< horreo, horrere + -idus) harsh, severe

durus, -a, -um strict, austere

ut (conj.) considering, taking into account (*OLD* 22)

licentia, -ae (f.) (< licens + -ia) lack of restraint, immoderate behavior {> license}

III.III.6

quantum . . . ualeat indir. quest. (AG #574) ff. *credere*; *quantum* (interr. adv.) (< quam + -to + -um) how much, how greatly; eloquentia, -ae (f.) (< pres. ptc. of eloquor + -ia) speaking ability, eloquence

plures, plura subst.: more/many people

facultas, facultatis (f.) ability, power {> faculty}

apertus, -a, -um (< ppp. of aperio, aperire) open, visible to all (*OLD* 9)

expositus, -a, -um (< ppp. of ex + pono, ponere) plain, w/ no concealment {> expository}

cerno, cernere distinguish, discern, perceive

recessus magnasque latebras habet, cuius pro Genitore me
sponsorem accipe. Nihil ex hoc uiro filius tuus audiet nisi
profuturum, nihil discet quod nescisse rectius fuerit, nec
minus saepe ab illo quam a te meque admonebitur, quibus
imaginibus oneretur, quae nomina et quanta sustineat.

7　Proinde fauentibus dis trade eum praeceptori, a quo mores
primum mox eloquentiam discat, quae male sine moribus
discitur. Vale.

vi—DEDICATING A STATUE

C. PLINIVS ANNIO SEVERO SVO S.

1　Ex hereditate quae mihi obuenit, emi proxime Corinthium
signum, modicum quidem sed festiuum et expressum, quan-

---

recessus, -us (m.) (< re + cedo, cedere + -tus) place of withdrawal or seclusion, recess

latebra, -ae (f.) (< lateo, latere) hiding place {> latent}

cuius (relat. pron.) anteced. *uita*

sponsor, sponsoris (m.) (< spondeo, spondere + -tor) guarantor, surety; *sponsorem*: appos. to *me*

prosum, prodesse, profui, profuturus (< pro + sum, esse) be useful, be beneficial

disco, discere learn

quod . . . fuerit relat. cl. of char. (AG #535); *nescisse* = contr. form of *nesciuisse* (AG #181); *rectius* (compar. adj.) (< rectus, -a, -um) more proper (morally)

admoneo, admonere (< ad + moneo, monere) remind {> admonish}

quibus . . . oneretur, quae . . . quanta sustineat indir. quest. (AG #574) ff. *admonebitur*; imago, imaginis (f.) ancestor's death mask; ancestor by METONYMY; onero (1) (< onus + -o) supply in abundance; quantus, -a, -um (interrog. adj.) (< quam + -to + -us) how great; sustineo, sustinere (< sub(s) + teneo, tenere) hold up, maintain {> sustain}; it was standard practice among elite Romans to display images (*imagines*) of their ancestors in their homes, using busts and death masks. These generally appeared in the atrium, into which friends and clients of the paterfamilias, the head of the family, came daily to visit or for the morning *salutatio*, a formalized practice in which clients would come to their patron's house early in the morning to greet him and to accompany him to the forum (*OCD* 1350). The primary function of the *imagines* was to remind the wider community of the family's status and achievements. Clearly any child living in the midst of these memorials to greatness would have been acutely aware of the expectations placed upon him.

III.III.7

fauentibus dis abl. abs. (AG #419); faueo, fauere: be favorably inclined, approve; *dis* = *deis*

trado, tradere (< trans + do, dare) hand over, surrender {> tradition}

a quo . . . discat relat. cl. of char. (AG #535); mos, moris (f.) custom, pl.: character, virtuous habits {> moral}

quae (relat. pron.) anteced. *eloquentiam*

III.VI: Pliny describes a statue he has purchased with an inheritance and asks his friend to make arrangements for its public display in Comum.

Addressee: Annius Severus was a fellow citizen of Comum and close friend of Pliny's who receives several letters about Pliny's inheritances (SW 185, AB 37).

tum ego sapio, qui fortasse in omni re, in hac certe perquam
exiguum sapio: hoc tamen signum ego quoque intellego. Est
enim nudum, nec aut uitia si qua sunt celat, aut laudes parum
ostentat. Effingit senem stantem; ossa musculi nerui, uenae
rugae etiam ut spirantis adparent; rari et cedentes capilli,

2

III.VI.1

hereditas, hereditatis (f.) (< heres + -tas) inheritance {> heredity}

obuenio, obuenire, obueni, obuentus (< ob + uenio, uenire) be assigned to (dat.), come one's (dat.) way

emo, emere, emi, emptus buy

proxime (adv.) very recently

Corinthius, -a, -um Corinthian; i.e. a type of bronze, one of several well-known varieties of bronze in the Mediterranean, made distinct by the amounts of copper and tin in the alloy and by the addition of other metals, both of which modified the resulting color of the bronze. In his *Natural History*, Pliny the Elder describes several types of Corinthian bronze as alloys produced w/ silver, gold, or a variety of metals (34.7).

signum, -i (n.) statue, sculpture (*OLD* 12a)

festiuus, -a, -um (< festus + -iuus) excellent, fine

expressus, -a, -um (< ppp. ex + premo, premere) clearly defined, distinct

quantum, -i (n.) (relat. pron.) (< quam + -to + -um) according to what (*OLD* 7a)

sapio, sapere understand, know {> sapient}

perquam (adv.) extremely, exceedingly

exiguus, -a, -um (< ex + ago, agere + -uus) small (in amount), scanty

quoque (adv.) even, indeed

intellego, intellegere (< inter + lego, legere) understand the value of, appreciate

III.VI.2

uitium, -i (n.) fault, defect

qua = *aliqua* (s. I.I.1n. on quas)

celo (1) hide

ostento (1) (< ob + tendo, tendere + -to) display {> ostentatious}

effingo, effingere (< ex + fingo, fingere) portray, depict

senex, senis (m.) old man {> senile}

os, ossis (n.) bone

musculus, -i (m.) (< mus + culus) muscle; lit. little mouse, because the shape of some muscles and their movement were thought to resemble those of mice

neruus, -i (m.) sinew

uena, -ae (f.) vein

ruga, -ae (f.) wrinkle

ut ... adparent *ut* w/ indic. "as" (AG #527f); spiro (1) breathe, i.e. be alive {> respiration}; *spirantis*: gen. of quality (AG #345), "of someone living"; adpareo, adparere (< ad + pareo, parere) be seen physically, appear; in this description, as often in Pliny, the use of ASYNDETON conveys a sense of excitement and even awe in what is described. The effect continues, heightened further by the ELLIPSIS of *esse* in the ff. phrases.

rarus, -a, -um thinly spaced, sparse

cedo, cedere withdraw, recede

capillus, -i (m.) hair

3

4

5

    lata frons, contracta facies, exile collum; pendent lacerti,
papillae iacent, uenter recessit; a tergo quoque eadem aetas
ut a tergo. Aes ipsum, quantum uerus color indicat, uetus et
antiquum; talia denique omnia, ut possint artificum oculos
tenere, delectare imperitorum. Quod me quamquam tirun-
culum sollicitauit ad emendum. Emi autem non ut haberem
domi (neque enim ullum adhuc Corinthium domi habeo),
uerum ut in patria nostra celebri loco ponerem, ac potissimum in Iouis templo; uidetur enim dignum templo dignum
deo donum. Tu ergo, ut soles omnia quae a me tibi iniungun-

---

frons, frontis (f.) forehead
contractus, -a, -um (< ppp. of con + traho, trahere) pinched, drawn together
facies, faciei (f.) face
exilis, exile thin, narrow
collum, -i (n.) neck
pendeo, pendere hang down loosely (*OLD* 5b)
lacertus, -i (m.) upper arm
papilla, -ae (f.) (< papula + -illa) nipple
uenter, uentris (m.) belly, abdomen
recedo, recedere, recessi, recessus (< re + cedo, cedere) draw back, recede

III.VI.3
tergum, -i (n.) back
ut a tergo "as (one might expect) from the back (of someone)"; i.e. the look of an old man
aes, aeris (n.) bronze
quantum, -i (n.) (relat. adv.) insofar as (*OLD* 7)
indico (1) (< in + dico, dicare) show, display
uetus, ueteris old, having been in existence a long time {> veteran}
ut ... imperitorum result cl. (AG #537); artifex, artificis (m.) (< ars + -fex) master craftsman, artist;
    imperitus, -a, -um (< in + peritus) unskilled, lacking knowledge

III.VI.4
Quod (relat. pron.) anteced. Pliny's description of the statue
tirunculus, -i (m.) (< tiro + -culus) beginner, recruit; appos. to *me*
sollicito (1) (< sollus + citus (ppp. of ciero, ciere) + -o) tempt, encourage {> solicit}
ad emendum gerv. purp. constr. w/ ad (AG #506)
non ut ... haberem ... uerum ut ... ponerem parallel and opposing purp. cls. (AG #531/1); i.e. Pliny
    has no personal collection of Corinthian bronzes; *uerum* (conj.) but in fact; *patria nostra*:
    i.e. Comum; celeber, celebris, celebre: much used, busy
potissimum (adv.) especially, above all
Iuppiter, Iouis (m.) Jupiter, whose temple precinct would have been in a prominent and easily visited
    location in Comum

III.VI.5
templo, deo abl. of specif. (AG #418b) w/ *dignum*
ut soles *ut* w/ indic. "as" (AG #527f); vb. like *agere* understood
iniungo, iniungere (< in + iungo, iungere) impose (+ dat. *tibi*)

tur, suscipe hanc curam, et iam nunc iube basim fieri, ex quo
uoles marmore, quae nomen meum honoresque capiat, si hos
quoque putabis addendos. Ego signum ipsum, ut primum   6
inuenero aliquem qui non grauetur, mittam tibi uel ipse
(quod mauis) adferam mecum. Destino enim, si tamen officii
ratio permiserit, excurrere isto. Gaudes quod me uenturum   7
esse polliceor, sed contrahes frontem, cum adiecero 'ad paucos dies': neque enim diutius abesse me eadem haec quae
nondum exire patiuntur. Vale.

---

iam nunc   at this point now

basis, basis (f.)   (< Gr. βάσις) base, pedestal

quo (indef. adj.)   = *aliquo*

marmor, marmoris (m.)   marble

quae . . . capiat   relat. cl. of char. (AG #535), anteced. *basim*

si . . . addendos   prot. of FMV condit. (AG #516a), whose apod. is relat. cl. that precedes it; *hos . . .*
   addendos: indir. disc. (AG #580), ELLIPSIS of *esse*; the location of the prot. after Pliny's dir. comm.
   suscipe and *iube* and the delay of *addendos* until the end of the sent. make it clear that his name and
   titles should appear on the pedestal.

III.VI.6

ut primum   as soon as

qui . . . grauetur   relat. cl. of char. (AG #535); grauo (1) (< grauis + -o) weigh down, pass.: feel
   inconvenienced, object

adfero, adferre   (< ad + fero, ferre) bring w/ [one]

destino (1)   intend, designate {> destination}

si . . . permiserit   mixed condit., prot. of FMV but w/ indic. apod. w/ a vb. indicating possibility
   (AG #516/2d); permitto, permittere, permisi, permissus (< per + mitto, mittere) allow

excurro, excurrere   (< ex + curro, currere) make an excursion, go

isto (adv.)   to the place where you are; iste, ista, istud: demon. adj. used to point to places and things
   connected to the pers. addressed, esp. w/ 2nd pers.

III.VI.7

me . . . esse   indir. disc. (AG #580) ff. *polliceor*; polliceor, polliceri, pollicitus sum: promise

contraho, contrahere   (< con + traho, trahere) draw together; contrahere frontem: scowl, frown

cum . . . dies   cum tmp. cl. (AG #545); *ad paucos dies*: for a few days; *ad* implies a set length of time
   (AG #424e)

diutius (compar. adv.)   (< diu) for a longer time

exeo, exire   (< ex + eo, ire) get away

neque . . . patiuntur   *haec*: subj. of *patiuntur*, read w/ *abesse me* and (*me*) *exire*; "For the same matters
   that do not yet allow me to get away also do not permit me to be away for much time."

xiv—SLAVES MURDER THEIR MASTER

C. PLINIVS ACILIO SVO S.

1   Rem atrocem nec tantum epistula dignam Larcius Macedo
uir praetorius a seruis suis passus est, superbus alioqui dominus et saeuus, et qui seruisse patrem suum parum, immo
2   nimium meminisset. Lauabatur in uilla Formiana. Repente
eum serui circumsistunt. Alius fauces inuadit, alius os uer-
berat, alius pectus et uentrem, atque etiam (foedum dictu)
uerenda contundit; et cum exanimem putarent, abiciunt in
feruens pauimentum, ut experirentur an uiueret. Ille siue
quia non sentiebat, siue quia se non sentire simulabat, im-

III.xiv: Pliny reports the horrific murder of a harsh master by his slaves. His horror and fear in describing the crime reflect well what must have been trepidation shared by many slave owners, even those
like him who considered themselves indulgent (s. VIII.XVI).

Addressee: Acilius, who may be the same person mentioned in *Ep.* I.XIV (S-W 246; AB 35). If so, he is
from Pliny's part of Italy, the city of Patavium in Cisalpine Gaul.

III.xiv.1

atrox, atrocis (< ater + -ox) dreadful, shocking

epistula abl. of specif. (AG #418) w/ *dignam*

Larcius Macedo a senator who was the son of the freedman A. Larcius Lydus (AB 68); his son
A. Larcius Macedo reached the suffect consulship under Hadrian (S-W 247).

praetorius, -i (m.) (< praetor + -ius) of praetorian rank (s. IV.XI.1n)

alioqui (adv.) as a general rule, otherwise

saeuus, -a, -um harsh {> savage}

qui . . . meminisset relat. cl. of char. (AG #535); *seruisse . . . parum*: indir. disc. (AG #580);
seruisse = *seruiuisse*; seruio, seruire, seruiui: serve in the capacity of a slave; *immo* (pcl.) rather,
more precisely; *nimium* (adv.) too much; memini, meminisse: remember; Pliny sets Macedo among
a specific milieu—sons of freedmen, and thus distances himself from poor treatment of slaves.

III.xiv.2

lauo, lauare wash, pass.: wash oneself

Formianus, -a, -um belonging to Formiae, a town on the coast of Latium

repente (adv.) suddenly, w/out warning

circumsisto, circumsistere (< circum + sisto, sistere) crowd around, surround; Pliny switches to the
hist. pres. tense to heighten the drama of his narrative.

fauces, faucium (f. pl.) throat

inuado, inuadere (< in + uado, uadere) assault, attack

os, oris (n.) mouth, face {> oral}

uerbero (1) (< uerber + -o) strike, beat

pectus, pectoris (n.) chest, breast {> pectoral}

uenter, uentris (m.) belly, abdomen

foedum dictu PARENTHESIS, ELLIPSIS of *est*; foedus, -a, -um: offensive, disgraceful, vile; *dictu*: supine,
abl. of specif. (AG #510)

mobilis et extentus fidem peractae mortis impleuit. Tum   3
demum quasi aestu solutus effertur; excipiunt serui fideliores,
concubinae cum ululatu et clamore concurrunt. Ita et uocibus excitatus et recreatus loci frigore sublatis oculis agitatoque
corpore uiuere se (et iam tutum erat) confitetur. Diffugiunt   4
serui; quorum magna pars comprehensa est, ceteri requi-
runtur. Ipse paucis diebus aegre focilatus non sine ultionis

---

uerendus, -a, -um (< gerv. of uereor) thing to be regarded w/ awe; n. pl. subst.: external sexual organs, private parts
contundo, contundere (< con + tundo, tundere) pound to pieces
cum ... putarent cum circumst. cl. (AG #546); exanimis, exanime (< ex + anima + -is) dead, lifeless; *eum* understood
abicio, abicere (< ab + iacio, iacere) throw down {> abject}
ferueo, feruere be intensely hot, boiling hot; presumably because the floor of the bath was heated (s. II.XVII.11 on balineum)
pauimentum, -i (n.) (< pauio, pauire + -mentum) paved floor, pavement
ut experirentur purp. cl. (AG #531/1)
an uiueret indir. quest. (AG #574); *an*: "whether" ("or not" implied)
simulo (1)   pretend
immobilis ... impleuit extendo, extendere, extendi, extentus (< ex + tendo, tendere) stretch out in death (OLD 2); perago, peragere, peregi, peractus (< per + ago, agere) carry out, finish; impleo, implere, impleui, impletus: provide, satisfy; "motionless and laid out, he satisfied their belief that they had accomplished his death."

III.XIV.3
demum (adv.) only
aestus, -us (m.) heat
solutus, -a, -um (< ppp. of soluo, soluere) weak, limp (OLD 5); *Macedo* understood
effero, efferre (< ex + fero, ferre) carry out
fidelis, fidele (< fides + -elis) faithful, loyal
ululatus, -us (m.) (< ululo, ululere + -tus) howling, drawn out cries
concurro, concurrere (< con + curro, currere) hurry together
excito (1) (< ex + cito, citare) rouse, stir
recreo (1) (< re + creo, creare) restore, pass.: recover, revive
frigor, frigoris (m.) cold
sublatis oculis, agitatoque corpore abl. abs. (AG #419); tollo, tollere, sustuli, sublatus: lift, raise; agito (1) (< ago, agere + -ito) set in motion, rouse
tutus, -a, -um (< ppp. tueor, tueri) safe
confiteor, confiteri, confessus sum (< con + fateor, fateri) admit

III.XIV.4
diffugio, diffugere (< dis + fugio, fugere) run away, scatter
comprehendo, comprehendere (< com + prehendo, prehendere) catch, seize, arrest
aegre (adv.) w/ difficulty, painfully
focilo (1) (< foueo, fouere + -culum) keep alive
ultio, ultionis (f.) (< ulciscor + -tio) revenge, retribution

5 solacio decessit ita uiuus uindicatus, ut occisi solent. Vides
quot periculis quot contumeliis quot ludibriis simus obnoxii;
nec est quod quisquam possit esse securus, quia sit remissus
et mitis; non enim iudicio domini sed scelere perimuntur.

6 Verum haec hactenus. Quid praeterea noui? Quid? Nihil,
alioqui subiungerem; nam et charta adhuc superest, et dies
feriatus patitur plura contexi. Addam quod opportune de
eodem Macedone succurrit. Cum in publico Romae lauaretur,
notabilis atque etiam, ut exitus docuit, ominosa res accidit.

---

decedo, decedere, decessi, decessus (< de + cedo, cedere) go away, die (*OLD* 7) {> decedent}

ita ... solent *ita ... ut*: correl. conj. (AG #323g) "while ... as"; uindico (1) (< uim + dico, dicere) avenge; occido, occidere, occidi, occisus (< ob + caedo, caedere) kill, slaughter; "avenged while living as those who have been murdered usually are"; the punishment for the murder of a master was the possible execution of all the slaves of the household, particularly any who had not come to his aid, exempting perhaps those who would have been manumitted in their master's will.

III.XIV.5

quot ... obnoxii indir. quest. (AG #574); *quot* (interrog. adj.) how many; *periculis, contumeliis, ludibriis*: dat. w/ adj. *obnoxii* (AG #384); contumelia, -ae (f.) insulting language, rough treatment {> contumely}; ludibrium, -i (n.) (< ludus) plaything, mockery, pl.: insults, outrages; obnoxius, -a, -um: subject to, exposed to

nec ... mitis causal cl. intro. denied reason (AG #540/2n.3); *nec est quod*: "nor is there any reason that"; securus, -a, -um (< se + cura + -us) free from care/anxiety; remissus, -a, -um (< ppp. of remitto, remittere) gentle, lenient {> remiss}; mitis, mite: kind, merciful

scelus, sceleris (n.) crime, wicked act

perimo, perimere (< per + emo, emere) destroy, deprive of life; subj. *domini*

III.XIV.6

haec hactenus enough of these things (*OLD* hactenus 4)

Quid ... noui *noui*: partit. gen. ff. n. pron. *quid* (AG #346/3), ELLIPSIS of *est*

subiungo, subiungere (< sub + iungo, iungere) attach, add; *subiungerem*: apod. of implied pres. C-to-F condit. (AG #517)

charta, chartae (f.) (< Gr. χάρτης) paper

supersum, superesse (< super + sum, esse) remain, be left over

dies feriatus festival, holiday (*OLD* feriatus 2)

contexo, contexere (< con + texto, texere) connect, compose {> context}

quod (relat. pron.) subst.: "that which"

opportune (adv.) (< opportunus) fittingly, in a manner fitting the occasion

succurro, succurrere (< sub + curro, currere) come to mind (*OLD* 5)

cum ... lauaretur cum circumst. cl. (AG #546); *in publico*: i.e. in one of a number of public baths in the city

notabilis, notabile (< noto, notare + -bilis) noteworthy

ut ... docuit *ut* w/ indic. "as" (AG #527f); exitus, -us (m.) (< exeo, exire + -tus) the end of one's life, death

ominosus, -a, -um (< omen + -osus) presaging ill, inauspicious

Eques Romanus a seruo eius, ut transitum daret, manu   7
leuiter admonitus conuertit se nec seruum, a quo erat
tactus, sed ipsum Macedonem tam grauiter palma per-
cussit ut paene concideret. Ita balineum illi quasi per   8
gradus quosdam primum contumeliae locus, deinde exitii
fuit. Vale.

xv—EVALUATING A FRIEND'S POETRY

C. PLINIVS SILIO PROCVLO SVO S.

Petis ut libellos tuos in secessu legam examinem, an edi-   1
tione sint digni; adhibes preces, adlegas exemplum: rogas
enim, ut aliquid subsiciui temporis studiis meis subtraham,

III.XIV.7

Eques Romanus a Roman knight (s. II.IV.2n. on milia)

ut . . . daret purp. cl. (AG #531/1); transitus, -us (m.) path through, passage

admoneo, admonere, admonui, admonitus (< ad + moneo, monere) remind {> admonish}

conuerto, conuertere (< con + uerto, uertere) turn about, turn around

palma, -ae (f.) palm of the hand

percutio, percutere, percussi, percussus (< per + quatio, quatere) strike forcefully {> percussion}

ut . . . concideret result cl. (AG #537); concido, concidere (< con + cado, cadere) fall down, collapse

III.XIV.8

illi dat. sg., i.e. Macedo

gradus, -us (m.) step, stage

III.XV: Pliny agrees to read through a book of poetry sent to him by the letter's recipient and offers
encouraging words.
Addressee: Silius Proculus, unknown outside of this letter.

III.XV.1

ut . . . examinem subst. cl. of purp. (AG #563) (= indir. comm.) ff. *petis;* examino (1) (< examen + -o)
evaluate, consider critically; ASYNDETON serves to unite the two verbs in a single activity.

an . . . digni indir. quest. (AG #574) ff. *examinem; an* (pcl.) whether ("or not" implied); editio, editionis
(f.) (< ex + do, dare + -tio) publication; *editione:* abl. of specif. (AG #418b) w/*digni*

adhibeo, adhibere (< ad + habeo, habere) apply, bring to bear, use

prex, precis (f.) prayer, entreaty

adlego (1) (< ad + lego, legare) employ, adduce in support

ut . . . tuis subst. cl. of purp. (AG #563) (= indir. comm.) ff. *rogas;* subsiciuus, -a, -um (< sub + seco,
secare + -iuus) left over, spare; *aliquid subsiciui temporis:* partit. gen. ff. n. pron. (AG #346/3), "some
spare time"; *studiis meis:* dat. of indir. obj. w/ compd. vb. *subtraham* (AG #370); subtraho, subtrahere
(< sub + traho, trahere) take away {> subtract}; impertio, impertire (< in + partio, partire) give a
share of, devote; *tuis (studiis)*

2   impertiam tuis, adicis M. Tullium mira benignitate poetarum ingenia fouisse. Sed ego nec rogandus sum nec hortandus; nam et poeticen ipsam religiosissime ueneror et te
ualdissime diligo. Faciam ergo quod desideras tam dili-

3   genter quam libenter. Videor autem iam nunc posse rescribere esse opus pulchrum nec supprimendum, quantum
aestimare licuit ex iis quae me praesente recitasti, si modo
mihi non imposuit recitatio tua; legis enim suauissime et
peritissime. Confido tamen me non sic auribus duci, ut omnes

4

M. Tullium ... fouisse indir. disc. (AG #580); benignitas, benignitatis (f.) (< benignus + -tas) kindness, generosity; foueo, fouere, foui, fotus: support, encourage (*OLD* 7a); Pliny here refers, of course,
to Marcus Tullius Cicero, the great orator and statesman of the Roman Republic. His accomplishments are a natural point of comparison for Pliny's own, as Cicero was known not only for his
speeches but also for his extensive writing, which included revised versions of his orations, hundreds
of letters, many philosophical works, and even poetry. While Pliny never undertakes to write philosophical treatises, his letters illuminate his interest in the other genres, nor does he hesitate to com-
pare his political career w/ that of his predecessor.

III.XV.2

rogandus ... hortandus 2nd (pass.) periphr. conjug. (AG #196 and 500/2)
poetice, poetices (f) = Gr. ποιητική: the poetic art; *poeticen*: Gr. acc. sg.
religiosissime (superl. adv.) (< religiosus, -a, -um) w/ great devotion or reverence
ueneror, uenerari, ueneratus sum hold in awe, revere {> venerate}
ualdissime (superl. adv.) (< ualdus, -a, -um) very intensely, tremendously
faciam ... libenter Pliny explains his easy compliance w/ Silius' request by playing particularly on
diligo w/ *diligenter*, an ex. of POLYPTOTON; *tam ... quam* (adv.) as ... as; *diligenter* (adv.) (< diligens,
diligentis) scrupulously, thoroughly; *libenter* (adv.) (< libens, libentis) w/ pleasure, willingly

III.XV.3

rescribo, rescribere (< re + scribo, scribere) write in response
esse ... supprimendum indir. disc. (AG #580) ff. *rescribere*; supprimo, supprimere (< sub + premo,
premere) hold back, suppress; *supprimendum esse*: 2nd (pass.) periphr. conjug. (AG #196 and 500/2)
aestimo (1) estimate, assess, judge
me praesente abl. abs. (AG #419); praesens, praesentis: present, face to face
recito (1) (< re + cito, citare) recite (before an audience) (s. I.XIII.1n. on quo ... aliquis); *recitasti* =
contr. form of pf. *recitauisti* (AG #181); in the next phrase, *si ... recitatio tua*, Pliny uses POLYPTOTON
to draw attention to the power of recitation; *si modo*: only provided that, if in fact (*OLD* modo 3a);
impono, imponere: deceive, trick (intr. use *OLD* 16) {> impose}, compd. vb + dat. *mihi* (AG #370)
suauissime (superl. adv.) (< suauis, suaue) most delightfully, pleasantly
peritissime (superl. adv.) (< peritus, -a, -um) w/ great experience, most expertly

III.XV.4

confido, confidere (< con + fido, fidere) trust, have confidence
me ... duci indir. disc. (AG #580)

aculei iudicii mei illarum delenimentis refringantur: hebetentur fortasse et paulum retundantur, euelli quidem ex-
torquerique non possunt. Igitur non temere iam nunc de   5
uniuersitate pronuntio, de partibus experiar legendo. Vale.

XXI—IN TRIBUTE TO MARTIAL

C. PLINIVS CORNELIO PRISCO SVO S.

Audio Valerium Martialem decessisse et moleste fero. Erat   1
homo ingeniosus acutus acer, et qui plurimum in scribendo et

---

ut . . . refringantur result cl. (AG #537); aculeus, -i (m.) (< acus + -leus) sting, sharp point or edge;
  illarum: i.e. *aurium*; delenimentum, -i (n.) (< de + lenio, lenire + -mentum) enticement, blandish-
  ment; refringo, refringere (< re + frango, frangere) break (by exerting pressure)

hebetentur . . . retundantur potent. subjv. w/ *fortasse* (AG #447/2b); hebeto (1) (< hebes + -o) make
  blunt or dull; *paulum* (adv.) somewhat, slightly; retundo, retundere (< re + tundo, tundere) reduce
  the edge of, weaken (*OLD* 2c); using ASYNDETON here and in the ff. cl., Pliny intensifies the confidence w/ which he begins.

euello, euellere (< e + uello, uellere) tear out, get rid of

extorqueo, extorquere (< ex + torqueo, torquere) remove w/ a twist, wrench away

III.XV.5

igitur (conj.) therefore

temere (adv.) recklessly, w/out reason

iam nunc at this point now

uniuersitas, uniuersitatis (f.) (< uniuersus + -tas) the whole, entirety

pronuntio (1) (< pro + nuntio, nuntiare) proclaim, state an opinion {> pronounce)

III.XXI: Pliny writes about the death of the poet Valerius Martial, whose extant poems number more
  than 1,500 and whose specialty was the witty epigram. Pliny expresses his admiration for the poetry,
  while focusing on his own generous response to the verses Martial wrote about him.
Addressee: Cornelius Priscus, identified as *consularis* in *Ep.* v.xx, may be a proconsul of Asia circa
  120 CE (SW 262, AB 52–3).

III.XXI.1

Valerium . . . decessisse indir. disc. (AG #580); decedo, decedere, decessi, decessus (< de + cedo,
  cedere) go away, die (*OLD* 7) {> decedent}; born in Spain, Martial came to Rome when he was in
  his mid-twenties, during the 2nd half of Nero's reign. Although he would eventually be awarded a
  tribunate and the concomitant privileges of equestrian rank, it is clear that he was dependent upon
  various patrons for financial support, among whom were Seneca the Younger and, of course, the
  younger Pliny (*OCD* 930–31).

moleste (adv.) (< molestus, -a, -um) in a distressing way

ingeniosus, -a, -um (< ingenium + -osus) talented, clever

acutus, -a, -um (< ppp. of acuo, acuere) sharp, keen-witted (*OLD* 8a)

acer, acris, acre shrewd, penetrating (*OLD* 5) {> acrid}; the staccato effect of ASYNDETON highlights
  the qualities that Pliny describes. He uses the device frequently to emphasize character traits.

2   salis haberet et fellis, nec candoris minus. Prosecutus eram
           uiatico secedentem; dederam hoc amicitiae, dederam etiam

3   uersiculis quos de me composuit. Fuit moris antiqui, eos qui
           uel singulorum laudes uel urbium scripserant, aut honoribus
           aut pecunia ornare; nostris uero temporibus ut alia speciosa
           et egregia, ita hoc in primis exoleuit. Nam postquam desiimus

4   facere laudanda, laudari quoque ineptum putamus. Quaeris,
           qui sint uersiculi quibus gratiam rettuli? Remitterem te ad
           ipsum uolumen, nisi quosdam tenerem; tu, si placuerint hi,

---

qui . . . minus relat. cl. of char. (AG #535); *plurimum . . . minus*: subst. use w/ partit. gen. (AG #346/3), *plurimum* w/ *salis . . . et felis*, *minus* w/ *candoris*; sal, salis (m.) salt, wit (*OLD* 6b); fel, fellis (n.) venom, bitterness; candor, candoris (m.) (< candeo, candere + -or) clearness, lucidity (*OLD* 5)

III.XXI.2
prosequor, prosequi, prosecutus sum (< pro + sequor, sequi) furnish (*OLD* 3a)
uiaticum, -i (n.) (< uia + -aticus) traveling allowance; *uiatico*: abl. of means (AG #409)
secedo, secedere (< se + cedo, cedere) withdraw (i.e. from Rome into the country) (*OLD* 3) {> secede}; *secedentem*: *eum* understood
amicitiae . . . uersiculis dat. of ref. (AG #376): "out of regard for . . ."; uersiculus, -i (m.) (< uersus + -culus) brief line, pl.: epigrams (*OLD* 2)

III.XXI.3
fuit moris mos, moris (m.) custom, practice, pl.: character {> moral}; *moris*: gen. of quality (AG #345); impers. n. subj. introd. acc. + inf. constr. *eos . . . ornare* (AG #455/2); honor, honoris (m.) political office; orno (1) (< ordo + -o) show respect to, honor (+ abl.) (*OLD* 6)
ut . . . ita (correl.) "as . . . so"
speciosa et egregia subst. use; speciosus, -a, -um (< species + -osus) appealing, impressive
in primis above all else, first and foremost
exolesco, exolescere, exoleui, exoletus fade away, fall out of use
laudanda, laudari POLYPTOTON, which stresses the importance of being praiseworthy; *laudanda*, subst. use: "things that should be praised"; *laudari . . . ineptum*: indir. disc. (AG #580) ff. *putamus*, ELLIPSIS of *esse*; ineptus, -a, -um (< in + aptus) foolish, silly

III.XXI.4
qui sint uersiculi indir. quest. (AG #574) ff. *Quaeris*
remitterem . . . tenerem pres. C-to-F condit. (AG #517); remitto, remittere (< re + mitto, mittere) send back, refer; uolumen, uoluminis (n.) (< uoluo, uoluere + -men) roll, book; teneo, tenere: retain (in the mind) (*OLD* 22); *uolumen* refers to a single roll of papyrus on which might be written as many as 1,500 lines of poetry. Pliny does not need to tell his addressee precisely which scroll or how it would have been distinguished, but likely it would have been labelled w/ Martial's name and perhaps the 1st words of the 1st poem it contained. (*OCD* s. Greek and Roman books, 250.)
si . . . requires FMV condit. (AG #516c); ceterus, -a, -um: the rest, the other

III.XXI.5
adloquor, adloqui, adlocutus sum (< ad + loquor, loqui) address, invoke
Musa, Musae (f.) Muse (s. II.XIII.7n. on ut . . . credas)
mando (1) give instructions, order {> mandate}

ceteros in libro requires. Adloquitur Musam, mandat ut   5
domum meam Esquiliis quaerat, adeat reuerenter:

> Sed ne tempore non tuo disertam
> pulses ebria ianuam, uideto.
> Totos dat tetricae dies Mineruae,
> dum centum studet auribus uirorum
> hoc, quod saecula posterique possint
> Arpinis quoque comparare chartis.
> Seras tutior ibis ad lucernas:
> haec hora est tua, cum furit Lyaeus,
> cum regnat rosa, cum madent capilli.
> Tunc me uel rigidi legant Catones.

---

ut . . . reuerenter subst. cl. of purp. (AG #563) (= indir. comm.); Esquiliae, -arum (f.) the Esquiline Hill in Rome; adeo, adire (< ad + eo, ire) approach {> adit}; *reuerenter* (adv.) (< reuerens, reuerentis) respectfully; one of the famous seven hills of Rome, the Esquiline was the 2nd most desirable place for the elite to live in Cicero's time, w/ the Palatine being the best. In Pliny's time imperial palaces had usurped most of the Palatine, leaving the Esquiline as the best address for those of high rank.

ne . . . ianuam subst. cl. of purp. (AG #563) (= indir. comm.) ff. *uideto* (fut. impv.); "see to it that . . ."; disertus, -a, -um: skilled in speaking or writing, learned; pulso (1) (< ppp. pello, pellere) knock on; ebrius, -a, -um: drunk; *disertam* is a TRANSFERRED EPITHET modifying the door but clearly describing its owner (Pliny), who is the subj. of *dat* and *studet* in the next sent.

tetricus, -a, -um stern, frowning; describes Minerva, whose dominion over the arts included writing (s. I.VI.3n. on Minerva)

studeo, studere concentrate on (w/ acc. *hoc*) (*OLD* 2)

centum . . . uirorum Martial is referring to the Centumviral Court (s. I.XVIII.6n. on iudicium centumuirale); *auribus*: dat. of ref. (AG #376)

quod . . . possint relat. cl. of char. (AG #535); saeculum, -i (n.) age, generation, pl.: future ages (*OLD* 8); posterus, -a, -um (< post) later, future, pl. subst.: descendents, posterity

Arpinus, -a, -um of Arpinum; Martial refers here to Cicero, who was from the town of Arpinum, and his speeches (s. III.XV.1n. on Cicero).

comparo (1) (< con + par + -o) align, treat as equal

charta, -ae (f.) (< Gr. χάρτης) paper, pl.: writings

serus, -a, -um late

tutus, -a, -um (< ppp. tueor, tueri) safe

lucerna, -ae (f.) (< lux, lucis) lamp; *ad lucernas*: "after dark"

cum . . . Lyaeus cum tmp. cl. (AG #545); furo, furere: rage, range wildly; Lyaeus, -i (m.) Bacchus; *Lyaeus*, mg. "releaser from cares," is one of number of cult names used for the god.

madeo, madere be wet, w/ *capilli*: be wet w/ oil or unguents/perfume (*OLD* 2d); capillus, -i (m.) hair

uel (pcl.) even (introd. an unlikely possibility *OLD* 5)

rigidus, -a, -um stiff, stern, inflexible

legant poten. subv. (AG #447/3)

Catones "The Catos"; Martial uses the names of M. Porcius Cato (Censorius) and his great-grandson M. Porcius Cato (Uticensis) to represent strict, stuffy Romans, who might not ordinarily choose to read his often ribald verses. The former was known for his literary works (esp. his *De Agricultura* and *Origines*) and particularly for his criticism of declining Roman morality, and the latter became famous for his unyielding defense of the Republican system, his defeat by Caesar at Utica in 46 BCE, and his subsequent suicide (*OCD* 1224–26).

6   Meritone eum qui haec de me scripsit et tunc dimisi amicis-
sime et nunc ut amicissimum defunctum esse doleo? Dedit
enim mihi quantum maximum potuit, daturus amplius si
potuisset. Tametsi quid homini potest dari maius, quam
gloria et laus et aeternitas? At non erunt aeterna quae
scripsit: non erunt fortasse, ille tamen scripsit tamquam
essent futura. Vale.

III.XXI.6

Merito (adv.) (< meritus, -a, -um) deservedly

eum ... defunctum esse indir. disc. (AG #580) ff. *doleo*; Pliny employs VARIATIO in describing the
reasons for his grief: a relat. cl. *qui ... scripsit*, then a shift to 1st pers. w/ *dimisi*, ending w/ a desc.
phase *nunc ... amicissimum*; dimitto, dimittere, dimisi, dimissus (< dis + mitto, mittere) pay off
(a creditor); *ut* (conj.) as; defungor, defungi, defunctum esse: come to an end, pf.: have died
{> defunct}; doleo, dolere: be in pain, grieve

amplior, amplius (compar. adj.) (< amplus, -a, -um) subst.: a greater amount

si potuisset prot. of past C-to-F condit.; apod. w/ fut. ptc. *daturus* substituting for plupf. subjv.
(AG #517d)

Tametsi (conj.) (< tam + etsi) yet, all the same

quid ... aeternitas RHETORICAL QUESTION; aeternitas, aeternitatis (f.) (< aeternus + -tas)
immortality (of fame)

quae (relat. pron.) subst.: "the things which"

tamquam essent futura condit. cl. of compar. (AG #524): "just as if they were going to be"

BOOK IV

11—REGULUS THE CONTEMPTIBLE MOURNER

C. PLINIVS ATTIO CLEMENTI SVO S.

Regulus filium amisit, hoc uno malo indignus, quod nescio   1
an malum putet. Erat puer acris ingenii sed ambigui, qui
tamen posset recta sectari, si patrem non referret. Hunc   2
Regulus emancipauit, ut heres matris exsisteret; mancipatum
(ita uulgo ex moribus hominis loquebantur) foeda et insolita

IV.11: Pliny reports the death of Regulus' son, focusing on the excessive behavior of his bereaved father, the same man Pliny had so forcefully criticized in II.xx.
Addressee: Attius Clemens, unknown outside of Pliny's letters.

IV.11.1
Regulus (s. II.xx.2n.)
amitto, amittere, amisi, amissus (< ab + mitto, mittere) incur the loss of, lose
indignus, -a, -us (< in + dignus, -a, -um) not deserving {> indignant}; w/ abl. of specif. (AG #418b)
    hoc uno malo
an ... putet indir. quest. (AG #574); *an*: "whether" ("or not" implied)
acris ingenii ... ambigui gen. of quality (AG #345); acer, acris, acre: shrewd, sharp {> acrid}; ambiguus, -a, -um (< ambi + ago, agere + -uus) undecided, untrustworthy (*OLD* 9)
qui ... referret *qui ... sectari*: relat. cl. of char. (AG #535), "the kind of boy who"; *recta*: subst. use; sector, sectari, sectatus sum (< ppp. of sequor, sequi) pursue, follow as a model; relat. cl.: apod. of pres. C-to-F condit. w/ prot. *si ... referret* (AG #517)

IV.11.2
emancipo (1) (< ex + mancipo, mancipare) release from control/power {> emancipate}; all Roman children were under the legal and financial control of their father until his death or, in the case of a female child, until she was married, and even then only if control of her affairs was transferred to her husband. Emancipation was a complicated process in Pliny's time that required the repeated 'sale' of the son or daughter. Once released from his father's power, a son became his own *paterfamilias* and was eligible to receive inheritances (*OCD* s. emancipation, 521–2).
ut ... exsisteret purp. cl. (AG #531/1); heres, heredis (m.) heir; exsisto, exsistere (< ex + sisto) appear, emerge
mancipo (1) (< manus + -ceps + -o) formally alienate, sell, surrender; *mancipatum: filium* understood
uulgo (adv.) (< uulgus + -o) commonly, publicly
mos, moris (m.) custom, practice, pl.: character {> moral}
foeda, insolita modify *simulatione*; foedus, -a, -um: offensive, disgraceful, vile; insolitus, -a, -um (< in + ppp. of soleo, solere) unaccustomed, strange, + dat. w/ adj. *parentibus* (AG #384); indulgentia, -ae (f.) (< indulgens + -ia) leniency, indulgence; *indulgentiae*: obj. gen. (AG #347) w/ *simulatione*; simulatio, simulationis (f.) (< simulo, simulare + -tio) pretence, show

3

4

parentibus indulgentiae simulatione captabat. Incredibile,
sed Regulum cogita. Amissum tamen luget insane. Habebat
puer mannulos multos et iunctos et solutos, habebat canes
maiores minoresque, habebat luscinias psittacos merulas:
omnes Regulus circa rogum trucidauit. Nec dolor erat ille,
sed ostentatio doloris. Conuenitur ad eum mira celebritate.
Cuncti detestantur oderunt, et quasi probent quasi diligant,
cursant frequentant, utque breuiter quod sentio enuntiem,

---

capto (1) (< capio, capere + -to) court the favor of in order to receive a legacy (*OLD* 9b); although
Regulus could not inherit from his son's mother, he could be left a legacy in his emancipated son's
will. With the use of *captabat*, Pliny equates Regulus' fawning treatment of his son w/ the unspeak-
ably crass legacy-hunting detailed in II.xx.

IV.II.3

amissum i.e. filium

lugeo, lugere mourn; it was considered unseemly for a Roman man to mourn excessively. The proper
rites were to be observed certainly, but open and extreme displays of grief were severely criticized.
Pliny himself reveals his concurrence w/ this assessment in his letters (s. v.xvi.8–10). The funeral
Pliny describes in this section is certainly a remarkable instance of outrageous spectacle, one that
brings nothing so much to mind as Homer's description of the rites performed by Achilles for Patroclus in *Iliad* 23.171–6, which included his slaughter of four horses and two of Patroclus' nine dogs,
not to mention twelve sons of Trojan nobles, all of whose bodies were thrown on the funeral pyre.

insane (adv.) (< insanus, -a, -um) wildly, extravagantly

mannulus, -i (m.) (< mannus + -ulus) little pony

iunctus, -a, -um (< ppp. of iungo, iungere) joined {> junction}, i.e. used for pulling a cart

solutus, -a, -um (< ppp. of soluo, soluere) not joined, i.e. for riding

luscinia, -ae (f.) nightingale

psittacus, -i (m.) (< Gr. ψίττακος) parrot

merula, -ae (f.) blackbird; Pliny's use of ANAPHORA (*habebat*) in the three cls., followed by ASYN-
DETON in the final cl., seems to expand the number of animals severalfold.

rogus, -i (m.) funeral pyre

trucido (1) slaughter

IV.II.4

dolor, doloris (m.) (< doleo, dolere + -or) grief, anguish

ostentatio, ostentationis (f.) (< ppp. of ostendo, ostendere + -tio) exhibition, display {> ostentatious)

conuenitur impers. use of pass., intr. vb. (AG #208d); *conuenitur ad eum*: "people visit him"

celebritas, celebritatis (f.) (< celeber + -tas) crowding, frequency

cunctus, -a, -um sg.: the whole, pl.: all

detestor, detestari, detestatus sum feel abhorrence for, loathe

odi, odisse hate; pf. w/ pres. sense

quasi probent quasi diligant condit. cl. of compar. (AG #524); probo (1) (< probus + -o) commend
{> probation}

curso (1) (< curro, currere + -to) rush about, hurry

frequento (1) (< frequens + -o) throng, crowd; here ASYNDETON seems to reproduce the frenetic
behavior of the crowds surrounding Regulus

ut ... enuntiem purp. cl. (AG #531/1); *breuiter* (adv.) (< breuis + -iter) in a few words {> brevity};
enuntio (1) (< ex + nuntio, nuntiare) express, articulate {> enunciate)

in Regulo demerendo Regulum imitantur. Tenet se trans   5
Tiberim in hortis, in quibus latissimum solum porticibus
immensis, ripam statuis suis occupauit, ut est in summa
auaritia sumptuosus, in summa infamia gloriosus. Vexat ergo   6
ciuitatem insaluberrimo tempore et, quod uexat, solacium
putat. Dicit se uelle ducere uxorem, hoc quoque sicut alia
peruerse. Audies breui nuptias lugentis nuptias senis;   7

---

in Regulo demerendo gerv. constr. (AG #503); demereo, demerere (< de + mereo, merere) oblige, win
  the favor of
imitor, imitari, imitatus sum copy the conduct of, imitate

IV.II.5
Tiberis, Tiberis (m.) the Tiber River; the river has its origin in the Apennine range near Arretium and
  flows through the city of Rome and into the Tyrrhenian Sea through the town of Ostia (*OCD* s.
  Tiber, 1522).
solum, -i (n.) soil, ground
porticus, -us (m./f.) covered walkway, colonnade
immensus, -a, -um (< in + ppp. of metior, metiri) immeasurable, huge
ripa, -ae (f.) riverbank
statuis suis i.e. statues of himself
ut . . . sumptuosus *ut* w/ indic. "as" (AG #527f); auaritia, -ae (f.) (< auarus, -a, -um + -ia) greed,
  avarice; sumptuosus, -a, -um (< sumo, sumere + -tus + -osus) extragavant
infamia, -ae (f.) (< infamis + -ia) bad reputation, notoriety, disgrace; the wd. *infamia* does not mean
  'bad reputation' per se but rather a lack of *fama* (s. II.IV.2n.) or reputation, certainly worse for most
  Romans. Without *fama*, a person could not participate in any legal proceeding on the behalf of another person. *Infamia* might be imposed following condemnation in the courts, and it was also in-
  herent for those in disreputable professions such as prostitution and virtually any entertainment
  (actors, dancers, and gladiators). Regulus is, of course, none of these and so is not technically *infamis*; however, his apparent lack of concern for maintaining a good reputation, makes him utterly vile
  in Pliny's estimation.
gloriosus, -a, -um (< gloria + -osus) boastful, vainglorious

IV.II.6
uexo (1) upset, distress, disturb
insaluberrimus, -a, -um (superl. adj.) (< insaluber, insalubris, insalubre) unhealthiest; late summer
  and early fall were, in fact, times in which the city was known by Pliny and his contemporaries to be
  prone to the spread of serious illness such as typhoid and malaria. Most elite Romans stayed outside
  of the city at their country homes in these months. Thus Regulus imperils his acquaintances by compelling them to seek him out at his city residence w/ their consolations.
quod (conj.) because
se . . . uxorem indir. disc. (AG #580); *uxorem ducere*: marry
sicut (conj.) just like
peruerse (adv.) (< peruersus, -a, -um) wrongly, perversely

IV.II.7
breui n. subst., abl. of time when (AG #423): "soon"
nuptias lugentis, nuptias senis nuptiae, -arum (f.) (< nubo, nubere + -ia) marriage ceremony, wedding {> nuptial} (s. I.IX.2n. on nuptiae); senex, senis (m.) old man {> senile}; here and in the ff. cl.
  Pliny uses ANAPHORA and ASYNDETON to stress his disapproval.

8 quorum alterum immaturum alterum serum est. Vnde hoc
augurer quaeris? Non quia adfirmat ipse, quo mendacius
nihil est, sed quia certum est Regulum esse facturum, quidquid fieri non oportet. Vale.

VIII—BECOMING AN AUGUR LIKE CICERO

C. PLINIVS MATVRO ARRIANO SVO S.

1 Gratularis mihi quod acceperim auguratum: iure gratularis, primum quod grauissimi principis iudicium in minoribus
etiam rebus consequi pulchrum est, deinde quod sacerdotium ipsum cum priscum et religiosum tum hoc quoque

---

immaturus, -a, -um ($<$ in + maturus, -a, -um) done prematurely

serus, -a, -um late

Vnde . . . augurer indir. quest. (AG #574) ff. *quaeris; Vnde* (interrog.) from what source; auguror, augurari, auguratus sum ($<$ augur + -or) predict, foretell

IV.II.8

adfirmo (1) ($<$ ad + firmo, firmare) confirm, corroborate

quo (relat. pron.) abl. of compar. (AG #406) w/ *mendacius; mendax,* mendicis ($<$ mendum + -ax) untruthful {$>$ mendacious}

certum . . . facturum impers. n. subj. introd. acc. + inf. constr. (AG #455/2)

quisquis, quidquid (indef. pron.) ($<$ quis, quid) anyone, anything, whatever

oportet it is proper, right, "ought"; impers. vb. w/ acc. + inf. constr. (AG #565n. 3)

IV.VIII: Pliny discusses the importance of the office of augur and his delight in having been appointed to it. Addressee: Maturus Arrianus, an equestrian from Altinum, for whom Pliny secures a position in Egypt (*Ep.* III.II). He receives six other letters from Pliny on a variety of topics.

IV.VIII.1

gratulor, gratulari, gratulatus sum congratulate (+ dat.)

quod acceperim causal cl., subjv. indicates another's opinion (AG #540/2)

auguratus, -us (m.) ($<$ auguror, augurari + -tus) office of augur; the *augures* were one of the four colleges of priests said by Roman tradition to have been instituted during the monarchical period. Their task was either to actively solicit signs w/ which they would determine the will of the gods in respect to the undertaking of a specific action, including elections and wars, or to interpret unexpected portents to determine if they signalled a disruption in the relationship between the *res publica* and the gods. Of special concern to augurs were birds and signs in the heavens, particularly lightning and thunder (*OCD* s. augures, 214, and divination, 488) (s. II.XX.4n. on haruspex).

iure (adv.) by reason, justly, deservedly

grauissimus, -a, -um (superl. adj.) ($<$ grauis, graue) most respected, venerable (*OLD* 13a) {$>$ gravity}

consequor, consequi, consecutus sum ($<$ con + sequor, sequi) acquire, follow, act in accordance w/ (*OLD* 11)

sacerdotium, -i (n.) ($<$ sacerdos + -ium) priesthood

cum . . . tum both . . . and

priscus, -a, -um ancient, long-standing, of old

sacrum plane et insigne est, quod non adimitur uiuenti. Nam   2
alia quamquam dignitate propemodum paria ut tribuuntur
sic auferuntur; in hoc fortunae hactenus licet ut dari possit.
Mihi uero illud etiam gratulatione dignum uidetur, quod   3
successi Iulio Frontino principi uiro, qui me nominationis
die per hos continuos annos inter sacerdotes nominabat,
tamquam in locum suum cooptaret; quod nunc euentus ita

---

religiosus, -a, -um (< religio + -osus) complying w/ religious duty

plane (adv.) (< planus, -a, -um) plainly, clearly

insignis, insigne (< in + signum + -is) noteworthy, distinguished

adimo, adimere (< ad + emo, emere) remove, take away; *uiuenti*: dat. of separ. (AG #381); i.e. the office of augur was a lifetime appointment

IV.VIII.2

dignitas, dignitatis (f.) (< dignus + -tas) excellence, rank, status (*OLD* 3a); *dignitate*: abl. of specif. (AG #418) w/ *paria*

propemodum (adv.) (prope + modus) virtually, just about

ut . . . sic correl. conj. (AG #323g), "as . . . so"

tribuo, tribuere grant, bestow on {> attribute}

aufero, auferre (< ab + fero, ferre) take away, remove

in . . . possit *hactenus* (adv.) to this extent; "In regard to this (honor/office) fortune is permitted only the means to grant it."

IV.VIII.3

illud points forward to the *quod* cl. (AG #297e)

gratulatio, gratulationis (f.) (< gratulor, gratulari + -tio) congratulations; *gratulatione*: abl. of specif. (AG #418b) w/ *dignum*

succedo, succedere, successi, successus (< sub + cedo, cedere) move up in position to, become successor to; compd. vb + dat. (AG #370)

Iulius Frontinus Pliny describes Sextus Iulius Frontinus elsewhere (*Ep.* v.i) as one of the two most respected men of his time and acknowledges his prominence again in IX.XIX. Frontinus served as consul an extraordinary three times and was also the author of the treatise *De Aquis* on aqueducts, regarding which he was well-versed, having also served as Rome's *curator aquarum* (SW 273, AB 64–5).

nominatio, nominationis (f.) (< nomino + -tio) nomination

continuus, -a, -um (< con + teneo, tenere + -uus) uninterrupted, w/ out pause

sacerdos, sacerdotis (m.) (< sacer) priest

nomino (1) (< nomen + -o) specify by name, name aloud

tamquam . . . cooptaret condit. cl. of compar. (AG #524); coopto (1) (< con + opto, optare) choose a colleague in office, elect

quod (relat. pron.) anteced. the preceding sent., i.e. Frontinus' persistent determination to make Pliny his successor

euentus, -us (m.) (< ex + uenio, uenire + -tus) outcome, occurrence

4   comprobauit, ut non fortuitum uideretur. Te quidem, ut
scribis, ob hoc maxime delectat auguratus meus, quod M.
Tullius augur fuit. Laetaris enim quod honoribus eius in-

5   sistam, quem aemulari in studiis cupio. Sed utinam ut
sacerdotium idem, ut consulatum multo etiam iuuenior
quam ille sum consecutus, ita senex saltem ingenium eius

6   aliqua ex parte adsequi possim! Sed nimirum quae sunt in
manu hominum et mihi et multis contigerunt; illud uero ut
adipisci arduum sic etiam sperare nimium est, quod dari
non nisi a dis potest. Vale.

---

comprobo (1) (< con + probo, probare) demonstrate the truth, confirm

ut ... uideretur result cl. (AG #537); fortuitus, -a, -um (< fors) determined by chance, fortuitous

iv.viii.4

ut scribis *ut* w/ indic. "as" (AG #527f); Pliny's repeated references to some previous communication from his addressee allows him to distance himself somewhat from what might otherwise seem obsessive self-praise.

hoc points forward to the *quod* cl. (AG #297e)

M. Tullius Cicero (s. iii.xv.1n. and iii.xxi.5n. on Arpinus, -a, -um)

augur, auguris (m.) augur, interpreter of the auspices

laetor, laetari, laetatus sum (< laetus, -a, -um + -o) be glad, be delighted

quod ... insistam causal cl., subjv. indicates another's opinion (AG #540/2); insisto, insistere (< in + sisto, sistere) stand on, pursue, compd. vb + dat. *honoribus* (AG #370)

quem (relat. pron.) anteced. *eius*

aemulor, aemulari, aemulatus sum (< aemulus + -o) emulate, take as a model {> emulate}

iv.viii.5

utinam (pcl.) if only

ut ... ut ... ita correl. conj. (AG #323g), "as ... as ... so"

consulatus, -us (m.) (< consul + -atus) office of consul

multo by much; abl. of deg. of diff. (AG #414) w/ *iuuenior*; Cicero was 43 years old when he became consul and 53 when he became augur; Pliny was consul at age 39 and augur at about 43.

senex, senis old man {> senile}; "as an old man"

saltem (adv.) at least

aliqua ex parte modifier of obj. of monosyl. prep. often precedes prep. (AG #599d)

adsequor, adsequi, adsecutus sum (< ad + sequor, sequi) catch up, achieve

possim opt. subjv. w/ *utinam* (AG #442)

iv.viii.6

nimirum (pcl.) w/ out doubt, of course

quae (relat. pron.) subst. use: "the things which"

contingo, contingere, contigi, contactus (< cum + tango, tangere) fall to one's lot, be granted to (dat.) (OLD 8a)

illud i.e. *ingenium*

uero (pcl.) (< uerus + -o) truly {> verify}

ut ... sic correl. conj. (AG #323g), "as ... so"

adipiscor, adipisci, adeptus sum (< ad + apio + -sco) reach, arrive at, obtain

arduus, -a, -um steep, difficult

nimium (adv.) too much

XI—DOMITIAN EXECUTES THE VESTAL CORNELIA

C. PLINIVS CORNELIO MINICIANO SVO S.

Audistine Valerium Licinianum in Sicilia profiteri? non-   1
dum te puto audisse: est enim recens nuntius. Praetorius hic
modo inter eloquentissimos causarum actores habebatur;
nunc eo decidit, ut exsul de senatore, rhetor de oratore fieret.
Itaque ipse in praefatione dixit dolenter et grauiter: 'Quos   2
tibi, Fortuna, ludos facis? facis enim ex senatoribus profes-
sores, ex professoribus senatores.' Cui sententiae tantum bilis,

---

IV.XI: Using comments on the exile of Valerius Licinianus as a frame for this letter, Pliny recounts the
trial and capital punishment of the Vestal Cornelia by the Emperor Domitian and casts doubt on the
rightness of his actions.

Addressee: Cornelius Minicianus, an equestrian from Bergamum, for whom Pliny seeks a military
tribunate in *Ep.* VII.XXII.

IV.XI.1

audisti = contr. form of pf. *audiuisti* (AG #181), followed by indir. disc. (AG #580) *Valerium . . . profiteri;* Valerius Licinianus: a Roman senator of praetorian rank known only from this letter; profiteor,
profiteri, professus sum (< pro + fateor, fateri) declare, teach professionally (*OLD* 5b)

te . . . audisse indir. disc. (AG #580) ff. *puto; audisse* = contr. form of *audiuisse* (AG #181)

recens, recentis recent, newly come

praetorius, -i (m.) (< praetor + -ius) of praetorian rank; mg. that Licinianus has served in the office of
praetor, which carried both judicial responsibilities and the burden of presiding over and funding
games. Former praetors might go on to serve as provincial governors or continue up the cursus hon-
orum to the consulship (*OCD* s. praetor, 1240). Licinianus apparently did neither.

modo (adv.) only recently

causa, -ae (f.) legal case; *causarum actores:* pleaders, advocates

habeo, habere have, treat (*OLD* 22), regard (*OLD* 24)

eo . . . fieret *eo* (adv.) to such a point; decido, decidere, decidi (< de + cado, cadere) fall down, sink; *ut
. . . fieret:* result cl. (AG #537); exsul, exsulis (m.) exile; rhetor, rhetoris (m.) (< Gr. ῥήτωρ) one who
teaches public speaking or the art of persuasion {> rhetoric}

IV.XI.2

praefatio, praefationis (f.) (< prae + for, fari + -tio) introduction, preface; as Pliny makes clear elsewhere in the letters (s. I.XIII), recitation of literary works had become quite popular in Rome in his
time. Such public presentations were sometimes preceded by an introduction that made preliminary
remarks about the text or its author (*OCD* 1295–96).

dolenter (adv.) (< pres. ptc. of doleo, dolere) w/ sorrow

grauiter (adv.) (< grauis) seriously

ludos facere (idiom.) amuse oneself (w/ reflex. pron. in dat.)

professor, professoris (m.) (< ppp. of pro + fateor + -or) teacher (of rhetoric)

Cui . . . inest sententia, -ae (f.) (< pres. ptc. of sentio, sentire + -ia) opinion, statement, observation;
bilis, amaritudinis: partit. gen. w/ *tantum* (AG #346/3); bilis, bilis (f.) bile, anger; amaritudo, amaritudinis (f.) (< amarus, -a, -um + -tudo) bitterness; insum, inesse (< in + sum, esse) belong to,
reside in, compd. vb + dat. (*cui sententiae*) (AG #370)

tantum amaritudinis inest, ut mihi uideatur ideo professus

3   ut hoc diceret. Idem cum Graeco pallio amictus intrasset

(carent enim togae iure, quibus aqua et igni interdictum est),

postquam se composuit circumspexitque habitum suum,

4   'Latine' inquit 'declamaturus sum.' Dices tristia et miseranda,

dignum tamen illum qui haec ipsa studia incesti scelere macu-

5   larit. Confessus est quidem incestum, sed incertum utrum

---

ut . . . diceret *ut . . . uideatur*: result cl. (AG #537); *ut hoc diceret*: purp. cl. (AG #531/1); "that he seems
to me to have become a teacher in order to say it."

IV.XI.3

cum . . . intrasset cum circumst. cl. (AG #546); pallium, -i (n.) outer garment, cloak; amicio, amicire,
amicui, amictus (< ambi + iacio, iacere) cover, clothe, dress; intro (1) (< intra + -o) enter; *intrasset* = contr. form of *intrauisset* (AG #181); a Greek garment, the pallium was a square or almost
square piece of cloth worn around the shoulders. It is appropriate for Licinianus to wear, since he is
now living in Sicily, which had been populated by Greek colonists for more than 800 years. Furthermore, from the reign of Tiberius onwards, exiles formally lost their citizenship and were thus
prohibited from wearing the toga (SW 281). There is also a dramatic flair to Licinianus' appearance,
as Roman adaptations of Greek comedies were called *fabulae palliatae*—"stories in Greek dress."

careo, carere lack, be w/ out, be deprived; w/ abl. of separ. *iure* (AG #401); ius, iuris (n.) the right {> jury}

interdico, interdicere, interdixi, interdictus (< inter + dico, dicere) forbid; w/ dat. of pers. *quibus*
(subst. "those for whom") and abl. of separ. *aqua et igni*; this is the language of a formal decree of
exile, which denied the condemned water and fire and thus a means of living.

circumspicio, circumspicere, circumspexi, circumspectus (< circum + specio, specere) examine,
consider

habitus, -us (m.) (< habeo, habere + -tus) state of being, style of dress {> habit}

Latine (adv.) (< Latinus, -a, -um) derived from adj. that denotes a population, used to denote language
that those people spoke; "in Latin"; in highlighting the incongruity of his language and clothing
Licinianus proclaims his status as exile.

declamo (1) (< de + clamo, clamare) make speeches {> declamation}

IV.XI.4

tristia et miseranda, dignum . . . illum indir. disc. (AG #580), ELLIPSIS of *esse*; tristis, triste: sad;
miserandus, -a, -um (< gerv. of miseror, miserari) pitiable; *tristia, miseranda*: subst. use

qui . . . macularit relat. cl. of char. (AG #535); incestum, -i (n.) (< in + castus) profanation of religious
rites, sexual impurity; scelus, sceleris (n.) crime, wicked act; maculo (1) (< macula + -o) stain, disgrace; *macularit* = contr. form of *maculauerit* (AG #181)

IV.XI.5

confiteor, confiteri, confessus sum (< con + fateor, fateri) admit

utrum . . . an whether . . . or

metuo, metuere (< metus + -o) fear, be afraid

si negasset prot. of past C-to-F condit. (AG #517), apod. implied by *grauiora*; *negasset* = contr. form of
negauisset (AG #181)

fremo, fremere roar, growl, clamor

Domitianus, -i (m.) Pliny consistently vilifies this emperor, offering him as a profoundly negat. ex.
in contrast w/ Trajan, the best of emperors. Indeed, w/ no evidence to suggest she was wrongly

quia uerum erat, an quia grauiora metuebat si negasset.
Fremebat enim Domitianus aestuabatque in ingenti inuidia
destitutus. Nam cum Corneliam Vestalium maximam defodere uiuam concupisset, ut qui inlustrari saeculum suum eiusmodi exemplis arbitraretur, pontificis maximi iure, seu potius
immanitate tyranni licentia domini, reliquos pontifices non
in Regiam sed in Albanam uillam conuocauit. Nec minore

6

---

convicted, it can be easily argued that Pliny has recast Cornelia's condemnation as a heinous act in
order to further blacken his portrayal of Domitian (C 196–201).

aestuo (1) (< aestus + -o) burn, seethe

inuidia, -ae (f.) (< inuidus, -a, -um + -ia) indignation, spite, jealousy

destitutus, -a, -um (< ppp. of de + statuo, statuere) deprived, left in isolation {> destitute)

IV.XI.6

cum ... concupisset cum circumst. cl. (AG #546)

Corneliam Vestalium maximam lit.: "Cornelia the greatest of the Vestals." She was, in fact, the senior
Vestal at the time of this 2nd trial, having been acquitted the 1st time. Under the purview of the pontifices and as one of the four original priestly colleges at Rome, the Vestals' chief charge was to maintain the fire in the hearth of Vesta's shrine, which represented the very life of the city. Symbolically
married to the city, they were required to maintain their chastity throughout their thirty years of
service, as any proper wife was expected to do. Breaking this vow was not only sacrilege, that is, a
great offense to the gods, but also a dire threat to Rome's continued existence.

defodio, defodere (< de + fodio, fodere) put underground, bury; *defodere*: compl. inf. (AG #456) w/
concupisset = contr. form of *concupiuisset* (AG #181); concupio, concupere, concupiui, concupitus
(< con + cupio, cupere) desire greatly

ut qui ... arbitraretur *ut* (conj.) as; *qui* (relat. pron.), "someone who"—intro. relat. cl. of char. (AG
#535), describing the sort of reign Domitian wanted to be remembered for; *inlustrari ... exemplis*:
indir. disc. (AG #580); inlustro (1) (< in + lustro, lustrare) illuminate, give glory to {> luster};
saeculum, -i (n.) age, generation; *eiusmodi* (gen.) of this kind (OLD modus 12c); *exemplis*: abl. of
means (AG #409); arbitror, arbitrari, arbitratus sum (< arbiter + -o) consider, judge, reckon

pontifex, pontificis (m.) (< pons, pontis + -fex) a priest from the college that had control over public
religion in Rome; Pontifex Maximus: the leading member of the college of pontifices, chosen originally by his fellow priests, oversaw the Vestals among other duties. By the middle of the Republic he
was elected by a select group of Roman tribes, until Augustus joined the power of the position and
that of other priesthoods w/ his political power, and thereafter each succeeding emperor held the
position, and thus controlled the religious practices of the state (OCD s. pontifex, 1219–20).

iure ... immanitate ... licentia abl. of manner omitting *cum* (AG #412b); *seu* (conj.) or rather (OLD
siue 9b); *potius* (adv.) more exactly; immanitas, immanitatis (f.) (< immanis + -tas) brutality, bar-
barity; licentia, -ae (f.) (< licens + -ia) lack of restraint, immoderate behavior {> license}

Regia, -ae (f.) Located in the Forum Romanum quite near the House of the Vestals, the Regia was by
tradition the home of Numa, Rome's 2nd king, who was credited w/ bringing the cult of Vesta to
Rome. After the monarchy, it became the office of the Pontifex Maximus (OCD s. Regia, 1297).

Albana uilla Domitian's residence in Alba Longa, a city that Roman tradition said had been founded
by Aeneas himself and cited as the birthplace of Romulus and Remus; the modern city of Albano
takes its name from the site of the villa (OCD s. Alba Longa, 50).

conuoco (1) (< con + uoco, uocare) call together

nec ... uidebatur ulciscor, ulcisci, ultus sum: exact retribution, take vengeance; "with no less a crime
than the one for which he seemed to exact retribution..."

7   scelere quam quod ulcisci uidebatur, absentem inauditamque
damnauit incesti, cum ipse fratris filiam incesto non pol-
luisset solum uerum etiam occidisset; nam uidua abortu
periit. Missi statim pontifices qui defodiendam necandamque
curarent. Illa nunc ad Vestam, nunc ad ceteros deos manus
tendens, multa sed hoc frequentissime clamitabat: 'Me
Caesar incestam putat, qua sacra faciente uicit triumphauit!'

---

inauditus, -a, -um (< in + ppp. of audio, audire) unheard; *absentem inauditamque: eam* understood

damno (1) (< damnum + -o) pass judgment, condemn; followed by *incesti*: gen. of the charge or penalty (AG #352)

cum ... occidisset cum conces. cl. (AG #549); *non ... solum uerum etiam*: not ... only but also; Pliny's use of HYPERBATON in the separation of *non* from *solum* heightens the drama of his accusation of incest and sends the reader headlong to the 2nd charge of murder; polluo, polluere, pollui, pollutus: violate, defile; occido, occidere, occidi, occisus (< ob + caedo, caedere) cause the death of, kill; Suetonius also tells the sordid tale of Domitian's relationship w/ his niece, whom he had refused to marry as a young woman, but then seduced as someone else's wife and impregnated as a widow (*Dom.* 22).

uiduus, -a, -um lacking a husband/wife

abortus, -us (m.) (< ab + orior, oriri + -tus) miscarriage, abortion; *abortu*: abl. of cause (AG #404)

pereo, perire, perii (< per + eo, ire) be lost, perish, die

IV.XI.7

missi ... pontifices ELLIPSIS of *sunt*

qui ... curarent relat. cl. of purp. (AG #531/2); *defodiendam necandamque*: gerv. w/ ELLIPSIS of *eam*; neco (1) (< nex, necis + -o) put to death, kill; Pliny's omission of words in this highly compressed sent. add to the gravity and shock of the sent.

ceterus, -a, -um the rest, the other

tendo, tendere extend, stretch out

frequentissime (superl. adv.) (< frequens, frequentis) constantly, persistently

clamito (1) (< clamo, clamare + -ito) shout repeatedly

me ... incestam indir. disc. (AG #580) ff. *putat*, ELLIPSIS of *esse*; incestus, -a, -um (< in + castus) sexually impure, polluted

qua sacra faciente abl. abs. (AG #419); *qua* (relat. pron.), anteced. *me*

uicit triumphauit ASYNDETON here seems to assure both victory and triumph; triumpho (1) (< triumphus + -o) celebrate a triumph; Cornelia's attention to the proper rituals would have been key to ensuring Domitian's success in war. Significant victory resulted in a triumph, an elaborate procession through the city of Rome held by a general in celebration of his victory. His retinue included his soldiers, enemy spoils, prisoners of war, Roman officials, entertainers, and animals that were to be sacrificed at the endpoint of the parade, the Temple of Capitoline Jupiter, who was the bringer of all victory.

IV.XI.8

blandiens ... dixerit indir. quest. (AG #574) ff. *dubium est*, w/ two pairs of alts., each separated by *an* (pcl.) "or" ("whether" implied); blandior, blandiri, blanditus sum (< blandus, -a, -um + -io) coax, flatter; inrideo, inridere (< in + rideo, ridere) laugh at, mock; fiducia, -ae (f.) (< fido, fidere) assurance, confident expectation of (+ gen.) {> fiduciary}; contemptus, -us (m.) (< con + temno, temnere + -tus) contempt, scorn

donec (conj.) until such time as, up to

supplicium, -i (n.) (< supplex, supplicis + -ium) punishment

Blandiens haec an inridens, ex fiducia sui an ex contemptu   8
principis dixerit, dubium est. Dixit donec ad supplicium,
nescio an innocens, certe tamquam innocens ducta est. Quin   9
etiam cum in illud subterraneum demitteretur, haesissetque
descendenti stola, uertit se ac recollegit, cumque ei manum
carnifex daret, auersata est et resiluit foedumque contactum
quasi plane a casto puroque corpore nouissima sanctitate
reiecit omnibusque numeris pudoris πολλὴν πρόνοιαν ἔσχεν
εὐσχήμων πεσεῖν. Praeterea Celer eques Romanus, cui Cornelia   10

---

innocens, innocentis (< in + pres. ptc. of noceo, nocere) not guilty, blameless, innocent
duco, ducere, duxi, ductus lead off to punishment (*OLD* 4b)

IV.XI.9

quin etiam moreover
cum … demitteretur, haesisset cum circumst. cl. (AG #546); subterraneus, -a, -um (< sub + terra + -aneus) underground; n. acc. subst. use: "place underground"; demitto, demittere (< de + mitto, mittere) cause to descend, make (acc.) descend; haereo, haerere, haesi, haesus: stick, cling {> adhesive}; *descendenti: ei* understood, dat. of ref. (AG #376); stola, -ae (f.) woman's garment, dress; in his biography of Numa, Plutarch, a contemporary of Pliny, describes the punishment of a disgraced Vestal, who was compelled to climb down a ladder into an underground chamber that had been fitted w/ a bed, a lamp, and some food and water, since it would be impious to starve a person who had been consecrated to a god. The location was then reburied and leveled w/ the surrounding ground so that its entrance would be obscured (*Numa* 10.5).
recolligo, recollegi (< re + con + lego, legere) gather up again; i.e. her *stola*
cum … daret cum circumst. cl. (AG #546); carnifex, carnificis (m.) (< caro + -fex) executioner (from the term for a butcher, 'meat-maker'); since a condemned Vestal entered the underground chamber alive, there was no need for an executioner per se. Thus Pliny is referring here to Domitian, at whose insistence she had been charged.
auerto, auertere, auerti, auersus (< ab + uerto, uertere) change direction, pass.: turn oneself away
resilio, resilire, resilui (< re + salio, salire) jump back, spring back in disgust, recoil
foedus, -a, -um offensive, vile
contactus, -us (m.) (< con + tango, tangere + -tus) touch, contact
plane (adv.) (< planus, -a, -um) plainly, clearly
castus, -a, -um free from vice, unstained, sexually pure
nouissima sanctitate abl. of manner (AG #412); sanctitas, sanctitatis (f.) (< sanctus + -tas) moral purity, integrity
reicio, reicere, reieci, reiectus (< re + iacio, iacere) refuse to accept (*OLD* 7a)
numerus, -i (m.) measure, cadence; *omnibus numeris*: abl. of manner omitting *cum* (AG #412b)
pudor, pudoris (m.) (< pudeo, pudere + -or) decency, honor
πολλὴν πρόνοιαν ἔσχεν εὐσχήμων πεσεῖν Gr.: "took great care to fall modestly"; a quotation from Euripides *Hecuba* (569) regarding the death of Polyxena, daughter of Hecuba, who was sacrificed at the tomb of Achilles.

IV.XI.10

Celer unknown; public execution by scourging was apparently the standard punishment for men who had been party to a Vestal's broken vow of chastity (Dion. Hal. *Ant. Rom.* 9.40.4).
eques Romanus a Roman knight (s. II.IV.2n. on milia)

11   obiciebatur, cum in comitio uirgis caederetur, in hac uoce
perstiterat: 'Quid feci? nihil feci.' Ardebat ergo Domitianus
et crudelitatis et iniquitatis infamia. Adripit Licinianum,
quod in agris suis occultasset Corneliae libertam. Ille ab iis
quibus erat curae praemonetur, si comitium et uirgas pati
nollet, ad confessionem confugeret quasi ad ueniam. Fecit.

12   Locutus est pro absente Herennius Senecio tale quiddam,
quale est illud: κεῖται Πάτροκλος. Ait enim: 'Ex aduocato

---

obicio, obicere (< ob + iacio, iacere) lay to one's charge, cite as a reason for condemnation (*OLD* 10);
cui: dat. of indir. obj. w/ compd vb. (AG #370)

cum . . . caederetur cum circumst. cl. (AG #546); comitium, -i (n.) (< con + eo, ire + -ium) place of
assembly, the assembly; uirga, -ae (f.) rod, switch; caedo, caedere: strike, beat

persto, perstare, perstiti, perstatus (< per + sto, stare) stand firm, persist

IV.XI.11

ardeo, ardere burn, rage {> ardent}

crudelitas, crudelitatis (f.) (< crudelis + -tas) cruelty, savagery

iniquitas, iniquitatis (f.) (< in + aequus + -tas) unfairness, adverse nature

infamia, -ae (f.) (< infamis + -ia) bad reputation, notoriety, disgrace (s. IV.II.5n.)

adripio, adripere (< ad + rapio, rapere) arrest, have arrested

quod . . . occultasset causal cl., subjv. indicates another's opinion (AG #540/2); occulto (1) (< ob +
celo, celare + -to) conceal, keep hidden {> occult}; *occultasset* = contr. form of *occultauisset* (AG #181)

liberta, -ae (f.) (< liber + -tus) freedwoman

quibus . . . curae dat. of ref. (AG #376) w/ dat. of purp. (AG #382) = dbl. dat.

praemoneo, praemonere (< prae + moneo, monere) warn in advance {> premonition}

si . . . nollet . . . confugeret fut. condit. cast back into past time (AG #516e), not C-to-F; condit., serves
as subst. cl. of purp. (AG #563) (= indir. comm.) ff. *praemonetur*; confessio, confessionis (f.) (< ppp.
of con + fateor, confateri + -io) admission, confession; confugio, confugere (< con + fugio, fugere)
flee for refuge (to)

IV.XI.12

pro absente i.e. Licinianus

Herennius Senecio Little known outside of Pliny's letters but prominent within them, Senecio hailed
from Hispania Baetica where he served a term as quaestor. He assisted Pliny in the prosecution
of the Baetican governor Baebius Massa in 93 CE and later that year was tried and executed by
Domitian, purportedly merely for writing a life of Helvidius Priscus, a staunch opponent of the
principate. Tacitus makes two brief mentions of his execution in *Agricola* (2 and 45).

tale . . . quale correl. w/ *quiddam . . . illud*, "some such thing as the following"

κεῖται Πάτροκλος Gr.: "Patroclus is dead"; *Iliad* 18.20; Quintilian offers this report of Patroclus'
demise as an ex. of brevity (*Inst. Orat.* x.1.49).

aduocatus, -i (m.) (< ppp. of ad + uoco, uocare) advocate, legal counsel

recedo, recedere, recessi, recessus (< re + cedo, cedere) withdraw {> recede}

IV.XI.13

gratum hoc ELLIPSIS of *erat*

adeo (adv.) to the extent that

ut . . . proderetur result cl. (AG #537); prodo, prodere (< pro + do, dare) betray

nuntius factus sum; Licinianus recessit.' Gratum hoc   13
Domitiano adeo quidem ut gaudio proderetur, diceretque:
'Absoluit nos Licinianus.' Adiecit etiam non esse uerecundiae
eius instandum; ipsi uero permisit, si qua posset, ex rebus
suis raperet, antequam bona publicarentur, exsiliumque
molle uelut praemium dedit. Ex quo tamen postea clementia   14
diui Neruae translatus est in Siciliam, ubi nunc profitetur
seque de fortuna praefationibus uindicat.

Vides quam obsequenter paream tibi, qui non solum res   15
urbanas uerum etiam peregrinas tam sedulo scribo, ut altius
repetam. Et sane putabam te, quia tunc afuisti, nihil aliud

---

absoluo, absoluere, absolui, absolutus (< ab + soluo, soluere) acquit

non . . . instandum indir. disc. (AG #580); uerecundia, -ae (f.) (< uereor + -cundus + -ia) restraint;
esse instandum: impers. use of 2nd (pass.) periphr. conjug. (AG #196 and 500/3); insto, instare (< in
+ sto, stare) press on, pursue, compd. vb + dat. *uerecundiae* (AG #370); "that his (Licinianus') restraint should not be pursued"; i.e. Domitian did not want anyone asking Licinianus why he had
withdrawn from the case rather than defending himself against the charges

ipsi i.e. Licinianus

permitto, permittere, permisi, permissus (< per + mitto, mittere) allow (+ dat.)

si qua posset prot. of simple condit., subjv. in subord. cl. (AG #512c n.); qua = *aliqua* (s. 1.1.1n. on quas)

ex . . . raperet subst. cl. of purp. (AG #563) (= indir. comm.) ff. *permisit, ut* omitted

antequam . . . publicarentur antequam w/ subjv. implies purp. or expectancy (AG #551b); publico
(1) (< publicus, -a, -um) make public property, confiscate

exsilium, -i (n.) (< exsul + -ium) exile

mollis, molle soft, tolerable, gentle

uelut (adv.) (< uel + ut) just like

IV.XI.14

quo (relat. pron.) anteced. *exsilium*

clementia, -ae (f.) (< clemens, clementis + -ia) clemency, leniency

Nerua, -ae (m.) Marcus Cocceius Nerva became emperor at the behest of the senators who had con-
spired to assassinate Domitian. With this in mind, he was careful to contrast his own behavior w/
that of his predecessor, doing away w/ treason trials and recalling many of those exiled. Nerva's decision not to recall Licinianus but rather merely to allow him to move suggests that the senator turned
teacher was not as innocent as he claimed and Pliny implies.

transfero, transferre, transtuli, translatus (< trans + fero, ferre) transport, transfer

uindico (1) (< uim + dico, dicere) lay claim, avenge

IV.XI.15

quam . . . paream indir. quest. (AG #574) ff. *Vides; quam* (interrog. adv.) how; *obsequenter* (adv.)
(< obsequens, obsequentis) obediently, compliantly {> obsequious}

urbanus, -a, -um (< urbs + -anus) pertaining to the city

peregrinus, -a, -um belonging to foreigners, of foreign origin

sedulo (adv.) diligently, zealously

ut . . . repetam result cl. (AG #537)

tunc (adv.) (< tum + -ce) at that moment

aliud . . . quam "other . . . than"

16 de Liciniano audisse quam relegatum ob incestum. Summam enim rerum nuntiat fama non ordinem. Mereor ut uicissim, quid in oppido tuo, quid in finitimis agatur (solent enim quaedam notabilia incidere) perscribas, denique quidquid uoles dum modo non minus longa epistula nuntia. Ego non paginas tantum sed uersus etiam syllabasque numerabo. Vale.

xix—CALPURNIA, THE IDEAL WIFE

C. PLINIVS CALPVRNIAE HISPVLLAE SVAE S.

1 Cum sis pietatis exemplum, fratremque optimum et amantissimum tui pari caritate dilexeris, filiamque eius ut tuam

---

relego (1) (< re + lego, legare) banish; *relegatum*: ELLIPSIS of *eum* and *esse*
summa, -ae (f.) w/ *rerum*: totality of a matter (*OLD* 4b) {> sum}
ordo, ordinis (m.) the steps or stages of a matter (*OLD* 9a) {> ordinal}

iv.xi.16
mereor, mereri, meritus sum earn, deserve {> merit}
ut ... perscribas subst. cl. of result showing accomplishment of an effort (AG #568); *uicissim* (adv.); in turn, reciprocally; *quid ... agatur*: indir. quest. (AG #574); finitimi, -orum (m. pl.) those living nearby, neighbors; notabilis, notabile (< noto, notare + -bilis) noteworthy; incido, incidere (< in + cado, cadere) occur (*OLD* 10a) {> incident}; perscribo, perscribere (< per + scribo, scribere) write in detail
quisquis, quidquid (indef. pron.) (< quis, quid) anyone, anything (AG #151b)
dum modo (adv.) so long as
nuntia pres. imperv. sg.; *longa epistula*: abl. of means (AG #409)
pagina, -ae (f.) column, page
uersus, -us (m.) (< uerto, uertere + -tus) line of writing
syllaba, -ae (f.) (< Gr. συλλαβή) syllable
numero (1) (< numerus + -o) count

iv.xix: Pliny praises the excellence of his young wife Calpurnia, whose qualities are a reflection of his own. Addressee: Calpurnia Hispulla, paternal aunt of Pliny's wife Calpurnia and daughter of Calpurnius Fabatus.

iv.xix.1
cum ... exemplum 1st cl. in series of 3 cum causal cls. (AG #549); pietas, pietatis (f.) (< pius + -tas) dutiful respect; this most Roman of virtues demanded a woman's unwavering devotion to her family and to the gods (s. also ii.xiii.4n.).
fratremque ... dilexeris 2nd cl.; *tui*: 2nd pers. sg. pron. objv. gen. (AG #347) w/ *amantissimum*; caritas, caritatis (f.) (< carus + -tas) affection, esteem; *pari caritate*: abl. of manner omitting *cum* (AG #412b); *ut tuam*: "as your own"
nec ... repraesentes 3rd cl.; amita, -ae (f.) paternal aunt; *ei*: 3rd pers. pron. dat. sg., i.e. Calpurnia; adfectus, -us (m.) (< adficio, adficere + -tus) devotion, affection; repraesento (1) (< re + praesens + -o) present in person, bring back into the present (*OLD* 6a)

diligas, nec tantum amitae ei adfectum uerum etiam patris
amissi repraesentes, non dubito maximo tibi gaudio fore cum
cognoueris dignam patre dignam te dignam auo euadere.
Summum est acumen summa frugalitas; amat me, quod   2
castitatis indicium est. Accedit his studium litterarum, quod
ex mei caritate concepit. Meos libellos habet lectitat ediscit
etiam. Qua illa sollicitudine cum uideor acturus, quanto cum   3
egi gaudio adficitur! Disponit qui nuntient sibi quem ad-
sensum quos clamores excitarim, quem euentum iudicii
tulerim. Eadem, si quando recito, in proximo discreta uelo

---

non ... fore inf. ff. *non dubito* (AG #558 n.2); *maximo tibi gaudio*: dat. of purp. (AG #382) w/ dat. of ref.
  (AG #376) = dbl. dat.
cum cognoueris cum circumst. cl. (AG #546); cognosco, cognoscere, cognoui, cognitus (< con +
  nosco, noscere) get to know, become aware
dignam ... euadere indir. disc. (AG #580), *eam* understood; *patre, te, auo*: abl. of specif. (AG #418b)
  w/ *dignam*; auus, -i (m.) grandfather; euado, euadere (< ex + uado, uadere) end up, emerge (*OLD* 8a);
  Pliny uses ANAPHORA and ASYNDETON here to emphasize his wife's excellence in measuring up to
  the standards of her father's family.

IV.XIX.2
acumen, acumenis (n.) (< acuo, acuere + -men) mental acuteness, judgment (*OLD* 4a)
frugalitas, frugalitatis (f.) (< frux + -alis + -tas) temperance, self-restraint (s. II.IV.3n.)
castitas, castitatis (f.) (< castus + -tas) moral purity, fidelity {> chastity}; *castitatis*: objv. gen.
  (AG #347) w/ *indicium*; indicium, -i (n.) (< index + -ium) sign, evidence (*OLD* 4a)
litterae, litterarum (f.) letters, literary works (*OLD* 8a) {> literature}
concipio, concipere, concepi, conceptus (< con + capio, capere) conceive, undertake (*OLD* 10)
lectito (1) (< leo, legere + -ito) read repeatedly
edisco, ediscere (< ex + disco, discere) learn by heart, memorize; his wife's devotion to his writings is
  demonstrated by Pliny's use of ASYNDETON in describing how she handles them.

IV.XIX.3
qua ... quanto interrog. used for emphasis in exclam. (AG #333n)
sollicitudo, sollicitudinis (f.) (< sollicitus, -a, -um + -tudo) anxiety
cum uideor ... cum egi cum tmp. cl. (AG #545); ago, agere, egi, actus: deliver a speech (*OLD* 43)
adficio, adficere (< ad + facio, facere) affect, stir/move (emotion)
dispono, disponere (< dis + pono, ponere) place here and there, station
qui ... sibi relat. cl. of purp. (AG #531/2)
quem ... tulerim indir. quest. (AG #574); adsensus, -us (m.) (< ad + sentio, sentire + -tus) approval,
  applause; excito (1) (< ex + cito, citare) rouse, stir; *excitarim* = contr. form of *excitauerim*
  (AG #181); euentus, -us (m.) (< ex + uenio, uenire + -tus) outcome, occurrence; Pliny again uses
  ASYNDETON to heighten his wife's engagement w/ his success.
si quando if ever
recito (1) (< re + cito, citare) recite (before an audience) (s. I.XIII.1n. on quo ... aliquis)
in proximo close at hand (*OLD* 2a)
discretus, -a, -um (< ppp. of dis + cerno, cernere) placed apart, separate
uelum, -i (n.) sail, curtain

4   sedet, laudesque nostras auidissimis auribus excipit. Versus
    quidem meos cantat etiam formatque cithara non artifice

5   aliquo docente, sed amore qui magister est optimus. His ex
    causis in spem certissimam adducor, perpetuam nobis maio-
    remque in dies futuram esse concordiam. Non enim aetatem
    meam aut corpus, quae paulatim occidunt ac senescunt, sed

6   gloriam diligit. Nec aliud decet tuis manibus educatam, tuis
    praeceptis institutam, quae nihil in contubernio tuo uiderit,
    nisi sanctum honestumque, quae denique amare me ex tua

7   praedicatione consueuerit. Nam cum matrem meam parentis
    loco uererere, me a pueritia statim formare laudare, talemque

---

auidus, -a, -um (< aueo + -idus) greedy, eager {> avid}
excipio, excipere (< ex + capio, capere) take out, receive, absorb (*OLD* 5c)

IV.XIX.4
uersus, -us (m.) (< uerto, uertere + -tus) line of writing
formo (1) shape, adapt, set (verses) to musical accompaniment (*OLD* 3)
cithara, -ae (f.) (< Gr. κιθάρα) lyre
artifice . . . docente abl. abs. (AG #419); artifex, artificis (m.) (< ars + -fex) skilled expert, musician

IV.XIX.5
his ex causis modifier of obj. of monosyl. prep. often precedes prep. (AG #599d)
spes, spei (f.) expectation (often used neutrally, w/ out either pos. or negat. inference)
adduco, adducere (< ad + duco, ducere) lead (into), draw
perpetuam . . . concordiam indir. disc. (AG #580) ff. *spem; in dies*: as the days proceed, daily (*OLD* 3a); concordia, -ae (f.) (< con + cor, cordis + -ia) mutual agreement, harmony; Pliny refers here to marital/family harmony, a state of unity that became famously celebrated by Livia, the wife of Augustus, w/ her dedication of a shrine to Concordia Augusta built in his honor in the portico that bore her name.
paulatim (adv.) (< paulus + -im) little by little, gradually
occido, occidere (< ob + cado, cadere) fall, come to grief
senesco, senescere (< seneo + -sco) grow old

IV.XIX.6
decet be right or fitting for; impers. vb. used only in 3rd pers.
educo (1) bring up, nurture {> educate}; *educatam*: subst. (AG #288)
praeceptum, -i (n.) (< ppp. of prae + capio, capere) piece of advice, rule {> precept}
instituo, instituere, institui, institutus (< in + statuo, statuere) set up, train, instruct (*OLD* 6a)
quae . . . consueuerit relat. cl. of char. (AG #535), anteced. (*eam*) *institutam*; contubernium, -i (n.) (< cum + taberna + -ium) cohabitation, living together; sanctus, -a, -um (< ppp. sancio, sancire) upright, virtuous; praedicatio, praedicationis (f.) (< prae + dico, dicare + -tio) commendation; consuesco, consuescere, consueui, consuetus (< con + suesco, suescere) become accustomed (to)

qualis nunc uxori meae uideor, ominari solebas. Certatim   8
ergo tibi gratias agimus, ego quod illam mihi, illa quod me
sibi dederis, quasi inuicem elegeris. Vale.

XXIII—PROPER RETIREMENT

C. PLINIVS POMPONIO BASSO SVO S.

Magnam cepi uoluptatem, cum ex communibus amicis   1
cognoui te, ut sapientia tua dignum est, et disponere otium
et ferre, habitare amoenissime, et nunc terra nunc mari corpus agitare, multum disputare, multum audire, multum
lectitare, cumque plurimum scias, cotidie tamen aliquid

IV.XIX.7

cum ... uererere cum causal cl. (AG #549); *loco*: abl. of place where w/ o prep. (AG #429)

pueritia, -ae (f.) (< puer + -itia) boyhood

talem qualis "the sort of man who"

ominor, ominari, ominatus sum (< omen + -o) presage, predict; *ominari* compl. inf. (AG #456) w/ *solebas*, along w/ *formare* and *laudare*; ASYNDETON emphasizes Pliny's longstanding and close connection w/ his wife's aunt.

IV.XIX.8

certatim (adv.) (< certo, certare + -im) in competition

quod me sibi dederis causal cl., subjv. indicates another's opinion (AG #540/2)

quasi ... elegeris condit. cl. of compar. (AG #524); *inuicem* (adv.) in turn, each for the other; eligo, eligere, elegi, electus (< ex + lego, legere) select, choose

IV.XXIII: Pliny describes the elements and proper timing of an ideal retirement and muses about his own future.

Addressee: Pomponius Bassus, suffect consul in 104 CE, who later serves Trajan by overseeing his alimentary program in central Italy (SW 301).

IV.XXIII.1

cum ... cognoui cum tmp. cl. (AG #545); cognosco, cognoscere, cognoui, cognitus (< con + nosco, noscere) get to know, become aware

te ... addiscere indir. disc. (AG #580), w/ *te* as subj. of each inf.

ut ... est *ut* w/ indic. "as" (AG #527f); *sapientia*: abl. of specif. (AG #418b) w/ *dignum*

dispono, disponere (< dis + pono, ponere) arrange, organize

amoenissime (superl. adv.) (< amoenus, -a, -um) most pleasantly, agreeably

agito (1) (< ago, agere + ito) set in motion, provide exercise for (*OLD* 7) {> agitate}

multum (adv.) (< multus) much, a lot

disputo (1) (< dis + puto, putare) debate, argue

lectito (1) (< leo, legere + -ito) read repeatedly

cum ... scias cum conces. cl. (AG #549); *plurimum*, subst. use: "the greatest amount"

2   addiscere. Ita senescere oportet uirum, qui magistratus am-
plissimos gesserit, exercitus rexerit, totumque se rei publicae

3   quam diu decebat obtulerit. Nam et prima uitae tempora et media patriae, extrema nobis impertire debemus, ut

4   ipsae leges monent, quae maiorem annis otio reddunt. Quando
mihi licebit, quando per aetatem honestum erit imitari istud
pulcherrimae quietis exemplum? quando secessus mei non
desidiae nomen sed tranquillitatis accipient? Vale.

---

addisco, addiscere (< ad + disco, discere) learn in addition

IV.XXIII.2
senesco, senescere (< seneo + -sco) grow old
oportet it is proper, right, "ought"; impers. vb. w/ acc. + inf. constr. (AG #565n. 3)
qui . . . obtulerit relat. cl. of char. (AG #535); magistratus, -us (m.) (< magister + -atus) office of a
     magistrate; amplus, -a, -um: great, distinguished {> ample}; *quam diu*: as long as; decet: be right or
     fitting for (impers. vb. used only in 3rd pers.); offero, offerre, obtuli, oblatus (< ob + fero, ferre)
     surrender, hand (oneself) over to (+ dat.) (*OLD* 7a/b)

IV.XXIII.3
extremus, -a, -um (< exter + -emus) occurring at the end, last
impertio, impertire (< in + partio, partire) give a share of, devote
ut . . . monent *ut* w/ indic. "as" (AG #527f)
annis abl. of specif. w/ *maiorem* (subst. use)

IV.XXIII.4
Quando . . . quando . . . quando RHETORICAL QUESTIONS
imitor, imitari, imitatus sum copy the conduct, imitate
quies, quietis (f.) rest, repose, relaxation
desidia, -ae (f.) (< desideo, desidere + -ia) idleness
tranquillitas, tranquillitatis (f.) quiet state of affairs, tranquillity

IV.XXV: Pliny expresses his disgust at improper behavior in the Senate and in so doing highlights his
     own integrity.
Addressee: Maesius Maximus, whose identity is not securely known, as Pliny addresses several other
     letters to various men named 'Maximus' without nomen or praenomen (SW 259–60, AB70).

IV.XXV.1
Scripseram Pliny refers here to *Ep.* III.XX (also sent to Maesius), in which he had complained about the
     intolerable disorder at recent elections that had prompted the Senate to institute secret balloting, a
     measure that had succeeded in the short term but that he had feared would lead to new types of bad
     behavior.
tibi uerendum esse impers. use of 2nd (pass.) periphr. conjug. (AG #196 and 500/3) in indir. disc.
     (AG #580); "that you ought to be afraid"
ne . . . exsisteret subst. cl. ff. vb. of fearing (AG #564); tacitus, -a, -um (< ppp. of taceo, tacere) silent;
     suffragium, -i (n.) vote {> suffrage}; uitium, -i (n.) defect, disorder, vice; exsisto, exsistere (< ex +
     sisto) appear, emerge
proximis comitiis abl. of time when (AG #423); comitium, -i (n.) (< con + eo, ire + -ium) place of
     assembly, election

xxv—ELECTORAL MISBEHAVIOR

C. PLINIVS MAESIO MAXIMO SVO S.

Scripseram tibi uerendum esse, ne ex tacitis suffragiis   1
uitium aliquod exsisteret. Factum est. Proximis comitiis in
quibusdam tabellis multa iocularia atque etiam foeda dictu,
in una uero pro candidatorum nominibus suffragatorum
nomina inuenta sunt. Excanduit senatus magnoque clamore   2
ei qui scripsisset iratum principem est comprecatus. Ille
tamen fefellit et latuit, fortasse etiam inter indignantes fuit.
Quid hunc putamus domi facere, qui in tanta re tam serio   3
tempore tam scurriliter ludat, qui denique omnino in senatu

---

tabella, -ae (f.) board, tablet used to record a vote (*OLD* 4)

iocularis, ioculare (< iocus +- ulus +- aris) humorous; n. pl. subst.: jokes

foedus, -a, -um offensive, disgraceful, obscene; *foeda*: w/ abl. of specif. (AG #418) *dictu* (supine form, "to say")

uero (pcl.) (< uerus + -o) in fact {> verify}

candidatus, -i (m.) (< candidus, -a, -um + -atus) candidate; the term derives from the bright color of the whitened toga worn by those seeking office.

suffragator, suffragatoris (n.) (< suffragor, suffragari + -tor) supporter of a candidate

IV.XXV.2

excandesco, excandescere, excandui (< ex + candeo, candere + -sco) burst into a rage, flare up

ei … principem indir. disc. (AG #580) ff. *comprecatus est*, ELLIPSIS of *fore*; *ei*: dat. sg.; *qui scripsisset*: relat. cl. in indir. disc., subjv. vb. when opinion is of someone other than the author (AG #591); comprecor, comprecari, comprecatus sum (< con + precor, precari) pray for, invoke

ille i.e. the naughty voter

fallo, fallere, fefelli, falsus trick, evade, go unnoticed

lateo, latere, latui hide, be invisible {> latent}

indignans, indignantis (< pres. ptc. of indignor, indignari) full of righteous anger, indignant

IV.XXV.3

qui … ludat relat. cl. of char. (AG #535), anteced. *hunc*, i.e., again, the miscreant; serius, -a, -um: weighty, important, serious; *scurriliter* (adv.) (< scurrilis, scurrile) in the manner of a scurra, w/ untimely humor {> scurrilous}; ludo, ludere: play, joke; *scurra* was a term used originally to describe an urbane and well-bred man, but by the later Republic and certainly during the Empire, it became highly derogatory, indicative of immoderate buffoonery rather than sophistication (*OLD*).

qui … est in this 2nd relat. cl., still about the villain, Pliny switches from subjv. to indic., because every member of the Senate on this occasion presented himself in this way, even the villain. The stmt. is thus factual; dicax, dicacis: having a ready tongue, tending to make witty remarks about others; urbanus, -a, -um (< urbs + -anus) elegant, sophisticated

4   dicax et urbanus et bellus est? Tantum licentiae prauis
           ingeniis adicit illa fiducia: 'quis enim sciet?' Poposcit tabellas,
           stilum accepit, demisit caput, neminem ueretur, se con-

5   temnit. Inde ista ludibria scaena et pulpito digna. Quo te
           uertas? quae remedia conquiras? Vbique uitia remediis
           fortiora. Ἀλλὰ ταῦτα τῷ ὑπὲρ ἡμᾶς μελήσει, cui multum cotidie
           uigiliarum, multum laboris adicit haec nostra iners et tamen
           effrenata petulantia. Vale.

IV.XXV.4

licentia, -ae (f.) (< licens + -ia) lack of restraint, immoderate behavior {> license}; *licentiae*: partit.
    gen. w/ *tantum* (AG #346/3)

prauus, -a, -um debased, perverse {> depraved}

prauis ingeniis dat. of indir. obj. w/ compd. vb. *adicit* (AG #370)

fiducia, -ae (f.) (< fido, fidere) assurance, confident expectation {> fiduciary}

stilus, -i (m.) stylus (for incising letters on wax tablets), pen

demitto, demittere, demisi, demissus (< de + mitto, mittere) cause to descend, bend down

nemo, neminis (m.) (< ne + homo, hominis) no one, nobody

contemno, contemnere (< con + temno, temnere) scorn, insult {> contempt}; Pliny dramatizes his
    description of corrupt behavior w/ his use of ASYNDETON.

IV.XXV.5

ludibrium, -i (n.) (< ludus) plaything, mockery, pl.: insults, outrages

scaena et pulpito abl. of specif. (AG #418b) w/ *digna*; scaena, -ae (f.) (< Gr.) stage, a spectacle worthy
    of the stage (*OLD* 5c); pulpitum, -i (n.) a wooden platform for dramatic performance; ELLIPSIS of
    sunt or *erant*

quo ... uertas quae ... conquiras delib. subjv. (AG #444); *quo* (interrog. adv.) where; remedium, -i
    (n.) remedy, means of preventing; conquiro, conquirere (< con + quaero, quaerere) search out,
    hunt down

Vbique (adv.) (< ubi + -que) everywhere {> ubiquitous}

remediis abl. of compar. (AG #406) w/ *fortiora*, ELLIPSIS of *sunt*

Ἀλλὰ ταῦτα τῷ ὑπὲρ ἡμᾶς μελήσει, Gr.: "But these things will be of concern to one above us"—not quite
    a dir. quote of Plato's *Phaedo* 95b, as he says more directly "to God:" τῷ θεῷ; the change suggests that
    Pliny may be referring to Trajan as judge.

cui (relat. pron.) anteced. "the one above"; dat. of indir. obj. w/ compd. vb. *adicit* (AG #370)

uigilia, -ae (f.) (< uigil + -ia) watchful attention, vigilance; *uigilarum, laboris*: partit. gen. w/ n. adj.
    multum used as pron. (AG #346/3): "much vigilance . . ."

iners, inertis (< in + ars) lacking skill, useless {> inert}

effrenatus, -a, -um (< ppp. of ex + frenus + -o) unrestrained, unbridled

petulantia, -ae (f.) (< petulans, petulantis + -ia) effrontery, offensive rudeness

BOOK v

xvi—MINICIA MARCELLA, THE IDEAL BETROTHED

C. PLINIVS AEFVLANO MARCELLINO SVO S.

Tristissimus haec tibi scribo, Fundani nostri filia minore   1
defuncta. Qua puella nihil umquam festiuius amabilius, nec
modo longiore uita sed prope immortalitate dignius uidi.
Nondum annos xiiii impleuerat, et iam illi anilis prudentia,   2
matronalis grauitas erat et tamen suauitas puellaris cum

---

v.xvi: Pliny reports the untimely death of a remarkable bride-to-be and in so doing offers an exemplum of the ideal maiden.

Addressee: Aefulius Marcellinus, unknown outside of Pliny's letters.

v.xvi.1

tristis, triste sad, gloomy

Fundani ... defuncta abl. abs. (AG #419); C. Minicius Fundanus also receives several letters from Pliny (s. 1.1x); defunctus, -a, -um (< ppp. of de + fungor, fungi) dead

Qua puella abl. of compar. (AG #406) w/ *festiuius, amabilius*, and *dignius*; although it may seem odd to speakers of E., it is not unusual for Pliny to praise or criticize a person's character w/ compar. adjs. and *nihil*.

festiuus, -a, -um (< festus + -ivus) companionable, genial

nec modo ... sed prope not only ... but almost

uita ... immortalitate abl. of specif. (AG #418b) w/ *dignius*

v.xvi.2

impleo, implere, impleui, impletus fill up, amount to, attain to the full; while Pliny sets Minicia Marcella's age at "not yet fourteen," her funerary urn, on which we find her name, reports that she was not yet thirteen (*ILS* 1030). But almost fourteen sets her nicely on the threshold of her 3rd septet of years, a traditional way to refer to stages in life, first explicated in a poem by the Athenian statesman and sage Solon (*fr.* 27 West) in the 6th century BCE.

illi dat. of poss. (AG #373)

anilis, anile (< anus + -ilis) belonging to an old woman

prudentia, -ae (f.) (< prudens, prudentis + -ia) wisdom, practical understanding

matronalis, matronale (< mater + -ona + -alis) befitting a married woman

grauitas, grauitatis (f.) (< grauis + -tas) dignity, seriousness of conduct

suauitas, suauitatis (f.) (< suauis + -tas) pleasantness, charm

puellaris, puellare (< puella + -aris) befitting a girl

3   uirginali uerecundia. Vt illa patris ceruicibus inhaerebat! ut
nos amicos paternos et amanter et modeste complectebatur!
ut nutrices, ut paedagogos, ut praeceptores pro suo quemque
officio diligebat! quam studiose, quam intellegenter lectita-
bat! ut parce custoditeque ludebat! Qua illa temperantia,
qua patientia, qua etiam constantia nouissimam ualetudinem

4   tulit! Medicis obsequebatur, sororem patrem adhortabatur
ipsamque se destitutam corporis uiribus uigore animi sustine-

---

uirginalis, uirginale (< uirgo, uirginis + -alis) befitting a girl of marriageable age

uerecundia, -ae (f.) (< uereor | -cundus | -ia) modesty, restraint; employing VARIATIO, Pliny
surprises the reader w/ a prep. phrase for Minicia's last quality rather than the expected nom. n.

v.xvi.3

Vt (adv.) exclam.: how, to what extent

ceruix, ceruicis (f.) neck (often used in pl. w/ same mg.); *ceruicibus*: dat. of indir. obj. w/ compd vb.
inhaerebat (AG #370); inhaereo, inhaerere (< in + haereo, haerere) cling, hold on tightly

amanter (adv.) (< amans, amantis) w/ love or affection

modeste (adv.) (< modestus, -a, -um) w/ respect for propriety

complector, complecti, complexus sum (< con + plecto, plectere) embrace, hug

nutrix, nutricis (f.) child's nurse

paedagogus, -i (m.) (< Gr. παιδαγωγός) a slave who oversaw children, esp. w/ schooling

praeceptor, praeceptoris (m.) (<prae + capio, capere + -tor) teacher, tutor

quique, quaeque, quodque (adj.) (< qui, quae, quod + -que) each

quam (interrog. adv.) how; interrog. used for emphasis in exclam. (AG #333n)

studiose (adv.) (< studiosus, -a, -um) ardently, attentively

intellegenter (adv.) (< intellegens, intellegentis) intelligently

lectito (1) (< lego, legere + -ito) read repeatedly

parce (adv.) (< parcus, -a, -um) sparingly, in a restricted manner

custodite (adv.) (< ppp. of custodio, custodire) guardedly, cautiously

ludo, ludere play

qua (interrog. adj.) s. *quam* above; "with what"

temperantia, -ae (f.) (< pres. ptc. of tempero, temperare + -ia) self-control

patientia, -ae (f.) (< pres. ptc. of patior, pati + -ia) endurance, patience

constantia, -ae (f.) (< pres. ptc. of consto, constare + -ia) steadiness, resolution

v.xvi.4

medicus, -i (m.) (< medeor, mederi + -cus) doctor {> medicine}; *medicis*: dat. of indir. obj. w/
compd. vb. *obsequebatur* (AG #370); obsequor, obsequi, obsecutus sum (< ob+ sequor, sequi)
comply, submit {> obsequious}

adhortor, adhortari, adhortatus sum (< ad + hortor, hortari) give encouragement to

destitutus, -a, -um (< ppp. of de + statuo, statuere) deprived of, left in isolation {> destitute); followed by abl. of separ. *uiribus*; uis, uis (f.) force, pl.: strength

uigor, uigoris (m.) (< uigeo, uigere + -or) energy; *uigore*: abl. of means (AG #409)

sustineo, sustinere (< sub(s) + teneo, tenere) hold up, maintain {> sustain}

v.xvi.5

duro (1) last, survive (*OLD* 7a/c)

hic i.e. *uigor animi*

illi dat. of ref. (AG #376)

bat. Durauit hic illi usque ad extremum, nec aut spatio   5
ualetudinis aut metu mortis infractus est, quo plures graui-
oresque nobis causas relinqueret et desiderii et doloris. O   6
triste plane acerbumque funus! o morte ipsa mortis tempus
indignius! iam destinata erat egregio iuueni, iam electus
nuptiarum dies, iam nos uocati. Quod gaudium quo maerore
mutatum est! Non possum exprimere uerbis quantum animo   7
uulnus acceperim, cum audiui Fundanum ipsum, ut multa
luctuosa dolor inuenit, praecipientem, quod in uestes margarita gemmas fuerat erogaturus, hoc in tus et unguenta et

---

usque (adv.) all the way (to), continually, persistently

extremum, -i (n.) (< extremus, -a, -um) final part, end

spatium, -i (n.) an expanse of physical space or time, length of time

infringo, infringere, infregi, infractus (< in + frango, frangere) crush, break, weaken

quo . . . doloris relat. result cl. (AG #537/2); *quo*: abl. of deg. of diff. but nearing abl. of cause
(AG #414a n.), "because of which"; anteced. *uigore animi*; desiderium, -i (n.) (< desidero + -ium)
desire (for something lost), longing; dolor, doloris (m.) (< doleo, dolere + -or) grief, anguish

v.xvi.6

plane (adv.) (< planus, -a, -um) plainly, clearly

funus . . . tempus acc. of exclam. (AG #397d); acerbus, -a, -um: bitter, cruel {> acerbic}; funus, funeris
(n.) funeral, death; indignus, -a, -um (< in + dignus, -a, -um) not deserving {> indignant}, w/ abl.
of specif. *morte*

iam . . . uocati w/ ANAPHORA (*iam, iam, iam*) and repeated ELLIPSIS of forms of *esse*, Pliny heightens
the pathos in this section of his narrative and creates an almost formal lament; destino (1) intend,
designate {> destination}, i.e. betrothe; eligo, eligere, elegi, electus (< ex + lego, legere) choose,
select {> eligible}; nuptiae, nuptiarum (f.) (< nubo, nubere + -ia) marriage ceremony, wedding
{> nuptial} (s. 1.ix.2n. on nuptiae); the wedding turned funeral was a long-standing motif in Greek
and Roman literature, beginning w/ Euripides' *Antigone*, of which only a few fragments survive.

quod . . . quo s. *quam* above

maeror, maeroris (m.) (< maereo, maerere + -or) sorrow, mourning

v.xvi.7

exprimo, exprimere (< ex + premo, premere) portray, describe

quantum . . . acceperim indir. quest. (AG #574); quantus, -a, -um (interr. adj.) how great

cum . . . audiui cum tmp. cl. (AG #545)

ut . . . inuenit *ut* w/ indic. "as" (AG #527f); luctuosus, -a, -um (< luctus + -osus) sorrowful,
distressing; *luctuosa*: n. pl. subst. use

praecipio, praecipere (< prae + capio, capere) order beforehand, give instruction

quod . . . erogaturus relat. cl., anteced. *hoc* (which follows); margarita, -ae (f.) (< Gr. μαργαρίτης)
pearl; gemma, -ae (f.) precious stone, jewel; erogo (1) (< ex + rogo, rogare) pay out, use for a
particular purpose; *fuerat erogaturus*: 1st periphr. conjug. (act. periphr.) (AG #195 and 498a)

hoc . . . impenderetur subst. cl. of purp. (AG #563) (= indir. comm.) ff. *praecipientem, ut* omitted; tus,
turis (n.) frankincense; unguentum, -i (n.) (< unguo, ungere) ointment; odor, odoris (m.) perfume,
spice; impendo, impendere (< in + pendo, pendere) pay out; ASYNDETON in the list of wedding
items suggests the excitement of the planning contrasted w/ the use of conjunctions in the list of
funereal items that slows the text to befit the somber reality.

8   odores impenderetur. Est quidem ille eruditus et sapiens, ut
qui se ab ineunte aetate altioribus studiis artibusque dediderit; sed nunc omnia, quae audiit saepe quae dixit, asper-

9   natur expulsisque uirtutibus aliis pietatis est totus. Ignosces,
laudabis etiam, si cogitaueris quid amiserit. Amisit enim
filiam, quae non minus mores eius quam os uultumque
referebat, totumque patrem mira similitudine exscripserat.

10   Proinde si quas ad eum de dolore tam iusto litteras mittes,
memento adhibere solacium non quasi castigatorium et
nimis forte, sed molle et humanum. Quod ut facilius admittat,

---

v.xvi.8

ille i.e. Minicius Fundanus, whom Pliny now describes

eruditus, -a, -um (< ppp. of ex + rudis + -io) learned {> erudition}

ut qui ... dediderit *ut qui*: "as the sort of man who"; relat. cl. of char. (AG #535); ineo, inire (< in + eo, ire) go in, begin (of a time period) (*OLD* 9a); *ab ineunte aetate*: "from an early age, from his youth"; dedo, dedere, dedidi, deditus (< de + do, dare) give up, surrender, w/ *se*: devote oneself

audiit = contr. form of *audiuit* (AG #181)

aspernor, aspernari, aspernatus sum push away, reject

expulsis uirtutibus aliis abl. abs. (AG #419); expello, expellere, expuli, expulsus (< ex + pello, pellere) drive out, banish

pietatis gen. of quality (AG #345) w/ *totus*, used as if adv. (BG #325 Remark 6): "entirely devoted to duty"

v.xvi.9

ignosces ... cogitaueris FMV condit. (AG #516c); ignosco, ignoscere (< in + (g)nosco, noscere) forgive

quid amiserit indir. quest. (AG #574); amitto, amittere, amisi, amissus (< ab + mitto, mittere) incur the loss of, lose

mos, moris (m.) custom, practice, pl.: character {> moral}

os, oris (n.) mouth, face {> oral}

uultus, -us (m.) countenance, facial expression

mira similitudine abl. of manner omitting *cum* (AG #412b); similitudo, similitudinis (f.) (< similis, simile + -tudo) resemblance, similarity

exscribo, exscribere, exscripsi, exscriptus (< ex + scribo, scribere) show a similarity to, resemble

v.xvi.10

si ... mittes, memento FMV condit. w/ impv. in apod. (AG #516d); *quas* = *aliquas* (s. I.I.1n.); memini, meminisse: remember; *memento*: fut. impv. sg., regularly used instead of pres. impv. (AG #449a)

adhibeo, adhibere (< ad + habeo, habere) hold out, bring to bear

castigatorius, -a, -um (< castigo, castigare + -torius) as a reprimand or correction; for the Roman attitude toward mourning s. iv.ii.3n. on lugeo

nimis (adv.) too

mollis, molle soft, tolerable, gentle

humanus, -a, -um kindly, indulgent (*OLD* 6 a/c)

Quod ... spatium *quod* (relat. pron.), anteced. *solacium*; *ut ... admittat*: subst. cl. of result (AG #568) ff. *faciet*; admitto, admittere (< ad + mitto, mittere) grant access, accept; *multum* (adv.) a lot, much; medius, -a, -um: intervening (*OLD* 11); "Some intervening time will make it much easier for him to accept this (solace)."

multum faciet medii temporis spatium. Vt enim crudum   11
adhuc uulnus medentium manus reformidat, deinde patitur
atque ultro requirit, sic recens animi dolor consolationes
reicit ac refugit, mox desiderat et clementer admotis adquiescit. Vale.

xix—PLINY'S FREEDMAN ZOSIMUS

C. PLINIVS VALERIO PAVLINO SVO S.

Video quam molliter tuos habeas; quo simplicius tibi   1
confitebor, qua indulgentia meos tractem. Est mihi semper   2

---

v.xvi.11

Vt . . . sic correl. conj. (AG #323g), "as . . . so"

crudus, -a, -um raw, bleeding

medens, medentis (m.) (< pres. ptc. of medeor, mederi) physician, doctor

reformido (1) (< re + formido, formidare) shrink from, recoil from

ultro (adv.) conversely

recens, recentis recent, newly come

consolatio, consolationis (f.) (< con + solor, solari + -atio) consolation

reicio, reicere (< re + iacio, iacere) refuse to accept (*OLD* 7a)

refugio, refugere (< re + fugio, fugere) flee from, avoid {> refuge}

clementer (adv.) (< clemens, clementis) kindly, mildly

admotis *consolationibus* understood, dat. of indir. obj. w/ compd. vb. *adquiescit* (AG #370); admoueo, admouere, admoui, admotus (< ad + moueo, mouere) move near, apply (as medication) (*OLD* 8a); adquiesco, adquiescere (< ad + quiesco, quiescere) relax, subside, find comfort

v.xix: Pliny sings the praises of his freedman Zosimus and asks that he be cared for at a friend's estate while he recovers from an ongoing and recurring illness. Pliny's concern not only contrasts with Macedo's cruelty in III.xiv but also clearly echoes Cicero's anxiety about the ongoing illness of his secretary Tiro, expressed in a great number of letters in Book 16 of *Ad Familiares*.

Addressee: Valerius Paulinus, suffect consul in 107 CE from Forum Julii in Narbonensis; he receives several letters from Pliny on various topics.

v.xix.1

quam . . . habeas indir. quest. (AG #574); *quam* (interrog. adv.) how; *molliter* (adv.) (< mollis, molle) gently; *tuos*, subst. use: the ones belonging to you, i.e. your slaves and freedmen

quo (relat. pron.) anteced. the previous stmt.; abl. of cause (AG #404)

simplicius (compar. adv.) (< simplex, simplicis) more candidly, openly

confiteor, confiteri, confessus sum (< con + fateor, fateri) admit

qua . . . tractem indir. quest. (AG #574); *qua* (interrog. adj.); indulgentia, -ae (f.) (< indulgens + -ia) leniency, indulgence; tracto (1) (< traho, trahere + -to) handle, manage; Pliny's gentle treatment of 'his own' is also the subj. of VIII.XVI.

v.xix.2

mihi dat. of poss. (AG #373)

3

in animo et Homericum illud πατὴρ δ' ὡς ἤπιος ἦεν et hoc
nostrum 'pater familiae'. Quod si essem natura asperior et
durior, frangeret me tamen infirmitas liberti mei Zosimi,
cui tanto maior humanitas exhibenda est, quanto nunc illa
magis eget. Homo probus officiosus litteratus; et ars quidem
eius et quasi inscriptio comoedus, in qua plurimum facit.
Nam pronuntiat acriter sapienter apte decenter etiam;
utitur et cithara perite, ultra quam comoedo necesse est.
Idem tam commode orationes et historias et carmina legit,

πατὴρ δ' ὡς ἤπιος ἦεν Gr.: "as a father he was gentle"—from Telemachus' description of Odysseus in
Homer, *Odyssey* II.47

quod (conj.) but even

si ... Zosimi pres. C-to-F condit. (AG #517); *natura*: abl. of specif. (AG #418) w/ *asperior et durior*;
asper, aspera, asperum: harsh, rough; frango, frangere: break, shatter, soften (*OLD* 10); infirmitas,
infirmitatis (f.) (< in + firmus + -tas) weakness, ill health; libertus, -i (m.) (< liber + -tus) freedman; as someone who had been Pliny's slave, Zosimus would have had an ongoing and close relationship w/ his former master, one that would have compelled Pliny to continue to view him as a
member of the household and that would have carried expectations of mutual concern, obligation,
and service, albeit w/ Pliny remaining very clearly in a controlling position (s. also II.vi.2n. on
libertus).

cui ... eget *tanto ... quanto*, correl. abl. of deg. of diff. w/ compar. *maior* (AG #414a n.), "as much ... as";
humanitas, humanitatis (f.) (< humanus + -tas) humane character, kindness; exhibeo, exhibere
(< ex + habeo, habere) present, show, practice {> exhibit}; *exhibenda est*: 2nd (pass.) periphr.
conjug. (AG #196 and 500/2); egeo, egere: need, require, be w/ out, w/ either gen. or dat.
(AG #356n.); "to whom much more kindness should be shown, as he now needs it so much more."

v.xix.3

probus, -a, -um of an upright character, honest

officiosus, -a, -um (< officium + -osus) dutiful, attentive

litteratus, -a, -um (< littera + -atus) well-versed in literature, erudite; Pliny's use of ASYNDETON here
and elsewhere in the letter and the ELLIPSIS of *est* emphasize these qualities.

et(iam) quasi "even as if"

inscriptio, inscriptionis (f.) (< in + scribo, scribere + -tio) brand, label; this term was used for the
signs that individuals for sale in the slave market would have worn to provide information about
their origins and to promote their skills to potential buyers.

comoedus, -i (m.) (< Gr. κωμῳδός) comic actor, comedic talent; *comoedus*: nom. sg., appos. to
inscriptio

qua (relat. pron.) anteced. *ars*

pronuntio (1) (< pro + nuntio, nuntiare) speak, pronounce {> pronounce)

apte (adv.) (< aptus, -a, -um) appropriately, properly

decenter (adv.) (< decens, decentis) in a way that conforms w/ good taste

cithara, -ae (f.) (< Gr. κιθάρα) lyre; *cithara*: w/ *utitur*, depon. vb. that takes abl. of means, not acc. dir.
obj. (AG #410)

perite (adv.) (< peritus, -a, -um) skillfully

ultra (adv.) to a point beyond, to a greater degree

commode (adv.) (< con + modus) properly, suitably, pleasingly {> commodious}

ut ... uideatur result cl. (AG #537)

ut hoc solum didicisse uideatur. Haec tibi sedulo exposui,　　　　4
quo magis scires, quam multa unus mihi et quam iucunda
ministeria praestaret. Accedit longa iam caritas hominis,
quam ipsa pericula auxerunt. Est enim ita natura com-　　　　5
paratum, ut nihil aeque amorem incitet et accendat quam
carendi metus; quem ego pro hoc non semel patior. Nam　　　　6
ante aliquot annos, dum intente instanterque pronuntiat,
sanguinem reiecit atque ob hoc in Aegyptum missus a me post
longam peregrinationem confirmatus rediit nuper; deinde
dum per continuos dies nimis imperat uoci, ueteris infirmitatis tussicula admonitus rursus sanguinem reddidit. Qua ex　　　　7

V.XIX.4

sedulo (adv.) diligently, zealously

expono, exponere, exposui, expositus (< ex + pono, ponere) put out, explain (*OLD* 6) {> expository}

quo … scires relat. cl. of purp., introd. by *quo* because of compar. *magis* (AG #531/2a); *quo*: abl. of deg. of diff. (AG #414a n.)

quam … praestaret indir. quest. (AG #574); *quam* (interrog. adv.) how; ministerium, -i (n.) (< minister + -ium) service, function; praesto (1) (< prae + sto, stare) make available, furnish (*OLD* 9a)

caritas, caritatis (f.) (< carus + -tas) affection, esteem

V.XIX.5

comparo (1) (< con + paro, parare) prepare, arrange, constitute (*OLD* 7a); *natura*: abl. of means (AG #409)

ut … metus result cl. (AG #537); *aeque* (adv.) (< aequus, -a, -um) to an equal degree, as much, w/ *quam*: "as much as"; incito (1) (< in + cito, citare) urge, make more intense (*OLD* 4) {> incite}; accendo, accendere: kindle, arouse (*OLD* 4); careo, carere: lack, be w/ out, be deprived; *carendi*: ger. objv. gen. (AG #347) w/ *metus*

semel (adv.) one time, once

V.XIX.6

aliquot (indecl. adj.) a number of, some

dum … pronuntiat *dum* w/ pres. indic. vb. for continuous action in past (AG #556); *intente* (adv.) (< intentus, -a, -um) w/ concentrated attention, intently; *instanter* (adv.) (< instans, instantis) vehemently

sanguis, sanguinis (m.) blood

reicio, reicere, reieci, reiectus (< re + iacio, iacere) throw out, bring up, vomit (*OLD* 5)

peregrinatio, peregrinationis (f.) (< peregrinor, peregrinari + -tio) act of traveling or staying abroad

confirmo (1) (< con + firmo, firmare) strengthen

redeo, redire, redii, reditus (< re + eo, ire) return

nuper (adv.) recently

continuus, -a, -um (< con + teneo, tenere + -uus) uninterrupted, w/ out pause

nimis (adv.) too much

uoci dat. w/ intr. vb. *imperat* (AG #367)

uetus, ueteris old, having been in existence a long time {> veteran}

tussicula, -ae (f.) (< tussis + culus) slight cough; *tussicula*: abl. of means (AG #409)

admoneo, admonere, admonui, admonitus (< ad + moneo, monere) remind {> admonish}

V.XIX.7

Qua ex causa modifier of obj. of monosyl. prep. often precedes prep. (AG #599d)

causa destinaui eum mittere in praedia tua, quae Foro Iulii
possides. Audiui enim te saepe referentem esse ibi et aera
salubrem et lac eiusmodi curationibus accommodatissimum.

8 Rogo ergo scribas tuis, ut illi uilla, ut domus pateat, offerant
9 etiam sumptibus eius, si quid opus erit. Erit autem opus
modico; est enim tam parcus et continens, ut non solum
delicias uerum etiam necessitates ualetudinis frugalitate
restringat. Ego proficiscenti tantum uiatici dabo, quantum
sufficiat eunti in tua. Vale.

---

destino (1) intend, make up one's mind {> destination}; w/ compl. inf. *mittere*
praedium, -i (n.) estate
Foro Iulii locat.; Forum Iulii was a colony founded by Julius Caesar in Gallia Narbonensis, the
modern-day town of Fréjus, and the birthplace of Tacitus' father-in-law Gnaeus Julius Agricola.
possideo, possidere (< potis + sedeo, sedere) have (land) in one's control, hold
esse … accommodatissimum indir. disc. (AG #580) ff. *referentem*; aer, aeris (m.) (< Gr. ἀήρ) air;
aera: Gr. acc. sg., modified by *salubrem*; saluber, salubris: healthy, beneficial {> salubrious}; lac,
lactis (n.) milk; *eiusmodi*: of this kind (*OLD* modus 12c); curatio, curationis (f.) (< curo + -tio)
method of treatment; *curationibus*: dat. w/ adj. *accommodatissimum* (AG #384); accommodatus, -a,
-um (< ppp. of ad + com + modus + -o) suitable, appropriate; perhaps Zosimus was suffering
from tuberculosis, which tends to recur and which was thought to respond well to milk and fresh
air (SW 350–1).

v.xix.8
scribas tuis subst. cl. of purp. (AG #563) (= indir. comm.) ff. *rogo, ut* omitted
ut … offerant subst. cl. of purp. (AG #563) (= indir. comm.) ff. *scribas*; *illi*: dat. sg. (i.e. Zosimus);
pateo, patere: be open, offer free access; offero, offerre (< ob + fero, ferre) provide, supply, compd.
vb + dat. *sumptibus* (AG #370); sumptus, -us (m.) (< sumo, sumere + -tus) expenditure
si … erit prot. of FMV condit. (AG #516c); *quid = aliquid* (s. 1.1.1n. on quas); opus, operis (n.) that
which needs to be done, is needed (*OLD* 12)

v.xix.9
modico n. abl. subst. w/ *opus* (AG #411)
parcus, -a, -um thrifty, careful
continens, continentis (< pres. ptc. of con + teneo, tenere) restrained, not indulging in excesses,
moderate (*OLD* 5)
ut … restringat result cl. (AG #537); delicia, -ae (f.) (< de + lacio, lacere + -ia) pleasure, delight, pl.:
luxuries {> delicious}; necessitas, necessitatis (f.) (< necesse + -tas) requirement, need; frugalitas,
frugalitatis (f.) (< frux + -alis + -tas) temperance, self-restraint (s. ii.iv.3n.); restringo, restringere
(< re + stringo, stringere) restrain, restrict
proficiscor, proficisci, profectus sum (< pro + facio + -sco) set out, start on a journey; *proficiscenti*:
ei understood here and w/ *eunti* ff.
tantum, -i (n.) … **quantum, -i** (n.) correl., "as much (w/ partit. gen. *uiatici*) … as"; uiaticum, -i (n.)
(< uia + -aticus) traveling allowance; *quantum … sufficiat*: relat. cl. of char. (AG #535)
in tua "to your estates"

BOOK VI

IV—1ST LOVE LETTER TO CALPURNIA

C. PLINIVS CALPVRNIAE SVAE S.

Numquam sum magis de occupationibus meis questus,   1
quae me non sunt passae aut proficiscentem te ualetudinis
causa in Campaniam prosequi aut profectam e uestigio subsequi. Nunc enim praecipue simul esse cupiebam, ut oculis   2

VI.IV: In language that recalls both the "excluded lover" theme of elegiac poetry and Cicero's anxiety about Tiro's illness (s. V.XIX and C 165–71), Pliny expresses his love and longing for his wife in the 1st of three letters (s. VI.VII; the 3rd is *Ep.* VII.V, not included in this volume).
Addressee: Calpurnia, Pliny's 2nd (C 104–5) or 3rd (SW 71, 264, 559–60) wife, parents deceased, granddaughter of Calpurnius Fabatus, niece of Calpurnia Hispulla.

VI.IV.1
occupatio, occupationis (f.) (< occupo, occupare + -tio) preoccupation w/ business, employment
queror, queri, questus sum complain, grumble {> querulous}
quae...passae (< patior) introd. acc. + inf. constr. (AG #565c): *me...aut...prosequi...aut... subsequi*
proficiscor, proficisci, profectus sum (< pro + facio + -sco) set out, start on a journey; Pliny's expresses his distress at Calpurnia's departure w/ his repetition of this vb. in both its pres. (*proficiscentem*) and pf. participial (*profectam*) forms to describe her (*te*), an ex. of POLYPTOTON.
ualetudinis gen. w/ *causa* (AG #359b)
Campania, -ae (f.) a region of western central Italy that was a popular location for elite villas, including such places as Baiae, Herculaneum, Stabiae, Pompeii, and Naples.
prosequor, prosequi, prosecutus sum (< pro + sequor, sequi) accompany
uestigium, -i (n.) footprint, track, path {> vestige}
subsequor, subsequi, subsecutus sum (< sub + sequor, sequi) follow immediately or closely {> subsequent}

VI.IV.2
praecipue (adv.) (< prae + capio, capere + -uus) especially
ut...crederem purp. cl. (AG #531/1)

meis crederem quid uiribus quid corpusculo adparares, ecquid denique secessus uoluptates regionisque abundantiam
3   inoffensa transmitteres. Equidem etiam fortem te non sine
cura desiderarem; est enim suspensum et anxium de eo quem
4   ardentissime diligas interdum nihil scire. Nunc uero me cum
absentiae tum infirmitatis tuae ratio incerta et uaria sollicitudine exterret. Vereor omnia, imaginor omnia, quaeque
natura metuentium est, ea maxime mihi quae maxime
5   abominor fingo. Quo impensius rogo, ut timori meo cottidie
singulis uel etiam binis epistulis consulas. Ero enim securior
dum lego, statimque timebo cum legero. Vale.

---

quid ... adparares 1st indir. quest. (AG #574) ff. *crederem*; *quid* (interrog. pron.) to what extent (*OLD* quis 15); uis, uis (f.) force, pl.: strength; corpusculum, -i (n.) (< corpus + -culum) small body, plumpness {> corpuscle}; *uiribus ... corpusculo*: dat. of indir. obj. w/ compd. vb. *adparares* (AG #370); adparo (1) (< ad + paro, parare) prepare, add to (+ dat.) (*OLD* 4)

ecquid ... transmitteres 2nd indir. quest. (AG #574); *ecquid* (interrog. pcl.), "whether it is true that"; abundantia, -ae (f.) (< pres. ptc. of abundo, abundere + -ia) excessive amount, wealth; inoffensus, -a, -um (< in + ppp. of offendo, offendere) unharmed; transmitto, transmittere (< trans + mitto, mittere) let (time, experiences) pass by (*OLD* 7); Pliny's old-fashioned sense of restraint and abstemiousness reflects a long-held Roman suspicion of the harmful power of luxurious living.

VI.IV.3

te ... desiderarem apod. of pres. C-to-F condit. (AG #517) w/ *etiam fortem* replacing the prot.: "even if you were strong"

est ... scire subj. of *est*: *nihil scire*; suspensus, -a, -um (< ppp. of sub + pendo, pendere) in anxious uncertainty; anxius, -a, -um: worried, uneasy; *ardentissime* (superl. adv.) (< ardens, ardentis) most passionately, zealously; *quem ... diligas*: relat. cl. of char. (AG #535); *interdum* (adv.) (< inter + dum) now and then, in the meantime

VI.IV.4

cum ... tum both ... and

infirmitas, infirmitatis (f.) (< in + firmus + -tas) weakness, ill health

incerta et uaria abl. sg. modifying *sollicitudine*; uarius, -a, -um: changeable, fluctuating (*OLD* 5a); sollicitudo, sollicitudinis (f.) (< sollicitus, -a, -um + -tudo) anxiety

exterreo, exterrere (< ex + terreo, terrere) drive to distraction, terrify

imaginor, imaginari, imaginatus sum (< imago, imaginis + -o) imagine

metuo, metuere (< metus + -o) fear, be afraid

ea ... quae ... abominor *ea*, acc. pl. subst. use: "those things"; abominor, abominari, abominatus sum (< ab + omen + -o) avert by prayer, detest {> abominate}

fingo, fingere form, create, invent, imagine; Pliny pours out his fears, piling them up through ASYNDETON rather than separating them w/ conjunctions.

VI.IV.5

Quo (relat. pron.) abl. of deg. of diff. w/ compar. (AG #414a n.), anteced. preceding sent.; *impensius* (compar. adv.) (< impensus, -a, -um) more lavishly, unendingly

ut ... consulas subst. cl. of purp. (AG #563) (= indir. comm.) ff. *rogo*; bini, -ae, -a (< bis + -nus) two, a pair {> binary}; *timori*: dat. of indir. obj. w/ *consulas* as intr. vb. (AG #367c)

securus, -a, -um (< se + cura + -us) free from care/anxiety

cum legero cum tmp. cl. (AG #545); *legero*: fut. pf. indic.

VII—2ND LETTER TO CALPURNIA

C. PLINIVS CALPVRNIAE SVAE S.

Scribis te absentia mea non mediocriter adfici unumque   1
habere solacium, quod pro me libellos meos teneas, saepe
etiam in uestigio meo colloces. Gratum est quod nos requiris,   2
gratum quod his fomentis adquiescis; inuicem ego epistulas
tuas lectito atque identidem in manus quasi nouas sumo.
Sed eo magis ad desiderium tui accendor: nam cuius litte-   3
rae tantum habent suauitatis, huius sermonibus quantum
dulcedinis inest! Tu tamen quam frequentissime scribe, licet
hoc ita me delectet ut torqueat. Vale.

VI.VII: Pliny again tells his wife how important her letters are to him in this 2nd of three letters
addressed to her.
Addressee: Calpurnia, s. VI.IV.

VI.VII.1
te ... solacium indir. disc. (AG #580); *mediocriter* (adv.) (< mediocris) moderately, w/ negat.: to no
small extent, exceedingly; adficio, adficere (< ad + facio, facere) affect, stir/move (emotion)
quod ... colloces subst. cl. introd. by *quod* (AG #572), "that," subord. cl. in indir. disc. takes subjv. vb.
(AG #580); uestigium, -i (n.) footprint, track, place where one has stood {> vestige}; colloco
(1) (< con + loco, locare) set in place, position; *te* understood

VI.VII.2
fomentum, -i (n.) (< foueo, fouere + -mentum) remedy, solace
adquiesco, adquiescere (< ad + quiesco, quiescere) relax, find comfort
inuicem (adv.) in turn
lectito (1) (< leo, legere + -ito) read repeatedly
identidem (< idem + et + idem) again and again, repeatedly
sumo, sumere take up (into one's hands)

VI.VII.3
eo magis (adv.) all the more, so much more (*OLD* 2); *eo*: abl. of deg. of diff. w/ compar. (AG #414a n.)
desiderium, -i (n.) (< desidero + -ium) desire (for something lost), longing; *tui*: objv. gen. (AG #347)
accendo, accendere kindle, arouse (*OLD* 4)
cuius = *tuae* relat. pron., anteced. *tui*
tantum, -i (n.) ... **quantum, -i** (n.) correl., "as much (w/ partit. gen. *suauitatis*) ... as (w/ partit. gen.
dulcedinis)"; suauitas, suauitatis (f.) (< suauis + -tas) pleasantness, charm; *huius*: again referring to
Calpurnia; *sermonibus*: dat. of indir. obj. w/ compd. vb. *inest* (AG #370); dulcedo, dulcedinis (f.)
(< dulcis + -edo) charm, pleasurableness; *nam ... inest*: "for your letters have as as much charm as
there is in your manner of speaking"
quam + superl. as ... as possible; *frequentissime* (superl. adv.) (< frequens, frequentis) constantly,
persistently
hoc ita me delectet subst. cl. of purp. ff. *licet, ut* omitted (AG #565)
ut torqueat result cl. (AG #537); torqueo, torquere: twist tightly, torture mentally

x—DISGRACE OF AN UNFINISHED TOMB

C. PLINIVS ALBINO SVO S.

1   Cum uenissem in socrus meae uillam Alsiensem, quae aliquamdiu Rufi Vergini fuit, ipse mihi locus optimi illius et
maximi uiri desiderium non sine dolore renouauit. Hunc
enim colere secessum atque etiam senectutis suae nidulum

2   uocare consueuerat. Quocumque me contulissem, illum
animus illum oculi requirebant. Libuit etiam monimentum

3   eius uidere, et uidisse paenituit. Est enim adhuc imper-

---

vi.x: Pliny writes about his distress that the tomb of his guardian Verginius Rufus remains unfinished. Addressee: Albinus, perhaps Lucceius Albinus, suffect consul circa 102 CE and fellow prosecutor with Pliny of Caecilius Classicus (SW 232, AB 69).

vi.x.1
cum . . . Alsiensem cum circumst. cl. (AG #546); socrus, -us (f.) mother-in-law; Alsiensis, Alsiensie: Alsian; Alsium was a town on the coast of Tuscany, a day's journey from Rome (SW 365)
aliquamdiu (adv.) for some time, for a considerable time
Verginius Rufus While he came to his 1st consulship late, at the age of 49, Verginius would serve in the office three times, twice as consul ordinarius, the most prestigious office an elite Roman could achieve, other than emperor. His renown came from his refusal of the principate twice, once following the death of Nero and a 2nd time following Otho's suicide. Pliny reports (*Ep.* II.I) that when his father died, Verginius was appointed in his will as Pliny's guardian. We can be sure, though, that Pliny was not among his heirs, as he would surely have seen to the completion of the unfinished monument that so upsets him.
desiderium, -i (n.) (< desidero + -ium) desire (for something lost), longing; *uiri*: objv. gen. (AG #347)
dolor, doloris (m.) (< doleo, dolere + -or) grief, anguish
renouo (1) (< re + nouo, nouare) restore, renew {> renovate}
Hunc i.e. *locum*; *secessum*: appos. to *Hunc*
senectus, senectutis (f.) (< senex + -tus) period of old age
nidulus, -i (m.) (< nidus + -ulus) little nest
consuesco, consuescere, consueui, consuetus (< con + suesco, suescere) become accustomed (+ compl. inf.)

vi.x.2
Quocumque . . . contulissem condit. relat. cl. (AG #542); *quocumque* (adv.): wherever
illum i.e. Verginius
libet, libuit impers. vb. (AG #208c): it is/was pleasing
monimentum, -i (n.) (< moneo, monere + -mentum) sepulchral monument, tomb
paeniteo, paenitere, paenitui cause dissatisfaction or regret {> penitent}; impers. vb. of feeling (AG #354b) {> penitent}

vi.x.3
imperfectus, -a, -um (< in + ppp. of per + facio, facere) incomplete, unfinished; i.e. *monimentum*
in causa (esse) be the cause/reason, be responsible (*OLD* causa 11b); ELLIPSIS of *est*
potius (adv.) rather, more exactly

fectum, nec difficultas operis in causa, modici ac potius exigui,
sed inertia eius cui cura mandata est. Subit indignatio cum
miseratione, post decimum mortis annum reliquias neglectum-
que cinerem sine titulo sine nomine iacere, cuius memoria
orbem terrarum gloria peruagetur. At ille mandauerat   4
caueratque, ut diuinum illud et immortale factum uersibus
inscriberetur:

> Hic situs est Rufus, pulso qui Vindice quondam
> imperium adseruit non sibi sed patriae.

Tam rara in amicitiis fides, tam parata obliuio mortuorum,   5
ut ipsi nobis debeamus etiam conditoria exstruere omniaque

---

exiguus, -a, -um (< ex + ago, agere + -uus) small (in amount), scanty

inertia, -ae (f.) (< iners, inertis + -ia) idleness, disinclination for activity

mando (1) give instructions, order (+ dat.) {> mandate}

subeo, subire, subii, subitus (< sub + eo, ire) steal in on, come over (a person's mind) (*OLD* 11)

indignatio, indignationis (f.) (< in + dignor, dignari + -tio) resentment, anger

miseratio, miserationis (f.) (< miseror, miserari + -tio) expression of grief, pity

post ... iacere indir. disc. (AG #580); reliquiae, reliquiarum (f.) (< reliquus + -ia) the remains
(of one who has died); neglectus, -a, -um (ppp. of neglego, neglegere < nec + lego, legere)
neglected, ignored; cinis, cineris (m.) ashes; titulus, -i (m.) identification, inscription

cuius ... peruagetur relat. cl. of char. (AG #535), anteced. Verginius Rufus understood; orbis terrarum: the world (*OLD* orbis 12); peruagor, peruagari, peruagatus sum (< per + uagor, uagari) range
over, spread through

VI.X.4

caueo, cauere, caui, cautus take precautions, make legal provision, stipulate (*OLD* 7a)

ut ... inscriberetur subst. cl. of purp. (AG #563) (= indir. comm.); uersus, -us (m.) (< uerto, uertere +
-tus) line of text, verse; the epitaph that follows is, naturally, an elegiac couplet, which Pliny will cite
again in IX.XIX.

situs, -a, -um (< ppp. of sino, sinere) laid in the grave, buried

pulso ... Vindice abl. abs. (AG #419); Vindex, Vindicis (m.). His defeat of Julius Vindex, who had pro-
mulgated a revolt of the troops against Nero, led Verginius' troops to offer repeatedly to raise him up
as emperor; he insisted instead on supporting whomever the Senate chose.

quondam (adv.) formerly, once

adsero, adserere, adserui, adsertus (< ad + sero, serere) lay claim to

VI.X.5

tam ... tam Pliny's use of ANAPHORA and the ELLIPSIS of *est* make these cls. more like exclams. and
even, given their mg., laments.

obliuio, obliuionis (f.) (< obliuiscor, obliuisci + -io) act of forgetting, oblivion

ut ... praesumere result cl. (AG #537); conditorium, -i (n.) (< condo, condere + -torium) burial
place, tomb; exstruo, exstruere (< ex + struo, struere) build up, construct; heres, heredis (m.) heir;
praesumo, praesumere (< prae + sumo, sumere) take up or perform beforehand

6   heredum officia praesumere. Nam cui non est uerendum,
     quod uidemus accidisse Verginio? cuius iniuriam ut indignio-
     rem, sic etiam notiorem ipsius claritas facit. Vale.

XI—PRAISE OF PLINY'S PROTÉGÉS

C. PLINIVS MAXIMO SVO S.

1   O diem laetum! Adhibitus in consilium a praefecto urbis
     audiui ex diuerso agentes summae spei summae indolis

VI.X.6

cui (interrog. pron.) dat. of agent w/ *est uerendum*, impers. use of 2nd (pass.) periphr. conjug. (AG #196
  and 500/3)

quod (relat. pron.) subst. use: "that which"

cuius . . . facit *cuius*: relat. pron.; indignus, -a, -um (< in + dignus, -a, -um) not deserving {> indig-
  nant}; *ut . . . sic*: correl. conj. (AG #323g), "as . . . as"; notus, -a, -um (< ppp. of nosco, noscere) known,
  notorious (*OLD* 7); claritas, claritatis (f.) (< clarus + -tas) renown, fame; "His fame makes his mistreatment even more notorious as it is so unwarranted."

VI.XI: Pliny expresses his delight at the success of two of his protégés in the courtroom, Fuscus
  Salinator and Ummidius Quadratus.

Addressee: Maximus, likely Novius Maximus, who receives a number of letters from Pliny on literary
  topics (SW 367, AB 76).

VI.XI.1

O . . . laetum acc. of exclam. (AG #397d)

adhibeo, adhibere, adhibui, adhibitus (< ad + habeo, habere) call in, bring in

in consilium into consultation (s. I.IX.2n.)

praefectus, -i (m.) (< ppp. of prae + facio, facere) prefect; under the emperors, the Praefectus Urbi(s),
  the City Prefect, served as the emperor's deputy at Rome; his duties included maintaining order in
  the city, using force if necessary. Generally a man of consular rank, he also presided over his own
  court. It is presumably to this court that Pliny is called (*OCD* s. praefectus urbi, 1239).

ex diuerso on opposite sides (*OLD* diuersus 7a)

ago, agere deliver a speech (*OLD* 43)

summae spei summae indolis gen. of quality (AG #345); spes, spei (f.) expectation, future promise
  (*OLD* 3a); indoles, indolis (f.) (< indu + -alies) innate character, nature

Fuscus Salinator Gnaeus Pedanius Fuscus Salinator, one of Pliny's pupils, would later marry
  Hadrian's niece (mentioned in *Ep.* VI.XXVI) and serve as his 1st colleague (*consul ordinarius*) in the
  consulship in 118 CE, a man of great promise indeed, but nothing is known of his subsequent career
  (SW 386, AB 77–8). He receives several letters from Pliny that suggest topics for study and detail
  how Pliny spends his time away from Rome, including IX.XXXVI.

iuuenes, Fuscum Salinatorem et Vmmidium Quadratum,
egregium par nec modo temporibus nostris sed litteris ipsis
ornamento futurum. Mira utrique probitas, constantia salua,   2
decorus habitus, os Latinum, uox uirilis, tenax memoria,
magnum ingenium, iudicium aequale; quae singula mihi
uoluptati fuerunt, atque inter haec illud, quod et ipsi me ut
rectorem, ut magistrum intuebantur, et iis qui audiebant me
aemulari, meis instare uestigiis uidebantur. O diem (repetam   3
enim) laetum notandumque mihi candidissimo calculo! Quid
enim aut publice laetius quam clarissimos iuuenes nomen et

Vmmidius Quadratus Gaius Ummidius Quadratus Sertorius Severus also depended on Pliny's guidance (s. VII.XXIV). He too would serve in office alongside the Emperor Hadrian, as suffect consul in
118. He may have been married to the younger sister of the future emperor Marcus Aurelius (SW
431, AB 96). Ummidius is also the addressee of letters from Pliny regarding the role of the advocate.
par, paris (n.) pair
temporibus . . . futurum *temporibus . . . litteris*: dat. of ref. (AG #376) w/ *ornamento*, dat. of purp. (AG
  #382) = dbl. dat.; ornamentum, -i (n.) (< orno, ornare + -mentum) adornment, enhancement

VI.XI.2
utrique dat. of poss. (AG #373), ELLIPSIS of *sunt*
mira . . . aequale probitas, probitatis (f.) (< probus + -tas) moral integrity, honesty; constantia, -ae (f.)
  (< pres. ptc. of consto, constare + -ia) steadiness, resolution; saluus, -a, -um: safe, unimpaired; decorus, -a, -um; (< decor + -us) handsome, honorable; habitus, -us (m.) (< habeo, habere + -tus)
  physical bearing, style of dress {> habit}; os, oris (n.) mouth, eloquence {> oral}; tenax, tenacis
  (< teneo, tenere + -ax) holding fast, retentive {> tenacious}; using ASYNDETON for this long list of
  qualities, Pliny gives the reader a sense of his breathless enthusiasm for these two young men
quae (relat. pron.) anteced. the preceding list of qualities
mihi uoluptati *mihi*: dat. of ref. (AG #376) w/ *uoluptati*, dat. of purp. (AG #382) = dbl. dat.
illud points forward to the *quod* cl. (AG #297e)
ut rectorem, ut magistrum *ut* (conj.) "as"; rector, rectoris (m.) (< rego, regere + -tor) guide, tutor
intueor, intueri, intuitus sum (< in + tueor, tueri) look at, look upon, regard (as)
aemulor, aemulari, aemulatus sum imitate, emulate
insto (1) (< in + sto, stare) stand on, pursue; compd. vb + dat. *uestigiis* (AG #370); uestigium, -i (n.)
  footprint, track, path {> vestige}

VI.XI.3
noto (1) mark as important; *notandum*: gerv. w/ dat. of agent *mihi* (AG #374)
candidus, -a, -um (< candeo + -idus) bright, white
calculus, -i (m.) (< calx, calcis + -ulus) small stone. It was Roman custom to mark out days on the
  calendar that were fortunate or favorable w/ white stones. In addition, white and black stones were
  used at trials in early Rome (and among the Athenian Greeks) to vote for acquittal or condemnation
  respectively (s. Martial IX.53.5 and Ovid *Met.* 15.41).
Quid . . . laetius ELLIPSIS of *est*; impers. n. subj. introd. acc. + inf. constr. (AG #455/2)
clarus, -a, -um bright {> clarity}

4 famam ex studiis petere, aut mihi optatius quam me ad recta
tendentibus quasi exemplar esse propositum? Quod gaudium
ut perpetuo capiam deos oro; ab isdem teste te peto, ut
omnes qui me imitari tanti putabunt meliores esse quam me
uelint. Vale.

XVI—ERUPTION OF VESUVIUS AND THE ELDER PLINY

C. PLINIVS TACITO SVO S.

1 Petis ut tibi auunculi mei exitum scribam, quo uerius
tradere posteris possis. Gratias ago; nam uideo morti eius si

---

optatius (compar. adj.) (< ppp. of opto, optare) more desired; *mihi*: dat. of agent w/ ppp. (AG #375)
ad recta subst. use: "for proper ways"
tendo, tendere stretch out, strive; *tendentibus*: dat. of agent w/ ppp. *propositum* (AG #375)
propono, proponere, proposui, propositus (< pro + pono, ponere) hold up, offer, suggest

VI.XI.4
Quod . . . oro *Quod gaudium*: dir. obj. of *capiam*; *Quod*: connecting relat., gener. translated "this" (AG
#308f); *ut . . . capiam*: subst. cl. of purp. (AG #563) (= indir. comm.) ff. *oro*; *perpetuo* (adv.) (< per +
poto, petere + -uus) continuously, w/ out pause
teste te abl. abs. (AG #419); testis, testis (m.) witness
ut . . . uelint subst. cl. of purp. (AG #563) (= indir. comm.) ff. *peto*; imitor, imitari, imitatus sum: copy
the conduct of, imitate; *tanti*: gen. of quality (price) (AG #345), used instead of abl. of price w/ indef.
value (AG #417), "worth so much"

VI.XVI: From the town of Misenum, Pliny offers the only extant eyewitness account of the eruption of
Mount Vesuvius in 79 CE, focusing on his observations and the actions of his Uncle Pliny. This is the
1st of two letters regarding the event (s. also VI.XX), both of which, Pliny notes, have been solicited
by Tacitus as sources for his *Historiae*. The letters, however, are not mere evidence; rather they are
carefully composed historical narrative in their own right.
Addressee: Cornelius Tacitus, s. I.VI.

VI.XVI.1
ut . . . scribam subst. cl. of purp. (AG #563) (= indir. comm.) ff. *petis*; auunculus, -i (m.) (< auus +
culus) maternal uncle {> avuncular}; exitus, -us (m.) (< exeo, exire + -tus) departure, the end of
one's life, death; this is, of course, Gaius Plinius Secundus (Pliny the Elder), who posthumously adopted his nephew—Pliny the Younger.
quo . . . possis relat. cl. of purp., introd. by *quo* because of compar. *uerius* (AG #531/2a); posterus, -a,
-um (< post) later, future, pl. subst.: descendents, posterity; the account of the eruption was, we may
assume, in the lost portion of Tacitus' *Historiae*.
morti . . . propositam indir. disc. (AG #580); *si celebretur*: prot. of a FMV condit. subjv. in indir. disc.,
apod. uses inf. (AG #589/1); celebro (1) (< celeber + -o) crowd, praise, extol (*OLD* 6a); propono,
proponere, proposui, propositus (< pro + pono, ponere) set forth, offer

celebretur a te immortalem gloriam esse propositam. Quam-   2
uis enim pulcherrimarum clade terrarum, ut populi ut urbes
memorabili casu, quasi semper uicturus occiderit, quamuis
ipse plurima opera et mansura condiderit, multum tamen
perpetuitati eius scriptorum tuorum aeternitas addet. Equi-   3
dem beatos puto, quibus deorum munere datum est aut
facere scribenda aut scribere legenda, beatissimos uero quibus
utrumque. Horum in numero auunculus meus et suis libris
et tuis erit. Quo libentius suscipio, deposco etiam quod
iniungis.
Erat Miseni classemque imperio praesens regebat. Nonum   4

VI.XVI.2

quamuis ... occiderit 1st of 2 conces. cls. (AG #527a); *quamuis* (relat. adv.) even though; clades, cladis
(f.) calamity, disaster; *ut* (conj.) "as"; casus, -us (m.) (< cado, cadere + -tus) occurrence, misfortune,
fall; uicturus, -a, -um; fut. ptc. of uiuo, uiuere, uixi, uictus (not uinco, uincere, uici, uictus); occido,
occidere, occidi, occisus (< ob + cado, cadere) die, come to grief

quamuis ... condiderit 2nd conces. cl.; condo, condere, condidi, conditus: store up, put away, compose, write (*OLD* 14a); s. Intro. re: the works of Pliny the Elder

perpetuitas, perpetuitatis (f.) (< per + peto + -uus + -tas) continuity, permanence, perpetuity

aeternitas, aeternitatis (f.) (< aeternus + -tas) immortality

---

VI.XVI.3

beatus, -a, -um fortunate

munus, muneris (n.) something freely bestowed, duty, gift

scribenda ... legenda subst. use: "things that must be written about" ... "things that must be read
about"

libris abl. of cause (AG #404)

quo (relat. pron.) abl. of deg. of diff. but nearing abl. of cause (AG #414a n.); "because of which"

libentius (compar. adv.) (< libens, libentis) quite willingly

deposco, deposcere (< de + posco, poscere) demand

quod iniungis *quod = id quod*; iniungo, iniungere (< in + iungo, iungere) impose

---

VI.XVI.4

Misenum, -i (n.) Misenum; the promontory and town at the end of the northern arm of the Bay of
Naples, Misenum and its harbor became one of Rome's main naval bases under Augustus (*OCD* s.
Misenum, 989). Pliny's uncle, Pliny the Elder, was the commander of the fleet stationed there.

classis, classis (f.) fleet

imperio abl. of means (AG #409); Uncle Pliny had full military authority over the fleet, as denoted by
the word *imperium*, a term that indicated supreme power within parameters specified by the office or
specific situation w/ which it was connected (*OCD* s. imperium, 751–2).

praesens, praesentis present, in person, face to face

kal. Septembres hora fere septima mater mea indicat ei
adparere nubem inusitata et magnitudine et specie. Vsus ille
sole, mox frigida, gustauerat iacens studebatque; poscit
soleas, ascendit locum ex quo maxime miraculum illud con-
spici poterat. Nubes—incertum procul intuentibus ex quo
monte (Vesuuium fuisse postea cognitum est)—oriebatur,
cuius similitudinem et formam non alia magis arbor quam

5

Nonum kal. Septembres Roman dates were reckoned by counting backwards from the three named
days of each month—the Kalends (the 1st day), the Nones (the fifth or seventh day, depending on
the day of the Ides), and the Ides (the thirteenth day, except in March, May, July, and October when
it was the fifteenth day). Romans counted both the starting day and the ending day. Thus the ninth
day before the Kalends of September was August 24. Omitted here is the standard abbreviation a.d.
(ante diem), which would illuminate Pliny's use of the acc. case of *Nonum* and *Septembres*.

fere (adv.) almost, virtually

septima hora the Roman day was divided into two twelve-hour time periods, one for day and one for
night, but the length of each hour was determined by daylight and darkness, rather than by any
standard period. As a result the twelve daytime hours were substantially longer in summer and
shorter in winter. The 1st hour began w/ daybreak; thus in late August w/ the Roman hour equal to
about 66 minutes of our time, the seventh hour would have begun at about 30 minutes past midday.

indico (1) (< in + dico, dicare) point out, show; Pliny enlivens his narrative here and throughout the
account of the eruption w/ the hist. use of the pres. tense (AG #469); *ei*: dat. sg. m., i.e. Uncle Pliny

adparere . . . specie indir. disc. (AG #580); adpareo, adparere (< ad + pareo, parere) be seen physically, appear; nubes, nubis (f.) cloud, cloud-like formation; *inusitata et magnitudine et specie*: abl.
of specif. (AG #418); inusitatus, -a, -um (< in + usitatus) unusual, strange; species, speciei (f.)
(< specio, specere + -ies) appearance, semblance

VI.XVI.5

Vsus sole . . . frigida i.e. he was sunbathing; *sole . . . frigida*: abl. w/ *usus*, depon. vb. that takes abl. of
means, not acc. dir. obj. (AG #410); frigidus, -a, -um (< frigus + -idus) cold; *frigida (aqua* understood): referring to the frigidarium, the cold water bath in a Roman bathing complex (s. II.XVII.11
on balineum)

gusto (1) taste, have a bite, take food

solea, -ae (f.) (< solum) sandal

miraculum, -i (n.) (< miror, mirari + -culum) amazing sight or circumstance

conspicio, conspicere (< con + specio, specere) catch sight of, pass.: be visible

procul (adv.) some way off, far away; *incertum*: ELLIPSIS of *erat*

intueor, intueri, intuitus sum (< in + tueor, tueri) look at, look upon, regard (as)

cognosco, cognoscere, cognoui, cognitus (< con + nosco, noscere) find to be, recognize

orior, oriri, ortus sum rise, come into existence

cuius . . . expresserit relat. cl. of char. (AG #535), anteced. *nubes*; similitudo, similitudinis (f.)
(< similis, simile + -tudo) resemblance, similarity; pinus, pinus (f.) pine tree; exprimo, exprimere,
expressi, expressus (< ex + premo, premere) portray, produce; the tree that Pliny refers to is the
Italian Umbrella Pine, also called the stone pine, which has a long straight branchless trunk topped
by a broad circle of foliage.

pinus expresserit. Nam longissimo uelut trunco elata in altum 6
quibusdam ramis diffundebatur, credo quia recenti spiritu
euecta, dein senescente eo destituta aut etiam pondere suo
uicta in latitudinem uanescebat, candida interdum, interdum sordida et maculosa prout terram cineremue sustulerat.
Magnum propiusque noscendum ut eruditissimo uiro uisum. 7
Iubet liburnicam aptari; mihi si uenire una uellem facit
copiam; respondi studere me malle, et forte ipse quod

VI.XVI.6

uelut (adv.) (< uel + ut) just as

truncus, -i (m.) trunk of a tree

effero, efferre, extuli, elatus (< ex + fero, ferre) bring forth, raise, lift (*OLD* 9); *elata: nubes* understood

ramus, -i (m.) branch

diffundo, diffundere (< dis + fundo, fundere) spread widely, spread out

recens, recentis recent, newly come

spiritus, -us (m.) (< spiro, spirare + -tus) breath, current of air, wind

eueho, euehere, euexi, euectus (< ex + ueho, uehere) carry out, carry up

senescente eo abl. abs. (AG #419); senesco, senescere (< seneo + -sco) grow old, deteriorate, die down, weaken; *eo*: i.e. *spiritu*

destituo, destituere, destitui, destitutus (< de + statuo, statuere) deprive of support, abandon {> destitute}

pondus, ponderis (n.) weight, bulk, mass {> ponderous}

uanesco, uanescere (< uanus + -esco) become insubstantial, vanish

candidus, -a, -um (< candeo + -idus) bright, white

interdum (adv.) (< inter + dum) sometimes

sordidus, -a, -um (< sordeo, sordere + -idus) dirty, discolored {> sordid}

maculosus, -a, -um (< macula + -osus) covered w/ blotches, spotted

prout (conj.) (< pro + ut) according to whether . . . or (-*ue*)

cinis, cineris (m.) ashes

tollo, tollere, sustuli, sublatus pick up, raise into the air

VI.XVI.7

magnum . . . uisum ELLIPSIS of *est*; nosco, noscere: examine, inspect; eruditus, -a, -um (< ppp. of ex + rudis + -io) learned {> erudition}; *ut eruditissimo uiro*: "to a man as exceptionally learned as he was"

liburnica, -ae (f.) a light fast-sailing warship; this type of ship was developed by the Liburni, who lived in Illyria on the northeast coast of the Adriatic Sea. They were well known for their skill on the water, especially as pirates, and for particularly fast ships, whose style Augustus adopted for his own fleet (*OCD* s. Liburni, 855).

apto (1) bring into position, make ready

si . . . uellem prot. of pres. C-to-F condit. w/ indic. apod. showing what was intended (AG #517b); *una* (adv.) together, along (w/)

copiam facere provide the means (*OLD* copia 7, facio 14a)

studere . . . malle indir. disc. (AG #580)

forte (adv.) (< fors) by chance, as luck would have it

quod . . . scriberem relat. cl. of char. (AG #535)

8   scriberem dederat. Egrediebatur domo; accipit codicillos
            Rectinae Tasci imminenti periculo exterritae (nam uilla eius
            subiacebat, nec ulla nisi nauibus fuga): ut se tanto discrimini

9   eriperet orabat. Vertit ille consilium et quod studioso animo
            incohauerat obit maximo. Deducit quadriremes, ascendit ipse
            non Rectinae modo sed multis (erat enim frequens amoenitas

10   orae) laturus auxilium. Properat illuc unde alii fugiunt,
            rectumque cursum recta gubernacula in periculum tenet

---

VI.XVI.8

egredior, egredi, egressus sum ($<$ ex + gradior, gradi) go out, leave

codicillus, -i (m.) pl.: writing tablets {$>$ codicil}

Rectina Tasci Rectina (wife) of Tascius; unknown outside of Pliny's letters; it was standard Roman
    practice to refer to a married woman by her gentilicium followed by her husband's name in the
    poss. gen.

immineo, imminere press closely, menace, impend {$>$ imminent}

exterreo, exterrere, exterrui, exterritus ($<$ ex + terreo, terrere) drive to distraction, terrify

subiaceo, subiacere ($<$ sub + iaceo, iacere) lie underneath, lie at the foot

nec ... fuga ELLIPSIS of *erat*

ut ... eriperet subst. cl. of purp. (AG #563) (= indir. comm.) ff. *orabat; tanto discrimini:* abl. of separ.
    (AG #401); discrimen, discriminis (n.) ($<$ dis + cerno, cernere + -men) dividing point, critical
    point, dangerous situation {$>$ discriminate}; eripio, eripere ($<$ ex + rapio, rapere) snatch away,
    rescue

VI.XVI.9

uerto, uertere, uerti, uersus change the course, turn in another direction (*OLD* 11) {$>$ vertex}

quod ... incohauerat *quod = id quod; studioso animo:* abl. of manner (AG #412); studiosus, -a, -um
    ($<$ studium + -osus) scholarly; incoho (1) start, initiate {$>$ incohate}

obeo, obire ($<$ ob + eo, ire) go to meet, take on (a task) (*OLD* 5a); the word can also mean to go to
    one's death

maximo *animo* understood

deduco, deducere ($<$ de + duco, ducere) bring away, launch (a ship)

quadriremis, quadriremis (f.) ($<$ quadri- + remus + -is) a large warship, galley; the quadrireme had
    two banks of oars w/ two rowers for each oar. Because it had fewer banks than other heavy warships,
    it sat lower in the water and was particularly suited for sailing near the coast.

frequens, frequentis crowded

amoenitas, amoenitatis (f.) ($<$ amoenus + -tas) pleasantness

ora, orae (f.) seacoast

VI.XVI.10

cursus, -us (m.) ($<$ curro, currere + -tus) course

gubernaculum, -i (n.) ($<$ guberno, gubernare + -culum) steering oar, rudder

adeo (adv.) to such an extent

solutus, -a, -um ($<$ ppp. of soluo, soluere) freed, unfettered; *metu:* abl. of separ.

ut ... enotaretque result cl. (AG #537); motus, -us (m.) ($<$ moueo, mouere + -tus) movement,
    motion; *illius mali:* i.e. the volcano; figura, -ae (f.) characteristic; *ut ... oculis:* tmp. use of *ut* w/ indic.
    (AG #543), "while"; deprendo, deprendere, deprendi, deprensus (de + prendo, prendere) come
    upon, detect; dicto (1) ($<$ dico + -to) dictate; enoto (1) ($<$ ex + noto, notare) write down, record

adeo solutus metu, ut omnes illius mali motus omnes figuras
ut deprenderat oculis dictaret enotaretque.

Iam nauibus cinis incidebat, quo propius accederent, cali-   11
dior et densior; iam pumices etiam nigrique et ambusti
et fracti igne lapides; iam uadum subitum ruinaque montis
litora obstantia. Cunctatus paulum an retro flecteret, mox
gubernatori ut ita faceret monenti 'Fortes' inquit 'fortuna
iuuat: Pomponianum pete.' Stabiis erat diremptus sinu medio   12
(nam sensim circumactis curuatisque litoribus mare infundi-

VI.XVI.11

iam ... iam ... iam With ANAPHORA and ELLIPSIS of the vb. to be, Pliny emphasizes the rapidly deteriorating conditions that his uncle was facing.

incido, incidere (< in + cado, cadere) fall {> incident}; *nauibus*: dat. of indir. obj. w/ compd vb.
(AG #370)

quo ... accederent relat. cl. of char. (AG #535); *quo* (relat. adv.) wherever

calidus, -a, -um (< caleo, calere + -idus) hot

pumex, pumicis (m.) pumice or similar volcanic rock

amburo, amburere, ambussi, ambustus (< ambi + uro, urere) scorch, char

fractus, -a, -um (< ppp. of frango, frangere) broken {> fracture}

lapis, lapidis (m.) stone, pebble

uadum, -i (n.) shallow water

subitus, -a, -um w/ out warning, suddenly appearing; perhaps < ppp. of subeo, subire (*OLD*) but
clearly evolved into stand-alone adj.

ruina, -ae (f.) (< ruo, ruere + -ina) headlong rush, collapse; *ruina*: abl. of cause (AG #404)

litus, litoris (n.) shore, coast

obsto (1) (< ob + sto, stare) stand in the way, obstruct

cunctor, cunctari, cunctatus sum delay, hesitate

an ... flecteret indir. quest. (AG #574) introd. by *cunctatus*; *an*: "whether" ("or not" implied); *retro*
(adv.) backwards, back; flecto, flectere: bend, alter course

gubernator, gubernatoris (m.) (< guberno, gubernare + -tor) helmsman {> gubernatorial}

ut ... faceret subst. cl. of purp. (AG #563) (= indir. comm.) ff. *monenti*

Pomponianus unknown outside of this letter

VI.XVI.12

Stabiae, -arum (f.) Stabiae, one of several Roman towns that became popular locations for summer
villas of well-to-do Romans, now the modern town of Castellammare (*OCD* 1437)

dirimo, dirimere, diremi, diremptus (< dis + emo, emere) separate, cut off; *diremptus erat*: subj.
Pomponianus

sinus, -us (m.) fold, hollow, bay (*OLD* 11)

sensim (adv.) gradually, little by little

circumago, circumagere, circumegi, circumactus (< circum + ago, agere) lead around, bend or
form round

curuatus, -a, -um (< ppp. of curuo, curuare) curved, bent

infundo, infundere (< in + fundo, fundere) pour in; compd vb + dat. *litoribus* (AG #370)

tur); ibi quamquam nondum periculo adpropinquante, conspicuo tamen et cum cresceret proximo, sarcinas contulerat in naues, certus fugae si contrarius uentus resedisset. Quo tunc auunculus meus secundissimo inuectus, complectitur trepidantem consolatur hortatur, utque timorem eius sua securitate leniret, deferri in balineum iubet; lotus accubat cenat, aut hilaris aut (quod aeque magnum) similis hilari.

13   Interim e Vesuuio monte pluribus locis latissimae flammae altaque incendia relucebant, quorum fulgor et claritas tenebris noctis excitabatur. Ille agrestium trepidatione ignes

---

periculo adpropinquante abl. abs. (AG #419)

conspicuo . . . proximo both adjs. modify *periculo*; conspicuus, -a, -um (< con + specio, specere + -uus) clearly seen, visible

cum cresceret cum circumst. cl. (AG #546); cresco, crescere: increase

sarcina, -ae (f.) pack, pl.: belongings

si . . . resedisset prot. of past C-to-F condit. (AG #517); contrarius, -a, -um: opposite, adverse, harmful; resido, residere, resedi (< re + sido, sidere) fall back, diminish

quo (relat. pron.) anteced. *uentus*

secundus, -a, -um (< sequor) following, favorable (wind); i.e. the same wind drove Uncle Pliny onto the shore at Stabiae that was preventing Pomponianus from leaving

inueho, inuehere, inuehi, inuectus (< in + ueho, uehere) carry in

complector, complecti, complexus sum (< con + plecto, plectere) embrace, hug

trepido (1) (< trepidus + -o) panic, tremble

consolor, consolari, consolatus sum (< con + solor, solari) comfort, console

ut . . . leniret purp. cl. (AG #531/1); securitas, securitatis (f.) (< se + curus + -tas) freedom from anxiety, assurance; lenio, lenire (< lenis + -io) soften, calm {> lenient}

defero, deferre (< de + fero, ferre) carry down; *deferri*: *se* understood

balineum, -i (n.) (< Gr. βαλανεῖον) baths

lauo, lauare, laui, lotus wash

accubo (1) (< ad + cubo, cubare) recline

ceno (1) (< cena + -o) dine

hilaris, hilare cheerful, lighthearted

VI.XVI.13

incendium, -i (n.) (< incendo, incendere + -ium) fire, conflagration {> incendiary}

reluceo, relucere (< re + luceo, lucere) shine out

fulgor, fulgoris (m.) (< fulg(e)o, fulgere + -or) brightness

claritas, claritatis (f.) (< clarus + -tas) clarity

tenebrae, -arum (f.) darkness

excito (1) (< ex + cito, citare) rouse, heighten

ille i.e. Uncle Pliny

agrestium . . . ardere indir. disc. (AG #580); agrestis, agrestis (m.) (< ager + -estris) countryman, peasant; trepidatio, trepidationis (f.) (< trepido, trepidare + -tio) state of alarm; solitudo, solitudinis (f.) (< solus + -tudo) uninhabited state; ardeo, ardere: burn

relictos desertasque uillas per solitudinem ardere in remedium formidinis dictitabat. Tum se quieti dedit et quieuit
uerissimo quidem somno; nam meatus animae, qui illi propter
amplitudinem corporis grauior et sonantior erat, ab iis qui
limini obuersabantur audiebatur. Sed area ex qua diaeta   14
adibatur ita iam cinere mixtisque pumicibus oppleta sur-
rexerat, ut si longior in cubiculo mora, exitus negaretur.
Excitatus procedit, seque Pomponiano ceterisque qui per-
uigilauerant reddit. In commune consultant, intra tecta   15
subsistant an in aperto uagentur. Nam crebris uastisque tre-

---

remedium, -i (n.) (< re + medeor, mederi + -ium) means of counteracting, remedy

formido, formidinis (f.) terror, horror {> formidable}

dictito (1) (< dico, dicere + -ito) keep saying, say repeatedly

quieti . . . quieuit POLYPTOTON here emphasizes Uncle Pliny's calm in the face of peril; quies, quietis
   (f.) rest, repose, relaxation

somnus, -i (m.) sleep {> somnolent}

meatus, -us (m.) (< meo, meare + -tus) movement

anima, -ae (f.) breath

amplitudo, amplitudinis (f.) (< amplus + -tudo) size, bulk

grauis, graue low in pitch, deep (OLD 9a)

sonans, sonantis (< pres. ptc. of sono, sonare) noisy, resonant

limen, liminis (n.) threshold, i.e. the household (METONYMY) {> liminal}; limini: dat. of indir.
   obj. w/ compd. vb. obseruabantur (AG #370); obuersor, obuersari, obuersatus sum: move about,
   go to and fro

VI.XVI.14

diaeta, -ae (f.) (< Gr. δίαιτα) annex, room

adeo, adire (< ad + eo, ire) approach {> adit}

misceo, miscere, miscui, mixtus mix, share (OLD 6)

oppleo, opplere, oppleui, oppletus (< ob + pleo, plere) fill up w/, cover completely

surgo, surgere, surrexi, surrectus (< sub + rego, regere) rise above the normal level (OLD 9)

ut . . . negaretur result cl. (AG #537); si . . . mora: prot. of a pres. C-to-F cond., esset understood; exitus,
   -us (m.) (< exeo, exire + -tus) departure, the end of one's life, death

procedo, procedere (< pro + cedo, cedere) move forward, advance

ceterus, -a, -um the rest, the other; used in pl. as pron.

peruigilo (1) (< per + uigil + -o) stay awake all night

VI.XVI.15

in commune together, jointly

consulto (1) deliberate, debate

intra . . . uagentur indir. quest. (AG #574) introd. by consultant; an: "or" (utrum omitted); tectum, -i
   (n.) (< ppp. of tego, tegere) roof, building, house; subsisto, subsistere (< sub + sisto, sistere) stand
   firm, remain; apertum, -i (n.) (< ppp. of aperio, aperire) the open; uagor, uagari, uagatus sum:
   wander, go from place to place

creber, crebra, crebrum frequent, in short intervals

uastus, -a, -um immense, intense

16 moribus tecta nutabant, et quasi emota sedibus suis nunc huc nunc illuc abire aut referri uidebantur. Sub dio rursus quam- quam leuium exesorumque pumicum casus metuebatur, quod tamen periculorum collatio elegit; et apud illum quidem ratio rationem, apud alios timorem timor uicit. Cer- uicalia capitibus imposita linteis constringunt; id muni-

17 mentum aduersus incidentia fuit. Iam dies alibi, illic nox omnibus noctibus nigrior densiorque; quam tamen faces multae uariaque lumina soluebant. Placuit egredi in litus, et ex proximo adspicere, ecquid iam mare admitteret; quod

---

tremor, tremoris (m.) (< tremo, tremere + -or) quaking, shuddering

nuto (1) nod, sway

emoueo, emouere, emoui, emotus (< ex + moueo, mouere) shift, displace, thrust from

sedes, sedis (f.) seat, foundation (*OLD* 10); *sedibus*: abl. of separ. (AG #401)

abeo, abire (< ab + eo, ire) go away, depart

VI.XVI.16

sub dio in the open air; dium, -i (n.) open sky

rursus (adv.) on the other hand (*OLD* 6)

quamquam leuium exesorumque phrase qualifies *pumicum*; exedo, exedere, exedi, exesus (< ex + edo, edere) eat up, eat away w/ fire

metuo, metuere (< metus + -o) fear

quod (relat. pron.) anteced. *dio*

collatio, collationis (f.) (< con + fero, ferre + -tio) comparison

eligo, eligere, elegi, electus (< ex + lego, legere) select, choose

apud illum on his (Uncle Pliny's) side, in his case

ceruical, ceruicalis (n.) (< ceruix + -alis) pillow, cushion (ceruix: neck) {> cervical}

impono, imponere, imposui, impositus lay on, place on {> impose}; compd. vb + dat. *capitibus* (AG #370)

linteum, -i (n.) (< linum + -eus) piece of linen, sail

constringo, constringere (< con +stringo, stringere) tie tightly

munimentum, -i (n.) (< munio, munire + mentum) defense, safeguard

aduersus (prep.) against (+ acc.); *incidentia*: n. acc. pl. subst.

VI.XVI.17

alibi (adv.) elsewhere; ELLIPSIS of *erat*

quam (relat. pron.) anteced. *nox*

fax, facis (f.) torch

lumen, luminis (n.) source of illumination, lamp

soluo, soluere (< se + luo, luere) remove, break up and scatter, diffuse (*OLD* 12a)

ex proximo close at hand

adspicio, adspicere (< ad + specio, specere) observe, investigate

ecquid ... admitteret indir. quest. (AG #574); *ecquid* (interrog. pcl.) whether; admitto, admittere (< ad + mitto, mittere) grant access, accept

aduersus, -a, -um (< ppp. of ad + uerto, uertere) unfavorable

permaneo, permanere (< per + maneo, manere) remain, persist {> permanent}

adhuc uastum et aduersum permanebat. Ibi super abiectum   18
linteum recubans semel atque iterum frigidam aquam popo-
scit hausitque. Deinde flammae flammarumque praenuntius
odor sulpuris alios in fugam uertunt, excitant illum. Innitens   19
seruolis duobus adsurrexit et statim concidit, ut ego colligo,
crassiore caligine spiritu obstructo, clausoque stomacho qui
illi natura inualidus et angustus et frequenter aestuans erat.
Vbi dies redditus (is ab eo quem nouissime uiderat tertius),   20
corpus inuentum integrum inlaesum opertumque ut fuerat
indutus: habitus corporis quiescenti quam defuncto similior.

VI.XVI.18

abicio, abicere, abieci, abiectus (< ab + iacio, iacere) throw down {> abject}

recubo (1) (< re + cubo, cubare) lie back, lie as ease

semel (adv.) one time, once

frigidus, -a, -um (< frigus + -idus) cold

haurio, haurire, hausi draw, drink

praenuntius, -a, -um (< prae + nuntius) announcing, heralding

sulpur, sulpuris (n.) sulphur

VI.XVI.19

innitor, inniti, innixus sum (< in + nitor, niti) lean on; *seruolis*: dat. of indir. obj. w/ compd. vb.
  innitens (AG #370)

seruolus, -i (m.) (< seruus + -olus) young slave

adsurgo, adsurgere, adsurrexi, adsurrectus (< ad + surgo, surgere) stand up

concido, concidere, concidi (< con + cado, cadere) fall down, collapse

ut . . . colligo *ut* w/ indic. "as" (AG #527f); colligo, colligere (< con + lego, legere) gather {> collect}

crassiore caligine abl. of means (AG #409); crassus, -a, -um: thick; caligo, caliginis (f.) fog, murky
  smoke

spiritu obstructo, clausoque stomacho abl. abs. (AG #419); obstruo, obstruere, obstruxi, obstructus
  (< ob + struo, struere) block, impede, stifle (*OLD* 2b); stomachus, -i (m.) (< Gr. στόμαχος) gullet,
  esophagus

qui (relat. pron.) anteced. *stomacho*

inualidus, -a, -um (< in + ualidus) weak, infirm; *illi*: dat. of ref. (AG #376)

angustus, -a, -um narrow, congested

aestuo (1) (< aestus + -o) be excessively hot, seethe; perhaps Uncle Pliny suffered from asthma.

VI.XVI.20

Vbi . . . redditus ELLIPSIS of *est*

tertius, -a, -um i.e. the 3rd day since the eruption had begun, and so August 26 (counting inclusively).

corpus . . . opertum *inuentum*: ELLIPSIS of *est*; inlaesus, -a, -um (< in + ppp. of laedo, laedere)
  unharmed, intact; opertus, -a, -um (< ppp. of operio, operire) covered

ut . . . indutus *ut* w/ indic. "as" (AG #527f); induo, induere, indui, indutus: clothe, dress

habitus, -us (m.) (< habeo, habere + -tus) state of being {> habit}; ELLIPSIS of *est*

defunctus, -a, -um (< ppp. of de + fungor, fungi) dead; *quiescenti . . . defuncto*: dat. w/ adj. *similior*
  (AG #384)

21 Interim Miseni ego et mater—sed nihil ad historiam, nec
    tu aliud quam de exitu eius scire uoluisti. Finem ergo faciam.

22 Vnum adiciam, omnia me quibus interfueram quaeque
    statim, cum maxime uera memorantur, audieram, perse-
    cutum. Tu potissima excerpes; aliud est enim epistulam aliud
    historiam, aliud amico aliud omnibus scribere. Vale.

xx—ERUPTION OF VESUVIUS AND THE YOUNGER PLINY

C. PLINIVS TACITO SVO S.

1 Ais te adductum litteris quas exigenti tibi de morte
   auunculi mei scripsi, cupere cognoscere, quos ego Miseni

VI.XVI.21
nihil ad historiam "that does not pertain to history"

VI.XVI.22
omnia ... persecutum indir. disc. (AG #580); intersum, interesse, interfui, interfuturus (< inter +
  sum, esse) attend as a participant, take part in (*OLD* 4), compd. vb + dat. *quibus* (AG #370); *cum ...*
  memorantur: cum tmp. cl. (AG #545); memoro (1) (< memor + -o) talk about, recall; *audieram* =
  contr. form of *audiueram* (AG #181); persequor, persequi, persecutus sum (< per + sequor, sequi)
  follow persistently, go over (*OLD* 8) {> persecute}; *persecutum*: ELLIPSIS of *esse*
potissimus, -a, -um (superl. adj.) (< potis) foremost, most powerful; *potissima*: n. pl. subst.
excerpo, excerpere (< ex + carpo, carpere) pick out, select {> excerpt}
aliud ... aliud "one thing ... another thing"

VI.XX: In this 2nd letter regarding the eruption of Mount Vesuvius in 79 (s. also VI.XVI), Pliny reports
  his personal experiences at Misenum following the departure of his uncle.
  Addressee: Cornelius Tacitus, s. I.VI.

VI.XX.1
te ... cognoscere indir. disc. (AG #580); adduco, adducere, adduxi, adductus (< ad + duco, ducere)
  lead (into), draw; *litteris*: i.e. VI.XVI; exigo, exigere (< ex + ago, agere) find out by inquiry, inquire
  (*OLD* 10a); auunculus, -i (m.) (< auus + culus) maternal uncle {> avuncular}; cognosco, cognoscere (< con + nosco, noscere) get to know, learn
quos ... pertulerim indir. quest. (AG #574); *quos* (interrog. adj.) modifying *metus* and *casus*;
  Misenum, -i (n.) (s. VI.XVI.4n.); ingredior, ingredi, ingressus sum (in + gradior, gradi) go on to,
  begin; abrumpo, abrumpere, abrupi (< ab + rumpo, rumpere) break off, cut short {> abrupt};
  casus, -us (m.) (< cado, cadere + -tus) occurrence, misfortune; perfero, perferre, pertuli, perlatus
  (< per + fero, ferre) endure, undergo (*OLD* 7a)
"Quamquam ... incipiam" quoting *Aeneid* II.12–13, where Aeneas begins telling Dido the story of
  the fall of his beloved Troy; w/ this quote Pliny signals the epic nature of the events that he is about
  to describe, which include an attempted journey and a series of trials and near disasters; memini,
  meminisse: remember; horreo, horrere: shudder, tremble, dread {> horror}; incipio, incipere (< in
  + capio, capere) begin {> incipient}

relictus (id enim ingressus abruperam) non solum metus
uerum etiam casus pertulerim. 'Quamquam animus meminisse
horret, . . . incipiam.'

Profecto auunculo ipse reliquum tempus studiis (ideo enim   2
remanseram) impendi; mox balineum cena somnus inquietus
et breuis. Praecesserat per multos dies tremor terrae, minus   3
formidolosus quia Campaniae solitus; illa uero nocte ita
inualuit, ut non moueri omnia sed uerti crederentur. Inrupit   4
cubiculum meum mater; surgebam inuicem, si quiesceret
excitaturus. Resedimus in area domus, quae mare a tectis
modico spatio diuidebat. Dubito, constantiam uocare an   5

VI.XX.2

profecto auunculo abl. abs. (AG #419); proficiscor, proficisci, profectus sum: (< pro + facio + -sco)
    set out, start on a journey

remaneo, remanere, remansi, remansus (< re+ maneo, manere) stay behind

impendo, impendere, impendi, impensus (< in + pendo, pendere) pay out, expend, devote

balineum, -i (n.) (< Gr. βαλανεῖον) baths; ASYNDETON and the ELLIPSIS of *erant* in this passage give
    the reader an impression of unusually hurried activities

somnus, -i (m.) sleep {> somnolent}

inquietus, -a, -um (< in + ppp. of quiesco, quiescere) restless, unsettled

VI.XX.3

praecedo, praecedere, praecessi, praecessus (< prae + cedo, cedere) come or occur before

tremor, tremoris (m.) (< tremo, tremere + -or) quaking, shuddering

formidolosus, -a, -um (< formido + -olus + -osus) causing fear, alarming

Campania, ae (f.) (s. VI.IV.1n); because this part of Italy sits astride the intersection of the African and
    Eurasian tectonic plates, it remains extremely prone to earthquakes and volcanoes; *Campaniae*: dat.
    w/ adj. *solitus* (AG #384); solitus, -a, -um (< ppp. of soleo, solere) customary, usual, normal

inualesco, inualescere, inualui (< in + ualeo, ualere) become strong

ut . . . crederentur result cl. (AG #537); uerto, uertere: cause to turn, overturn {> vertex}

VI.XX.4

inrumpo, inrumpere, inrupi, inruptus (< in + rumpo, rumpere) burst in, rush in

surgo, surgere (< sub + rego, regere) rise, get up

inuicem (adv.) in turn

si . . . quiesceret prot. of pres. C-to-F condit. (AG #517), w/ fut. act. ptc. *excitaturus* as apod.; excito
    (1) (< ex + cito, citare) rouse, stir

resido, residere, resedi (< re + sido, sidere) sit down, take up a position {> reside}

area, -ae (f.) open space, courtyard; *domus*: gen. sg.

tectum, -i (n.) (< ppp. of tego, tegere) roof, building, house

spatium, -i (n.) an expanse of physical space or time, length of time

diuido, diuidere separate, divide

VI.XX.5

constantiam . . . debeam indir. quest. (AG #574) ff. *dubito*; *an*: "or" (utrum omitted); constantia,
    -ae (f.) (< pres. ptc. of consto, constare + -ia) steadiness, resolution; imprudentia, -ae (f.)
    (< in + prudens + -ia) lack of judgment, ignorance

imprudentiam debeam (agebam enim duodeuicensimum
annum): posco librum Titi Liui, et quasi per otium lego
atque etiam ut coeperam excerpo. Ecce amicus auunculi qui
nuper ad eum ex Hispania uenerat, ut me et matrem sedentes,
me uero etiam legentem uidet, illius patientiam securitatem
meam corripit. Nihilo segnius ego intentus in librum.

6   Iam hora diei prima, et adhuc dubius et quasi languidus
dies. Iam quassatis circumiacentibus tectis, quamquam in
aperto loco, angusto tamen, magnus et certus ruinae metus.

7   Tum demum excedere oppido uisum; sequitur uulgus attoni-

---

duodeuicensimus, -a, -um ($<$ duo + de + uicensimus) eighteenth; i.e. Pliny was seventeen years old.

posco Pliny switches to the hist. pres. to heighten the drama of his narrative.

Titus Liuius the author of a monumental work on the history of Rome from its founding to 9 BCE entitled *Ab urbe condita*. Of its 142 books, only 1–10 and 21–45 survive, although there are summaries of almost all of the other books. Pliny would have been selecting particularly interesting points or well-phrased passages from Livy's work.

ut coeperam *ut* w/ indic. "as" (AG #527f); coepi, coepisse (pf. stem only) begin

excerpo, excerpere ($<$ ex + carpo, carpere) pick out, select {$>$ excerpt}

Ecce in vivid narrative: "Lo and behold" or "Up came"

nuper (adv.) recently

ut . . . uidet tmp. use of *ut* w/ indic. (AG #543), "when"

illius i.e. Pliny's mother

patientia, -ae (f.) ($<$ pres. ptc. of patior, pati + -ia) endurance, patience

securitas, securitatis (f.) ($<$ se + curus + -tas) freedom from anxiety, assurance

corripio, corripere ($<$ con + rapio, rapere) rebuke, find fault w/ (*OLD* 6)

nihilo (minus) nonetheless

segnius (compar. adv.) ($<$ segnis, segne) rather sluggishly, w/ out moving; the ELLIPSIS of the vb. (*est* or *remanebat*) here emphasizes Pliny's inaction.

intentus, -a, -um ($<$ ppp. of intendo, intendere) keenly occupied

VI.XX.6

hora . . . prima dawn (s. VI.XVI.4n. on septima hora); ELLIPSIS of *erat*

dubius, -a, -um uncertain

languidus, -a, -um ($<$ langueo, languere + -idus) faint, feeble

quassatis . . . tectis abl. abs. (AG #419); quasso (1) ($<$ quatio + -to) shake repeatedly, batter, weaken; circumiaceo, circumiacere ($<$ circum + iaceo, iacere) lie nearby

in aperto loco ELLIPSIS of *eramus* here and *erat* in the next cl.

angustus, -a, -um narrow, congested

ruina, -ae (f.) ($<$ ruo, ruere + -ina) collapse

VI.XX.7

tum . . . uisum ELLIPSIS of *est*; *tum demum*: not until then, only then (*OLD* s. demum 1b); excedo, excedere ($<$ ex + cedo, cedere) go out, depart

uulgus, -i (n.) common people, crowd {$>$ vulgar}

attonitus, -a, -um ($<$ ppp. of attono, attonare) stunned, frenzied

quod (relat. pron.) subst. use: "something which"

pauor, pauoris (m.) ($<$ paueo, pauere + -or) fright, panic

tum, quodque in pauore simile prudentiae, alienum consilium
suo praefert, ingentique agmine abeuntes premit et impellit.
Egressi tecta consistimus. Multa ibi miranda, multas formi-   8
dines patimur. Nam uehicula quae produci iusseramus,
quamquam in planissimo campo, in contrarias partes age-
bantur, ac ne lapidibus quidem fulta in eodem uestigio
quiescebant. Praeterea mare in se resorberi et tremore terrae   9
quasi repelli uidebamus. Certe processerat litus, multaque
animalia maris siccis harenis detinebat. Ab altero latere nubes
atra et horrenda, ignei spiritus tortis uibratisque discursibus

---

prudentia, -ae (f.) (< prudens + -ia) wisdom, practical understanding; *prudentiae*: dat. w/ adj. *simile*
  (AG #384), ELLIPSIS of *est*
praefero, praeferre (< prae + fero, ferre) attach more value to or prefer (acc.) over (dat.) (*OLD* 7)
agmen, agminis (n.) (< ago, agere + -men) stream, throng, horde
abeo, abire (< ab + eo, ire) go away, depart
premo, premere press, push
impello, impellere (< in + pello, pellere) push forward

VI.xx.8
egredior, egredi, egressus sum (< ex + gradior, gradi) go out, leave
consisto, consistere (< con + sisto, sistere) stop moving, come to a halt
formido, formidinis (f.) terror, horror {> formidable}
uehiculum, -i (n.) (< ueho, uehere + -culum) wheeled vehicle, wagon
produco, producere (< pro + duco, ducere) bring forth
planus, -a, -um smooth, level, flat
contrarius, -a, -um opposite, opposing
lapis, lapidis (m.) stone, pebble
fulcio, fulcire, fulsi, fultus support, brace
uestigium, -i (n.) footing, track, path {> vestige}; *in uestigio*: in position

VI.xx.9
mare . . . repelli indir. disc. (AG #580) ff. *uidebamus*; resorbeo, resorbere (< re + sorbeo, sorbere)
  swallow down, absorb; repello, repellere (< re + pello, pellere) drive back
procedo, procedere, processi, processus (< pro + cedo, cedere) move forward, advance
litus, litoris (n.) shore, coast
siccus, -a, -um dry {> desiccate}
harena, -ae (f.) sand
detineo, detinere (< de + tineo, tinere) cause to remain, retain
latus, lateris (n.) side
nubes, nubis (f.) cloud, cloud-like formation
ater, atra, atrum dark-colored
horrendus, -a, -um (< gerv. of horreo, horrere) terrible, fearful
igneus, -a, -um (< ignis + -eus) fiery, consisting of fire {> igneous}
spiritus, -us (m.) (< spiro, spirare + -tus) breath, wind, current
torqueo, torquere, torsi, tortus twist, hurl, whirl
uibro (1) move rapidly, shake, shoot out
discursus, -us (m.) (< dis + curro, currere + -tus) the act of running in different directions
  {> discursive}

10   rupta, in longas flammarum figuras dehiscebat; fulguribus
illae et similes et maiores erant. Tum uero idem ille ex Hispania amicus acrius et instantius 'Si frater' inquit 'tuus, tuus
auunculus uiuit, uult esse uos saluos; si periit, superstites
uoluit. Proinde quid cessatis euadere?' Respondimus non
commissuros nos ut de salute illius incerti nostrae consulere-
11   mus. Non moratus ultra proripit se effusoque cursu periculo
aufertur. Nec multo post illa nubes descendere in terras,
operire maria; cinxerat Capreas et absconderat, Miseni quod
12   procurrit abstulerat. Tum mater orare hortari iubere, quo-

---

rumpo, rumpere, rupi, ruptus break, split open, burst

figura, -ae (f.) form, outline, shape

dehisco, dehiscere (< de + hisco, hiscere) split open, gape

fulgur, fulguris (n.) flash of lightning; *fulguribus*: both a dat. w/ adj. *similes* (AG #384) and abl. of compar. w/ *maiores* (AG #406)

illae i.e. *figurae flammarum*

VI.xx.10

acrius (compar. adv.) (< acer) more forcefully

instantius (compar. adv.) (< pres. ptc. of insto, instare) more urgently

si . . . uiuit, uult; si periit, . . . uoluit simple condit. (indic.) (AG #514a); saluus, -a, -um safe, secure; pereo, perire, perii (< per + eo, ire) be lost, perish; superstes, superstitis: remaining alive, surviving; *uos* understood

quid (interrog. adv.) why (*OLD* quis, quid 16a)

cesso (1) (< cedo, cedere + -to) hold back, fail {> cessation}

euado, euadere (< ex + uado, uadere) escape

non . . . nos indir. disc. (AG #580); *commissuros*: ELLIPSIS of *esse*; committo, committere (< con + mitto, mittere) entrust, bring about, begin

ut . . . consuleremus subst. cl. of result (AG #568 n.); *nostrae* (*saluti* understood) dat. of indir. obj. w/ *consuleremus* as intr. vb. (AG #367c)

VI.xx.11

ultra (adv.) to a point beyond, to a greater degree

proripio, proripere (< pro + rapio, rapere) w/ reflex: rush forth

effusus, -a, -um (< ppp. of ex + fundo, fundere) headlong, unrestrained {> effuse}

cursus, -us (m.) (< curro, currere + -tus) course, act of running, speed

aufero, auferre (< ab + fero, ferre) take away, remove; *periculo*: abl. of separ. (AG #401)

multo by much; abl. of deg. of diff. (AG #414)

descendere, operire hist. inf. (AG #463); operio, operire, operui, opertus: cover, overspread

cingo, cingere, cinxi, cinctus encircle, surround

Capreae, -arum (f.) the island of Capri, known in Pliny's time for its imperial villas, in which Tiberius resided for a substantial portion of his rule (*OCD* 289)

abscondo, abscondere, abscondi, absconditus (< ab + condo, condere) conceal from view, hide

Miseni quod procurrit i.e. the promontory at Misenum; *quod* = *id quod*; procurro, procurrere (< pro + curro, currere) run ahead, project, extend

quo modo fugerem; posse enim iuuenem, se et annis et corpore grauem bene morituram, si mihi causa mortis non
fuisset. Ego contra saluum me nisi una non futurum; dein
manum eius amplexus addere gradum cogo. Paret aegre
incusatque se, quod me moretur.

Iam cinis, adhuc tamen rarus. Respicio: densa caligo tergis   13
imminebat, quae nos torrentis modo infusa terrae sequebatur.
'Deflectamus' inquam 'dum uidemus, ne in uia strati comitantium turba in tenebris obteramur.' Vix consideramus, et   14

VI.XX.12

quoquo modo fugerem subst. cl. of purp. (AG #563) (= indir. comm.) ff. hist. inf. *orare, hortari, iubere*

posse … morituram indir. disc. (AG #580), supply *dicens* or similar; grauis, grauis: weighed down; *morituram (fuisse)* serves as apod. w/ *si … fuisset* as prot. of past C-to-F condit. (AG #517)

contra (adv.) in reply, by way of objection (*OLD* 6a/b)

saluum … futurum indir. disc. (AG #580) ff. implied vb. of saying; saluus, -a, -um: safe, secure, unimpaired; *una* (adv.) together; *futurum*: ELLIPSIS of *esse*; Pliny's refusal to abandon his mother is proof of his *pietas* (s. II.XIII.4n.) and reminiscent of Aeneas' determination in *Aeneid* II to save his father, as are the fires and chaos that surround them.

amplector, amplecti, amplexus sum (< ambi + plecto, plectare) embrace, seize eagerly upon

addo, addere (< ad + do, dare) increase (*OLD* 5c); *eam* understood

gradus, -us (m.) step, pace

aegre (adv.) (< aeger) painfully, grudgingly

incuso (1) (< in + causa + -o) find fault w/, reproach

quod … moretur causal cl., subjv. indicates another's opinion (AG #540/2)

VI.XX.13

cinis, cineris (m.) ashes; ELLIPSIS of *erat*

rarus, -a, -um sparse, infrequent

respicio, respicere (< re + specio, specere) look back

caligo, caliginis (f.) fog, murky smoke

tergum, -i (n.) back

immineo, imminere press closely, menace {> imminent}

torrens, torrentis (m.) (< pres. ptc. of torreo, torrere) rushing stream {> torrent}

modo abl. of manner omitting *cum* (AG #412b)

infundo, infundere, infudi, infusus (< in + fundo, fundere) pour on; compd. vb. + dat. *terrae* (AG #370)

deflecto, deflectere (< de + flecto, flectere) change course; *deflectamus*: hort. subjv. (AG #439)

ne … obteramur purp. cl. (AG #531/1); sterno, sternere, straui, stratus: scatter, knock down (*OLD* 6a); comito (1) accompany, follow (as military camp followers [*comites*] would do); *comitantium*: pres. ptc. gen. pl., subst. use w/ *turba*; turba, -ae (f.) crowd; tenebrae, -arum (f.) darkness; obtero, obterere (< ob + tero, terere) crush, trample

VI.XX.14

Vix (adv.) scarcely

consido, considere, considi (< con + sido, sidere) sit down

nox non qualis inlunis aut nubila, sed qualis in locis clausis
lumine exstincto. Audires ululatus feminarum, infantum
quiritatus, clamores uirorum; alii parentes alii liberos alii
coniuges uocibus requirebant, uocibus noscitabant; hi suum
casum, illi suorum miserabantur; erant qui metu mortis
15   mortem precarentur; multi ad deos manus tollere, plures
nusquam iam deos ullos aeternamque illam et nouissimam
noctem mundo interpretabantur. Nec defuerunt qui fictis
mentitisque terroribus uera pericula augerent. Aderant qui
Miseni illud ruisse illud ardere falso sed credentibus nun-

---

nox ELLIPSIS of *erat*; here and in the next phrases, Pliny's omission of verbs and use of ASYNDETON
heighten the reader's sense of the speed w/ which conditions were deteriorating and the overwhelm-
ing fear that accompanied these changes

qualis (relat. adj.) of the sort/kind which; introd. relat. cl. of char. (AG #535) w/ ELLIPSIS of *esset*

inlunis, inlune (< in + luna + -is) moonless

nubilus, -a, -um (< nubes + -ilus) cloudy

lumine exstincto abl. abs. (AG #419); lumen, luminis (n.) source of illumination, lamp; exstinguo,
exstinguere, exstinxi, exstinctus (< ex + stinguo, stinguere) extinguished, put out

audires apod. of implied past C-to-F condit., impf. subjv. indicating repeated or continued action
(AG #517a); "(If you had been there), you would have heard . . ."

ululatus, -us (m.) (< ululo, ululere + -tus) howling, drawn out cries

quiritatus, -us (m.) (< quirito, quiritare + -tus) protesting cry

coniunx, coniugis (m./f.) partner in marriage, spouse {> conjugal}

noscito (1) (< nosco, noscere + -ito) be familiar w/, recognize

miseror, miserari, miseratus sum (< miser + -o) pity, express sorrow

qui . . . precarentur relat. cl. of char. (AG #535); *metu*: abl. of cause (AG #404); precor, precari, preca-
tus sum: pray for

VI.xx.15

tollo, tollere raise into the air; *tollere*: hist. inf. (AG #463)

nusquam . . . mundo indir. disc. (AG #580), ELLIPSIS of *esse*; *nusquam* (adv.) nowhere; *mundo*: dat. of
ref. (AG #376); mundus, -i (m.) universe, world

interpretor, interpretari, interpretatus sum (< interpres + -o) regard, comprehend

desum, deesse, defui, defuturus (< de + sum, esse) be lacking or missing

qui . . . augerent relat. cl. of char. (AG #535); *qui*, subst. use: "those who"

fictus, -a, -um (< ppp. fingo, fingere) untrue, false {> fiction}

mentior, mentiri, mentitus sum (< mens + -io) misrepresent, invent

Miseni . . . ardere indir. disc. (AG #580); *illud . . . illud:* "one part . . . another part"; ruo, ruere, rui,
rutus; be brought to ruin, collapse (*OLD* 7); ardeo, ardere: burn

falso (adv.) (< falsus) erroneously, mistakenly

credentibus pres. ptc. subst. use; indir. obj. of *nuntiabant*

VI.xx.16

paulum (adv.) somewhat, slightly

reluceo, relucere, reluxi (< re + luceo, lucere) give out light again

quod (relat. pron.) anteced. the previous phrase

tiabant. Paulum reluxit, quod non dies nobis, sed aduentantis   16
ignis indicium uidebatur. Et ignis quidem longius substitit;
tenebrae rursus cinis rursus, multus et grauis. Hunc identidem
adsurgentes excutiebamus; operti alioqui atque etiam oblisi
pondere essemus. Possem gloriari non gemitum mihi, non   17
uocem parum fortem in tantis periculis excidisse, nisi me cum
omnibus, omnia mecum perire misero, magno tamen mor-
talitatis solacio credidissem.
Tandem illa caligo tenuata quasi in fumum nebulamue dis-   18
cessit; mox dies uerus; sol etiam effulsit, luridus tamen qualis
esse cum deficit solet. Occursabant trepidantibus adhuc oculis
mutata omnia altoque cinere tamquam niue obducta. Re-   19

---

aduento (1) (< aduenio, aduenire + -to) approach, draw near

indicium, -i (n.) (< index + -ium) sign, evidence (+ obj. gen.) (*OLD* 4a)

subsisto, subsistere, substiti (< sub + sisto, sistere) stand firm, remain

tenebrae ... grauis ELLIPSIS of *erant*

hunc i.e. *cinis*

identidem (< idem + et + idem) again and again, repeatedly

adsurgo, adsurgere (< ad + surgo, surgere) stand up, rise up

excutio, excutere (< ex + quatio, quatere) shake off

operti ... essemus apod. of implied past C-to-F condit. (AG #517), prot. omitted (AG #522); *alioqui*
(adv.) otherwise; oblido, oblidere, oblisi, oblisus (< ob + laedo, laedere) crush; pondus, ponderis
(n.) weight, bulk, mass {> ponderous}

VI.XX.17

possem ... credidissem mixed C-to-F condit. (AG #517), describing a pres. condit. that is the result of
a past inaction; glorior, gloriari, gloriatus sum (< gloria + -o) pride myself, boast; *non ... excidisse*:
indir. disc. (AG #580); gemitus, -us (m.) (< gemo, gemere + -tus) groan, moan; excido, excidere,
excidi (< ex + cado, cadere) fall out, slip out; *me ... perire*: indir. disc. (AG #580) ff. *credidissem*, read
perire twice, w/ *me* and *omnia*; *misero ... solacio*: dat. of purp. (AG #382)

VI.XX.18

tandem (adv.) after some time, at last

tenuo (1) (< tenuis + -o) make thin or slender, diminish {> tenuous}

fumus, -i (m.) smoke

nebula, -ae (f.) mist {> nebulous}

effulgeo, effulgere, effulsi, effulsus (< ex + fulgeo, fulgere) shine forth

luridus, -a, -um sickly yellow in color, sallow

cum deficit cum tmp. cl. (AG #545); deficio, deficere (< de + facio, facere) fail, suffer eclipse
(*OLD* 8b)

occurso (1) (< ob + curro, currere + -to) present itself (to the eyes), be found (*OLD* 3, 4); compd. vb
+ dat. *trepidantibus oculis* (AG #370); trepido (1) (< trepidus + -o) panic, tremble

niuis, niuis (f.) snow

obduco, obducere, obduxi, obductus (< ob + duco, ducere) cover on the surface (*OLD* 6a)

gressi Misenum curatis utcumque corporibus suspensam
dubiamque noctem spe ac metu exegimus. Metus praeuale-
bat; nam et tremor terrae perseuerabat, et plerique lymphati
terrificis uaticinationibus et sua et aliena mala ludificabantur.

20 Nobis tamen ne tunc quidem, quamquam et expertis periculum et exspectantibus, abeundi consilium, donec de
auunculo nuntius.

Haec nequaquam historia digna non scripturus leges et tibi
scilicet qui requisisti imputabis, si digna ne epistula quidem
uidebuntur. Vale.

VI.XX.19

regredior, regredi, regressus sum (< re + gradior, gradi) return, go back

curatis . . . corporibus abl. abs. (AG #419); *utcumque* (adv.) by whatever means possible, as best one
can

suspensus, -a, -um (< ppp. of sub + pendo, pendere) anxious

spe ac metu abl. of manner omitting *cum* (AG #412b)

exigo, exigere, exegi, exactus (< ex + ago, agere) pass, spend, undergo

praeualeo, praeualere (< prae + ualeo, ualere) have the upper hand, prevail {> prevalent}

perseuero (1) (< per + seuerus + -o) persist, continue

plerusque, -aque, -umque (< plerus + -que) the greater part, most of, m. pl.: "most people"

lymphatus, -a, -um (< ppp. of lympho, lymphare) frenzied, frantic

terrificus, -a, -um (< terreo, terrere + -ficus) terrifying

uaticinatio, uaticinationis (f.) (< uates + -cinor + -tio) prediction, prophecy

ludificor, ludificari, ludificatus sum (< ludus + ficus + -o) make sport of, make fun of; i.e. make dire
predictions about what was yet to come.

VI.XX.20

nobis dat. of poss. (AG #373); modified by *expertis* and *exspectantibus*

abeundi consilium ELLIPSIS of *erat*

donec (conj.) until such time as, up to; ELLIPSIS of *erat*

haec . . . uidebuntur FMV condit. (AG #516a); *nequaquam* (adv.) by no means, not at all, read w/ *digna*
and abl. of specif. *historia* (AG #418b); *scilicet* (pcl.) (< prob. scire + licet) it is clear (that), you may
be sure (that); imputo (1) (< in + puto, putare) enter as a debt, charge; "You will read these things
that are not at all worthy of a history, w/ out intending to write about them, and, since you asked for
them, it is clear that you must charge the debt to yourself, if they seem not even worthy of a letter."

VI.XXVII: Pliny describes the approach he took in the speech he gave to thank the Emperor Trajan for
choosing him to serve as consul (his *gratiarum actio*). Pliny published a revised and expanded version of his speech, which survives and is known as the *Panegyricus*.
Addressee: Severus, perhaps C. Vettenius Severus, suffect consul 107 CE (SW 387, AB 89).

VI.XXVII.1

ut cogitem subst. cl. of purp. (AG #563) (= indir. comm.) ff. *rogas*

quid . . . censeas indir. quest. (AG #574); designo (1) (< de + signo, signare) designated, appointed;
i.e. chosen for the office but not yet serving; censeo, censere: give one's opinion, assess

XXVII—HOW TO PRAISE TRAJAN

C. PLINIVS SEVERO SVO S.

Rogas ut cogitem, quid designatus consul in honorem   1
principis censeas. Facilis inuentio, non facilis electio; est enim
ex uirtutibus eius larga materia. Scribam tamen uel (quod
malo) coram indicabo, si prius haesitationem meam ostendero.
Dubito num idem tibi suadere quod mihi debeam. Desi-   2
gnatus ego consul omni hac, etsi non adulatione, specie tamen
adulationis abstinui, non tamquam liber et constans, sed tamquam intellegens principis nostri, cuius uidebam hanc esse
praecipuam laudem, si nihil quasi ex necessitate decernerem.
Recordabar etiam plurimos honores pessimo cuique delatos,   3

---

inuentio, inuentionis (f) (< in + uenio, uenire + -tio) discovery, (in rhetoric) the devising of subject
matter; ELLIPSIS of *est*; *inuentio* was the 1st step in the rhetorical process, which entailed discovering
the points of argument for the speech. The other parts of an effective speech were *dispositio, elocutio,
memoria*, and *pronuntiatio* (arrangement, style, memory, and delivery).

electio, electionis (f.) (< ex + lego, legere + -tio) choice, act of selecting

materia, -ae (f.) (< mater + -ia) material, means, potential (*OLD* 8)

scribam ... ostendero FMV condit. (AG #516c); *coram* (adv.) face to face, in person; indico (1) (< in
+ dico, dicare) reveal, disclose; *prius* (compar. adv.) (< primus) first; haesitatio, haesitationis (f.)
(< haereo, haerere + -to + -tio) hesitation; ostendo, ostendere, ostendi, ostentus (< ob + tendo,
tendere) present, reveal

VI.XXVII.2

num ... debeam indir. quest. (AG #574); *num*: whether (AG #332b n.); suadeo, suadere: recommend,
advise (+ dat. *tibi* and *mihi*)

omni hac ... specie abl. of separ. (AG #401); *etsi non adulatione*: appos. to *specie*, "even if not (meant)
as flattery"; *etsi* (conj.) even if, although; adulatio, adulationis (f.) (< adulor, adulari + -tio) obsequious or servile flattery

abstineo, abstinere, abstinui, abstentus (< ab + teneo, tenere) keep away

constans, constantis (< pres. ptc. of consto, constare) resolute, unchanging {> constant}

intellegens, intellegentis (< pres. ptc. of inter + lego, legere) understanding keenly, appreciating;
principis nostri: gen. w/ pres. ptc. (BG #375)

hanc ... laudem indir. disc. (AG #580); *hanc* points forward to the *si* cl. (AG #297e); praecipuus, -a,
-um (< prae + capio, capere + -uus) surpassing all others, exceptional

si ... decernerem prot. of a pres. gen. condit., subjv. in indir. disc. (AG #589/1); necessitas, necessitatis
(f.) (< necesse + -tas) requirement, obligation; decerno, decernere (< de + cerno, cernere) settle
on, decide, propose

VI.XXVII.3

recordor, recordari, recordatus sum (< re + cor + -o) call to mind, give one's thoughts to

pessimo cuique superl. w/ quisque (AG #313b); "to all the worst men"

defero, deferre, detuli, delatus (< de + fero, ferre) carry down, confer, grant

a quibus hic optimus separari non alio magis poterat, quam
diuersitate censendi; quod ipsum non dissimulatione et silentio praeterii, ne forte non iudicium illud meum sed obliuio

4   uideretur. Hoc tunc ego; sed non omnibus eadem placent,
ne conueniunt quidem. Praeterea faciendi aliquid non faci-
endiue ratio cum hominum ipsorum tum rerum etiam ac

5   temporum condicione mutatur. Nam recentia opera maximi
principis praebent facultatem, noua magna uera censendi.
Quibus ex causis, ut supra scripsi, dubito an idem nunc tibi
quod tunc mihi suadeam. Illud non dubito, debuisse me in
parte consilii tui ponere, quid ipse fecissem. Vale.

---

quibus (relat. pron.) abl. of separ. (AG #401)

separo (1) (< se + paro, parare) separate, differentiate

non alio magis "by nothing more"

diuersitas, diuersitatis (f.) (< diuersus + -tas) different method

quod ipsum i.e. the previous explanation

dissimulatio, dissimulationis (f.) (< dis + simulo, simulare + -tio) concealment, pretended
    ignorance

silentium, -i (n.) (< silens + -ium) absence of sound, silence

praetereo, praeterire, praeterii, praeteritus (< praeter + eo, ire) pass over, omit to mention; Pliny
    here uses a vb. that refers to a common rhetorical practice, PRAETERITIO, in which the speaker refers
    to a potential topic or point of discussion by saying he will pass it by, thus bringing it obliquely into
    his argument. He says that he did not employ this in his speech but told Trajan directly that his
    observations were sincere, rather than compelled, and that he was intentionally forgoing such false
    praise.

ne . . . uideretur purp. cl. (AG #531/1); *forte* (adv.) (< fors) by chance, as luck would have it; obliuio,
    obliuionis (f.) (< obliuiscor, obliuisci + -io) act of forgetting, forgetfulness

VI.XXVII.4

hoc tunc ego ELLIPSIS of vb. like *constitui*; the clipped nature of this stmt. stresses that this approach to
    praising the emperor is Pliny's alone, at least thus far.

aliquid dir. obj. of both instances of *faciendi* (ger.)

cum . . . tum . . . etiam ac both . . . and . . . and even

condicio, condicionis (f.) (< con + dico, dicere + -io) situation, state of health (*OLD* 6a and d)

VI.XXVII.5

recens, recentis recent, newly come

praebeo, praebere (< prae + habeo, habere) present, provide

facultas, facultatis (f.) ability, opportunity {> faculty}; *censendi*: objv. gen. (AG #347) w/ dir. obj.
    noua magna uera

ut . . . scripsi *ut* w/ indic. "as" (AG #527f); *supra* (adv.) above

an . . . suadeam indir. quest. (AG #574) ff. *dubito*; *an*: "whether" ("or not" implied)

Illud points forward (AG #297e)

debuisse . . . ponere indir. disc. (AG #580); *in parte consilii tui ponere*: "explain as part of your advice"

quid . . . fecissem indir. quest. (AG #574)

BOOK VII

XVIII—CREATING LASTING GENEROSITY

C. PLINIVS CANINIO SVO S.

Deliberas mecum quemadmodum pecunia, quam muni-   1
cipibus nostris in epulum obtulisti, post te quoque salua sit.
Honesta consultatio, non expedita sententia. Numeres rei
publicae summam: uerendum est ne dilabatur. Des agros: ut
publici neglegentur. Equidem nihil commodius inuenio,   2
quam quod ipse feci. Nam pro quingentis milibus nummum,

VII.XVIII: Pliny offers advice on how best to make a lasting monetary commitment for the public good by explaining his own astute generosity in setting up an alimentary program for the children of Comum.

Addressee: Caninius (Rufus), a fellow townsman from Comum, who receives several other letters from Pliny that focus on literary pursuits.

VII.XVIII.1

delibero (1) (< de + libra + -o) weigh the pros and cons, consider, consult

quemadmodum ... sit indir. quest. (AG #574); *quemadmodum* (interrog. adv.) (< quem + ad + modum) how; municeps, municipis (m.) (< munia + -ceps) fellow townsman {> municipal}; epulum, -i (n.) public feast, banquet; although Pliny does not offer specific details, this unusual word is used to refer to the banquet associated w/ a yearly religious festival; offero, offerre, obtuli, oblatus (< ob + fero, ferre) supply, provide (+ dat.); saluus, -a, -um: safe, secure

consultatio, consultationis (f.) (< con + sulo, sulare + -to + tio) consultation; ELLIPSIS of *est*

expeditus, -a, -um (< ppp. of ex + pes + -io) quick, ready

sententia, -ae (f.) (< pres. ptc. of sentio, sentire + -ia) opinion

numero (1) (< numerus + -o) count out, make payment; *numeres*: potent. subjv. (AG #447)

summa, -ae (f.) totality, whole amount

uerendum est impers. use of 2nd (pass.) periphr. conjug. (AG #500/3)

ne dilabatur subst. cl. ff. vb. of fearing (AG #564); dilabor, dilabi, dilapsus sum (< di + labor, labi) melt away, flow away

des potent. subjv. (AG #447)

ut ... neglegentur result cl. (AG #537); *publici*: "as public lands"; neglego (1) (< nec + lego, legere) neglect, ignore

VII.XVIII.2

commodius (compar. adj.) (< commodus) more suitable, advantageous, agreeable

quod = id quod

pro ... nummum quingenti, -ae, -a: 500; milia, milium (n.) thousands; *nummum*: gen. pl.; nummus, -i (m.) coin, sesterce (s. II.XX.1n. on as)

quae in alimenta ingenuorum ingenuarumque promiseram,
agrum ex meis longe pluris actori publico mancipaui; eundem

3   uectigali imposito recepi, tricena milia annua daturus. Per
hoc enim et rei publicae sors in tuto nec reditus incertus, et
ager ipse propter id quod uectigal large supercurrit, semper

4   dominum a quo exerceatur inueniet. Nec ignoro me plus
aliquanto quam donasse uideor erogauisse, cum pulcherrimi

5   agri pretium necessitas uectigalis infregerit. Sed oportet

---

alimentum, -i (n.) (< alo, alere + -mentum) food, provisions, pl.: sustenance, maintenance {> alimentary}; *alimenta* were a civic benefaction that appeared in the mid-1st century CE. Elite citizens established foundations through which allowances were provided for feeding the local children. Pliny is thus following a recent, but established practice, one which was also taken up by the emperor Nerva and expanded by his successor Trajan in Italian towns (*OCD* s. alimenta, 63).

ingenuus, -a, -um native-born, freeborn; *ingenuorum, ingenuarum*: subst. use

promitto, promittere, promisi, promissus (< pro + mitto, mittere) promise, guarantee

agrum ... mancipaui ager, agri (m.) farmable land; *ex meis*: i.e. from Pliny's acreage; *pluris*: describes *agrum*, gen. of quality (price) (AG #345), used instead of abl. of price w/ indef. value (AG #417), i.e. the land is more valuable than the amount Pliny has promised; actor, actoris (m.) (< ago, agere + -tor) manager, agent; mancipo (1) (< manus + -ceps + -o) surrender (+ dat.)

eundem i.e. *agrum*; Pliny rents back the land that he has given to the town for the *alimenta*

uectigali imposito abl. abs. (AG #419); uectigal, uectigalis (n.) annual payment (for use of public lands, similar to rent); impono, imponere, imposui, impositus: lay on (as a burden) {> impose}

triceni, -ae, -a 30

annuus, -a, -um (< annus + -uus) annual, paid yearly {> annuity}

VII.XVIII.3

sors, sortis (f.) lot, allocation; *rei publicae*: dat. of ref. (AG #376), "for the town"

in tuto subst. use of tutus, -a, -um: "in a safe place"; ELLIPSIS of *est*

reditus, -us (m.) (< redeo, redire + -tus) return, revenue

supercurro, supercurrere (< super + curro, currere) outstrip in yield

a quo exerceatur relat. cl. of char. (AG #535); exerceo, exercere (< ex + arceo, arcere) work, occupy, cultivate (land)

VII.XVIII.4

ignoro (1) be unaware of, fail to recognize

me ... erogauisse indir. disc. (AG #580); *aliquanto* (adv.) (< alius + quantus) to some extent, somewhat; dono (1) (< donum + -o) grant, present; *donasse* = contr. form of *donauisse* (AG #181); erogo (1) (< ex + rogo, rogare) pay out, disperse

cum ... infregerit cum causal cl. (AG #549); pretium, -i (n.) reward, price, value; necessitas, necessitatis (f.) (< necesse + -tas) requirement, need; infringo, infringere, infregi, infractus (< in + frango, frangere) impair, reduce, diminish

VII.XVIII.5

oportet it is proper, right, "ought"; impers. vb. w/ acc. + inf. constr. (AG #565n. 3)

utilitas, utilitatis (f.) (< utilis + -tas) interest, advantage; *utilitatibus*: read w/ all four adjs., opposing acc. forms w/ dat. ones: *publicas ... priuatis, aeternas ... mortalibus*

antefero, anteferre (< ante + fero, ferre) give precedence to (acc.) over (dat.)

priuatis utilitatibus publicas, mortalibus aeternas anteferre,
multoque diligentius muneri suo consulere quam facultatibus.
Vale.

XIX—FANNIA, THE IDEAL MATRON

C. PLINIVS PRISCO SVO S.

Angit me Fanniae ualetudo. Contraxit hanc dum adsidet   1
Iuniae uirgini, sponte primum (est enim adfinis), deinde
etiam ex auctoritate pontificum. Nam uirgines, cum ui morbi   2
atrio Vestae coguntur excedere, matronarum curae custodiae-
que mandantur. Quo munere Fannia dum sedulo fungitur,

---

multo by much; abl. of deg. of diff. (AG #414)

muneri . . . facultatibus dat. of indir. obj. w/ *consulere* as intr. vb. (AG #367c); munus, muneris (n.)
something freely bestowed, duty, gift; facultas, facultatis (f.) ability, power, pl.: resources {> faculty}

VII.XIX: Pliny worries about the illness of an upstanding matron, for whom he offers exceptional praise
and whom he considers an exemplar of excellence for both men and women.
Addressee: Priscus, perhaps Cornelius Priscus (AB 52), s. III.XXI.

VII.XIX.1

ango, angere (< Gr. ἄγχω) choke, cause anguish, distress

Fannia Clodia Fannia, associated both by birth and marriage w/ men condemned for opposition to the
principate.

contraho, contrahere, contraxi, contractus (< con + traho, trahere) catch (an illness), contract
(*OLD* 8b)

dum . . . uirgini *dum* w/ pres. indic. vb. for continuous action in past (AG #556); adsido, adsidere
(< ad + sido, sidere) sit near (+ dat.); Iunia uirgo: i.e. Junia was a Vestal Virgin (s. IV.XI.6n. on
Cornelia Vestalium)

sponte of her own will

adfinis, adfine (< ad + finis) related by marriage

auctoritas, auctoritatis (f.) (< auctor + -tas) authorization, command

pontifex, pontificis (m.) (< pons, pontis + -fex) a priest from the college that had control over public
religion in Rome (s. IV.XI.6n.)

VII.XIX.2

cum . . . excedere cum tmp. cl. (AG #545); uis, uis (f.) force, potency; morbus, -i (m.) disease, illness
{> morbid}; atrium Vestae: the house of Vesta, the building in which the Vestal Virgins lived; it was
situated immediately adjacent to the Temple of Vesta in the Roman Forum; cogo, cogere (< con +
ago, agere) compel; excedo, excedere (< ex + cedo, cedere) leave, withdraw from

custodia, -ae (f.) (< custos + -ia) protection, safekeeping, responsibility {> custody}

mando (1) hand over, commit {> mandate} (+ dat.)

quo munere i.e. the task of caring for Junia; munus, muneris (n.) duty, service; *munere*: abl. of means,
not acc. dir. obj. w/ depon. vb. *fungitur* (AG #410); *sedulo* (adv.) diligently; fungor, fungi, functus
sum: perform, discharge

3   hoc discrimine implicita est. Insident febres, tussis increscit;
summa macies summa defectio. Animus tantum et spiritus
uiget Heluidio marito, Thrasea patre dignissimus; reliqua
labuntur, meque non metu tantum, uerum etiam dolore con-

4   ficiunt. Doleo enim feminam maximam eripi oculis ciuitatis,
nescio an aliquid simile uisuris. Quae castitas illi, quae sancti-

---

discrimen, discriminis (n.) (< dis + cerno, cernere + -men) critical point, dangerous situation
{> discriminate}

implico, implicare, implicui, implicitus (< in + plico, plicare) entwine, involve {> implicate};
i.e. she became ill

VII.XIX.3

insido, insidere (< in + sido, sidere) settle in

febris, febris (f.) fever

tussis, tussis (f.) cough

incresco, increscere (< in + cresco, crescere) develop, become stronger

macies, maciei (f.) thinness, wasting of the body

defectio, defectionis (f.) (< de + facio, facere + -tio) failing, weakness; ELLIPSIS of *est* and
ASYNDETON emphasize the speed w/ which the illness came on

animus, -i (m.) mind (as opposed to body)

uigeo, uigere flourish, thrive {> vigor}

Heluidio ... dignissimus *marito ... patre*: abl of specif. (AG #418b) w/ *dignissimus*; maritus, -i (m.)
husband {> marital}; Helvidius Priscus was a persistent critic of the principate and advocate of
senatorial independence. As such, he ran afoul of both Nero and Vespasian and was banished on
separate occasions by each emperor and executed on orders from the latter (*OCD* 680–1). Publius
Clodius Thrasea Paetus was also a strong believer in the freedom of the senate, so much so that he
refused to participate in what he perceived as acts of subservience to the imperial family. His absten-
tion resulted in his condemnation and subsequent suicide (*OCD* 351).

labor, labi, lapsus sum slip or pass away, fail

dolor, doloris (m.) (< doleo, dolere + -or) grief, anguish

conficio, conficere (< con + facio, facere) overwhelm, consume (*OLD* 14a/15)

VII.XIX.4

doleo, dolere be in pain, grieve; Pliny's use of POLYPTOTON (*dolore, doleo*) reinforces the focus of the
letter on his emotions, expressed immediately at the beginning of the letter w/ *angit me*.

feminam ... eripi indir. disc. (AG #580); eripio, eripere (< ex + rapio, rapere) snatch away; *oculis*: abl.
of separ. (AG #401), modified by *uisuris*

quae ... quae ... quanta ... quanta interrog. used for emphasis in exclam. (AG #333n)

castitas, castitatis (f.) (< castus + -tas) moral purity {> chastity}; *illi*: dat. of poss. (AG #373); Pliny's
praise and his anxiety are heightened by the staccato effect of ASYNDETON and ELLIPSIS in this list
of qualities.

sanctitas, sanctitatis (f.) (< sanctus + -tas) integrity

tas, quanta grauitas quanta constantia! Bis maritum secuta
in exsilium est, tertio ipsa propter maritum relegata. Nam   5
cum Senecio reus esset quod de uita Heluidi libros composuis-
set rogatumque se a Fannia in defensione dixisset, quaerente
minaciter Mettio Caro, an rogasset respondit: 'Rogaui'; an
commentarios scripturo dedisset: 'Dedi'; an sciente matre:
'Nesciente'; postremo nullam uocem cedentem periculo
emisit. Quin etiam illos ipsos libros, quamquam ex neces-   6

---

grauitas, grauitatis (f.) (< grauis + -tas) weight, seriousness of conduct, influence
constantia, -ae (f.) (< pres. ptc. of consto, constare + -ia) steadiness, resolution
bis (adv.) twice
exsilium, -i (m.) (< exsul + -ium) exile
tertio supply *tempore*
relego (1) (< re + lego, legare) banish; ELLIPSIS of *est*

VII.XIX.5

cum ... esset cum circumst. cl. (AG #546); *Senecio*: Herennius Senecio (s. IV.XI.12n.); reus, -i (m.)
    defendant, the accused
quod ... dixisset causal cl., subjv. indicates another's opinion (AG #540/2); *rogatum ... Fannia*: indir.
    disc. (AG #580), ELLIPSIS of *esse*; defensio, defensionis (f.) (< defendo, defendere + -tio) defense,
    justification
quaerente ... Caro abl. abs. (AG #419); quaero, quaerere: search for, seek; *minaciter* (adv.) (< minax)
    in a threatening/menacing manner; Mettius Carus is unknown outside of Pliny's letters, but was
    apparently one of the infamous *delatores* under Domitian and clearly the lead accuser against Fannia
    and the six others accused of treason in 93 CE. These included Arulenus Rusticus, his brother Junius
    Mauricus and his wife Gratilla, Herennius Senecio, the younger Helvidius Priscus (Fannia's step-
    son), and the younger Arria (Fannia's mother). Mauricus and the women were relegated, while the
    remaining men were executed.
an rogasset ... an dedisset 2 indir. quests. (AG #574) ff. *quaerente, an*: "whether (or not)"; *respondit*:
    subj. *Fannia*; commentarius, commentarii (m.) notebook, journal; *scripturo, Senecioni* understood;
    the term *commentarius* originally referred to records of business, political, or military actions or
    notes for speeches or teaching. By the late Republic, *commentarii* became more like memoirs than
    practical notes. The most famous of these were, of course, those written by Caesar on his conquest of
    Gaul and his civil war w/ Pompey (*OCD* s. commentarii, 373).
an sciente matre abl. abs. (AG #419), a surprise 3rd member of this series, ff. two indir. quests., an ex.
    of Pliny's VARIATIO.
postremo (adv.) in the end, in fact
cedo, cedere submit, yield (*OLD* 10)
emitto, emittere, emisi, emissus (< ex + mitto, mittere) send out, utter (*OLD* 6d)

VII.XIX.6

quin etiam moreover
necessitas, necessitatis (f.) (< necesse + -tas) requirement, need

sitate et metu temporum abolitos senatus consulto, publicatis bonis seruauit habuit, tulitque in exsilium exsili

7 causam. Eadem quam iucunda quam comis, quam denique
(quod paucis datum est) non minus amabilis quam ueneranda!
Eritne quam postea uxoribus nostris ostentare possimus? Erit
a qua uiri quoque fortitudinis exempla sumamus, quam sic

8 cernentes audientesque miremur, ut illas quae leguntur? Ac
mihi domus ipsa nutare, conuulsaque sedibus suis ruitura supra
uidetur, licet adhuc posteros habeat. Quantis enim uirtutibus
quantisque factis adsequentur, ut haec non nouissima occi-

---

aboleo, abolere, aboleui, abolitus destroy

consultum, -i (n.) (< ppp. of consulo, consulere) decision to act, plan; senatus consultum: resolution of the senate; while these did not have the force of law per se, in practice they were treated as binding (*OCD* s. senatus consultum, 1388).

publicatis bonis abl. abs. (AG #419); publico (1) (< publicus, -a, -um) make public property, confis-cate; bona, bonorum (n.) possessions

exsilium exsili w/ this use of POLYPTOTON, Pliny both stresses Fannia's unflagging determination to preserve her husband's memoirs and identifies these books as the sole source of her banishment.

VII.XIX.7

quam interrog. used for emphasis in exclam. (AG #333n); as above in section 4, Pliny employs ASYNDETON and ELLIPSIS to create a series of breathless exclams. to praise Fannia and to demon-strate his own distress.

comis, come kind, gracious

ueneror, uenerari, ueneratus sum hold in awe, revere {> venerate}

Eritne . . . leguntur In this series of RHETORICAL QUESTIONS, Pliny creates a ritualized lament for Fannia, employing ANAPHORA and ASYNDETON.

quam . . . possimus, a qua . . . sumamus, quam . . . miremur relat. cl. of char. (AG #535); *quam, qua = aliquam, aliqua* (s. 1.1.1n. on quas)

ostento (1) (< ob + tendo, tendere + -to) display, hold up, point out {> ostentatious}

fortitudo, fortitudinis (f.) (< fortis + -tudo) strength, courage

sumo, sumere take up, adopt/take (as an example)

cerno, cernere distinguish, discern, perceive

ut illas quae leguntur *ut* w/ indic. "as" (AG #527f); lit. "as those who are read," i.e. "as we do the famous women of the past"

VII.XIX.8

nuto (1) nod, sway

conuello, conuellere, conuelli, conuulsus (< con + uello, uellere) pull or shake violently, uproot {> convulsion}; *sedibus suis*: abl. of separ. (AG #401); sedes, sedis (f.) seat, foundation (*OLD* 10)

ruo, ruere, rui, ruiturus be brought to ruin, collapse (*OLD* 7)

supra (adv.) further, in addition

posterus, -a, -um (< post) later, future, pl. subst.: descendents, posterity

adsequor, adsequi, adsecutus sum (< ad + sequor, sequi) carry out successfully, succeed, achieve; compd. vb + dat. *Quantis . . . uirtutibus, quantisque factis* (AG #370)

derit? Me quidem illud etiam adfligit et torquet, quod   9
matrem eius, illam (nihil possum inlustrius dicere) tantae
feminae matrem, rursus uideor amittere, quam haec, ut reddit
ac refert nobis, sic auferet secum, meque et nouo pariter et
rescisso uulnere adficiet. Vtramque colui utramque dilexi: 10
utram magis nescio, nec discerni uolebant. Habuerunt officia
mea in secundis, habuerunt in aduersis. Ego solacium relega-
tarum, ego ultor reuersarum; non feci tamen paria atque eo
magis hanc cupio seruari, ut mihi soluendi tempora supersint.
In his eram curis, cum scriberem ad te; quas si deus aliquis in   11
gaudium uerterit, de metu non querar. Vale.

---

ut . . . occiderit result cl.; occido, occidere, occidi, occisus (< ob + cado, cadere) be struck down, die;
i.e. Pliny finds it hard to imagine that her descendants could match her character and deeds; she will
thus be the last of her kind.

VII.XIX.9

illud points forward to the *quod* cl. (AG #297e)
adfligo, adfligere (< ad + fligo, fligere) vex, distress
torqueo, torquere twist tightly, torture mentally
inlustrius (compar. adj.) (< inlustris) more distinguished
amitto, amittere (< ab + mitto, mittere) incur the loss of, lose
quam (relat. pron.) anteced. *matrem*; *haec*: Fannia
ut . . . sic correl., as . . . so
aufero, auferre (< ab + fero, ferre) take away, remove
rescindo, rescindere, rescidi, rescissus (< re + scindo, scindere) tear open
adficio, adficere (< ad + facio, facere) affect, stir/move (emotion)

VII.XIX.10

colo, colere, colui cultivate, be a devotee of, cherish, respect
discerno, discernere (< dis + cerno, cernere) separate, distinguish
secundus, -a, -um (< sequor) following, favorable
aduersus, -a, -um (< ppp. of ad + uerto, uertere) unfavorable
ultor, ultoris (m.) (< ulciscor, ulcisci + -tor) avenger, ELLIPSIS of *erat*
reuertor, reuerti, reuersus sum (< re + uertor, uerti) come back, return
eo magis (adv.) all the more, so much more (*OLD* 2); *eo*: abl. of deg. of diff. w/ compar. (AG #414a n.)
ut . . . supersint purp. cl. (AG #531/1); *soluendi*: ger., gen. of specif. (BG #361) w/ *tempora*; soluo,
soluere (< se + luo, luere) pay (a debt) (*OLD* 18 and 19) {> solvent}; supersum, superesse
(< super + sum, esse) remain, be left over

VII.XIX.11

cum . . . scriberem cum circumst. cl. (AG #546); *eram, scriberem*: epistolary past tense
quas (relat. pron.) anteced. *curis*
si . . . querar FMV condit. (AG #516c); queror, queri, questus sum: complain, grumble {> querulous}

xxiv—UMMIDIUS QUADRATUS' FEISTY GRANDMOTHER

C. PLINIVS GEMINO SVO S.

1   Vmmidia Quadratilla paulo minus octogensimo aetatis
anno decessit usque ad nouissimam ualetudinem uiridis, atque
etiam ultra matronalem modum compacto corpore et robusto.

2   Decessit honestissimo testamento: reliquit heredes ex besse
nepotem, ex tertia parte neptem. Neptem parum noui,
nepotem familiarissime diligo, adulescentem singularem nec
iis tantum, quos sanguine attingit, inter propinquos aman-

VII.XXIV: Pliny reports the death of a prominent Roman matron, who is fond of her leisure time and
whose grandson is one of his protégés.

Addressee: (Rosianus) Geminus, suffect consul circa 125 CE, who had served as Pliny's quaestor in
100 CE (SW 402, AB 85); receives several letters from Pliny on illness and death.

VII.XXIV.1

Vmmidia Quadratilla The daughter of a senator from Casinum (modern day Cassino), she is also
known from several inscriptions found there that indicate her ongoing benefactions to the
community, including the funding of an amphitheater and a temple and the restoration of a
theater.

paulo somewhat, by a little; abl. of deg. of diff. (AG #414)

octogensimus, -a, -um 80th

decedo, decedere, decessi, decessus (< de + cedo, cedere) go away, die (*OLD* 7) {> decedent}

usque (adv.) all the way (to), continually, persistently

uiridis, uiride green, youthful, healthy

ultra (prep. + acc.) beyond, to a point beyond

matronalis, matronale (< mater + -ona + -alis) of a matron

compacto corpore et robusto abl. of quality (AG #415a); compactus, -a, -um (< ppp. of con + pango,
pangere) well-set, compact; robustus, -a, -um (< robur + -tus) strong, firm, solid

VII.XXIV.2

honesto testamento abl. of quality (AG #415a); testamentum, -i (n.) (< testor + -mentum) will, testament (s. I.IX.2n.)

heres, heredis (f.) heir

bes, bessis (m.) two-thirds (of any whole); *ex besse*: in the proportion of two-thirds (*OLD* 2a)

nepotem . . . neptem appos. to *heredes*; nepos, nepotis (m.) grandson; neptis, neptis (f.)
granddaughter

nosco, noscere, noui, notus become acquainted w/, pf.: know (have become acquainted w/)

familiarissime (superl. adv.) (< familiaris) very intimately

singularis, singulare (< singuli + -aris) special, unique, remarkable

iis dat. of agent (AG #374) w/ *amandum*; anteced. of *quos*

sanguis, sanguinis (m.) blood

attingo, attingere (< ad + tango, tangere) touch, be related to (by blood) (*OLD* 12a)

propinquus, -a, -um living nearby, neighbors

dum. Ac primum conspicuus forma omnes sermones mali- 3
gnorum et puer et iuuenis euasit, intra quartum et uicensimum
annum maritus, et si deus adnuisset pater. Vixit in contubernio auiae delicatae seuerissime, et tamen obsequentissime.
Habebat illa pantomimos fouebatque, effusius quam principi 4
feminae conuenit. Hos Quadratus non in theatro, non domi
spectabat, nec illa exigebat. Audiui ipsam cum mihi com- 5

VII.XXIV.3

conspicuus, -a, -um (< con + specio, specere + -uus) notable, famous; *forma*: abl. of specif.
(AG #418)

malignus, -a, -um spiteful, harmful {> malign}; subst. use: "spiteful people"

euado, euadere, euasi, euasus (< ex + uado, uadere) escape

uicensimus, -a, -um 20th

maritus, -i (m.) husband {> marital}; ELLIPSIS of *erat*; Augustan marriage laws (Lex Iulia de
maritandis ordinibus, 18 BCE, and Lex Papia Poppaea, 9 CE) imposed penalties, such as restrictions
on inheritance, on those who were unmarried and/or childless at the age of 25 and granted
privileges to those who had at least three children.

si . . . adnuisset prot. of past C-to-F condit. (AG #517); adnuo, adnuere, adnui, adnutus (< ad + nuo,
nuere) nod assent, grant (a prayer); (*pater*) *esset* implied in apod. rather than *fuisset* because it
expresses a pres. condit.

contubernium, -i (n.) (< con + taberna + -ium) cohabitation, lodging

auia, -ae (f.) grandmother

delicatus, -a, -um addicted to pleasure, self-indulgent

seuerissime (superl. adv.) (< seuerus) most strictly

obsequentissime (superl. adv.) (< pres. ptc. of obsequor, obsequi) most obediently

VII.XXIV.4

pantomimus, -i (m.) (< Gr. παντόμιμος) pantomime performer; a pantomime troupe included a solo
dancer who, w/ a variety of masks and movements, represented the characters and actions of a story,
w/ the support of a chorus and musicians. Tragic subjects were particularly popular. Close association w/ pantomime actors could seriously threaten the reputation of anyone of senatorial rank.
There was so much concern about their debilitating effect on their fans that legal restrictions were
placed on performances and interactions between pantomime performers and Roman citizens outside of the theater (Tacitus *Ann.* 1.77).

foueo, fouere support, favor, indulge

effusus, -a, -um (< ppp. of effundo, effundere) extravagant, immoderate

principi feminae dat. of indir. obj. w/ compd. vb. *conuenit* (AG #370)

hos i.e. *pantomimos*

Quadratus Ummidius Quadratus (s. VI.XI.1n.)

exigo, exigere (< ex + ago, agere) compel, demand, require (*OLD* 9a)

VII.XXIV.5

Audiui ipsam followed by 3 indir. disc. (AG #580)

cum . . . studia cum circumst. cl. (AG #546); commendo (1) (< con + mando, mandare) entrust,
compd. vb + dat. *mihi* (AG #370)

mendaret nepotis sui studia, solere se, ut feminam in illo otio
sexus, laxare animum lusu calculorum, solere spectare pantomimos suos, sed cum factura esset alterutrum, semper se
nepoti suo praecepisse abiret studeretque; quod mihi non
amore eius magis facere quam reuerentia uidebatur.

6   Miraberis, et ego miratus sum. Proximis sacerdotalibus
ludis, productis in commissione pantomimis, cum simul theatro ego et Quadratus egrederemur, ait mihi: 'Scis me hodie
primum uidisse saltantem auiae meae libertum?' Hoc nepos.

---

solere ... calculorum 1st indir. disc.; *ut ... sexus*: *ut* w/ indic. "as" (AG #527f); sexus, -us (m.) state of
being male or female; laxo (1) (< laxus + -o) release, relax; lusus, -us (m.) (< ludo, ludere + -tus)
game; calculus, -i (m.) (< calx + -ulus) small stone, board game marker; *calculi* were used in games
such as *duodecim scripta* or *latrunculi*, which may be precursors of backgammon and chess respectively. Such unproductive activities constituted a poor use of *otium* (s. Freq. Vocab.) for Roman men
and were frowned upon.

solere ... suos 2nd indir. disc.

cum ... alterutrum cum circumst. cl. (AG #546); alteruter, -utra, -utrum: one or the other

se ... praecepisse 3rd indir. disc.; praecipio, praecipere, praecepi (< prae + capio, capere) order
beforehand, give instruction

abiret studeretque subst. cl. of purp. (AG #563) (= indir. comm.) ff. *praecepisse*, *ut* omitted; abeo,
abire (< ab + eo, ire) go away, depart

quod (rel pron.) anteced. preceding cl.

reuerentia, -ae (f.) (< reuerens + -ia) deference, respect; *amore, reuerentia*: abl. of cause (AG #404)

VII.XXIV.6

miror, mirari, miratus sum (< mirus + -o) be surprised, amazed; *miraberis ... miratus*: Pliny's use of
POLYPTOTON signals his awareness of the likely reaction of his reader to the improbability of what
he is reporting.

proximis sacerdotalibus ludis abl. of time when (AG #423); sacerdotalis, sacrerdotale (< sacerdos +
-alis) connected w/ priests, priestly; ludus, -i (m.) game, recreation, pl.: set of festival or public
games; the term *ludi* describes various types of competitions held in conjunction w/ Roman religious festivals. The oldest, most popular, and longest lasting were the *ludi circenses*, chariot racing.
Theater games, *ludi scaenici*, began in the middle of the 4th century BCE and included plays, Atellan
farce, mime, and pantomime. The latecomer to festival games were *munera*, gladiatorial competition,
which had only been offered at private funerals to honor the deceased before 42 BCE, when they were
first officially incorporated into regularly scheduled games. During the Republic, the games at Rome
were presided over by various magistrates, but beginning early in the imperial period the emperor
took control of their oversight and funding. It is difficult to know precisely how many days a year
games were offered in Rome in Pliny's time, but the number is likely to have been at least 100.

productis ... pantomimis abl. abs. (AG #419); produco, producere, produxi, productus (< pro + duco,
ducere) bring forth; commissio, commissionis (f.) (< con + mitto, mittere + -tio) commencement/
opening of the games

cum ... egrederemur cum circumst. cl. (AG #546); *theatro*: abl. of place from which w/ out prep.
(AG #428g); egredior, egredi, egressus sum (< ex + gradior, gradi) go out, leave

me ... libertum indir. disc. (AG #580); salto (1) (< salio, salire + -to) dance; libertus, -i (m.) (< liber
+ -tus) freedman (s. II.VI.2n.); Pliny refers here specifically to the main performer of the troupe.

Hoc nepos vb. of saying understood

At hercule alienissimi homines in honorem Quadratillae   7
(pudet me dixisse honorem) per adulationis officium in theatrum cursitabant exsultabant plaudebant mirabantur ac deinde
singulos gestus dominae cum canticis reddebant; qui nunc
exiguissima legata, theatralis operae corollarium, accipient
ab herede, qui non spectabat. Haec, quia soles si quid incidit   8
noui non inuitus audire, deinde quia iucundum est mihi quod
ceperam gaudium scribendo retractare. Gaudeo enim pietate
defunctae, honore optimi iuuenis; laetor etiam quod domus
aliquando C. Cassi, huius qui Cassianae scholae princeps et

VII.XXIV.7

at hercule *At* (conj.) and yet (expresses contrast); *hercule:* voc.; appeal to Hercules, used for emphasis
    or to express strong feelings, *at* w/ *hercule* intensifies imprecation and has expletive force (*OLD* s.
    at 11b)

alienus, -a, -um (< alius + -enus) foreign, unrelated by blood, distasteful (*OLD* 8c)

pudeo, pudere fill w/ shame, make ashamed

adulatio, adulationis (f.) (< adulor, adulari + -tio) obsequious flattery

cursito (1) (< curro, currere + -to + -ito) hurry, rush constantly about; Pliny employs ASYNDETON to
    present these actions and so heightens the sense of frenetic movement among the performers.

exsulto (1) (< ex + salto, saltare) leap about, dance

plaudo, plaudere clap one's hands, applaud

gestus, -us (m.) (< gero, gerere + -tus) movement of the limbs, gesture

canticum, -i (n.) (< cantus + -icum) a passage of song

qui (relat. pron.) anteced. *homines*

exiguus, -a, -um (< ex + ago, agere + -uus) small (in amount), scanty

legatum, -i (n.) (< ppp. of lego, legare) legacy, bequest

opera, -ae (f.) activity, work, service; *theatralis operae:* objv. gen. (AG #347) w/ *corollarium;*
    corollarium, -i (n.) (< corolla + -arium) gratuity

VII.XXIV.8

Haec i.e. the preceding story; vb. of telling/relating understood

si ... noui simple condit. (indic.) (AG #514a); *quid = aliquid* (s. 1.1.1n. on quas); incido, incidere (< in
    + cado, cadere) occur (*OLD* 10a) {> incident}; *noui:* partit. gen. ff. n. pron. *quid* (AG #346/3)

inuitus, -a, -um unwilling, reluctant

quod (relat. pron.) anteced. *gaudium*

retracto (1) (re + traho, trahere + -to) re-examine, review, recollect (*OLD* 7)

pietate, honore abl. of cause (AG #404)

defunctus, -a, -um (< ppp. of de + fungor, fungi) dead

laetor, laetari, laetatus sum (< laetus, -a, -um + -o) be glad, be delighted

aliquando (adv.) once, formerly

C. Cassius Gaius Cassius Longinus was a juriconsult of consular rank in the mid-1st century CE. He
    was exiled by Nero but recalled by Vespasian. He founded the *scola Cassiana,* a group of legal advo-
    cates who held to strict and traditional application of the law (*OCD* 301).

9 parens fuit, seruiet domino non minori. Implebit enim illam
Quadratus meus et decebit, rursusque ei pristinam digni-
tatem celebritatem gloriam reddet, cum tantus orator inde
procedet, quantus iuris ille consultus. Vale.

XXVII—DO GHOSTS EXIST?

C. PLINIVS SVRAE SVO S.

1 Et mihi discendi et tibi docendi facultatem otium praebet.
Igitur perquam uelim scire, esse phantasmata et habere pro-
priam figuram numenque aliquod putes an inania et uana ex

2 metu nostro imaginem accipere. Ego ut esse credam in primis

---

seruio, seruire (< seruus + -io) serve; *domino non minori*: dat. w/ intr. vb. (AG #367)

VII.XXIV.9
impleo, implere fill up
illam i.e. *domus*
decet be right or fitting for; impers. vb. used only in 3rd pers.
ei i.e. *illa domus*
pristinus, -a, -um belonging to a previous time, former
dignitas, dignitatis (f.) (< dignus + -tas) excellence, status (*OLD* 3a)
celebritas, celebritatis (f.) (< celeber + -tas) reputation, renown
cum ... procedet cum tmp. cl. (AG #545); *tantus ... quantus*: correl., "as great ... as"; procedo, procedere (< pro + cedo, cedere) come forth, advance
iuris consultus, -i (m.) jurisconsult; an expert on Roman law, whose advice would be sought on the
proper application of laws

VII.XXVII: Pliny contemplates whether ghosts exist and tells a series of stories about them.
Addressee: (Licinius) Sura, suffect consul circa 93 CE, ordinary consul in both 102 and 107 CE; of
Spanish origin, he funded buildings at various cities there; a close associate and supporter of the
Emperor Trajan (SW 309–10, AB 69)

VII.XXVII.1
disco, discere learn; *discendi, docendi*: objv. gen. (AG #347) w/ *facultatem*; facultas, facultatis (f.)
ability, power, opportunity {> faculty}
praebeo, praebere (< prae + habeo, habere) present, provide
perquam (adv.) extremely, exceedingly
uelim potent. subjv. (AG #447)
esse ... accipere compd. indir. disc. (AG #580) ff. *putes*, which signals an indir. quest. (AG #574) ff.
scire; an: "or" *utrum* ("whether") implied; *esse ... aliquod*: explains the 1st of two possible opinions
that Pliny's addressee may hold; phantasma, phantasmatis (n.) (< Gr. φάντασμα) ghost, apparition;
proprius, -a, -um: its own, one's own; numen, numinis (n.) divine or supernatural power; *inania ...*
accipere: explaining the 2nd possibility; inanis, inane: unsubstantial, illusory (*OLD* 10/11); uanus,
-a, -um: imaginary; imago, imaginis (f.) likeness, appearance

eo ducor, quod audio accidisse Curtio Rufo. Tenuis adhuc et
obscurus, obtinenti Africam comes haeserat. Inclinato die
spatiabatur in porticu; offertur ei mulieris figura humana
grandior pulchriorque. Perterrito Africam se futurorum
praenuntiam dixit: iturum enim Romam honoresque ge-
sturum, atque etiam cum summo imperio in eandem prouinciam reuersurum, ibique moriturum. Facta sunt omnia.
Praeterea accedenti Carthaginem egredientique naue eadem
figura in litore occurrisse narratur. Ipse certe implicitus

3

VII.XXVII.2

ut ... credam subst. cl. of purp. (AG #563) (= indir. comm.) ff. *ducor; esse*: echoing the 1st option:
"that they exist"

in primis above all else, first and foremost

quod (relat. pron.) anteced. *eo*: "(by that) which"; *Curtio Rufo*: dat. of indir. obj. w/ compd. vb. *accidisse*
(AG #370)

Curtius Rufus a senator said to be of humble background, who scholars now believe should be identified w/ the like-named author of a history of Alexander the Great (AB 54–5, OLD 415–6)

tenuis, tenue modest, of little importance

obscurus, -a, -um little known, undistinguished; i.e. early in Curtius Rufus' career

obtineo, obtinere (< ob + teneo, tenere) be in charge of, control, govern; *obtinenti*: dat. sg. pres. ptc.
subst., "the man governing"

comes, comitis (m.) companion, staff member (*OLD* 4a)

haereo, haesi stick, cling, be attached to {> adhesive}

inclinato die abl. abs. (AG #419); inclino (1) lean to one side, bend downwards; "in the afternoon"

spatior, spatiari, spatiatus sum (< spatium + -o) walk about

porticus, -us (m./f.) covered walkway, colonnade

offero, offerre (< ob + fero, ferre) put in the path of, pass.: present oneself (+ dat.)

grandis, grande full grown, tall, large; *humana*: abl. of compar. (AG #406)

perterreo, perterrere, perterrui, perterritus (< per + terreo, terrere) terrify; *perterrito*: dat. of indir.
obj. (AG #362), i.e. *Rufo*

Africam ... praenuntiam indir. disc. (AG #580), ELLIPSIS of *esse*; praenuntius, -a, -um: announcing in
advance; *praenuntiam*: appos. to *Africam*, subst. use: harbinger, herald

(eum) iturum ... moriturum indir. disc. (AG #580) ff. *praenuntiam; cum summo imperio*: i.e. as governor; reuertor, reuerti, reuersus sum (< re + uertor, uerti) come back, return

VII.XXVII.3

Carthago, Carthaginis (f.) Carthage; this is, of course, not Phoenician Carthage, which had been
destroyed in 146 BCE, but rather the Roman colony intended by Caesar and established by Augustus.
It was the capital of the province Africa Proconsularis (*OCD* s. Carthage, 295–6).

egredior, egredi, egressus sum (< ex + gradior, gradi) leave, disembark; *naue*: abl. of place from
which w/ o prep. (AG #428g)

litus, litoris (n.) shore, coast

occurro, occurrere, occurri (< ob + curro, currere) hurry to meet; compd. vb. + dat. *accedenti,
egredienti* (AG #370), *Rufo* understood

implico, implicare, implicui, implicitus (< in + plico, plicare) entwine, hem in {> implicate};
w/ abl. of thing *morbo* (AG #364n); morbus, -i (m.) disease, illness

morbo futura praeteritis, aduersa secundis auguratus, spem
salutis nullo suorum desperante proiecit.

4 Iam illud nonne et magis terribile et non minus mirum est

5 quod exponam ut accepi? Erat Athenis spatiosa et capax
domus sed infamis et pestilens. Per silentium noctis sonus
ferri, et si attenderes acrius, strepitus uinculorum longius
primo, deinde e proximo reddebatur: mox adparebat idolon,
senex macie et squalore confectus, promissa barba horrenti
capillo; cruribus compedes, manibus catenas gerebat quatie-

---

futura ... auguratus praetereo, praeterire, praeterii, praeteritus (< praeter + eo, ire) go by, pass; aduersus, -a, -um (< ppp. of ad + uerto, uertere) unfavorable; secundus, -a, -um (< sequor) favorable; auguror, augurari, auguratus sum (< augur + -or) predict, foretell; "after predicting future events by what had passed and unfavorable outcomes by favorable ones"

nullo ... desperante abl. abs. (AG #419); despero (1) (< de + spero, sperare) give up hope (of a cure); trans. as conces. "although"; *suorum*: i.e. his family and members of his staff

proicio, proicere, proieci, proiectus (< pro + iacio, iacere) discard, abandon (*OLD* 6 a/b)

VII.XXVII.4

illud points forward to the *quod* cl. (AG #297e)

terribilis, terribile (< terreo, terrere + -bilis) frightening

expono, exponere, exposui, expositus (< ex + pono, ponere) describe, explain (*OLD* 6) {> expository}

ut accepi *ut* w/ indic. (AG #527f), "as it came to me"

VII.XXVII.5

spatiosus, -a, -um (< spatium + -osus) expansive

capax, capacis (< capio + -ax) roomy {> capacity}

infamis, infame (< in + fama + -is) having a bad name/reputation

pestilens, pestilentis unhealthy, causing danger to life or health

silentium, -i (n.) (< silens + -ium) absence of sound, silence

sonus, -i (m.) sound, noise; ELLIPSIS of *erat*

si attenderes ... reddebatur gen. condit. using 2nd pers. sg. impf. subjv. in prot. and indic. in apod. to show repeated action (AG #518c); attendo, attendere (< ad + tendo, tendere) pay attention, listen carefully; strepitus, -us (m.) (< strepo, strepere + -tus) noise, din; uinculum, -i (n.) (< uincio, uincire + -ulum) chain, shackle; *primo* (adv.) at first, firstly; *e proximo*; close at hand

adpareo, adparere (< ad + pareo, parere) be seen physically, appear

idolon, -i (n.) (< Gr. εἴδωλον) apparition, ghost, image

macies, maciei (f.) thinness, wasting of the body

squalor, squaloris (m.) (< squaleo, squalere + -or) filth

conficio, conficere, confeci, confectus (< con + facio, facere) overwhelm, consume (*OLD* 14a/15)

promissa barba horrenti capillo abl. of quality (AG #415a); promitto, promittere, promisi, promissus (< pro + mitto, mittere) let loose, stream forth; barba, -ae (f.) beard; horreo, horrere: stand on end, bristle; capillus, -i (m.) hair; Pliny uses ASYNDETON to heighten the drama of his horrifying description.

crus, cruris (n.) leg

compes, compedis (f.) pl.: shackles for the feet, fetters

catena, -ae (f.) chain

quatio, quatere shake

batque. Inde inhabitantibus tristes diraeque noctes per   6
metum uigilabantur; uigiliam morbus et crescente formidine
mors sequebatur. Nam interdiu quoque, quamquam absces-
serat imago, memoria imaginis oculis inerrabat, longiorque
causis timoris timor erat. Deserta inde et damnata solitudine
domus totaque illi monstro relicta; proscribebatur tamen, seu
quis emere seu quis conducere ignarus tanti mali uellet.
Venit Athenas philosophus Athenodorus, legit titulum audito-   7
que pretio, quia suspecta uilitas, percunctatus omnia docetur

---

VII.XXVII.6

inhabito (1) (< in + habito, habitare) inhabit, occupy; *inhabitantibus*: dat. of ref. (AG #376)

tristis, triste gloomy, grim

dirus, -a, -um awful, dreadful, frightful

uigilabantur ... uigiliam POLYPTOTON; uigilo (1) (< uigil + -o) stay awake, spend (a night) awake; uigilia, -ae (f.) (< uigil + -ia) watchful attention, wakefulness

crescente formidine abl. abs. (AG #419); cresco, crescere: increase; formido, formidinis (f.) terror, horror {> formidable}

interdiu (adv.) in the daytime, by day

abscedo, abscedere, abscessi, abscessus (< ab + cedo, cedere) go away, withdraw

imago, imaginis (f.) likeness, image

inerro (1) (< in + erro, errare) wander or roam in {> errant}; compd. vb. + dat. *oculis* (AG #370)

causis abl. of compar. (AG #406)

desertus, -a, -um (< ppp. of desero, deserere) deserted, abandoned

damno (1) (< damnum + -o) pass judgment, condemn; *solitudine*: abl. of price/penalty (AG #353/1); solitudo, solitudinis (f.) (< solus + -tudo) the state of being alone, solitude

monstrum, -i (n.) unnatural thing, monstrosity; *relicta*: ELLIPSIS of *est*

proscribo, proscribere, proscripsi, proscriptus (< pro + scribo, scribere) announce publicly, advertise

seu ... seu (conj.) whether ... or

quis ... uellet indir. quest. (AG #574); *quis = aliquis* (s. 1.1.1n. on quas); emo, emere: buy; conduco, conducere (< con + duco, ducere) hire, rent (*OLD* 4a); ignarus, -a, -um (< in + gnarus) having no knowledge, unaware; *tanti mali*: objv. gen. (AG #350) w/ *ignarus*

VII.XXVII.7

philosophus, -i (m.) (< Gr. φιλόσοφος) philosopher; here Pliny begins the use of the hist. pres. to enliven the narrative.

Athenodorus a philosopher who paid court to Augustus and whose ethical writings were a source for the younger Seneca (*OCD* 203)

titulus, -i (m.) identification, notice

audito pretio abl. abs. (AG #419); pretium, -i (n.) reward, price, value

suspectus, -a, -um (< ppp. of sub + specio, specere) suspected; ELLIPSIS of *est*

uilitas, uilitatis (f.) (< uilis + -tas) low price, cheapness

percunctor, percunctari, percunctatus sum (< per + contus + -o) make inquiries, investigate

ac nihilo minus, immo tanto magis conducit. Vbi coepit
aduesperascere, iubet sterni sibi in prima domus parte, poscit
pugillares stilum lumen, suos omnes in interiora dimittit;
ipse ad scribendum animum oculos manum intendit, ne
uacua mens audita simulacra et inanes sibi metus fingeret.

8   Initio, quale ubique, silentium noctis; dein concuti ferrum,
uincula moueri. Ille non tollere oculos, non remittere stilum,
sed offirmare animum auribusque praetendere. Tum crebrescere fragor, aduentare et iam ut in limine, iam ut intra limen
audiri. Respicit, uidet agnoscitque narratam sibi effigiem.

---

nihilo minus nonetheless

immo (pcl.) rather, more precisely

tanto magis so much the more; *tanto*: abl. of deg. of diff. (AG #414)

coepi, coepisse (pf. stem only) begin

aduesperascit, aduesperascere (< ad + uesperascit) impers. use only: it draws toward evening,
evening comes on

sterno, sternere spread out (blankets), lay out (a couch); Pliny employs ASYNDETON to rattle off
Athenodorus' orders here and his subsequent actions when left alone below, highlighting the delib-
erateness of his behavior.

pugillares, pugillarium (m.) (< pugnus + -illus + -aris) writing tablets; (s. I.VI.1n. on *pugillares*)

stilus, -i (m.) stylus (for incising letters on wax tablets), pen

lumen, luminis (n.) source of illumination, lamp

suos *seruos* or *familiares* understood

interior, interius interior, inner

dimitto, dimittere (< dis + mitto, mittere) dismiss, send away

intendo, intendere (< in + tendo, tendere) keenly occupy, direct (one's eyes, mind, etc.) (*OLD* 6c)

ne ... fingeret negat. purp. cl. (AG #531/1); uacuus, -a, -um (< uaco, uacare + -uus) empty, unoccu-
pied {> vacuum}; simulacrum, -i (n.) image, phantom; fingo, fingere: create, invent, imagine

VII.XXVII.8

initium, -i (n.) (< ineo + -ium) beginning, start; *initio*: abl. of time when (AG #423)

quale ubique "the kind that is everywhere," i.e. nothing extraordinary; *ubique* (adv.) (< ubi + -que)
everywhere {> ubiquitous}; ELLIPSIS of *est* or *esse*

dein ... audiri Pliny shifts to the hist. inf. (AG #463) here to describe what happens when
Athenodorus has set himself in place, unmoving; concutio, concutere (< con + quatio, quatere)
shake; tollo, tollere: raise; remitto, remittere (< re + mitto, mittere) release, let go; offirmo
(1) (< ob + firmo, firmare) make firm (one's mind); praetendo, praetendere (< prae + tendo,
tendere) extend in front as a protection, i.e. block, shut out, compd vb. + dat. of indir. obj. *auribus*
(AG #370); crebresco, crebrescere (< creber + -esco) increase; fragor, fragoris (m.) crash, roar;
aduento (1) (< ad + uenio, uenire + -to) approach, draw near; *ut* (conj.) as; limen, liminis (n.)
threshold {> liminal}

respicio, respicere (< re + specio, specere) look back; *respicit*: subj. *Athenodorus*

agnosco, agnoscere (< ad + nosco, noscere) recognize, identify

effigies, effigiei (f.) (< ex + fingo, fingere + -ies) specter, ghost

Stabat innuebatque digito similis uocanti. Hic contra ut
paulum exspectaret manu significat rursusque ceris et stilo
incumbit. Illa scribentis capiti catenis insonabat. Respicit
rursus idem quod prius innuentem, nec moratus tollit lumen
et sequitur. Ibat illa lento gradu quasi grauis uinculis. Postquam deflexit in aream domus, repente dilapsa deserit comi-
tem. Desertus herbas et folia concerpta signum loco ponit.
Postero die adit magistratus, monet ut illum locum effodi
iubeant. Inueniuntur ossa inserta catenis et implicita, quae

9

10

11

---

innuo, innuere (< in + nuo, nuere) make signs, beckon to; *stabat innuebatque*: subj. *effigies*
digitus, -i (m.) finger {> digital}; *digito*, abl. of means (AG #409) w/ *uocanti*: subst. use, dat. w/ adj.
  similis (AG #384)

VII.XXVII.9
Hic i.e. Athenodorus
contra (adv.) in reply
ut … expectaret subst. cl. of purp. (AG #563) (= indir. comm.) ff. *significat*; *paulum* (adv.) a little
significo (1) (< signum + -fico) indicate
cera, -ae (f.) beeswax, wax; writing-tablet (s. I.VI.1n. on cera)
incumbo, incumbere bend or lean over
illa i.e. *effigies*
insono (1) (< in + sono, sonare) make a loud noise at; compd. vb. + dat. *capiti* (AG #370)

VII.XXVII.10
lento gradu abl. of manner; lentus, -a, -um: slow, sluggish; gradus, -us (m.) step, pace
grauis, graue heavy, weighed down (*OLD* 7)
deflecto, deflectere, deflexi, deflexus (< de + flecto, flectere) change course
area, -ae (f.) open space, forecourt
repente (adv.) suddenly, w/ out warning
dilabor, dilabi, dilapsus (< di + labor, labi) melt away, dissolve
deserit … desertus using POLYPTOTON, Pliny emphasizes the disappearance of the ghost and the
  shift in action from its disappearance to Athenodorus' response; desero, deserere, deserui, desertus
  (< de + sero, serere) withdraw from, abandon; comes, comitis (m.) companion
herba, -ae (f.) plant, weed
folium, -i (n.) leaf
concerpo, concerpere, concerpsi, concerptus (< con + carpo, carpere) pluck off, pick

VII.XXVII.11
posterus, -a, -um (< post) later, following
adeo, adire (< ad + eo, ire) go to, approach {> adit}
magistratus, -us (m.) (< magister + -atus) office of a magistrate, magistrate; *magistratus*: acc. pl.
ut … iubeant subst. cl. of purp. (AG #563) (= indir. comm.) ff. *monet*
effodio, effodere (< ex + fodio, fodere) dig up
os, ossis (n.) bone
insero, inserere, inserui, insertus (< in + sero, serere) put in, thrust in, joined; compd. vb + dat.
  catenis (AG #370)
implico, implicare, implicui, implicitus (< in + plico, plicare) entwine {> implicate}

corpus aeuo terraque putrefactum nuda et exesa reliquerat
uinculis; collecta publice sepeliuntur. Domus postea rite
conditis manibus caruit.

12 Et haec quidem adfirmantibus credo; illud adfirmare aliis
possum. Est libertus mihi non inlitteratus. Cum hoc minor
frater eodem lecto quiescebat. Is uisus est sibi cernere quendam in toro residentem, admouentemque capiti suo cultros,
atque etiam ex ipso uertice amputantem capillos. Vbi inluxit,
ipse circa uerticem tonsus, capilli iacentes reperiuntur.

13 Exiguum temporis medium, et rursus simile aliud priori
fidem fecit. Puer in paedagogio mixtus pluribus dormiebat.

---

aeuum, -i (n.) long period of time

putrefacio, putrefacere, putrefeci, putrefactus (< putris + facio, facere) cause to rot or decay

exedo, exedere, exedi, exesus (< ex + edo, edere) eat up, eat away

colligo, colligere, collexi, collectus (< con + lego, legere) gather, assemble {> collect}

sepelio, sepelire dispose of remains in a proper fashion, bury

rite (adv.) w/ the proper rites

condo, condere, condidi, conditus put away, lay to rest (*OLD* 4a)

manes, manium (m. pl.) spirits of the dead; *manibus*: abl. of separ. w/ vb. of privation *caruit*
   (AG #401); careo, carere, carui: lack, be w/ out

VII.XXVII.12

haec i.e. the story just told

adfirmo (1) (< ad + firmo, firmare) confirm, corroborate

illud i.e. the story that follows; *aliis*: dat. of ref. (AG #376)

libertus, -i (m.) (< liber + -tus) freedman (s. II.VI.2n.); *mihi*: dat. of poss. (AG #373)

inlitteratus, -a, -um (< in + litteratus) uneducated, unlearned

lectus, -i (m.) bed, couch; *eodem lecto*: abl. of place where w/ out prep. (AG #429)

cerno, cernere distinguish, discern, perceive

torus, -i (m.) cushion (used on a dining couch or bed)

resido, residere (< re + sido, sidere) take a seat, sit down

admoueo, admouere (< ad + moueo, mouere) move near; compd. vb + dat. *capiti* (AG #370)

culter, cultri (m.) knife (esp. for cutting hair)

uertex, uerticis (m.) crown of the head

amputo (1) cut off

inluceo, inlucere, inluxi (< in + luceo, lucere) shine; impers.: grow light, dawn

tondeo, tondere, totondi, tonsus cut or trim the hair; *tonsus*: ELLIPSIS of *est*

reperio, reperire (< re + pario, parire) discover, find by looking

VII.XXVII.13

exiguus, -a, -um (< ex + ago, agere + -uus) small (in amount); subst. use: "a small amount (of time)";
   ELLIPSIS of *erat*

prior, prius (compar. adj.) (< primus) previous, earlier

fidem facere (idiom.) induce belief (+ dat.) (*OLD* fides 11)

paedagogium, -i (n.) (< Gr. παιδαγωγεῖον) training place for slave boys

Venerunt per fenestras (ita narrat) in tunicis albis duo cuban-
temque detonderunt et qua uenerant recesserunt. Hunc quoque tonsum sparsosque circa capillos dies ostendit. Nihil   14
notabile secutum, nisi forte quod non fui reus, futurus, si
Domitianus sub quo haec acciderunt diutius uixisset. Nam in
scrinio eius datus a Caro de me libellus inuentus est; ex quo
coniectari potest, quia reis moris est summittere capillum,
recisos meorum capillos depulsi quod imminebat periculi
signum fuisse.

Proinde rogo, eruditionem tuam intendas. Digna res est   15
quam diu multumque consideres; ne ego quidem indignus,

---

misceo, miscere, miscui, mixtus mix, share (*OLD* 6); w/ abl. of accomp. *pluribus, cum* omitted
   (AG #413a n.)
cubo (1) lie down, sleep
detondo, detondere, detondi (< de + tondeo, tondere) shear, cut the hair off
qua (relat. adv.) where, by which way
recedo, recedere (< re + cedo, cedere) draw back, move away, depart {> recede}
spargo, spargere, sparsi, sparsus scatter, spread about
ostendo, ostendere present, reveal

VII.XXVII.14
secutum ELLIPSIS of *est*
forte (adv.) (< fors) by chance, as luck would have it
quod...reus subst. cl. introd. by *quod* (AG #572), "that"; reus, -i (m.) defendant, the accused
futurus...uixisset *fuissem* understood; past C-to-F condit. (AG #517); for Pliny's need to recast his
   relationship w/ Domitian, s. Intro.
scrinium, -i (n.) writing case, receptacle for holding scrolls
Carus Mettius Carus (s. VII.XIX.5n.)
coniecto (1) (< con + iacio, iacere + -to) draw a conclusion, infer
moris gen. of quality (price) (AG #345) w/ *est*: "it is customary"
summitto, summittere (< sub + mitto, mittere) allow hair to grow long
recisos...fuisse indir. disc. (AG #580) ff. *coniectari*
recido, recidere, recidi, recisus (< re + caedo, caedere) cut back, cut away
depello, depellere, depuli, depulsus (< de + pello, pellere) drive off, repel, avert; *depulsi*: modifies
   periculi
quod (relat. pron.) anteced. *periculi*
immineo, imminere press closely, menace, impend {> imminent}

VII.XXVII.15
eruditionem...intendas subst. cl. of purp. (AG #563) (= indir. comm.) ff. *rogo, ut* omitted; eruditio,
   eruditionis (f.) (< erudio, erudire + -tio) knowledge, learning
quam...consideres relat. cl. of char. (AG #535), anteced. *res*; considero (1) (< con + sidus + -o)
   examine, contemplate
indignus, -a, -um (< in + dignus, -a, -um) not deserving {> indignant}; ELLIPSIS of *est*

16   cui copiam scientiae tuae facias. Licet etiam utramque in
partem (ut soles) disputes, ex altera tamen fortius, ne me
suspensum incertumque dimittas, cum mihi consulendi
causa fuerit, ut dubitare desinerem. Vale.

---

cui . . . facias   relat. cl. of char. (AG #535), anteced. *ego*

VII.XXVII.16

utramque . . . disputes   subst. cl. of purp. ff. *licet* (AG #565); *utramque in partem*: modifier of obj. of
monosyl. prep. often precedes prep. (AG #599d); *ut soles*: *ut* w/ indic. "as" (AG #527f); Pliny uses
this PARENTHESIS to encourage a response from his addressee; disputo (1) (< dis + puto, putare)
debate, argue

ne . . . dimittas   negat. purp. cl. (AG #531/1); suspensus, -a, -um (< ppp. of sub + pendo, pendere) in
anxious uncertainty

cum . . . fuerit   cum causal cl. (AG #549); *mihi*: dat. of poss. (AG #373)

ut . . . desinerem   purp. cl. (AG #531/1)

BOOK VIII

xii—LITERARY OBLIGATIONS

C. PLINIVS MINICIANO SVO S.

Hunc solum diem excuso: recitaturus est Titinius Capito,   1
quem ego audire nescio magis debeam an cupiam. Vir est optimus et inter praecipua saeculi ornamenta numerandus. Colit
studia, studiosos amat fouet prouehit, multorum qui aliqua
componunt portus sinus gremium, omnium exemplum, ipsa-

VIII.XII: Pliny discusses the various reasons he must attend a particular public reading, giving his
reader deeper insight into the interchange of services and obligations in the literary community
(s. I.XIII.1n.).
Addressee: (Cornelius) Minicianus, s. IV.XI.

VIII.XII.1
excuso (1) ($<$ ex + causa + -o) excuse, exempt from a task
recito (1) ($<$ re + cito, citare) recite (before an audience)
Titinius Capito Of equestrian rank, Capito served as an imperial secretary to several emperors,
including Trajan (SW 333, AB 92); he would thus have been well-placed to support the lively literary
atmosphere Pliny describes.
magis . . . cupiam indir. quest. (AG #574) introd. by *nescio an*, "or" (*utrum* omitted); "whether it is
more my duty or my desire (to hear)"
praecipuus, -a, -um ($<$ prae + capio, capere + -uus) surpassing all others, exceptional
saeculum, -i (n.) age, generation
ornamentum, -i (n.) ($<$ orno, ornare + -mentum) embellishment, distinction
numero (1) ($<$ numerus + -o) count
colo, colere cultivate, be a devotee of, cherish, respect
studia, studiosos studiosus, -a, -um ($<$ studium + -osus) scholarly; subst.: "those who pursue
literature"; Pliny's use of both POLYPTOTON and ASYNDETON focuses the reader's attention on
literature and emphasizes Capito's devotion to the creation of a community of *studiosi*.
foueo, fouere support, encourage (*OLD* 7a)
proueho, prouehere ($<$ pro + ueho, uehere) carry forward, promote
portus, -us (m.) harbor, refuge, haven; ELLIPSIS of *est*
sinus, -us (m.) shelter
gremium, -i (n.) bosom, heart

2

3

4

rum denique litterarum iam senescentium reductor ac reformator. Domum suam recitantibus praebet, auditoria non apud
se tantum benignitate mira frequentat; mihi certe, si modo
in urbe, defuit numquam. Porro tanto turpius gratiam non
referre, quanto honestior causa referendae. An si litibus
tererer, obstrictum esse me crederem obeunti uadimonia mea,
nunc, quia mihi omne negotium omnis in studiis cura, minus
obligor tanta sedulitate celebranti, in quo obligari ego, ne
dicam solo, certe maxime possum? Quod si illi nullam uicem
nulla quasi mutua officia deberem, sollicitarer tamen uel

---

litterae, -arum (f. pl.) letters, literary works (*OLD* 8a) {> literature}

senesco, senescere (< seneo + -sco) grow old

reductor, reductoris (m.) (< re + duco, ducere + -tor) restorer

reformator, reformatoris (m.) (< re + formo, formare + -tor) reshaper, reformer; unsaid but implied is literature's need for a savior following the execution of several senators in 93 CE purportedly for treasonous writings that were likely accompanied by treasonous activities (C 34). Pliny's hostility toward Domitian is shared by Tacitus and colors his characterization of the emperor, who was, in fact, a literary patron.

VIII.XII.2

praebeo, praebere (< prae + habeo, habere) present, provide

auditorium, -i (n.) (< audio, audire + -torium) lecture hall, place for recitation

apud se "at his residence"

benignitas, benignitatis (f.) (< benignus + -tas) kindness, generosity

frequento (1) (< frequens + -o) visit or attend regularly

si modo only provided that, if in fact (*OLD* modo 3a); ELLIPSIS of *est*

desum, deesse, defui, defuturus (< de + sum, esse) fail, neglect to support (+ dat.)

porro . . . referendae *porro* (adv.) further, besides; ELLIPSIS of *est*; *tanto . . . quanto*: correl., abl. of deg. of diff. w/ compar. (AG #414a n.); turpis, turpe: ugly, shameful {> turpitude}; honestus, -a, -um (< honor + -tus) upright, worthy; "Besides, it is all the more shameful not to show my gratitude, given how truly worthy is the reason for rendering it."

VIII.XII.3

an (interrog. pcl.) here introd. a pair of RHETORICAL QUESTIONS (AG #335b).

si . . . mea pres. C-to-F condit. (AG #517); lis, litis (f.) lawsuit {> litigation}; tero, terere: wear away; *obstrictum . . . mea*: indir. disc. (AG #580) ff. *crederem*; obstringo, obstringere, obstrinxi, obstrictus (< ob + stringo, stringere) oblige, bind, compd. vb. + dat. *obeunti* (AG #370); obeo, obire (< ob + eo, ire) go to meet, take on (a task) (*OLD* 5a); uadimonium, -i (n.) (< uas, uadis + -monium) guarantee that defendant will appear, surety; *uadimonia*: abl. of price (AG #353/1)

negotium, -i (n.) (< neg (neque) + otium) business; ELLIPSIS of *est*

obligo (1) (< ob + ligo, ligare) tie, place under a moral obligation {> obligate}; compd. vb + dat. *celebranti* (AG #370); celebro (1) (< celeber + -o) celebrate, praise, extol (*OLD* 6a)

sedulitas, sedulitatis (f.) (< sedulus + -tas) painstaking attention; *tanta sedulitate*: abl. of manner (AG #412)

in quo (relat. pron.) "in whose case" (AG #221/12/2); anteced. *celebranti*; i.e. Capito

ne dicam solo negat. hort. subjv. as conces. (AG #440); "although I do not say the only one"

ingenio hominis pulcherrimo et maximo et in summa seueri-
tate dulcissimo, uel honestate materiae. Scribit exitus inlu-
strium uirorum, in his quorundam mihi carissimorum. Videor   5
ergo fungi pio munere, quorumque exsequias celebrare non
licuit, horum quasi funebribus laudationibus seris quidem
sed tanto magis ueris interesse. Vale.

xvi—HUMANE TREATMENT OF SLAVES

C. PLINIVS PATERNO SVO S.

Confecerunt me infirmitates meorum, mortes etiam, et   1
quidem iuuenum. Solacia duo nequaquam paria tanto dolori,

VIII.XII.4

si... deberem prot. of pres. C-to-F condit. (AG #517); —, uicis (f.) repayment (of a good turn)
(*OLD* 5), nom. form not extant, 1st wd. in phrase *uice uersa*; *quasi* (adv.) as it were; mutuus, -a, -um
(< muto, mutare + -uus) mutual, reciprocal

sollicitarer... materiae apod. of pres. C-to-F condit. (AG #517); sollicito (1) (< so llus + citus (ppp.
of ciero, ciere) + -o) arouse, stir up {> solicit}; seueritas, seueritatis (f.) (< seuerus + -tas) strictness,
austerity (of style) (*OLD* 4); dulcis, dulce: charming, pleasing {> dulcet}; honestas, honestatis (f.)
(< honestus + -tas) integrity, decency, dignity; materia, -ae (f.) (< mater + -ia) material, means,
potential (*OLD* 8); "I would still be aroused by the poetic talent of the man, which is exceptionally fine
and certainly exceedingly pleasing even within its greatest austerity, or by the dignity of his material."

exitus, -us (m.) (< exeo, exire + -tus) the end of one's life, death

inlustris, inlustre brilliant, famous, distinguished {> illustrious}

VIII.XII.5

fungor, fungi, functus sum perform, discharge; depon. vb. that takes abl. of means *munere*, not acc.
dir. obj. (AG #410); munus, muneris (n.) duty, gift (often used to describe funeral rites)

quorum (relat. pron.) anteced. *horum*

exsequiae, -arum (f.) (< ex + sequor, sequi + -ia) funeral procession or rites

funebribus laudationibus dat. of indir. obj. w/ compd. vb. *interesse* (AG #370); funebris, funebre:
funerary; laudatio, laudationis (f.) (< laudo + tio) commendation, eulogy; intersum, interesse
(< inter + sum, esse) attend as a participant, take part in (*OLD* 4); serus, -a, -um: late; *tanto magis*:
so much more; *tanto*: abl. of deg. of diff. (AG #414)

VIII.XVI: Pliny confesses his indulgent treatment of his slaves, echoing the sensitivity to the needs of his
household that he displayed in v.xix and contrasting with Macedo's mistreatment of his slaves in III.XIV.

Addressee: Paternus, probably Plinius Paternus from Comum, who may be a kinsman of Pliny from his
mother's family (SW 135, AB 78–9).

VIII.XVI.1

conficio, conficere, confeci, confectus (< con + facio, facere) overwhelm, consume (*OLD* 14a/15)

infirmitas, infirmitatis (f.) (< in + firmus + -tas) weakness, ill health

meorum i.e. the members of his *familia*, his slaves

nequaquam (adv.) by no means, not at all

dolor, doloris (m.) (< doleo, dolere + -or) grief, anguish; *tanto dolori*: dat. w/ adj. *paria* (AG #384),
ELLIPSIS of *sunt*

solacia tamen: unum facilitas manumittendi (uideor enim
non omnino immaturos perdidisse, quos iam liberos perdidi),
alterum quod permitto seruis quoque quasi testamenta facere,

2   eaque ut legitima custodio. Mandant rogantque quod uisum;
pareo ut iussus. Diuidunt donant relinquunt, dumtaxat intra
domum; nam seruis res publica quaedam et quasi ciuitas

3   domus est. Sed quamquam his solaciis adquiescam, debilitor
et frangor eadem illa humanitate, quae me ut hoc ipsum permitterem induxit. Non ideo tamen uelim durior fieri. Nec

---

unum ... alterum i.e. *solacium*; ELLIPSIS of *est*

facilitas, facilitatis (f.) (< facio, facere + -ilis + -tas) readiness, ability

manumitto, manumittere (< manus + mitto, mittere) manumit, set free

immaturus, -a, -um (< in + maturus, -a, -um) prematurely, before the proper time

perdo, perdere, perdidi, perditus (< per + do, dare) lose, be deprived of {> perdition}

permitto, permittere (< per + mitto, mittere) allow (+ dat.), intr. vb. (AG #367); followed by inf. (AG #563/2c)

quasi (adv.) "more or less" (*OLD* 8)

testamentum, -i (n.) (< testor + -mentum) will, testament

ut legitima *ut* (conj.) "as"; legitimus, -a, -um (< lex + -timus) legal, legally recognized {> legitimate}

custodio, custodire (< custos + -io) preserve, follow out, observe

VIII.XVI.2

mando (1) give instructions, order {> mandate}

quod uisum ELLIPSIS of *est*; "that which seems best"

diuido, diuidere separate, divide

dono (1) (< donum + -o) grant, present

dumtaxat (adv.) provided that, as long as; under this proviso, Pliny loses nothing, as anything that remained in the household belonged to him.

VIII.XVI.3

quamquam (conj.) conces. cl. w/ subjv. (usu. indic. w/ *quamquam*) (AG #527e)

adquiesco, adquiescere (< ad + quiesco, quiescere) find comfort

debilito (1) (< debilis + -ito) weaken

frango, frangere break, shatter, soften (*OLD* 10)

humanitas, humanitatis (f.) (< humanus + -tas) humane character, kindness

ut ... permitterem purp. cl. (AG #531/1) ff. *induxit*; induco, inducere, induxi, inductus (< in + duco, ducere) influence, bring in

uelim potent. subjv. (AG #447)

ignoro (1) be unaware of, fail to recognize

alios ... uideri indir. disc. (AG #580)

casus, -us (m.) (< cado, cadere + -tus) occurrence, misfortune

amplus, -a, -um large, great {> ample}

damnum, -i (n.) financial loss

eo (adv.) therefore, thereby

qui ... sint indir. quest. (AG #574) ff. *nescio*

ignoro alios eius modi casus nihil amplius uocare quam damnum, eoque sibi magnos homines et sapientes uideri. Qui an
magni sapientesque sint, nescio; homines non sunt. Hominis   4
est enim adfici dolore sentire, resistere tamen et solacia
admittere, non solaciis non egere. Verum de his plura fortasse   5
quam debui; sed pauciora quam uolui. Est enim quaedam
etiam dolendi uoluptas, praesertim si in amici sinu defleas,
apud quem lacrimis tuis uel laus sit parata uel uenia. Vale.

VIII.XVI.4

hominis gen. of quality (AG #345)

adficio, adficere (< ad + facio, facere) affect, stir/move (emotion)

admitto, admittere (< ad + mitto, mittere) grant access, accept; s. v.xvi.10–11 on consolation and
solace

egeo, egere need, require w/ either gen. or dat. (AG #356n.); *non ... non*: use of a dbl. negat. for emphasis is not uncommon in Latin.

VIII.XVI.5

de his plura vb. like *dixi* or *scripsi* understood

doleo, dolere be in pain, grieve; *dolendi*: obj. gen. w/ *uoluptas*

praesertim (adv.) (< prae + sero + -im) especially

si ... defleas prot. of a FLV condit. (AG #516b); sinus, -us (m.) bosom, shelter (*OLD* 11); defleo, deflere
(< de + fleo, flere) weep abundantly (for the dead)

apud ... uenia relat. cl. of char. (AG #535), anteced. *amici*; lacrima, -ae (f.) tear, weeping; *lacrimis tuis*:
dat. of ref. (AG #376); w/ this closing SENTENTIA, Pliny embraces the reader w/ whom he has just
shared his emotions.

BOOK IX

III—PURSUING IMMORTAL FAME

C. PLINIVS PAVLINO SVO S.

Alius aliud: ego beatissimum existimo, qui bonae man-   1
suraeque famae praesumptione perfruitur, certusque posteritatis cum futura gloria uiuit. Ac mihi nisi praemium aeternitatis
ante oculos, pingue illud altumque otium placeat. Etenim   2
omnes homines arbitror oportere aut immortalitatem suam
aut mortalitatem cogitare, et illos quidem contendere eniti,
hos quiescere remitti, nec breuem uitam caducis laboribus

IX.III: Pliny describes his own quest for immortal fame in a letter that does much to explain his motivation for writing.
Addressee: Paulinus, s. v.XIX.

IX.III.1
alius aliud consecutive forms of *aliud* = dbl. stmt. (AG #315c); vb. omitted, mg. clarified by ff. cl.; "one
person thinks one thing, another something else"
beatus, -a, -um fortunate; subst. use
existimo (1) (< ex + aestimo, aestimare) consider, hold the opinion that
praesumptio, praesumptionis (f.) (< prae + sumo, sumere + -tio) anticipation, presumption; *praesumptione*: abl. of means, not acc. dir. obj., w/ depon. vb. *perfruitur* (AG #410); perfruor, perfrui,
perfructus sum (< per + fruor, frui) have full enjoyment, enjoy
posteritas, posteritatis (f.) (< posterus + -tas) posthumous fame, immortality (of reputation); *posteritatis*: objv. gen. (AG #347) w/ *certus*
nisi ... oculos prot. of pres. C-to-F condit. (AG #517), ELLIPSIS of *esset*
pinguis, pingue rich, comfortable
placeat potent. subjv. (AG #447)

IX.III.2
etenim (conj.) (< et + enim) and indeed, the fact is
arbitror, arbitrari, arbitratus sum (< arbiter + -o) consider, judge, reckon
omnes homines ... cogitare 1st indir. disc. (AG #580); oportet, oportere: it is proper, right, "ought,"
impers. vb. w/ acc. + inf. constr. *immortalitatem ... mortalitatem cogitare* (AG #565n. 3); *immortalitatem* here refers to a lasting reputation, while *mortalitatem* describes the fleeting nature of the body;
Pliny plays w/ these words that at first glance seem to be opposites, but in fact are not meant as such.
et ... remitti 2nd indir. disc., in 2 parts: *illos ... hos*: "the former ... the latter," i.e. those considering
their lasting fame ... those remembering their mortality; contendo, contendere (< con + tendo,
tendere) press forward, make an effort, compete; *contendere*: compl. inf. (AG #456) w/ *eniti*; enitor,
eniti, enixus sum (< ex + nitor, niti) struggle, strive, exert oneself; *quiescere remitti*: read together:
"rest and relax"; remitto, remittere (< re + mitto, mittere) relax (*OLD* 8)
nec ... fatigare appos. to *hos ... remitti*, still in indir. disc; caducus, -a, -um: fleeting, vain, futile; fatigo
(1) tire out, exhaust

3   fatigare, ut uideo multos misera simul et ingrata imagine
     industriae ad uilitatem sui peruenire. Haec ego tecum quae
     cotidie mecum, ut desinam mecum, si dissenties tu; quam-
     quam non dissenties, ut qui semper clarum aliquid et immor-
     tale meditere. Vale.

VI—CHARIOT RACING'S BAFFLING ALLURE

C. PLINIVS CALVISIO SVO S.

1   Omne hoc tempus inter pugillares ac libellos iucundissima
     quiete transmisi. 'Quemadmodum' inquis 'in urbe potuisti?'
     Circenses erant, quo genere spectaculi ne leuissime quidem

---

ut uideo ... peruenire *ut* w/ indic. "as" (AG #527f); *multos ... peruenire*: indir. disc. (AG #580);
   ingratus, -a, -um: displeasing, disagreeable {> ingratitude}; imago, imaginis (f) likeness, appearance; industria, -ae (f.) diligent activity, industry; uilitas, uilitatis (f.) (< uilis + -tas) worthlessness,
   low price; *sui*: objv. gen. (AG #347); peruenio, peruenire (< per + uenio, uenire) come to, arrive at

IX.III.3
haec ... mecum vb. like *considero* understood
ut desinam purp. cl. (AG #531/1)
si ... tu prot. of a FMV condit. (AG #516d); dissentio, dissentire (< dis + sentio, sentire) differ in
   opinion, disagree
ut qui ... meditere "as someone who ..."; relat. cl. of char. (AG #535); clarus, -a, -um: bright, famous
   {> clarity}; meditor, meditari, meditatus sum: contemplate, ponder {> meditate}

IX.VI: Pliny expresses his disinterest in chariot racing—an improper use of *otium* (s. Freq. Vocab.)—
   and his surprise at the interest it compels in some of his peers. His disdain echoes that expressed by
   Cicero in *Ad Familiares* VII.1 for the inaugural games in Pompey's theater, which brought nothing
   new and whose excess was tiresome rather than amusing.
Addressee: Calvisius, s. II.XX.

IX.VI.1
pugillares, pugillarium (m.) (< pugnus + -illus + -aris) writing tablets (s. I.VI.1n. on pugillares)
quies, quietis (f.) rest, repose, relaxation; *iucundissima quiete*: abl. of manner omitting *cum* (AG #412b)
transmitto, transmittere, transmisi, transmissus (< trans + mitto, mittere) cause to pass, let (time,
   experiences) pass by (*OLD* 7)
quemadmodum (interrog. adv.) (< quem + ad + modum) how
Circenses, Circensium (m. pl.) Circus Games; the oldest and most popular of the Roman games,
   chariot racing was a team sport, w/ each team designated by a color: blue, green, red, or white.
   Domitian tried briefly but unsuccessfully to add two new colors—gold and purple. But the strong
   tradition of the four colors, which fed both fanatical devotion and the Romans' fondness for betting,
   simply would not admit such change. Unlike Greek chariot racing, in which the owner of the win-
   ning team received the glory, the best Roman charioteers and their horses became famous, w/ some
   charioteers amassing enormous wealth as well.

teneor. Nihil nouum nihil uarium, nihil quod non semel
spectasse sufficiat. Quo magis miror tot milia uirorum tam

2

pueriliter identidem cupere currentes equos, insistentes curribus homines uidere. Si tamen aut uelocitate equorum aut
hominum arte traherentur, esset ratio non nulla; nunc fauent
panno pannum amant, et si in ipso cursu medioque certamine
hic color illuc ille huc transferatur, studium fauorque trans-
ibit, et repente agitatores illos equos illos, quos procul nosci-
tant, quorum clamitant nomina relinquent. Tanta gratia

3

---

genus, generis (n.) a kind or sort of thing (*OLD* 9) {> generic}

spectaculum, -i (n.) (< specto, spectare + -culum) spectacle, performance

uarius, -a, -um changeable, different; ELLIPSIS of *est*

quod . . . sufficiat relat. cl. of char. (AG #535); *spectasse* = contr. form of pf. inf. *spectauisse* (AG #181); *semel* (adv.) one time, once

IX.VI.2

quo magis (adv.) all the more; *quo*: relat. pron., abl. of deg. of diff. w/ compar. (AG #414a n.)

tot . . . uidere indir. disc. (AG #580); milia, milium (n.) thousands; *pueriliter* (adv.) (< puer + -ilis) childishly; *identidem* (< idem + et + idem) again and again, repeatedly; insisto, insistere (< in + sisto, sistere) stand on; compd. vb + dat. *curribus* (AG #370); currus, -us (m.) (< curro, currere) chariot; racing chariots consisted of little other than a board on top of an axle, w/ just a small frame that gave the chariot some stability; thus the charioteer stood 'on' the chariot.

si . . . nulla pres. C-to-F condit. (AG #517); uelocitas, uelocitatis (f.) (< uelox + -tas) swiftness, speed; *non nulla*: the dbl. negat. is often used for emphasis in Latin.

faueo, fauere be favorably inclined, approve; intr. vb. w/ dat. *panno* (AG #367); pannus, -i (m.) piece of cloth, colored shirt of a charioteer (*OLD* 2b); *panno pannum*: POLYPTOTON, w/ whose use Pliny spotlights the importance of the team colors. ASYNDETON throughout his description of the scene heightens its frenetic nature.

si . . . relinquent mixed condit., prot. of FLV but w/ indic. apod. used to emphasize change in point of view (AG #516/2b n.)

cursus, -us (m.) (< curro, currere + -tus) course, act of running, speed

certamen, certaminis (n.) (< certo, certare + -men) competition, contest

transfero, transferre (< trans + fero, ferre) transport, transfer

studium, -i (n.) (< studeo, studere + -ium) zeal, devotion; gener. used by Pliny to denote commitment to intellectual pursuits (s. studium in Freq. Vocab.), but here to offer a counterpoint, an ex. of misplaced focus

fauor, fauoris (m.) (< faueo, fauere + -or) enthusiastic support, partiality

transeo, transire (< trans + eo, ire) cross over, transfer support (*OLD* 3a)

repente (adv.) suddenly, w/ out warning

agitator, agitatoris (m.) (< ago, agere + -ito + -tor) driver, charioteer

procul (adv.) some way off, far away

noscito (1) (< nosco, noscere + -ito) be familiar w/, recognize

clamito (1) (< clamo, clamare + -ito) shout repeatedly

tanta auctoritas in una uilissima tunica, mitto apud uulgus,
quod uilius tunica, sed apud quosdam graues homines; quos
ego cum recordor, in re inani frigida adsidua, tam insatia-
biliter desidere, capio aliquam uoluptatem, quod hac uolu-

4   ptate non capior. Ac per hos dies libentissime otium meum in
litteris colloco, quos alii otiosissimis occupationibus perdunt.
Vale.

xvii—TO EACH HIS OWN TASTE

C. PLINIVS GENITORI SVO S.

1   Recepi litteras tuas quibus quereris taedio tibi fuisse quamuis lautissimam cenam, quia scurrae cinaedi moriones mensis

---

IX.VI.3

auctoritas, auctoritatis (f.) (< auctor + -tas) authority, command; ELLIPSIS of *est*

uilis, uile cheap, ordinary

mitto apud uulgus mitto, mittere: release, pay no heed to, disregard (*OLD* 8); uulgus, -i (n.) common
    people, crowd {> vulgar}; w/ this phrase, Pliny uses PRAETERITIO as a means of comparing to the
    mob the elite men he will now discuss, while denying doing so.

quod (relat. pron.) anteced. *uulgus*; ELLIPSIS of *est*

grauis, graue serious, respected {> gravity}

quos . . . desidere indir. disc. (AG #580) ff. *recordor*; *cum recordor*: cum tmp. cl. (AG #545); recordor,
    recordari, recordatus sum (< re + cor + -o) call to mind; *in . . . adsidua*: Pliny expresses his passion-
    ate opinion through his use of ASYNDETON in this series of negat. adjs.; inanis, inane: empty, serving
    no purpose (*OLD* 13); frigidus, -a, -um (< frigus + -idus) cold, lacking warmth or passion, tedious
    (*OLD* 8c); adsiduus, -a, -um (< ad + sideo, sidere + -uus) incessant, ordinary; *insatiabiliter* (adv.)
    (< in + satio, satiare + bilis) insatiably; desideo, desidere (< de + sideo, sidere) remain seated,
    hang about

IX.VI.4

libentissime (superl. adv.) (< libens, libentis) most willingly, gladly

litterae, litterarum (f.) letters, literary works (*OLD* 8a) {> literature}

colloco (1) (< con + loco, locare) put in place, devote (*OLD* 12)

quos (relat. pron.) anteced. *dies*

otiosus, -a, -um (< otium + -osus) at leisure; sometimes pejorative, implying that the one it describes
    is not pursuing any valuable activity (s. otium in Freq. Vocab.)

occupatio, occupationis (f.) (< occupo, occupare + -tio) preoccupation

perdo, perdere (< per + do, dare) ruin, waste {> perdition}

IX.XVII: Pliny notes his lack of interest in the types of popular entertainments offered at dinner parties,
    but without the kind of criticism he levels at the host of the gathering discussed in II.VI nor with the
    disdain he expresses for chariot racing in IX.VI.

Addressee: (Julius) Genitor, the strict tutor whom Pliny recommends highly in III.III.

IX.XVII.1

queror, queri, questus sum complain, grumble {> querulous}

inerrabant. Vis tu remittere aliquid ex rugis? Equidem nihil
tale habeo, habentes tamen fero. Cur ergo non habeo? Quia
nequaquam me ut inexspectatum festiuumue delectat, si quid
molle a cinaedo, petulans a scurra, stultum a morione profertur. Non rationem sed stomachum tibi narro. Atque adeo
quam multos putas esse, quos ea quibus ego et tu capimur et
ducimur, partim ut inepta partim ut molestissima offendant!
Quam multi, cum lector aut lyristes aut comoedus inductus
est, calceos poscunt aut non minore cum taedio recubant,

2

3

---

taedio ... cenam indir. disc. (AG #580); taedium, -i (n.) (< taedet + -ium) object of disgust, offensive
condition; *taedio*: dat. of purp. (AG #382) w/ *tibi*, dat. of ref. (AG #376) = dbl. dat.; *quamuis* (relat.
adv.) even though; lautus, -a, -um (< ppp. of lauo, lauare) splendid, luxurious
scurra, -ae (f.) buffoon, clown (s. IV.XXV.3n. on scurriliter)
cinaedus, -i (m.) (< Gr. κίναιδος) catamite, young male sexual partner
morio, morionis (m.) (< morus + -io) idiot, fool; ASYNDETON in this list of entertainers fits the carni-
val atmosphere that their presence must have created.
inerro (1) (< in + erro, errare) wander or roam in {> errant}; compd. vb + dat. *mensis* (AG #370)

IX.XVII.2

uis ... rugis remitto, remittere (< re + mitto, mittere) release, relax; ruga, -ae (f.) wrinkle; *ex rugis*: i.e.
lines caused by frowning; "Do you want to stop frowning?"
habentes pres. ptc. subst. use: "those who do have (such things)," i.e. at their dinner parties
nequaquam (adv.) by no means, not at all
ut inexpectatum festiuumue *ut* (conj.) "as"; inexpectatus, -a, -um (< in + ppp. of exspecto, exspect-
are) unforeseen, i.e. new; festiuus, -a, -um (< festus + -iuus) excellent, amusing
si quid ... profertur simple condit. (indic.) (AG #514a); *quid = aliquid* (s. I.I.1n. on quas); mollis,
molle: soft, voluptuous; petulans, petulantis: rude, insolent; stultus, -a, -um: foolish, silly; profero,
proferre (< pro + fero, ferre) bring forth, show, display

IX.XVII.3

stomachus, -i (m.) (< Gr. στόμαχος) gullet, one's tastes or likings
quam multos esse indir. disc. (AG #580) ff. *putas*; *quam* (interrog. adv.) interrog. used for emphasis
(AG #333n), "how"; *multos*: subst. use
quos ... offendant relat. cl. of char. (AG #535); *partim* (adv.) in part; "some ... others" (OLD 1b); *ut
inepta ... ut molestissima*: Pliny's use of *ut* here echoes his earlier stmt. about his own tastes; ineptus,
-a, -um (< in + aptus) foolish, silly; molestus, -a, -um: troublesome, annoying; offendo, offendere:
displease, annoy
cum ... est cum tmp. cl. (AG #545); lyristes, lyristae (m.) (< Gr. λυριστής) lyre player; comoedus,
-i (m.) (< Gr. κωμῳδός) comic actor; induco, inducere, induxi, inductus (< in + duco, ducere)
bring in, introduce
calceus, -i (m.) (< calx, calcis) shoe; a soft shoe especially in red worn by men of senatorial rank
recubo (1) (< re + cubo, cubare) lie back, lie as ease

4   quam tu ista (sic enim adpellas) prodigia perpessus es! Demus
igitur alienis oblectationibus ueniam, ut nostris impetremus.
Vale.

xix—QUEST FOR IMMORTALITY

C. PLINIVS RVSONI SVO S.

1   Significas legisse te in quadam epistula mea iussisse Verginium Rufum inscribi sepulcro suo:

>Hic situs est Rufus, pulso qui Vindice quondam
>imperium adseruit non sibi sed patriae.

Reprehendis quod iusserit, addis etiam melius rectiusque
Frontinum, quod uetuerit omnino monumentum sibi fieri,

---

sic … adpellas PARENTHESIS w/ which Pliny can distance himself from the condemnation that
follows; *enim* (pcl.) for (here explaining the reason for the ff. stmt.)
prodigium, -i (n.) unnatural event, monstrosity
perpetior, perpeti, perpessus sum (< per + patior, pati) experience, put up w/

IX.XVII.4
Demus hort. subjv. (AG #439)
igitur (conj.) therefore
alienus, -a, -um (< alius + -enus) belonging to another
oblectatio, oblectationis (f.) (< ob + lacto, lactare + -tio) delight, pleasure
ut … impetremus purp. cl. (AG #531/1); impetro (1) (< in + patro, patrare) obtain by request, gain

IX.XIX: Refering to his earlier letter on the tomb of Verginius Rufus (s. VI.x), Pliny writes about two
different but equally acceptable paths to securing lasting fame.
Addressee: Ruso, identity uncertain; SW suggests Cremutius Ruso, a protégé of Pliny's, while Syme
suggests P. Calvisius Ruso Julius Frontinus or his son (SW 302, AB 47).

IX.XIX.1
significo (1) (< signum + -fico) indicate
legisse … mea indir. disc. (AG #580); Pliny is referring to VI.x
iussisse … suo indir. disc. (AG #580) ff. *legisse*
Verginius Rufus (s. VI.x.1n.)
sepulcrum, -i (n.) (< sepelio, sepelire + -crum) tomb; *sepulcro*: dat. of indir. obj. w/ compd. vb.
    inscribi (AG #370)
situs, -a, -um (< ppp. of sino, sinere) laid in the grave, buried
pulso Vindice abl. abs. (AG #419); for Vindex, s. VI.x.4n.
quondam (adv.) formerly, once
adsero, adserere, adserui, adsertus (< ad + sero, serere) lay claim to
reprehendo, reprehendere (< re + prehendo, prehendere) find fault w/ (*OLD* 5)
quod iusserit relat. cl. of char. (AG #535); *quod*, subst. use: "the sort of thing that"

meque ad extremum quid de utroque sentiam consulis.

Vtrumque dilexi, miratus sum magis quem tu reprehendis,   2
atque ita miratus ut non putarem satis umquam posse laudari,

cuius nunc mihi subeunda defensio est. Omnes ego qui ma-   3
gnum aliquid memorandumque fecerunt, non modo uenia
uerum etiam laude dignissimos iudico, si immortalitatem
quam meruere sectantur, uicturique nominis famam supre-
mis etiam titulis prorogare nituntur. Nec facile quemquam   4
nisi Verginium inuenio, cuius tanta in praedicando uerecundia quanta gloria ex facto. Ipse sum testis, familiariter ab eo   5

---

melius ... Frontinum indir. disc. (AG #580), *iussisse* understood; for Sextus Iulius Frontinus, s. IV.VIII.3n.

quod uetuerit subord. cl. in indir. disc. takes subjv. vb. (AG #580); ueto, uetare, uetui, uetitus: forbid, introd. acc. + inf. constr. *monumentum ... fieri* (AG #563a)

extremum, -i (n.) (< extremus, -a, -um) final part, end (of a document)

quid ... sentiam indir. quest. (AG #574) ff. *consulis*; sentio, sentire: hold an opinion

IX.XIX.2

miror, mirari, miratus sum (< mirus + -o) hold in awe, revere

quem (relat. pron.) subst. use: "the man whom"

ut ... putarem result cl. (AG #537); (*eum*) *satis ... laudari*: indir. disc. (AG #580)

subeo, subire (< sub + eo, ire) approach, undergo, sustain; *subeunda ... est*: 2nd (pass.) periphr. conjug. (AG #196 and 500/2); *mihi*: dat. of agent (AG #374)

defensio, defensionis (f.) (< defendo, defendere + -tio) defense, justification

IX.XIX.3

memorandus, -a, -um (< gerv. of memor + -o) noteworthy, memorable

uenia, laude abl. of specif. (AG #418b) w/ *dignissimos*

iudico (1) (< iudex + -o) judge, express an opinion

si ... sectantur simple condit. (indic.) (AG #514a); mereo, merere, merui: earn, deserve {> merit}; *meruere = meruerunt*; sector, sectari, sectatus sum (< ppp. of sequor, sequi) pursue

uicturus, -a, -um fut. act. ptc. of uiuo, uiuere, uixi, uictus; modifies *nominis*

supremus, -a, -um (< super + -us + -emus) highest, latest, at the end of one's existence

titulus, -i (m.) identification, inscription

prorogo (1) (< pro + rogo, rogare) prolong; *prorogare*: compl. inf. w/ *nituntur* (AG #456); nitor, niti, nixus sum: incline, strive, exert oneself

IX.XIX.4

tanta ... quanta correl., "as great ... as"

praedico (1) (< prae + dico, dicare) make known, proclaim

uerecundia, -ae (f.) (< uereor + -cundus + -ia) modesty, restraint; ELLIPSIS of *erat/esset*

IX.XIX.5

testis, testis (m.) witness

familiariter (< familia + -aris) as a close friend, thoroughly

dilectus probatusque, semel omnino me audiente prouectum,
ut de rebus suis hoc unum referret, ita secum aliquando
Cluuium locutum: 'Scis, Vergini, quae historiae fides debeatur; proinde si quid in historiis meis legis aliter ac uelis
rogo ignoscas.' Ad hoc ille: 'Tune ignoras, Cluui, ideo me
fecisse quod feci, ut esset liberum uobis scribere quae libuis-

6   set?' Age dum, hunc ipsum Frontinum in hoc ipso, in quo
tibi parcior uidetur et pressior, comparemus. Vetuit exstrui
monumentum, sed quibus uerbis? 'Impensa monumenti super-

---

probo (1) (< probus + -o) commend {> probation}

semel … prouectum indir. disc. (AG #580) after *testis*; *semel* (adv.) one time, once; *me audiente*: abl. abs. (AG #419); prouecho, prouehere, prouexi, prouectus (< pro + ueho, uehere) carry forward (to a particular degree); *(eum) prouectum (esse)*

ut … referret purp. cl. (AG #531/1); *hoc*: points forward to the next cl. (AG #297e); *ita … locutum*: indir. disc. (AG #580) after *referret*, ELLIPSIS of *esse*; *aliquando* (adv.) at some time in the past; Cluvius Rufus, of consular rank, was an imperial historian, w/ the major part of his work covering the reign of Nero (*OCD* 353).

quae … debeatur indir. quest. (AG #574)

si … uelis, rogo mixed condit., prot. of FLV but w/ indic. apod. used to emphasize change in point of view (AG #516/2b n.); *quid = aliquid* (s. 1.1.1n. on quas); *aliter ac*: otherwise than (AG #324c)

ignoscas subst. cl. of purp. (AG #563) (= indir. comm.) ff. *rogo*, *ut* omitted; ignosco, ignoscere (< in + (g)nosco, noscere) forgive

ignoro (1) be unaware of, fail to recognize

me fecisse indir. disc. (AG #580)

ut … libuisset purp. cl. (AG #531/1); *esset liberum*: impers. use w/ dat. of ref. *uobis* (AG #376), "you would be free"; *quae libuisset*: relat. cl. of char. (AG #535); libet, libuit: impers. vb. (AG #208c): it is pleasing

IX.XIX.6

Age dum come then

parcior (compar. adj.) (< parcus) more moderate

pressior (compar. adj.) (< pressus) more restrained

comparo (1) (< con + par + -o) estimate, evaluate; *comparemus*: hort. subjv. (AG #439)

exstrui monumentum acc. + inf. constr. w/ *uetuit* (AG #563a); exstruo, exstruere (< ex + struo, struere) build up, construct

impensa, -ae (f.) (< in + pendo, pendere) cost, expense

superuacuus, -a, -um (< uaco, uacare + -uus) excessive, unnecessary

nostri objv. gen. (AG #347) w/ *memoria*

duro (1) last, survive (*OLD* 7a/c)

si … meruimus simple condit. (indic.) (AG #514a); *uita*: abl. of specif. (AG #418)

an (pcl.) when introd. a dir. quest.: "Can it really be that …"

restrictius … signare indir. disc. (AG #580); *restrictius* (compar. adj.) (< ppp. of restringo, restringere) more modest, w/ more reticence; arbitror, arbitrari, arbitratus sum (< arbiter + -o) consider, judge, reckon

uacua est; memoria nostri durabit, si uita meruimus.' An
restrictius arbitraris per orbem terrarum legendum dare
duraturam memoriam suam quam uno in loco duobus uersi-
culis signare quod feceris? Quamquam non habeo propositum   7
illum reprehendendi, sed hunc tuendi; cuius quae potest apud
te iustior esse defensio, quam ex collatione eius quem praetulisti? Meo quidem iudicio neuter culpandus, quorum uterque   8
ad gloriam pari cupiditate, diuerso itinere contendit, alter
dum expetit debitos titulos, alter dum mauult uideri con-
tempsisse. Vale.

---

per . . . suam orbis terrarum: the world (*OLD* orbis 12); do, dare: communicate, put forward (*OLD* 28);
legendum, subst. use of gerv.: "something to be read"; *duraturam . . . suam*: indir. disc. (AG #580) after
legendum, ELLIPSIS of *esse*

quam . . . signare 2nd half of indir. disc.; *quam* (conj.) w/ compar. *restrictius*; *uno in loco*: modifier of
obj. of monosyl. prep. often precedes prep. (AG #599d); uersiculus, -i (m.) (< uersus + -culus) brief
line, pl.: epigrams (*OLD* 2); *duobus uersiculis*: "with a single epigram"; signo (1) (< signum + -o)
indicate

quod feceris relat. cl. of char. (AG #535)

IX.XIX.7

propositum, -i (n.) (< ppp. of propono, proponere) objective, intention

illum . . . hunc i.e. Frontinus . . . Verginius

tueor, tueri, tutus sum watch over, preserve, safeguard

cuius . . . praetulisti collatio, collationis (f.) (< con + fero, ferre + -tio) comparison; praefero, praeferre, praetuli, praelatus (< prae + fero, ferre) attach more value to or prefer (*OLD* 7); "What could
be a more fitting defense of that man in your presence than one drawn from a comparison with the
man whom you prefer?"

IX.XIX.8

culpo (1) (< culpa + -o) blame, find fault w/; *culpandus*: 2nd (pass.) periphr. conjug. (AG #196 and
500/2), ELLIPSIS of *est*

cupiditas, cupiditatis (f.) (< cupidus + -tas) desire, yearning

diuersus, -a, -um (< ppp. of diuerto, diuertere) different

contendo, contendere, contendi, contentus (< con + tendo, tendere) press forward, make an effort,
compete

alter . . . alter one . . . the other

expeto, expetere (< ex + peto, petere) ask for, request

contemno, contemnere, contempsi, contemptus (< con + temno, temnere) scorn, despise
{> contempt}

xxiii—ACHIEVING LITERARY FAME

C. PLINIVS MAXIMO SVO S.

1   Frequenter agenti mihi euenit, ut centumuiri cum diu se
intra iudicum auctoritatem grauitatemque tenuissent, omnes
repente quasi uicti coactique consurgerent laudarentque;

2   frequenter e senatu famam qualem maxime optaueram ret-
tuli: numquam tamen maiorem cepi uoluptatem, quam nuper
ex sermone Corneli Taciti. Narrabat sedisse secum circen-
sibus proximis equitem Romanum. Hunc post uarios erudi-
tosque sermones requisisse: 'Italicus es an prouincialis?' Se

3   respondisse: 'Nosti me, et quidem ex studiis.' Ad hoc illum:
'Tacitus es an Plinius?' Exprimere non possum, quam sit
iucundum mihi quod nomina nostra quasi litterarum propria,

IX.XXIII: Pliny expresses his delight in being identified by his written works and in the same breath as
Tacitus (s. I.VI).

Addressee: Maximus; proposed by SW (506) and AB (76) to be Novius Maximus, who receives other
letters from Pliny about court appearances and literature.

IX.XXIII.1

frequenter (adv.) on many occasions, repeatedly (*OLD* 2)

ago, agere deliver a speech (*OLD* 43); *agenti mihi:* dat. of ref. (AG #376)

euenio, euenire (< ex + uenio, uenire) happen, come about {> event}

ut...laudarentque subst. cl. of result (AG #567) ff. *euenit; centumuiri:* the judges of the Centumviral
Court (s. I.XVIII.6n.); *cum...tenuissent:* cum circumst. cl. (AG #546); iudex, iudicis (m.) judge; auctoritas, auctoritatis (f.) (< auctor + -tas) authority; grauitas, grauitatis (f.) (< grauis + -tas) seriousness of conduct; teneo, tenere, tenui: keep in check (*OLD* 19); *repente* (adv.) suddenly; cogo, cogere,
coegi, coactus (< con + ago, agere) compel; consurgo, consurgere (< con + surgo, surgere) stand up

IX.XXIII.2

opto (1) desire

nuper (adv.) recently

sedisse...Romanum indir. disc. (AG #580); circenses, circensium (m. pl.) circus games (s. IX.VI.1n.);
for eques Romanus, s. II.IV.2n. on milia

hunc...requisisse, se...respondisse indir. disc. (AG #580); Pliny continues to report what Tacitus
had told him; eruditus, -a, -um (< ppp. of ex + rudis + -io) learned {> erudition}

prouincialis, prouinciale (< prouincia + -alis) pertaining to or from a province

nosco, noscere, noui, notus become acquainted w/, pf.: know; *nosti* = contr. form of pf. *nouisti* (AG #181)

IX.XXIII.3

an (pcl.) or (introd. the 2nd of two options in a quest.)

exprimo, exprimere (< ex + premo, premere) express in words, describe

quam...mihi indir. quest. (AG #574); *quam* (interrog. adv.) how

quod...notus subst. cls. introd. by *quod* (AG #572), "that"; proprius, -a, -um: appropriate to, followed
by gen. of poss. (AG #385c); *his:* subst. use, dat. w/ adj. *notus* (AG #384); notus, -a, -um
(< ppp. of nosco, noscere) known

non hominum, litteris redduntur, quod uterque nostrum his
etiam ex studiis notus, quibus aliter ignotus est.

Accidit aliud ante pauculos dies simile. Recumbebat mecum   4
uir egregius, Fadius Rufinus, super eum municeps ipsius, qui
illo die primum uenerat in urbem; cui Rufinus demonstrans
me: 'Vides hunc?' Multa deinde de studiis nostris; et ille
'Plinius est' inquit. Verum fatebor, capio magnum laboris   5
mei fructum. An si Demosthenes iure laetatus est, quod illum
anus Attica ita noscitauit: Οὗτός ἐστι Δημοσθένης, ego celebritate nominis mei gaudere non debeo? Ego uero et gaudeo

---

quibus (relat. pron.) anteced. *his*; dat. w/ adj. (AG #384)

aliter (adv.) otherwise

ignotus, -a, -um unknown, unfamiliar

IX.XXIII.4

pauculus, -a, -um (< paucus, -a, -um + -ulus) pl.: a few

recumbo, recumbere (< re + cumbo, cumbere) recline {> recumbent} (s. II.VI.3n. on Roman dining)

Fadius Rufinus Lucius Fadius Rufinus, suffect consul in 113 CE (SW 507, AB 59); the middle of the three diners

municeps, municipis (m.) (< munia + -ceps) fellow townsman {> municipal}

cui . . . me *cui*: anteced. *municeps*; ELLIPSIS of vb.; Pliny recounts the conversation omitting some verbs of speaking to create a sense of witty repartee.

ille i.e. the unnamed *municeps*

IX.XXIII.5

fateor, fateri, fassus sum concede, acknowledge

fructus, -us (m.) (< fruor, frui + -tus) pleasure, gratification, reward

an (pcl.) when introd. a dir. quest.: "Can it really be that . . ."

si . . . debeo simple condit. (indic.) (AG #514a)

Demosthenes often described as the greatest Athenian orator. He was best known for the clarity and focus of his argument and for varying his style according to the topic and circumstances at hand (*OCD* 456–8). His work had a profound influence on Cicero. Thus reference to him here is particularly appropriate for Pliny.

iure (adv.) by reason, justly, deservedly

laetor, laetari, laetatus sum (< laetus, -a, -um + -o) be glad, be delighted

quod (conj.) subst. cl. introd. by *quod* (AG #572), "that"

anus, -i (f.) old woman

Atticus, -a, -um from Attica, Athenian; this adj. refers not only to the city but also to the surrounding territory that was controlled by Athens

noscito (1) (< nosco, noscere + -ito) be familiar w/, recognize

Οὗτός ἐστι Δημοσθένης Gr.:"That man is Demosthenes"; Pliny quotes from Cicero (*Tusc.* v.103) but translates the latter's "hic est ille Demosthenes" back into Greek.

celebritas, celebritatis (f.) (< celeber + -tas) renown, fame; *celebritate*: abl. of cause (AG #404)

6   et gaudere me dico. Neque enim uereor ne iactantior uidear,
     cum de me aliorum iudicium non meum profero, praesertim
     apud te qui nec ullius inuides laudibus et faues nostris. Vale.

XXXVI—A DAY AWAY FROM ROME

C. PLINIVS FVSCO SVO S.

1   Quaeris, quemadmodum in Tuscis diem aestate disponam.
     Euigilo cum libuit, plerumque circa horam primam, saepe
     ante, tardius raro. Clausae fenestrae manent; mire enim
     silentio et tenebris ab iis quae auocant abductus et liber et mihi
     relictus, non oculos animo sed animum oculis sequor, qui

---

gaudere me indir. disc. (AG #580)

IX.XXIII.6

ne . . . uidear subst. cl. ff. vb. of fearing (AG #564); iactans, iactantis (< pres. ptc. of iacto, iactare)
     boastful, proud

cum . . . profero cum tmp. cl. (AG #545); profero, proferre (< pro + fero, ferre) bring forth, make
     known

praesertim (adv.) (< prae + sero + -im) especially

apud te in your presence (*OLD* 8a)

inuideo, inuidere (< in + uideo, uidere) envy, begrudge (*OLD* 2c) {> invidious}; intr. vb. w/ dat.
     laudibus (AG #367)

faueo, fauere be favorably inclined; intr. vb. w/ dat. *nostris* (*laudibus*) (AG #367)

IX.XXXVI: Pliny describes a typical day spent away from the business of Rome at his Tuscan estate,
     described in *Ep.* v.vi, which is not included in this volume, but s. II.XVII offers a tour of another of
     his villas. The activities Pliny outlines reflect well the benefits of the *otium* (s. Freq. Vocab.) he extols
     in I.IX.

Addressee: Pliny's protégé Fuscus Salinator, s. VI.XI.1n.

IX.XXXVI.1

quaero, quaerere search for, seek

quemadmodum . . . disponam indir. quest. (AG #574); *quemadmodum* (interrog. adv.) (< quem +
     ad + modum) how; Tuscus, -a, -um: Etruscan; here Pliny refers to his villa in Etruria at Tifernum
     Tiberinum; dispono, disponere (< dis + pono, ponere) arrange, organize

euigilo (1) (< ex + uigilo, uigilare) wake up

cum libuit cum tmp. cl. (AG #545); libet, libuit, impers. vb. (AG #208c): it is/was pleasing

plerumque (adv.) generally, on most occasions

hora prima (s. VI.XVI.4n. on septima hora)

tardius (compar. adv.) (< tardus) later

raro (adv.) seldom

silentio et tenebris abl. of means (AG #409); silentium, -i (n.) (< silens + -ium) absence of sound,
     silence; tenebrae, -arum (f.) darkness

auoco (1) (< ab + uoco, uocare) distract {> avocation}

eadem quae mens uident, quotiens non uident alia. Cogito si   2
quid in manibus, cogito ad uerbum scribenti emendantique
similis, nunc pauciora nunc plura, ut uel difficile uel facile
componi teneriue potuerunt. Notarium uoco et die admisso
quae formaueram dicto; abit rursusque reuocatur rursusque
dimittitur. Vbi hora quarta uel quinta (neque enim certum   3
dimensumque tempus), ut dies suasit, in xystum me uel
cryptoporticum confero, reliqua meditor et dicto. Vehicu-
lum ascendo. Ibi quoque idem quod ambulans aut iacens;
durat intentio mutatione ipsa refecta. Paulum redormio, dein

---

abduco, abducere, abduxi, abductus (< ab + duco, ducere) lead away, remove

quotiens (relat. adv.) (< quot + -iens) whenever; Pliny here is describing the concept of the mind's
  eye, which can produce a mental vision when deprived of direct input from the eyes.

IX.XXXVI.2

si … manibus simple condit. (AG #514a), ELLIPSIS of *est*; *quid = aliquid* (s. 1.1.1n. on quas); i.e. if he is
  in the middle of writing something

ad uerbum word by word (*OLD* 8b)

emendo (1) (< ex + menda + -o) correct, revise; *scribenti emendantique*: subst. use, dat. w/ adj.
  (AG #384)

ut … potuerunt *ut* w/ indic. "as" (AG #527f); i.e. Pliny's success at mental editing depends upon the
  complexity of the task

notarius, -i (m.) (< nota + -arius) stenographer, writer of shorthand

die admisso abl. abs. (AG #419); admitto, admittere, admisi, admissus (< ad + mitto, mittere) allow
  to enter, grant access; i.e. the shutters on the windows are opened

quae (relat. pron.) subst. use: "the things which"

formo (1) shape, adapt

dicto (1) (< dico + -to) dictate

abeo, abire (< ab + eo, ire) go away, depart; *abit*: subj. *notarius*

dimitto, dimittere (< dis + mitto, mittere) discharge, dismiss

IX.XXXVI.3

dimensus, -a, -um (< ppp. of dimetior, dimetiri) regular, measured; ELLIPSIS of *est*

ut … suasit *ut* w/ indic. "as" (AG #527f); perhaps depending on the weather

xystus, -i (m.) (< Gr. ξυστός) garden walkway, terrace

cryptoporticus, -us (f.) (< Gr. κρυπτός + porticus) covered gallery, cloister

meditor, meditari, meditatus sum contemplate, ponder {> meditate}

uehiculum, -i (n.) (< ueho, uehere + -culum) wheeled vehicle, wagon

Ibi … iacens vb. of doing understood

duro (1) last, survive (*OLD* 7a/c)

intentio, intentionis (f.) (< intendo, intendere + -tio) mental effort, concentration

mutatio, mutationis (f.) (< muto, mutare + -tio) change

reficio, reficere, refeci, refectus (< re + facio, facere) restore, refresh; *refecta*: modifies *intentio*

paulum (adv.) a little

4

ambulo, mox orationem Graecam Latinamue clare et intente
non tam uocis causa quam stomachi lego; pariter tamen et
illa firmatur. Iterum ambulo ungor exerceor lauor. Cenanti
mihi, si cum uxore uel paucis, liber legitur; post cenam
comoedia aut lyristes; mox cum meis ambulo, quorum in
numero sunt eruditi. Ita uariis sermonibus uespera extendi-

5

tur, et quamquam longissimus dies bene conditur. Non numquam ex hoc ordine aliqua mutantur; nam, si diu iacui uel
ambulaui, post somnum demum lectionemque non uehiculo
sed, quod breuius quia uelocius, equo gestor. Interueniunt
amici ex proximis oppidis, partemque diei ad se trahunt
interdumque lasso mihi opportuna interpellatione subueni-

---

intente (adv.) (< intentus, -a, -um) w/ concentrated attention, intently
tam ... quam (adv.) correl., so much ... as
stomachus, -i (m.) (< Gr. στόμαχος) gullet, stomach
et illa = *etiam illa*; i.e. Pliny's voice
firmo (1) (< firmus + -o) make strong, support

IX.XXXVI.4
ungo, ungere rub w/ oil
exerceo, exercere (< ex + arceo, arcere) exercise, train
lauo (1) wash, pass.: wash oneself; ASYNDETON here suggests no particular order of these activities
ceno (1) (< cena + -o) dine
si ... uel whether ... or
paucis *amicis* understood
comoedia, -ae (f.) (< Gr. κωμῳδία) comedy
lyristes, lyristae (m.) (< Gr. λυριστής) lyre player; ELLIPSIS of *est*; Pliny has already mentioned in
   IX.XVII.3 that these are among his preferred entertainments.
eruditus, -a, -um (< ppp. of ex + rudis + -io) learned {> erudition}
uarius, -a, -um changing, different
uespera, -ae (f.) (< Gr. ἕσπερος) evening
extendo, extendere (< ex + tendo, tendere) continue, prolong
condo, condere compose, construct (*OLD* 12)

IX.XXXVI.5
non numquam sometimes; Latin often uses the dbl. negat. for emphasis.
ordo, ordinis (m.) order, arrangement {> ordinal}
demum (adv.) only
lectio, lectionis (f.) (< lego, legere + -tio) reading
quod ... uelocius ELLIPSIS of *est*; uelox, uelocis: swift, speedy
gesto (1) (< gero, gerere + -to) carry about, take for a ride
interuenio, interuenire (< inter + uenio, uenire) drop in, come by
interdum (adv.) (< inter + dum) now and then, in the meantime
lassus, -a, -um tired, weary
opportuna interpellatione abl. of means (AG #409); opportunus, -a, -um: convenient, advantageous;
   interpellatio, interpellationis (f.) (< inter + pello, pellere + -tio) interruption
subuenio, subuenire (< sub + uenio, uenire) provide help or relief; compd. vb + dat. *mihi* (AG #370)

unt. Venor aliquando, sed non sine pugillaribus, ut quamuis   6
nihil ceperim non nihil referam. Datur et colonis, ut
uidetur ipsis, non satis temporis, quorum mihi agrestes
querelae litteras nostras et haec urbana opera commendant.
Vale.

XXXIX—REBUILDING THE TEMPLE OF CERES

C. PLINIVS MVSTIO SVO S.

Haruspicum monitu reficienda est mihi aedes Cereris in   1
praediis in melius et in maius, uetus sane et angusta, cum sit

---

IX.XXXVI.6

uenor, uenari, uenatus sum hunt

aliquando (adv.) at times, from time to time

pugillares, pugillarium (m.) (< pugnus + -illus + -aris) writing tablets (s. I.VI.1n. on pugillares)

ut . . . referam purp. cl. (AG #531/1); Pliny expresses the same sentiment about hunting in I.VI.3; *quamuis* (relat. adv.) even though

Datur et colonis subj. *non satis temporis*; *et = etiam*; colonus, -i (m.) (< colo, colere + -nus) tenant farmer; *quorum* (relat. pron.) anteced. *colonis*

agrestis, agreste (< ager + estris) of the countryside, boorish

querela, -ae (f.) (< queror, queri + -ela) complaint, grievance

urbanus, -a, -um (< urbs + -anus) pertaining to the city, witty, urbane

commendo (1) (< con + mando, mandare) recommend, make attractive (*OLD* 6)

IX.XXXIX: Pliny writes about his need to rebuild a Temple of Ceres at one of his estates and gives instructions to his agent regarding plans and materials. His commitment not only to restore but also to embellish the shrine offers a model of his *pietas* (s. II.XIII.4n.).
Addressee: Mustius, unknown outside of this letter

IX.XXXIX.1

haruspex, haruspicis (m.) diviner (s. II.XX.4n.)

monitus, -us (m.) (< moneo, monere + -tus) warning, advice; *monitu*: abl. of cause (AG #404)

reficio, reficere (< re + facio, facere) restore, remade; *reficienda est*: 2nd (pass.) periphr. conjug. (AG #196 and 500/2); *mihi*: dat. of agent (AG #374)

aedes, aedis (f.) temple, shrine; *templum* refers to the entire consecrated area, while *aedes* denotes the building within the *templum* that houses the statue of the god or goddess. It was not unusual for temples to be located on private property, as many Roman families acknowledged and worshiped particular deities as their patrons. Furthermore, the worship of a number of Roman gods began as private cult practice, w/ Hercules as the foremost example.

Ceres one of the most ancient of the Roman deities, as shown by the fact that she was assigned one of the *flamines*—the oldest priestly order. Ceres was the goddess of growth. Her major festival, the Cerialia, was celebrated in April, but other rituals for her were required during the growing season (*OCD* 313).

praedium, -i (n.) estate

in melius et in maius "into something better and bigger"

uetus, ueteris old, having been in existence a long time {> veteran}

angustus, -a, -um narrow, congested

cum . . . frequentissima cum circumst. cl. (AG #546); *alioqui* (adv.) as a general rule; *stato die*: i.e. the day of the festival; frequens, frequentis: crowded

161

2   alioqui stato die frequentissima. Nam idibus Septembribus
magnus e regione tota coit populus, multae res aguntur,
multa uota suscipiuntur, multa redduntur; sed nullum in

3   proximo suffugium aut imbris aut solis. Videor ergo munifice
simul religioseque facturus, si aedem quam pulcherrimam ex-
struxero, addidero porticus aedi, illam ad usum deae has ad

4   hominum. Velim ergo emas quattuor marmoreas columnas,
cuius tibi uidebitur generis, emas marmora quibus solum,
quibus parietes excolantur. Erit etiam faciendum ipsius
deae signum, quia antiquum illud e ligno quibusdam sui par-

IX.XXXIX.2

Idus Septembres September 13 (s. VI.XVI.4n. on Nonum Kal. Septembres); the gathering Pliny refers
to is clearly not the Cerialia. It is apparently a regional festival for the goddess, held on the same day
as the great *Epulum Iouis*, feast of Jupiter.

coeo, coire (< con + eo, ire) come together, gather round

uotum, -i (n.) vow

in proximo close at hand (*OLD* 2a)

suffugium, -i (n.) (< sub + fugo, fugere + -ium) shelter, refuge; ELLIPSIS of *est*

imber, imbris (m.) rain; *imbris . . . solis*: objv. gen. (AG #347)

IX.XXXIX.3

Videor . . . facturus apod. of FMV condit. using fut. ptc. (AG #516d); *munifice* (adv.) (< munificus)
dutifully, generously {> munificent}; *religiose* (adv.) (< religiosus) in accordance w/ religious law,
reverently

si . . . hominum prot. of FMV condit.; *quam* + superl.: "as . . . as possible"; exstruo, exstruere, exstruxi,
exstructus (< ex + struo, struere) build up, construct; *aedi* dat. of indir. obj. w/ compd. vb. *addidero*
(AG #370); porticus, -us (m./f.) covered walkway, colonnade; *illam . . . has*: the former . . . the latter;
usus, -us (m.) (< utor, uti + -tus) enjoyment, use

IX.XXXIX.4

Velim . . . emas opt. subjv. (AG #442b); emo, emere: buy; i.e. a polite request: "I would like for you
to buy"

quattuor . . . excolantur marmoreus, -a, -um (< marmor + -eus) of marble; genus, generis (n.) type
{> generic}; *cuius generis*: gen. of quality (AG #345); marmor, marmoris (n.) marble; *quibus . . .*
excolantur: relat. cl. of char. (AG #535); solum, -i (n.) soil, ground; paries, parietis (m.) wall of a
building; excolo, excolere (< ex + colo, colere) improve, decorate; Pliny's use of both the adj. and n.
forms for marble (POLYPTOTON) draws particular attention to this luxury material w/ which he will
embellish the temple.

erit . . . faciendum 2nd (pass.) periphr. conjug. (AG #196 and 500/2)

signum, -i (n.) statue (*OLD* 12a)

lignum, -i (n.) wood

quibusdam . . . partibus abl. of specif. (AG #418)

tibus uetustate truncatum est. Quantum ad porticus, nihil   5
interim occurrit, quod uideatur istinc esse repetendum,
nisi tamen ut formam secundum rationem loci scribas.
Neque enim possunt circumdari templo: nam solum templi
hinc flumine et abruptissimis ripis, hinc uia cingitur. Est ultra   6
uiam latissimum pratum, in quo satis apte contra templum
ipsum porticus explicabuntur; nisi quid tu melius inuenies,
qui soles locorum difficultates arte superare. Vale.

---

uetustas, uetustatis (f.) (< uetus + -tas) old age; *uetustate*: abl. of cause (AG #404)
trunco (1) (< truncus + -o) cut off, lop off

IX.XXXIX.5
occurro, occurrere (< ob + curro, currere) occur, present itself
quod uideatur relat. cl. of char. (AG #535), anteced. *nihil*; *istinc* (adv.) from over there; *esse repetendum*:
    2nd (pass.) periphr. conjug. (AG #196 and 500/2)
ut . . . scribas subst. cl. of purp. (AG #563) (= indir. comm.) ff. *repetendum*; forma, -ae (f.) shape,
    configuration (*OLD* 6); *secundum* (prep.) in accordance w/
circumdo, circumdare (< circum + do, dare) place around, surround, enclose; compd. vb + dat.
    templo (AG #370); *possunt*: subj. *porticus* implied
hinc . . . hinc on one side . . . on another side
abruptus, -a, -um (< ppp. of ab + rumpo, rumpere) steep
ripa, -ae (f.) riverbank
cingo, cingere encircle, lie round

IX.XXXIX.6
ultra (prep.) beyond
pratum, -i (n.) meadow
apte (adv.) (< aptus, -a, -um) appropriately, properly
explico (1) (< ex + plico, plicare) spread out, extend
nisi . . . inuenies prot. of FMV condit. (AG #516c); *quid* = *aliquid* (s. 1.1.1n. on quas)

BOOK x

xxxix—SHODDY BUILDING PRACTICES

C. PLINIVS TRAIANO IMPERATORI

Theatrum, domine, Nicaeae maxima iam parte con-   1
structum, imperfectum tamen, sestertium (ut audio; neque
enim ratio operis excussa est) amplius centies hausit: uereor
ne frustra. Ingentibus enim rimis desedit et hiat, siue in   2

---

x.xxxix: Now serving as an imperial legate in Bithynia-Pontus, Pliny seeks advice from the emperor regarding shoddy and disorganized building projects in Nicea and Claudiopolis.
Addressee: the Emperor Trajan

x.xxxix.1
domine Pliny's use of this form of personal address does not indicate servility but rather respect. By his time, it had become a common way for one man of rank to address another, particularly if the latter enjoyed more elevated status. Although Domitian had demanded to be addressed as "Dominus et Deus," *Dominus* would not become an official title of the emperor until the Severan Dynasty in the early 3rd century CE.
Nicea, -ae (f.) Nicea, a Hellenistic city founded w/ the name Antigoneia by Antigonus Monopthalmos, a Macedonian nobleman. In modern times, it is best known as the location of Constantine's 1st ecumenical church council, held in 325 CE, and in connection w/ the Nicene Creed that was its result (*OCD* s. Niceae (1), 1040).
construo, construere, construxi, constructus (< con + struo, struere) put together, build
imperfectus, -a, -um (< in + per + facio, facere) unfinished, not completed
sestertium, -i (n.) 100,000 sesterces (s. II.xx.1n. on as)
ut audio *ut* (conj.) "as"; as he goes on to explain, Pliny has not yet examined the books.
excutio, excutere, excussi, excussus (< ex + quatio, quatere) scrutinize
centies (adv.) a hundred times; *centies sestertium*: 10 million sesterces
haurio, haurire, hausi, hausus draw, swallow, consume
ne frustra subst. cl. ff. vb. of fearing (AG #564), ELLIPSIS of *fuerit*; frustra (adv.) to no purpose, in vain; (*sit* understood)

x.xxxix.2
rima, -ae (f.) crack, fissure; *ingentibus rimis*: abl. of cause (AG #404)
desido, desidere, desedi (< de + sido, sidere) sink
hio (1) be wide open, gape
siue ... siue whether ... or

causa solum umidum et molle, siue lapis ipse gracilis et putris:
dignum est certe deliberatione, sitne faciendum an sit re-
linquendum an etiam destruendum. Nam fulturae ac sub-
structiones, quibus subinde suscipitur, non tam firmae mihi

3   quam sumptuosae uidentur. Huic theatro ex priuatorum
pollicitationibus multa debentur, ut basilicae circa, ut porticus supra caueam. Quae nunc omnia differuntur cessante

4   eo, quod ante peragendum est. Iidem Nicaeenses gymnasium
incendio amissum ante aduentum meum restituere coeperunt,
longe numerosius laxiusque quam fuerat, et iam aliquantum

---

in causa (esse) be the cause (*OLD* causa 11b), ellipsis of *est*

solum, -i (n.) soil, ground

umidus, -a, -um (< umeo, umere + -idus) wet, moist

mollis, molle soft

lapis, lapidis (m.) stone, pebble

gracilis, gracile thin, w/ little density

putris, putre rotten, crumbly

deliberatio, deliberationis (f.) (< de + libra + -o + -tio) careful consideration; *deliberatione*: abl. of
    specif. (AG #418b) w/ *dignum*

sitne … destruendum indir. quest. (AG #574); 2nd (pass.) periphr. conjug. (AG #196 and 500/2); *an*
    (pcl.) "or"; destruo, destruere (< de + struo, struere) demolish, pull down

fultura, -ae (f.) that which supports, a prop

substructio, substructionis (f.) (< sub + struo, struere + -tio) substructure

subinde (adv.) (< sub + inde) at intervals

tam … quam (adv.) correl., so much … as

firmus, -a, -um strong, durable

sumptuosus, -a, -um (< sumo, sumere + -tus + -osus) costly, expensive

x.xxxix.3

pollicitatio, pollicitationis (f.) (< polliceor, polliceri + -to + -tio) promise; *priuatorum*: subst. use,
    i.e. "private citizens"

ut (adv.) such as, like

basilica, -ae (f.) colonnaded hall

circa (adv.) on either side (*OLD* 4)

porticus, -us (m./f.) covered walkway, colonnade

cauea, -ae (f.) seating area of a theater

quae (relat. pron.) anteced. the promised additions to the theater

differo, differre (< dis + fero, ferre) postpone, delay (*OLD* 4)

cessante eo abl. abs. (AG #419); cesso (1) (< cedo, cedere + -to) hold back, delay {> cessation}; *eo*:
    i.e. the building of the theater itself

perago, peragere (< per + ago, agere) carry through, finish; *peragendum est*: 2nd (pass.) periphr.
    conjug. (AG #196 and 500/2)

x.xxxix.4

Nicaeensis, Nicaeense from Nicea; subst. m. pl.: the inhabitants of Nicea

gymnasium, -i (n.) ancient public gymnasia began simply, as open areas designated for exercise w/
    access to water nearby. The location was often associated w/ the shrine or sanctuary of a deity or

erogauerunt; periculum est, ne parum utiliter; incompositum
enim et sparsum est. Praeterea architectus, sane aemulus eius
a quo opus incohatum est, adfirmat parietes quamquam
uiginti et duos pedes latos imposita onera sustinere non posse,
quia sint caemento medii farti nec testaceo opere praecincti.
Claudiopolitani quoque in depresso loco, imminente etiam
monte ingens balineum defodiunt magis quam aedificant, et

5

---

hero. Over time gymnasia were used for mental as well as physical training and became intellectual centers, w/ the exercise area surrounded by a portico, behind which was a variety of rooms, sometimes even including bathing facilities (*OCD* s. gymnasium, 659–60).

incendium, -i (n.) (< incendo, incendere + -ium) fire, conflagration {> incendiary}

amitto, amittere, amisi, amissus (< ab + mitto, mittere) incur the loss of, lose

aduentus, -us (m.) (< ad + uenio, uenire + -tus) arrival

restituo, restituere (< re + statuo, statuere) restore, rebuild

coepi, coepisse (pf. stem only) begin

numerosius laxiusque modifying *gynasium*; numerosus, -a, -um (< numerus + -osus) abundant, varied, prolific; laxus, -a, -um: spacious, roomy

aliquantum, -i (n.) a considerable amount

erogo (1) (< ex + rogo, rogare) pay out

ne ... utiliter subst. cl. ff. vb. of fearing (AG #564), ELLIPSIS of *sit*; *utiliter* (adv.) (< utilis) usefully, to their advantage

incompositus, -a, -um (< in + ppp. of con + pono, ponere) not well put together

spargo, spargere, sparsi, sparsus scatter, spread about

aemulus, -i (m.) rival, competitor {> emulate}

incoho (1) start, initiate {> incohate}

adfirmo (1) (< ad + firmo, firmare) confirm, corroborate

parietes ... posse indir. disc. (AG #580); paries, parietis (m.) wall of a building; *uiginti et duos pedes*: acc. of extent of space (AG #425); impono, imponere, imposui, impositus: lay on, place on {> impose}; onus, oneris (n.) burden, load; sustineo, sustinere (< sub(s) + teneo, tenere) hold up, maintain {> sustain}

quia ... praecincti subord. cl. in indir. disc. takes subjv. vb. (AG #540/2b and 580)

caemento medii farti The walls Pliny describes consist of parallel stone walls between which small stones and rubble are poured; the technique substantially increased the thickness of a wall, but required mortared brick walls on either side for it to have sufficient support; caementum, -i (n.) (< caedo, caedere + -mentum) small stones, rubble; medium, -ii (n.) middle part; fartus, -a, -um (< ppp. of farcio, farcire) stuffed, crammed

testaceus, -a, -um (< testa + -aceus) made of brick

praecingo, praecingere, praecinxi, praecinctus (< prae + cingo, cingere) encircle, gird

x.xxxix.5

Claudiopolitani, -orum (m. pl.) residents of Claudiopolis (the modern day city of Bolu in Turkey); it was also called Bithynium and was one of at least five cities in the region that took the name Claudiopolis.

depressus, -a, -um (< ppp. of de + premo, premere) having a low elevation

imminente ... monte abl. abs. (AG #419); immineo, imminere: press closely, impend {> imminent}

balineum, -i (n.) (< Gr. βαλανεῖον) baths (s. II.XVII.11 on balineum)

defodio, defodere (< de + fodio, fodere) excavate

6   quidem ex ea pecunia, quam buleutae additi beneficio tuo
aut iam obtulerunt ob introitum aut nobis exigentibus con-
ferent. Ergo cum timeam ne illic publica pecunia, hic, quod
est omni pecunia pretiosius, munus tuum male collocetur,
cogor petere a te non solum ob theatrum, uerum etiam ob
haec balinea mittas architectum, dispecturum utrum sit
utilius post sumptum qui factus est quoquo modo consum-
mare opera, ut incohata sunt, an quae uidentur emendanda
corrigere, quae transferenda transferre, ne dum seruare
uolumus quod impensum est, male impendamus quod
addendum est.

---

buleuta, -ae (m.) (< Gr. βουλευτής) member of a Greek council or senate

beneficium, -i (n.) (< bene + facio, facere + -ium) kindness, benefit {> beneficiary}; i.e. Trajan must
have appointed some of the local elite to the council.

offero, offerre, obtuli (< ob + fero, ferre) supply, hand over

introitus, -us (m.) (< intro + eo, ire + -tus) entrance, right of admittance; Pliny is referring here to
the *honorarium decurionatus*, that is the amount the officeholder was required to pay for the honor of
the position. This would not have seemed unreasonable to elite members of a Hellenized city, as
wealthy members of a Greek community had always been expected to fund its needs.

nobis exigentibus abl. abs. (AG #419); exigo, exigere (< ex + ago, agere) exact or enforce payment
(*OLD* 8a)

x.xxxix.6

cum timeam cum causal cl. (AG #549)

ne . . . collocetur subst. cl. ff. vb. of fearing (AG #564); *illic . . . hic*: "at the former place (Nicaea) . . . at
the latter place (Claudiopolis)"; *quod . . . pretiosius*: relat. cl. describing *munus*; *omni pecunia*: abl. of
compar. (AG #406) w/ *pretiosius*; pretiosus, -a, -um (< pretium + -osus) valuable; munus, muneris
(n.) gift, favor; colloco (1) (< con + loco, locare) spend, invest (*OLD* 10)

cogo, cogere (< con + ago, agere) compel

mittas architectum subst. cl. of purp. (AG #563) (= indir. comm.) ff. *petere, ut* omitted

dispicio, dispicere, dispexi, dispectus (< dis + specio, specere) consider; *dispecturum*: fut. act. ptc.,
trans. as relat. cl.: "who will consider"

utrum . . . sunt 1st half of indir. quest. (AG #574); sumptus, -us (m.) (< sumo, sumere + -tus) expenditure; *quoquo modo*: in whatever manner; "however it can be done"; consummo (1) (< con +
summa + -o) make complete, finish {> consummate}; *ut . . . sunt*: ut w/ indic. (AG #543) "as"

an . . . transferre 2nd half of indir. quest. (AG #574); *quae*, subst. use: "the things which"; emendo
(1) (< ex + menda + -o) correct; corrigo, corrigere (< con + rego, regere) straighten out, put right;
transfero, transferre (< trans + fero, ferre) change the location of

ne . . . impendamus negat. purp. cl. (AG #531/1); impendo, impendere, impendi, impensus (< in +
pendo, pendere) pay out, expend; "lest, in wishing to preserve that which has been paid out, we
waste what (moneys) must be added."

XL—TRAJAN RESPONDS

TRAIANVS PLINIO

Quid oporteat fieri circa theatrum, quod incohatum apud   1
Nicaeenses est, in re praesenti optime deliberabis et constitues. Mihi sufficiet indicari, cui sententiae accesseris. Tunc
autem a priuatis exige opera, cum theatrum, propter quod
illa promissa sunt, factum erit. Gymnasiis indulgent Graeculi;   2
ideo forsitan Nicaeenses maiore animo constructionem eius
adgressi sunt: sed oportet illos eo contentos esse, quod possit
illis sufficere. Quid Claudiopolitanis circa balineum quod   3

---

x.xl: The Emperor Trajan responds to Pliny's inquiries regarding the building projects in x.xxxix. Addressee: Pliny

x.xl.1

quid . . . theatrum indir. quest. (AG #574) ff. *constitues*; oportet; it is proper, right, "ought," impers. vb. gener. w/ acc. + inf. constr. (AG #565n. 3)

incoho (1) start, initiate {> incohate}

Nicaeensis, Nicaeense from Nicea; subst. m. pl.: the inhabitants of Nicea (s. x.xxxix.1n.)

praesens, praesentis present, face to face

delibero (1) (< de + libra + -o) weigh the pros and cons, consider, consult

indico (1) (< in + dico, dicare) give essential information about (*OLD* 1b)

cui . . . accesseris indir. quest. (AG #574); sententia, -ae (f.) decision; *sententiae*: dat. of indir. obj. w/ compd. vb. *accesseris* (AG #370)

exigo, exigere (< ex + ago, agere) exact or enforce payment (*OLD* 8a)

cum . . . factum erit cum tmp. cl. (AG #545); *propter quod*: for which reason; promitto, promittere, promisi, promissus (< pro + mitto, mittere) promise, guarantee

x.xl.2

gymnasium, -i (n.) (s. x.xxxix.4n.); *gymnasiis*: dat. w/ intr. vb. *indulgent* (AG #367); indulgeo, indulgere: take pleasure in, devote oneself to {> indulge}

Graeculus, -i (n.) (< Graecus + -ulus) little Greek; often a condescending or disparaging term

forsitan (adv.) it may be, perhaps

maiore animo "too ambitiously"

adgredior, adgredi, adgressus sum (< ad + gradior, gradi) approach, set about a task

quod . . . sufficere relat. cl. of char. (AG #535), anteced. *eo*: loc. abl. w/ *contentos* (AG #431a); *illis*: dat. of indir. obj. w/ compd. vb. *sufficere* (AG #370)

x.xl.3

quid . . . sit indir. quest. (AG #574) ff. *constitues*; Claudiopolitani, -orum (m. pl.) residents of Claudiopolis (s. x.xxxix.5n.); *Claudiopolitanis*: dat. w/ intr. vb. *suadendum sit* (AG #367); balineum, -i (n.) (< Gr. βαλανεῖον) baths, bathing complex; *ut scribis*: ut w/ indic. (AG #543) "as"; idoneus, -a, -um: appropriate, suitable; *loco*: abl. of place where w/o prep. (AG #429); *suadendum sit*: impers. use of 2nd (pass.) periphr. conjug. (AG #196 and 500/3); suadeo, suadere: recommend, advise

parum, ut scribis, idoneo loco incohauerunt suadendum sit,
tu constitues. Architecti tibi deesse non possunt. Nulla
prouincia non et peritos et ingeniosos homines habet; modo
ne existimes breuius esse ab urbe mitti, cum ex Graecia etiam
ad nos uenire soliti sint.

lxv—STATUS OF FREEBORN FOUNDLINGS

C. PLINIVS TRAIANO IMPERATORI

1   Magna, domine, et ad totam prouinciam pertinens
quaestio est de condicione et alimentis eorum, quos uocant
2   θρεπτούς. In qua ego auditis constitutionibus principum, quia
nihil inueniebam aut proprium aut uniuersale, quod ad
Bithynos referretur, consulendum te existimaui, quid obser-

---

desum, deesse (< de + sum, esse) be lacking be unavailable (+dat.)

peritus, -a, -um experienced, expert

ingeniosus, -a, -um (< ingenium + -osus) talented, clever

modo ne existimes negat. hort. subv. w/ *modo* as cl. of proviso (AG #528); existimo (1) (< ex + aestimo, aestimare) consider, hold the opinion that; "you shouldn't think that"

breuius . . . mitti indir. disc. (AG #580); *eis* understood

cum . . . sint cum causal cl. (AG #549)

x.lxv: Pliny seeks advice regarding the status of freeborn people who had been exposed as children and raised as slaves.
Addressee: the Emperor Trajan

x.lxv.1

domine (s.x.xxxix.1n.)

pertineo, pertinere (< per + teneo, tenere) relate, be of concern

quaestio, quaestionis (f.) (< quaero, quaerere + -tio) judicial inquiry

condicio, condicionis (f.) (< con + dico, dicere + -io) situation, state of health (*OLD* 6a and d)

alimentum, -i (n.) (< alo, alere + -mentum) food, provisions, pl.: sustenance, maintenance
{> alimentary}

θρεπτούς Gr. acc. pl. "adopted foundling"; these are children exposed by their families. In both Greece and Rome, a father might reject a newborn baby as his own and thus be freed of his obligation to raise that child. It is difficult to say w/ what frequency this occurred or what percentage of abandoned babies survived, but it is clear that at least some were picked up and raised as slaves.

x.lxv.2

qua (relat. pron.) anteced. *quaestio*

auditis constitutionibus principum abl. abs. (AG #419); constitutio, constitutionis (f.) (< constituo, constituere + -tio) decision, decree

proprius, -a, -um belonging to, appropriate

uari uelles; neque putaui posse me in eo, quod auctoritatem
tuam posceret, exemplis esse contentum. Recitabatur autem
apud me edictum, quod dicebatur diui Augusti, ad Andaniam
pertinens; recitatae et epistulae diui Vespasiani ad Lacedaemonios et diui Titi ad eosdem et Achaeos et Domitiani
ad Auidium Nigrinum et Armenium Brocchum proconsules,
item ad Lacedaemonios; quae ideo tibi non misi, quia et
parum emendata et quaedam non certae fidei uidebantur, et
quia uera et emendata in scriniis tuis esse credebam.

3

---

uniuersalis, uniuersale (< unus + uersus + -alis) having general application

quod…referretur relat. cl. of char. (AG #535); Bithyni, -orum (m. pl.) the people of Bithynia; refero,
referre (< res + fero, ferre) ascribe, apply (to) (*OLD* 11b)

consulendum te indir. disc. (AG #580) after *existimaui*, ELLIPSIS of *esse*; 2nd (pass.) periphr. conjug.
(AG #196 and 500/2); existimo (1) (< ex + aestimo, aestimare) consider, judge

quid…uelles indir. quest. (AG #574); obseruo (1) (< ob + seruo, seruare) carry out in practice,
adopt as a course of action (*OLD* 5)

posse…contentum indir. disc. (AG #580); *quod…posceret*: relat. cl. of char. (AG #535); auctoritas,
auctoritatis (f.) (< auctor + -tas) authorization, command; *exemplis*: loc. abl. w/ *contentum* (AG #431a)

X.LXV.3

recito (1) (< re + cito, citare) recite (before an audience) (s. I.XIII.1n. on quo…aliquis)

apud me in my presence (*OLD* 8a)

edictum, -i (n.) (< ppp. of ex + dico, dicere) proclamation

Andania, -ae (f.) a small Greek city in Messenia in the southern Peloponnese w/ a sanctuary of Deme-
ter, where mysteries were performed.; SW suggests that the sanctuary, acting as a place of asylum,
might have cared for a group of exposed children (652).

Lacedaemonii, -orum (m. pl.) the people of Sparta (Lacedaemon)

eosdem i.e. the Lacedaemonians

Achaei, -orum (m. pl.) the inhabitants of the Roman province of Achaia, which incorporated most of
Greece w/ the exception of some independent cities, including Sparta and Athens (*OCD* 6)

Auidius Nigrinus the date of his service as governor of Achaia is uncertain

Armenius Brocchus unknown outside of this letter

proconsul, proconsulis (m.) (< pro + consul) governor; one of several terms used to describe the
position; the word itself indicates that the office carried the power of the office of consul. Proconsuls
governed directly as opposed to imperial legates, who represented the power of the emperor in the
provinces over which he kept careful control.

quae (relat. pron.) anteced. *edictum* and *epistulae*

emendo (1) (< ex + menda + -o) correct, revise

certae fidei gen. of quality (AG #345); i.e. Pliny doubts their authenticity

uera…esse indir. disc. (AG #580) after *credebam*

scrinium, -i (n.) writing case, receptacle for holding scrolls; i.e. records or files

lxvi—TRAJAN RESPONDS

TRAIANVS PLINIO

1 Quaestio ista, quae pertinet ad eos qui liberi nati expositi, deinde sublati a quibusdam et in seruitute educati sunt, saepe tractata est, nec quicquam inuenitur in commentariis eorum principum, qui ante me fuerunt, quod ad omnes

2 prouincias sit constitutum. Epistulae sane sunt Domitiani ad Auidium Nigrinum et Armenium Brocchum, quae fortasse debeant obseruari: sed inter eas prouincias, de quibus rescripsit, non est Bithynia; et ideo nec adsertionem denegandam iis qui ex eius modi causa in libertatem uindicabuntur puto, neque ipsam libertatem redimendam pretio alimentorum.

---

x.lxvi: The Emperor Trajan renders his opinion on the rights of the exposed as requested by Pliny in x.lxv. Addressee: Pliny

x.lxvi.1

quaestio, quaestionis (f.) (< quaero, quaerere + -tio) judicial inquiry

pertineo, pertinere (< per + teneo, tenere) extend, relate, be of concern

nascor, nasci, natus sum be born

expono, exponere, exposui, expositus (< ex + pono, ponere) abandon, expose (children)

tollo, tollere, sustuli, sublatus pick up; the term was also used to describe the moment when a father picked up a newborn child, thus indicating his formal acceptance of the child as his own and acknowledging his obligation to raise it.

seruitus, seruitutis (f.) (< seruus + -tus) slavery

educo (1) bring up {> educate}

tracto (1) (< traho, trahere + -to) examine, consider (*OLD* 8a)

commentarius, commentarii (m.) notebook, journal (s. vii.xix.5n.)

quod . . . sit relat. cl. of char. (AG #535), anteced. *quicquam*

x.lxvi.2

Auidius Nigrinus (s. x.lxv.3n.)

Armenius Brocchus (s. x.lxv.3n.)

quae . . . obseruari relat. cl. of char. (AG #535), anteced. *epistulae*; obseruo (1) (< ob + seruo, seruare) carry out in practice, adopt as a course of action (*OLD* 5)

rescribo, rescribere (< re + scribo, scribere) reply, write back; i.e. Domitian's response to the same kind of inquiry regarding the treatment of provincials that Pliny is making

Bithynia, -ae (f.) Bithynia

nec . . . iis 1st indir. disc. (AG #580) ff. *puto*; adsertio, adsertionis (f.) (< adsero, adserere + -tio) declaration of free status {> assertion}; *denegandum*: ELLIPSIS of *esse*, 2nd (pass.) periphr. conjug. (AG #196 and 500/2); denego (1) (< de + nego, negare) deny, refuse, w/ dat. of separ. *iis* (AG #381)

uindico (1) (< uim + dico, dicere) lay claim; *in libertatem* uindicare: claim as free (in a legal proceeding)

ipsam . . . alimentorum 2nd indir. disc. ff. *puto*; *redimendam*: ELLIPSIS of *esse*, 2nd (pass.) periphr. conjug. (AG #196 and 500/2); redimo, redimere (< re + emo, emere) buy back, pay the cost of; pretium, -i (n.) price, value; alimentum, -i (n.) (< alo, alere + -mentum) food, provisions, pl.: sustenance, maintenance {> alimentary}

XCVI—HOW TO DEAL WITH CHRISTIANS

C. PLINIVS TRAIANO IMPERATORI

Sollemne est mihi, domine, omnia de quibus dubito ad te 1
referre. Quis enim potest melius uel cunctationem meam
regere uel ignorantiam instruere? Cognitionibus de Chri-
stianis interfui numquam: ideo nescio quid et quatenus aut
puniri soleat aut quaeri. Nec mediocriter haesitaui, sitne 2
aliquod discrimen aetatum, an quamlibet teneri nihil a robu-
stioribus differant; detur paenitentiae uenia, an ei, qui omnino

---

x.xcvi: In what is undoubtedly the best-known letter from his correspondence with Trajan, Pliny seeks the emperor's guidance and approval as to how he has and should treat confessed Christians and the accusations made against them.

Addressee: the Emperor Trajan

x.xcvi.1

sollemnis, sollemne traditional, customary

cunctatio, cunctationis (f.) (< cunctor, cunctari + -tio) hesitation

ignorantia, -ae (f.) (< pres. ptc. of ignoro, ignorare + -tia) lack of knowledge

instruo, instruere (< in + struo, struere) provide w/ information, instruct (*OLD* 8a)

cognitio, cognitionis (f.) (< cognosco, cognoscere + -tio) investigation, judicial inquiry; *cognitioni-bus*: dat. of indir. obj. w/ compd. vb. *interfui* (AG #370); intersum, interesse, interfui, interfuturus (< inter + sum, esse) attend as an onlooker, take part in (*OLD* 4)

Christiani, -orum (m. pl.) Christians; the Romans considered Christianity to be just another super-stitious Eastern cult, like those that worshiped Isis or Mithras; what made Christianity different was that it threatened the proper cultivation of the gods that the Romans believed were responsible for the success and survival of the empire. In Pliny's time Christian communities represented a very small percentage of the population and were located primarily in the eastern Mediterranean, w/ Rome as the notable exception. While there had been isolated incidents that resulted in the prosecu-tion of Christians, they had not yet suffered any systematic pursuit or persecution.

quid . . . quaeri indir. quest. (AG #574); *quatenus* (interrog. adv.) to what extent; punio, punire (< poena + -io) punish; quaero, quaerere: hold a judical inquiry into, investigate (*OLD* 10a)

x.xcvi.2

mediocriter (adv.) (< mediocris) moderately; w/ negat.: to no small extent, exceedingly

haesito (1) (< haereo, haerere + -to) be undecided or uncertain; followed by a series of indir. quest. (AG #574)

sitne . . . aetatum 1st quest.; discrimen, discriminis (n.) (< dis + cerno, cernere + -men) dividing point, critical point {> discriminate}

an . . . differant 2nd quest.; *quamlibet* (adv.) (< quam + libet) in whatever degree one likes, however much; tener, -a -um: soft, immature, of tender age; *nihil* (adj.): used w/ adv. force: in no respect, not at all (*OLD* 11a); robustus, -a, -um (< robur + -tus) strong, firm, solid; differo, differre (< dis + fero, ferre) be different (*OLD* 8a)

detur . . . uenia 3rd quest.; paenitentia, -ae (f.) (< paeniteo + -ia) regret {> penitent}

an . . . prosit 4th quest.; *ei*: dat. of indir. obj. w/ compd. vb. *prosit* (AG #370); prosum, prodesse (< pro + sum, esse) be useful, be beneficial

3   Christianus fuit, desisse non prosit; nomen ipsum, si flagitiis
careat, an flagitia cohaerentia nomini puniantur. Interim, <in>
iis qui ad me tamquam Christiani deferebantur, hunc sum
secutus modum. Interrogaui ipsos an essent Christiani. Confitentes iterum ac tertio interrogaui supplicium minatus:
perseuerantes duci iussi. Neque enim dubitabam, qualecumque esset quod faterentur, pertinaciam certe et inflexibilem

4   obstinationem debere puniri. Fuerunt alii similis amentiae,
quos, quia ciues Romani erant, adnotaui in urbem remittendos.
Mox ipso tractatu, ut fieri solet, diffundente se crimine plures

---

nomen . . . puniantur 5th quest.; *si . . . careat*: prot. of FLV condit. (AG #516b); flagitium, -i (n.) disgrace, shameful act; *flagitiis*: abl. of separ. (AG #401) w/ *careat*; careo, carere: lack, be w/ out; co- haereo, cohaerere (< co + haereo, haerere) be connected (to), compd. vb + dat. *nomini* (AG #370)

defero, deferre (< de + fero, ferre) report, accuse

hunc . . . modum points forward to the next section (AG #297e)

x.xcvi.3

an . . . Christiani indir. quest. (AG #574), 2nd alt. implied by *an*: "whether (or not)"

confiteor, confiteri, confessus sum (< con + fateor, fateri) admit; *confitentes*, subst. use: "those who admit (that they are Christians)"

supplicium, -i (n.) (< supplex, supplicis + -ium) punishment

minor, minari, minatus sum (< minae + -o) threaten, give an indication of

perseuerantes duci acc. + inf. constr (AG #563a) w/ *iussi*; perseuero (1) (< per + seuerus + -o) per- sist, continue; *perseuerantes*: subst. use; duco, ducere: lead off to punishment (*OLD* 4b)

qualecumque . . . esset relat. cl. of char. (AG #535); qualiscumque, qualecumque (relat. adj.) (< qualis + cumque) whatever kind or sort of

quod faterentur subjv. of integral part (also called subjv. by attraction) (AG #593); fateor, fateri, fassus sum: concede, acknowledge

pertinaciam . . . puniri indir. disc. (AG #580) ff. *dubitabam*; pertinacia, -ae (f.) (< pertinax + -ia) defiance; inflexibilis, inflexibile (< in + flecto, flectare + -bilis) unbending, stubborn; obstinatio, obstinationis (f.) (< obstino, obstinare + -tio) obstinacy, stubborn adherence

x.xcvi.4

amentia, -ae (f.) (< ab + mens + -ia) madness, frenzy, infatuation; *similis amentiae*: gen. of quality (AG #345)

adnoto (1) (< ad + noto, notare) put on record, designate

remitto, remittere (< re + mitto, mittere) send back; a Roman citizen living in the provinces who was condemned to death was almost always sent to Rome so that he could appeal his sentence. Paul of Tarsus, the author of many letters that are part of the Bible's New Testament, is the most prominent ex. Arrested and imprisoned in Jerusalem, he exercised his right as a Roman citizen to appeal to the emperor and was transported to Rome, where he was beheaded.

ipso tractatu abl. of cause (AG #404); tractatus, -us (m.) (< tracto, tractare + -tus) method of treatment

ut . . . solet *ut* w/ indic. (AG #543) "as"

diffundente se crimine abl. abs. (AG #419); diffundo, diffundere (< dis + fundo, fundere) spread widely, spread out; crimen, criminis (n.) indictment, charge

species inciderunt. Propositus est libellus sine auctore mul-   5
torum nomina continens. Qui negabant esse se Christianos
aut fuisse, cum praeeunte me deos adpellarent et imagini
tuae, quam propter hoc iusseram cum simulacris numinum
adferri, ture ac uino supplicarent, praeterea male dicerent
Christo, quorum nihil cogi posse dicuntur qui sunt re uera
Christiani, dimittendos putaui. Alii ab indice nominati esse   6
se Christianos dixerunt et mox negauerunt; fuisse quidem sed
desisse, quidam ante triennium, quidam ante plures annos,
non nemo etiam ante uiginti. <Hi> quoque omnes et imaginem
tuam deorumque simulacra uenerati sunt et Christo male

---

species, speciei (f.) (< specio, specere + -ies) appearance, type
incido, incidere (< in + cado, cadere) occur (*OLD* 10a) {> incident}

x.xcvi.5
propono, proponere, proposui, propositus (< pro + pono, ponere) put out, publish
libellus, -i (m.) (< liber + -lus) leaflet, pamphlet
auctor, auctoris (m.) (< augeo, augere + -tor) originator, source, author (*OLD* 10a)
contineo, continere (< con + teneo, tenere) contain, consist of (*OLD* 11b)
Qui (relat. pron.) subst. use: "those who"
se ... fuisse indir. disc. (AG #580)
cum ... Christo cum circumst. cl. (AG #546) in three parts
praeeunte ... adpellarent 1st part; *praeeunte me*: abl. abs. (AG #419); praeeo, praeire (< prae + eo,
    ire) lead the way, dictate a religious formula for repetition (*OLD* 3a)
imagini tuae ... supplicarent 2nd part; imago, imaginis (f.) likeness; simulacrum, -i (n.) image;
    numen, numinis (n.) god; adfero, adferre (< ad + fero, ferre) bring in, bring forward; tus, turis (n.)
    frankincense; supplico (1) make offerings (to a deity), compd. vb + dat. *imagini* (AG #370)
praeterea ... Christo 3rd part; male dicere: speak ill of, abuse, insult + dat. *Christo*
quorum (relat. pron.) anteced. the three preceding actions
cogo, cogere (< con + ago, agere) compel
qui (relat. pron.) subst. use: "those who"
re uera in actual fact, really (*OLD* uerus 2c)
dimitto, dimittere (< dis + mitto, mittere) discharge; *dimittendos*: indir. disc. (AG #580), *eos* under-
    stood (i.e. *Qui negabant*), ELLIPSIS of *esse*, 2nd (pass.) periphr. conjug. (AG #196 and 500/2)

x.xcvi.6
index, indicis (m.) informer
nomino (1) (< nomen + -o) specify by name, name aloud
esse ... Christianos indir. disc. (AG #580)
fuisse ... desisse indir. disc. (AG #580), *se* understood
triennium, -i (n.) (< tri- + annus + ium) a period of three years
nemo, neminis (m.) (< ne + homo, hominis) no one, nobody; *non nemo*: "some"; Latin often uses a
    dbl. negat. for emphasis.
ueneror, uenerari, ueneratus sum hold in awe, revere {> venerate}

7   dixerunt. Adfirmabant autem hanc fuisse summam uel culpae
suae uel erroris, quod essent soliti stato die ante lucem conuenire, carmenque Christo quasi deo dicere secum inuicem
seque sacramento non in scelus aliquod obstringere, sed ne
furta ne latrocinia ne adulteria committerent, ne fidem fal-
lerent, ne depositum adpellati abnegarent. Quibus peractis
morem sibi discedendi fuisse rursusque coeundi ad capiendum
cibum, promiscuum tamen et innoxium; quod ipsum facere
desisse post edictum meum, quo secundum mandata tua

8   hetaerias esse uetueram. Quo magis necessarium credidi ex

---

x.xcvi.7

adfirmo (1) (< ad + firmo, firmare) confirm, corroborate

hanc ... erroris indir. disc. (AG #580); *hanc*: points forward to the *quod* cl. (AG #297e); summa, -ae
(f.) full extent, the whole; culpa, -ae (f.) blame, wrongdoing, fault

quod ... obstringere subord. causal cl. in indir. disc. takes subjv. vb. (AG #540n.3b and 580); status,
-a, -um (< ppp. sisto, sistere) fixed, regular; *inuicem* (adv.) in turn, each for the other; sacramentum,
-i (n.) (< sacro, sacrare + -mentum) solemn oath; scelus, sceleris (n.) crime, wicked act; obstringo,
obstringere (< ob + stringo, stringere) place under moral obligation, bind

ne ... abnegarent a series of negat. purp. cls. (AG #531/1) that describe the things they did not gather
together to do; furtum, -i (n.) robbery; lactrocinium, -i (n.) (< latro, latrare + -cinium) banditry, pillag-
ing; adulterium, -i (n.) (< adulter + -ium) adultery; committo, committere (< con + mitto, mittere)
commit; fallo, fallere: trick, evade; depositum, -i (n.) (< ppp. of de + pono, ponere) deposit, money
placed in safekeeping; adpello (1) demand the payment of; abnego (1) (< ab + nego, negare) deny

quibus peractis abl. abs. (AG #419); perago, peragere, peregi, peractus (< per + ago, agere) carry
through, finish; i.e. the rituals just described

morem ... desisse Using indir. disc., Pliny continues to recount what the confessed Christians had
told him.

coeo, coire (< con + eo, ire) come together, gather round

ad capiendum cibum gerv. purp. constr. w/ *ad* (AG #506)

promiscuus, -a, -um (< pro + misceo, miscere + -uus) w/ out distinction, common, available to the
general public

innoxius, -a, -um (< in + noxius) innocent, harmless; among the rumors about Christians' practice
was that they ate babies and committed incest.

quod (relat. pron.) anteced. the preceding actions

edictum, -i (n.) (< ppp. of ex + dico, dicere) proclamation

secundum (prep.) in accordance w/

mandatum, -i (n.) (< ppp. of mando, mandare) order, imperial directive

hetaeria, -ae (f.) (< Gr. ἑταιρία) guild, fraternity

ueto, uetare, uetui forbid; introd. acc. + inf. constr (AG #563a)

x.xcvi.8

quo magis (adv.) all the more; *quo*: relat. pron., abl. of deg. of diff. w/ compar. (AG #414a n.)

necessarium ... quaerere indir. disc. (AG #580); necessarius, -a, -um (< necesse + -arius) essential,
necessary; ancilla, -ae (f.) female slave; ministra, -ae (f.) deaconess (in Christianity); *quid ... ueri*:
indir. quest. (AG #574); tormentum, -i (n.) (< torqueo, torquere + -mentum) torture, torment; the
use of torture indicates that these *ministrae* were not freeborn women, but rather slaves, who were
conventionally tortured to extract confessions or evidence from them in criminal proceedings
(*OCD* s. torture, 1535).

duabus ancillis, quae ministrae dicebantur, quid esset ueri,
et per tormenta quaerere. Nihil aliud inueni quam supersti-
tionem prauam et immodicam.

Ideo dilata cognitione ad consulendum te decucurri. Visa   9
est enim mihi res digna consultatione, maxime propter periclitantium numerum. Multi enim omnis aetatis, omnis ordinis,
utriusque sexus etiam uocantur in periculum et uocabuntur.
Neque ciuitates tantum, sed uicos etiam atque agros superstitionis istius contagio peruagata est; quae uidetur sisti et
corrigi posse. Certe satis constat prope iam desolata templa   10
coepisse celebrari, et sacra sollemnia diu intermissa repeti
passimque uenire <carnem> uictimarum, cuius adhuc raris-

---

superstitio, superstitionis (f.) ($<$ superstes $+$ -io) irrational religious awe or credulity
prauus, -a, -um debased, perverse {$>$ depraved}
immodicus, -a, -um ($<$ in $+$ modicus) excessive, unrestrained

x.xcvi.9
dilata cognitione abl. abs. (AG #419); differo, differre, distuli, dilatus ($<$ dis $+$ fero, ferre) postpone,
  delay (*OLD* 4)
ad consulendum te gerv. purp. constr. w/ *ad* (AG #506)
decurro, decurrere, decucurri, decursus ($<$ de $+$ curro, currere) run directly, turn to (*OLD* 9)
consultatio, consultationis (f.) ($<$ con $+$ sulo, sulare $+$ -to $+$ tio) consultation; *consultatione*: abl. of
  specif. (AG #418b) w/ *digna*
periclitor, periclitari, periclitatus sum ($<$ periculum $+$ -ito) be in danger or at risk; *periclitantium*:
  subst. use: "of those in danger"
ordo, ordinis (m.) rank, order {$>$ ordinal}
sexus, -us (m.) state of being male or female
uicus, -i (m.) village
contagio, contagionis (f.) ($<$ contages $+$ -io) infection
peruagor, peruagari, peruagatus sum ($<$ per $+$ uagor, uagari) range over, spread through
sisto, sistere bring to a standstill, stop (*OLD* 6a)
corrigo, corrigere ($<$ con $+$ rego, regere) straighten out, put right

x.xcvi.10
consto (1) ($<$ con $+$ sto, stare) stand together; *constat*: impers. use "it is plain" (AG #207)
prope . . . celebrari 1st of 3 indir. disc. (AG #580) ff. *constat*; *prope iam*: "to this point nearly"; desolo
  (1) ($<$ de $+$ solus $+$ -o) forsake, leave deserted; coepi, coepisse (pf. stem only) begin; celebro
  (1) ($<$ celeber $+$ -o) crowd
sacra . . . repeti 2nd indir. disc.; intermitto, intermittere, intermisi, intermissus ($<$ inter $+$ mitto, mittere) discontinue, interrupt
passimque . . . uictimarum 3rd indir. disc.; *passim* (adv.) ($<$ passus $+$ -im) all over the place, in every
  direction; ueneo, uenire ($<$ uenum $+$ eo, ire) be for sale; caro, carnis (f.) flesh (of animals); uictima,
  -ae (f.) sacrificial animal
cuius (relat. pron.) anteced. *carnem*; rarus, -a, -um: infrequent; emptor, emptoris (m.) ($<$ emo, emere $+$
  -tor) buyer

1   simus emptor inueniebatur. Ex quo facile est opinari, quae
turba hominum emendari possit, si sit paenitentiae locus.

XCVII—TRAJAN RESPONDS

TRAIANVS PLINIO

1   Actum quem debuisti, mi Secunde, in excutiendis causis
eorum, qui Christiani ad te delati fuerant, secutus es. Neque
enim in uniuersum aliquid, quod quasi certam formam habeat,

2   constitui potest. Conquirendi non sunt; si deferantur et
arguantur, puniendi sunt, ita tamen ut, qui negauerit se
Christianum esse idque re ipsa manifestum fecerit, id est

---

opinor, opinari, opinatus sum think, believe

quae . . . possit indir. quest. (AG #574) and apod. of FLV condit., prot. *si . . . locus* (AG #516b); turba, -ae (f.) crowd; emendo (1) (< ex + menda + -o) correct, revise

x.xcvii: The Emperor Trajan affirms the process Pliny has used against those charged as Christians in response to x.xcvi.

Addressee: Pliny

x.xcvii.1

actus, -us (m.) (< ago, agere + -tus) course of action

in excutiendis causis gerv. constr. (AG #503); excutio, excutere (< ex + quatio, quatere) search, scrutinize (*OLD* 9b)

defero, deferre, detuli, delatus (< de + fero, ferre) report, accuse

in uniuersum entirely, so as to apply universally (*OLD* 1d)

quod . . . habeat relat. cl. of char. (AG #535)

x.xcvii.2

conquirendi non sunt 2nd (pass.) periphr. conjug. (AG #196 and 500/2); conquiro, conquirere (< con + quaero, quaerere) search out, hunt down

si . . . sunt FLV condit., w/ pass. periphr. in apod. (AG #516b/d); arguo, arguere: prove guilty, condemn; punio, punire (< poena + -io) punish

ut . . . impetret result cl. (AG #537); *qui . . . fecerit*: relat. cl. of char. (AG #535); *qui*, subst. use: "he who"; *se . . . esse*: indir. disc. (AG #580); *re ipsa*: "by the act itself"; manifestus, -a, -um: clearly visible, unmistakeable; supplico (1) make offerings (to a deity), compd. vb + dat. *dis nostris* (AG #370); *quamuis* (relat. adv.) even though; praeteritus, -a, -um (< ppp. of praeter + eo, ire) past, former; n. subst. sg.: the past; paenitentia, -ae (f.) (< paeniteo + -ia) regret {> penitent}; impetro (1) (< in + patro, patrare) obtain by request, gain

supplicando dis nostris, quamuis suspectus in praeteritum,
ueniam ex paenitentia impetret. Sine auctore uero propositi
libelli <in> nullo crimine locum habere debent. Nam et pessimi
exempli nec nostri saeculi est.

---

auctor, auctoris (m.) (< augeo, augere + -tor) originator, source, author (*OLD* 10a)
propono, proponere, proposui, propositus (< pro + pono, ponere) put out, post, publish
libellus, -i (m.) (< liber + -lus) leaflet, pamphlet
crimen, criminis (n.) indictment, charge
et . . . nec both . . . and not
pessimi exempli, nostri saeculi gen. of qual. (AG #345); saeculum, -i (n.) age (*OLD* 8)

Printed in the USA/Agawam, MA
January 8, 2020

747663.013